1964

Ancrene Wisse

EARLY ENGLISH TEXT SOCIETY

No. 249

1962 (for 1960)

PRICE 30*s*.

Liber octauus

Þe feader ⁊ þe sune ⁊ þe hali gastes nome her biginneð ancrene wisse.

Recti diligunt te.
In canticis. spon
sa ad sponsum.
Est rectum gramaticum. Rectum
geometricum. Rectum theologicum.
Et sunt differencie totidem regularum. De recto theolo
gico sermo nobis est. cuius regule due sunt. Una circa
cordis directionem. altera uersatur circa exteriorum
rectificationem. Recti diligunt te. Lauerd seið go
des spuse to hire deorewurðe spus. þe rihte luuieð þe.
þeo beoð rihte þe luuieð efter riwle. ant ʒe mine leo
ue sustren habbeð moni dei icrauet on me efter riwle.
Monie cunne riwlen beoð. ah twa beoð bimong alle.
þ ich chulle speoken of þurh ower bone wið godes
grace. þe an riwleð þe heorte ⁊ makeð efne ⁊ smeðe wið
ute cnost ⁊ dolc of woh inwit ⁊ of wreiʒende þe segge.
her þu sunegest. oþer þis nis nawt ibet ʒet ase wel as
hit ahte. þeos riwle is eauer inwið ⁊ rihteð þe heorte.
Et hec est caritas quam describit apostolus. de corde puro et
consciencia bona ⁊ fide non ficta. þeos riwle is chearite
of schir heorte ⁊ cleane inwit ⁊ treowe bileaue. Preten
de inquit psalmista misericordiam tuam scientibus te per fidem non fictam.
⁊ iusticiam tuam. id est uite rectitudinem hiis qui recto
sunt corde. Qui scilicet omnes uoluntates suas dirigunt
ad regulam diuine uoluntatis. Isti dicuntur boni an
tonomasice. Psalmista. Benefac domine bonis et rectis corde. Istis di
citur ut glorientur testimonio uidelicet bone conscientie.
Gloriamini omnes recti corde. quos scilicet rectificauit

Liber ecclesie sancti Jacobi de Wygemore. quem Johannes Purcel dedit
eidem ecclesie ad instanciam fratris Walteri de Lodel' tunc prioris.
Si quis dictum librum alienauerit a predicta ecclesia uel titulum hunc maliciose
deleuerit anathema sit. Amen. fiat. fiat. fiat. Amen.

Corpus Christi College, Cambridge, MS. 402, f. 1a

þing þ me heateð. þeo þenne habbeð þe nebbes ƿrong ƿen
de euch frommard oðer: hƿen nan ne luueð oþer. ah bi
þe teiles ha beoð somet 7 beoreð þes deofles bleasen þe bru
ne of galnesse. On an oðer ƿise teil bitacneð ende. In þa
re ende ha schulen beon ibunden togederes as ƿeren
samsones foxes bi þe teiles. 7 iset bleasen þrin. þis is þ fur of helle.
All þis is iseid mine leoue sustren. þ oƿer leoue
nebbes beon eauer iƿent somet ƿið luuefule semblant. 7
ƿið swote chere. þ ȝe beon aa ƿið annesse of an heorte 7
of a ƿil iunnet togederes. as hit iƿritten is bi ure lauerdes
deore deciples. Multitudinis credentium erat cor unum
7 anima una. Pax uobis. þis ƿes godes gretunge to his
deore deciples. Grið beo bimong oƿ. ȝe beoð þe ancren of
englond sƿa feole togederes. tƿenti oðer ma. godd
i god ƿ mutli. þ meast grið is among. meast annesse 7
anrednesse. 7 sometreadnesse of anred lif efter a riule.
Sƿa þ alle teoð an. alle turnt anesƿeis. 7 nan frommard
oðer. efter þ ƿord is. forþi ȝe gað ƿel forð 7 spedeð in oƿ
er ƿei. for euch is ƿiðƿard oþer in an manere of lifiade.
as þah ȝe ƿeren an cuuent of lundene 7 of oxneford. of
schreobsburi. oðer of chester. þear as alle beoð an ƿið
an imeane manere. ant ƿið uten singularite. þ is anful
frommardschipe. lah þing i religiun. for hit toƿarpeð
annesse 7 manere imeane. þ ah to beon in ordre. þis
nu þenne þ ȝe beoð alle as an cuuent. is oƿer hehe fa
me. þis is godd icƿeme. þis is nunan ƿide cuð. sƿa þ ƿer
oƿer cuuent biginneð to spreaden toƿard englondes
ende. ȝe beoð as þe moder hus þ heo beoð of istreonet.

Corpus Christi College, Cambridge, MS. 402, f. 69a

THE ENGLISH TEXT OF THE
ANCRENE RIWLE

Ancrene Wisse

EDITED FROM
MS. CORPUS CHRISTI COLLEGE
CAMBRIDGE 402

BY

J. R. R. TOLKIEN

WITH AN INTRODUCTION BY

N. R. KER

Published for
THE EARLY ENGLISH TEXT SOCIETY
by the
OXFORD UNIVERSITY PRESS
LONDON NEW YORK TORONTO
1962

PRINTED IN GREAT BRITAIN

CONTENTS

MS. Corpus Christi College Cambridge 402, f. 1a and f. 69a — *Frontispiece*

PREFATORY NOTE, by J. R. R. TOLKIEN — vi

INTRODUCTION, by N. R. KER — ix

TEXT — 1

PREFATORY NOTE

THE text of the *Ancrene Wisse* is reproduced from MS. Corpus Christi College Cambridge 402 without emendation. Insertions of words or letters attributed to the original scribe are enclosed in angular brackets. Alterations or additions made by other hands are recorded in footnotes, except the late alterations on ff. 1 and 3, which are printed in heavy type. All letters expuncted are so printed. Words crossed out are retained, when their excision is clearly erroneous, as on f. 7b.28; otherwise they are removed to the footnotes, as on f. 3b.13.

The punctuation of the manuscript has been retained. An attempt has also been made to represent the capitalization, where this is significant,[1] though the similar shapes or enlargements used as space-fillers are not represented, except after coloured initials. All initial capitals in heavy type represent coloured letters.

Owing to the regularity of the hand it has been possible to preserve the lineation of the manuscript, but some change in the treatment of abbreviations has thus become necessary. These are usually, as in other versions, expanded without italics; but in a number of places the scribe used arbitrary contractions, reducing words to one or two initial letters, the expansion of which would require a full extra line, or more. In such cases the abbreviations are left in the text and are expanded in the footnotes. This occurs mostly where familiar passages in Latin are cited or repeated (especially in Part I): English examples occur on ff. 9b.20 and 10.2. Where the expansion of regular contractions, or the compression of the hand,[2] has made short over-runs necessary, these are ignored in the line-numbering. At these points hyphens are used in a few cases: they indicate that the word is *not* divided in the manuscript. The spacing between words is according to convenience in printing; but

[1] See p. xi. [2] See p. x.

actual joinings or disjoinings, whether correct or not, represent the procedure of the scribe.

As usual *þ̄* for *þet*; ⁊ for *ant* and Latin *et*; & for Latin *et*, are not expanded. The contraction *qđ*, used in every place, except *quođ* f. 67b.17, for Latin *quod*, is expanded, but the identical form used for English 'quoth' is retained, since its correct expansion is debatable: full writing occurs only in *cweđ* f. 33.28. In English *ih̄u* is expanded *iesu*, following the full spellings in ff. 67.25 and 110.4. In Latin *ih̄c*, *ih̄m*, *ih̄u* are expanded *iesus*, *iesum*, *iesu* according to better contemporary usage;[1] but *christus*, *christ-* is used to indicate that the manuscript (in Latin only) writes *xp̄c*, and *xp̄* (occasionally *x*) with added case-letter. As far as this text is concerned the single spelling in Latin *criste* (*cͥste*), beside the thirty-two examples of *xp̄*, *x*, is probably a casual intrusion of the vernacular form.[2] Similarly, *dauiđ*, the English form used thirty times, appears in the Latin context f. 11b.23; and *maria* in the English context f. 9b.11. *xp̄el* and *kyriel* have been expanded *christe eleison* and *kyrie eleison*; these correct forms are indicated by the spelling *x͛el* f. 11b.17, but the usual contractions may show the influence of the popular pronunciation of these familiar invocations.[3] Where the abbreviations for *er* are used in vernacular words whose full spelling normally shows *ear*, this is recorded in the footnotes, since the abbreviations have less value in considering the orthography of this text. Wyn (*ƿ*), which with one exception, the name *wilȝam* f. 92b.2, was used throughout by the scribe, is represented by *w*.

Members of the Council of the Early English Text Society have seen the volume in proof, and their comments have saved the editor from missing a number of misprints and from making several errors in his transcription. His thanks are especially due to Mr. N. R. Ker; to Mr. R. W. Burchfield;

[1] See pp. xii–xiii.

[2] But see p. xiii, footnote. In the early period, however, full writings such as *xpistus*, *xpisti*, &c., also appear.

[3] From *kiriel*(*eison*) such words as MHG. *kiriel*, *kirleis*, and French *kirielle* 'litany, long recital' are derived.

and to Professor N. Davis, who made a first correction of the latter half of the text. He has also been greatly assisted by the use of her word-list, now complete for more than half of the vocabulary of this text, kindly lent by Miss M. E. Griffiths; and by Professor A. H. Smith's kind loan of photographs of B.M. MS. Cotton Cleopatra C. VI.

The gratitude of the Society is due to the Master and Fellows of Corpus Christi College, Cambridge, for their permission to print and publish the text of this manuscript and to reproduce from it the two plates which form the frontispiece to the present edition.

J. R. R. T.

INTRODUCTION

1. The text of the *Ancrene Wisse* is written on 117 leaves of good parchment measuring now, after rebinding, 215×148 mm. The leaves were in twelve quires of ten, but two leaves of quire 2, the central opening, are now missing after f. 14. The last leaf of quire 12, no doubt a blank, is now missing. In quires 7–12 the central opening (ff. 63–64, 73–74, 83–84, 93–94, 103–4, 113–14) is not a single sheet, but consists of two separate leaves folded one within the other. There are no signs of ancient quire signatures. The only catchword is at f. 18b. A modern pencil numbering of the quires is in the bottom right-hand corner of the first recto of each quire. Small holes and splits, the latter mended with green silk, occur on some twenty leaves and were avoided by the scribe, if they fell within the written space. Apart from the loss of two leaves, the damage sustained by the manuscript since it was written is trifling. There are damp stains and associated creases on ff. 23, 24, 29–36, 43, 44, and a crease on f. 70. Folio 15 has at some time been folded vertically down the centre.

The written space on each page is about 156×95 mm. on ff. 1–68 and afterwards, from the beginning of quire 8, about 156×100 mm. The ruling is with pencil in a single column of 28 lines. A pair of lines set close together bounds the written space on each side. Of the horizontal lines, the first and third from the top and the first and third from the bottom are usually prolonged across the margins. Pricks to guide the ruling of the horizontal lines are not to be seen. They were presumably in the outer margins. There are no pricks in the inner margins, a position in which they are commonly found in manuscripts of the later twelfth century and the earlier thirteenth century of about this format or a larger format, and which indicates that the sheets were folded before the horizontal lines were ruled. The scribe used the first horizontal line as a line on which to write, following in this the practice of past scribes, but not the practice of up-to-date scribes of his own period, who kept all their writing within a frame of ruled lines.[1]

2. The hand is close and angular, but admirably clear. It is the same throughout. The letters are made to one pattern, but their size varies, so that the writing is not always uniform in appearance. For example, on f. 69 the minims are about 3 mm. high and the space between the lines is about 2½ mm., but on f. 75 the minims are about 2 mm. high and the space between the lines is about 3 mm. 'Bitings' and ligatures apart, the scribe had a repertory of thirty-five 'lower-case' letters. Twenty-three of them are the common letters of the Latin alphabet, *a–z*, eight are variants of one kind and another, and four are special letters used in writing English. Of the common letters, *d* is in the rounded form usual in thirteenth-century and later bookhand and usual in vernacular writing of all dates. The pointed angular impression given by the tops of minims and by the forms of *b, c, e, h, þ, p*, is modified by the rounding of bases, especially *r*, so that the script does not look as angular as some late-twelfth-century writing. The final stroke of *m* and *n* is often extended below the line for greater distinctness (f. 69.7). The biting of back-to-back curving strokes, for example *he* or *po*, and of a diagonal with a curve, for example *de*, is extremely common. The letters *st* form a ligature, as usual. Final *t* sometimes has a hairline descending from the bar (f. 69.28), but this ugly form is not usual. The scribe's *y* is ungainly (f. 9.10). The tongue of *e*, the head of *f*, the horizontal projection of *g*, and the head of *t* may be prolonged at a line-end to fill space (ff. 1.4, 24; 2.25; 4.24). Ascenders in the first line on a page are prolonged upwards.

The variant letters are:

Upright **d**. This, the traditional form of bookhand *d*, occurs now and then in Latin words, for example nine times on f. 1, but as a deliberate form in English only in *feaderes* (f. 1.1) and *eadínesses* (f. 7.28) and often in the word *leafdi* (e.g. f. 9.27).[2]

Small uncial **M**. For this form see below, p. xiv.

[1] N.R.Ker in *Celtica*, v (1960), 13–16.
[2] Cf. textual note to f. 1b.13.

N. Used commonly to take up space, the horizontal stroke being conveniently extendible (f. 69.5). To save space the scribe combined *N* with *d* at f. 84b.17 *forbearnd*, and with *s* at ff. 18b.8, 44b.4, 84.14, 97.17, 109.3, all at line-ends.

R. Used like *N* to take up space (f. 2.23).

2-shaped **r**. Used in its traditional place after *o*, and also commonly after other letters which have as their second stroke a curve more or less like the curve of *o* (as *b*, *d*, *p*). The later medieval form with a descending hairline occurs occasionally (f. 70.28 *forðre*).

Round **s**. Used like *N* and *R* to take up space at a line-end (f. 1.14, 17), but also as a mere alternative to the common *s* finally, initially (f. 11.8 *sanctus*), and—rarely—medially (f. 4.18 *leasse*). Used in a narrow and vertically elongated form to save space (f. 4b.13 *werkes*) and, also to save space, above the line in conjunction with a preceding *r* (f. 16b.13 *meonurs*). The ligature of *P* with round *s* followed by a mark of abbreviation denotes 'Psalmista' or the like (f. 1.26).

t. The special form of *t* after *c* (f. 1.20) is a relic of the ancient *ct* ligature. When *c* and *t* are divided at a line-end the memory of the ligature is preserved by the stroke attached to the head of *c* (f. 97.22–23 *resurrec/tionis*).

v. Used occasionally instead of *u* at the beginning of a word (f. 8.21 *víua*).

The four special letters are *ȝ*, *þ*, *ð*, *ƿ*. *ȝ* is used only for the palatal spirant, the other functions of Anglo-Saxon *ȝ* being fulfilled by *h* and caroline *g*. *þ* is used initially and *ð* finally and also in nearly all words medially. *w* (or *W*) is used instead of *ƿ* only once (f. 92b.2, *wilȝam* 'William').

Capital letters are used at the beginning of a sentence, commonly for the first letter of a personal name, and sometimes for the first letter of an important word, for example at ff. 54b.16–18, 82b.6–8. On f. 1.1 the second letter of *Recti* is a capital. *C*, *E*, *H*, *O* occur in two forms, one of them generally like the minuscule, but larger, the other similar, but with a distinguishing stroke, horizontal in *H* and an open downward curve in *C*, *E*, *O* (ff. 1.4, 69.4). *Q* is marked in the same way, under the influence of *O*. An *M* shaped like a conjoint *O* and *H* has both the downward and the horizontal stroke (f. 69.11), but this is not the normal form (cf. f. 1.13). *S* consists of two parallel curving strokes, but a plainer and smaller form of *S* is used sometimes as a capital. *V*, *Y*, capital yogh, and capital thorn are distinguished by their size.[1] Capital thorn is distinguished also by a horizontal tag to the left at the top of the upright (e.g. f. 12b.4). Capital wyn, larger than and of a different shape from the small letter, occurs at ff. 48b.20, 56b.27, 57b.28. A letter like *p* in size, but with a tag like that on capital thorn, appears to be meant as a capital thorn (ff. 32b.21, 26; 65b.8; 68b.5; 82b.8).

Capital letters are used also after a coloured initial and for *A*, *M*, and *N* in the word *Amen.* Their special character is shown by the fact that the scribe did not feel free to use the whole alphabet, but only nine letters, *A*, *D*, *I*, *M*, *N*, *O*, *R*, *S*, and *V*. These letters do not rise above or fall below the line, four of them, *D*, *I*, *O*, *S*, differing in this respect from the capitals normally used at the beginning of a sentence.

The common mark of abbreviation at the end of a word is usually a wavy stroke like that made in the twelfth century. Elsewhere it is usually a straight stroke with a downward hairline prong at each end (f. 1.22). Abbreviations in Latin include the tironian nota for *est* in an unusual form (f. 1.19) and at ff. 21b.24, 25.2, and 42.11 the tironian nota for *enim.* The nota for *et* (or in English *ant*) is regularly crossed (f.1.18). In English *qđ* is noteworthy.[2] Common Latin forms of abbreviation are used in vernacular contexts, where the orthography permits, but are sparingly employed, except in French or learned Latin words. Some examples are superior *a*, *e*, *i* to denote omission of *r* (ff. 73.7 *traitre*, 103b.1 *uttre*, 40.13 *priuement*) and the sign for *er* to represent *er* (or *ear*) in *sperklinde*, *lauerdes* (ff. 8b.20, 69.10). *d* with attached mark, used to abbreviate Latin words, is indistinguishable from đ. The form *iesu* is found written in full at ff. 67.25 and 110.4. We can therefore confidently expand the abbreviation *iħc* to *iesus*. This good spelling was becoming less common in

[1] See below, p. xiv. [2] See p. vii.

the thirteenth century, but it was not yet as rare as in the later Middle Ages, when almost all scribes, if they wrote the word in full, wrote *ihesus*. The abbreviation *xp̄c* or x^c is regular. The spelling 'c*ri*ste' at f. 4b.24 with superior *i* denoting omission of *r*, the form *crist* in English, and the almost universal usage of scribes leave no doubt that the correct extension is *cristus*.[1] An instance of *ierusalemes* written in full occurs at f. 56.20.

The punctuation is: (i) a mid or mid-low point for the full stop and for a minor pause within a sentence; (ii) the *punctus elevatus* (.͘) for a major pause within a sentence; (iii) the mark of interrogation. It has a squeezed-in appearance because the scribe did not as a rule leave a larger space between words separated by punctuation than between words not so separated. Points are also written in front of a run-over, after abnormal abbreviations by suspension (for example f. 6b.18), and on each side of a single-letter abbreviation (f. 1.23, 24). Points are also found occasionally separating words written very close together, but it is not certain that any of them are by the original scribe.

A hairline like an acute accent is written frequently above *i*, especially when *i* comes next to another minim (f. 69.19; cf. 18), and also sometimes above an *e* (ff. 66b.12 *wéte*, 69.9 *chére*, 104.28 *behé/ue*), *a* (f. 38.6 *iha/ten*), or *o* (f. 6.10 *nón*).

There are no hyphens. In order to avoid breaking a word at a line-end, and at the same time to fill the line, the scribe employed horizontally elongated letters (see p. xi above) and zigzag line-fillers (f. 15b.25). The last syllable of *stude* (f. 102.28) and of *bihéue* (f. 104.28) is dropped below the line and the last syllable of *silence* (f. 43b.19) is run over to the line below. The dropping of the two-letter words *te* and *is* below the last line on two recto pages, 8 and 56, are examples of the same sort of care for the reader's convenience.

[1] *Christus* occurs occasionally in the eleventh century and earlier. In Copenhagen GKS 10 fol. (s. xi), f. 55b, *christi* was written first and then altered to *cristi*. Apart from *antichristi* in a late-twelfth-century manuscript of Gregory, Moralia, from Villers (Ushaw College MS. 32, f. 91), I do not know any example of the spelling with *h* in the period 1100–1400. It reappears in the fifteenth century.

In dividing his words the scribe appears to have worked to rule, the rule being that every word should be separated from every other word by the same amount of space, irrespective of the sense and without taking the punctuation into account. Larger spaces were permissible only before a coloured initial. He was sometimes at fault with the enclitic *que*, separating it, for example, at f. 13b.14.

ti is written sometimes for *ci* in Latin words or in words derived from Latin, e.g. *faties* f. 21b.25, *spetial* f. 112b.11, 12. *ci* for classical Latin *ti* occurs mainly in the ending *-cia*.

Every letter of the script is clearly legible, except where there have been alterations. The reader's only uncertainties are these: whether, in places where he would expect a capital letter, *v*, *y*, *ȝ*, *þ* are majuscule or minuscule, whether *N*, *R*, and *S* at the beginning of a word within a sentence are meant as capitals or have the same minuscule value as they certainly have at the end of a word, and whether the small uncial *M* which the scribe uses a good deal initially within a sentence is always meant as a capital. In this transcript *V*, *Y*, *Ȝ*, *Þ* have been used when the letters in the manuscript are clearly larger than the normal minuscule, and *v*, *y*, *ȝ*, *þ* have been used when, as often, the letters are only very slightly larger or no larger than the normal minuscule, for example at ff. 69.12 *þis*, 69.13 *ȝe*, 96b.23 *ysa*. It is odd that such a competent scribe failed so often to make the distinction. Initial *M*, *N*, *R* within a sentence have been printed as *M*, *N*, *R*, since they seem to occur mainly in words where it is at least not unreasonable to use a capital, e.g. ff. 26.24, 41b.14, 52b.25, 54.7, 109.8. Probably more doubt attaches to *M* than to *N* and *R*: it is difficult to believe that a capital was intended in *Maht*, f. 75b.16.[1] *S* is doubtful only when it is in the simpler of the two forms noticed on p. xii. Its interpretation then is particularly difficult, because, though ultimately a majuscule form, it was commonly used as a minuscule in twelfth-century and earlier script. In this

[1] For small uncial *M* replacing minuscule *m* in the Peterborough Chronicle see Dorothy Whitelock's introduction to the facsimile edition (Copenhagen, 1954), p. 15.

matter of capitals no transcript can take the place of the original manuscript.

There is hardly anything in the script which could not be found in a late-twelfth-century manuscript. But even if there were no internal evidence one would not want to date it in the twelfth century. Two of its features, the cross through ʒ and the biting of back-to-back curving strokes, came into use only in the last decades of the twelfth century. Probably they would not be used regularly in a west-country manuscript until some time after 1200. Two occasional features, the *v* for *u* initially and the additional strokes in capital letters, have their origin in the current script used for documents. Their employment in bookhand is thirteenth-century rather than twelfth. The generalization of rounded *d* for Latin as well as for English and the absence of any of the distinctions between Latin and English observed by twelfth-century and earlier scribes point also to a date after 1200. The curved form of the common mark of abbreviation is traditional, but the angular form is typical of the thirteenth century. 'First half of the thirteenth century' is probably as near as one ought to go on palaeographical grounds. The internal evidence, the mention of the Dominican and Franciscan friars at f. 16b.13, suggests that the date of writing is likely to be after rather than before 1225.

3. A five-line initial in red and blue with ornament of both colours begins the text (f. 1). All other coloured initials are red or blue, the colours usually alternating, with ornament in blue and red respectively. The largest, six-line, is on f. 47b. Five more are four-line (ff. 12b, 32, 94, 104, 111) and one is three-line (f. 4b). The rest are all two-line or one-line. The two-line or larger initials begin a new line. A coloured paragraph is used before the heading on f. 12 and before the explicit on f. 117b. Elsewhere this mark is used only to separate a runover to the line below from the other words on the line. The rubricator failed to notice the runovers on ff. 8b, 43b, 91, 116b, and on ff. 6b and 7b he went wrong, putting a paragraph instead of a coloured initial. The paragraphs, like the coloured initials, are red or blue with

ornament of the other colour. More often than not the rubricator made a red paragraph after a blue initial and vice versa.

The scribe left spaces for headings on ff. 1, 4, 4b, 12, 26, 32, 47b, 94, 104, 111, and for a conclusion on f. 8b. He filled the spaces, using red ink, on ff. 1, 4, 4b, 8b, 12. The other spaces remain blank.

4. The manuscript was rebound in 1953 by J. P. Gray of Cambridge. The two unnumbered paper leaves at each end are of the date of binding. The next two leaves at the beginning, a bifolium (ff. i, ii), and a leaf at the end (f. 118) are parchment leaves taken over from the medieval binding. The recto of f. i and the verso of f. 118 were pasted to the covers of this binding, which had a strap-and-pin fastening: the attachment of the strap to the edge of the upper cover caused a rust-hole on ff. i, ii, 1 and the pin near the centre of the lower cover caused a similar hole on f. 118. Before the rebinding in 1953 some small fragments of a hardly legible Latin text were attached to the recto of f. 1. They are now missing. For ff. iii, iv see § 6 below.

5. The scribe corrected some of his own mistakes, either as he went along or soon afterwards. This is most evident where he has simply crossed out the wrong word and written the right word after it (f. 23.15) or above it (ff. 45b.27, 53b.13, 16, 103.19, 107.9, 116b.20). The other medieval corrections and alterations and marginalia are not easy to sort out or to date. They are not numerous, but they are sufficient to show that the text was read carefully in the thirteenth and fourteenth centuries. At least three are the work of one reader of the thirteenth century who was concerned to make details clearer: (*a*) f. 17.7, the expuncting of *oþer* and the substitution for it of *owðer* in the margin in pencil; (*b*) f.17b. 7, 8, the expuncting of *from non efter mete aðet* and the addition of *on easter* in the margin in pencil: (*c*) f. 18.5, the expuncting of *ane* and the addition of *bute* in the margin in pencil: further alteration here has produced the final reading 'forte *loken bute* hire and hire meidnes', the words in italics being partly in the margin and partly in the written

space over erasure.[1] Another reader (late-thirteenth-century?) disliked the words *priuement* and *proprement* and substituted for them *darnliche* and *ouneliche* (ff. 40.13, 52.2, 4): his hand occurs again, perhaps, in the correction at f. 82b.26, *dica* above expuncted *da*. A scribe writing in a current and probably late-fourteenth-century hand made a devastating series of alterations on ff. 1 and 3. The 147 'Nota' signs in the margins are also medieval, as are, probably, a couple of dozen pointing hands. One pointer occurs beside a 'Nota' (f. 53.12) and its relative position shows that it is later.

Palaeographically the alterations, apart from those on ff. 1 and 3, seem to be earlier than or of about the same date as the inscription (later thirteenth century ?) at the foot of f. 1, which records the gift of the manuscript by John Purcel to the house of Augustinian canons at Wigmore in Herefordshire. Two other Wigmore *ex libris* inscriptions, one in a Petrus Riga at Trinity College, Cambridge (MS. 66), the other in a handsome Isidore, Etymologiae, at St. John's College, Cambridge (MS. 214), are of about the same date, but in different hands. They are accompanied by a form of anathema in which is the same phrase as occurs in the Corpus manuscript, 'uel titulum hunc maliciose deleuerit'. The word *maliciose* is not common in this context and may have been used in order to cover the abbot and convent if they wished to alienate a book, not with evil intent, but for the profit of the house.[2] The gift to Wigmore was at the instance of the precentor, Walter de Ludlow senior. A Walter de Ludlow senior was, as Macaulay noticed, one of the principal monks of Wigmore in 1299. He was elected abbot in 1302, but refused to take office.[3] The Purcels were a south Shropshire

[1] Some 'corrections' (as at f. 17.7) are erroneous, and show misunderstanding of the text, or of its dialect, e.g. *marhe* ~~*ȝeuen*~~/*ȝeoue* (ff. 7b.28–8.1) where *ȝeuen* has been crossed out under the mistaken notion that it was the same as *ȝeoue*.

[2] A twelfth-century Augustine at Hereford (P.vi.3) has a cancelled Wigmore *ex libris*, followed by the words (also cancelled) 'Si quis eum alienauerit uel titulum deleuerit anathema sit'. It was at Hereford Cathedral by the fourteenth century.

[3] C. G. Macaulay, 'The "Ancren Riwle"', *Modern Language*

family. A John Purcel, head of one of its branches at the end of the thirteenth century, held land within some ten miles of Wigmore at Norbury, near Bishop's Castle, and at Diddlebury, near Ludlow. He occurs in records between 1272, when he was an infant, and 1306.[1]

6. The *Ancrene Wisse* was read again carefully in the sixteenth century. The many crosses in the margins and the marking of passages in the text by underlining and side-scoring in pale ink are of this date, as appears from the script and the ink of words which in four places accompany these marks (f. 44.16 *Eccl'*; f. 63.27 *Cantic'*; f. 70.7 *þreaȝendes*; f. 72b.1 *Josaphat*). Marginalia and underlining in red chalk, found in many of the manuscripts owned by Archbishop Parker, occur here only on ff. 1, 1b, 2, 2b, 12b, and 77.[2] One of Parker's expert scribes wrote on the flyleaf, f. iib, and also filled two inserted parchment leaves (ff. iii, iv) with a modernized version of the text on ff. 2.20–3b.1. Presumably earlier than this, but after the accession of Elizabeth, one John Mannyng wrote his name in a legal hand on f. 112b.

Parker's manuscripts were bequeathed to Corpus Christi College in 1575. The catalogue made at this time lists most of the 'Saxon' manuscripts under the letter *S* and among them, in fifteenth place, 'A rule for religious in Saxon, recti diligunt te'. S(5–9, 13, 14) are respectively volumes 1–7 of the series of sermons in Anglo-Saxon which Parker possessed. S(17) was the eighth volume of sermons, but this for some reason never came to Corpus, having been given by Parker himself in 1574 to Cambridge University Library, where it is now MS. Ii. 1. 33. The words 'Liber Octauus' at the head of f. 1 suggest that the *Ancrene Wisse* took the place of this missing volume in the series of sermons.

N. R. K.

Review, ix (1914), 145; *Registrum R. de Swinfield* (Canterbury and York Society, vi (1909), p. 363.

[1] R. W. Eyton, *Antiquities of Shropshire*, xi. 215. I owe the reference to Miss V. Bonnell.

[2] Cf. C. E. Wright in *Transactions of the Cambridge Bibliographical Society*, i (1951), 228.

MS. Corpus Christi College Cambridge 402

A Rule for Nunnes or Recluses

ANCRENE WISSE

f. iib

A Rule for Nunnes or Recluses
written in Saxon Charect. a
good time since the Conqueste. 5

In this may be notid howe the English tonge
is altered in time both in wordes Sentences
and Phrases.

Here may yowe note manie wordes mere 10
English w^c^h nowe be forgotten and Inkehorne
termes in their places / As

In witt.	*for Conscience.*
mans foundels.	*for mans Invencions*
fore dele.	*for the forth parte* 15
h d sinne	*for Capitall sinne*
bone.	*for desier.*
shir heorte.	*for puer hearte*
Domelick.	*for Iudiciall*
Licamlick	*for corporall* 20
Dedelick	*for mortall*
Ealderlick	*for principall*
flugol	*for fugitiue.*

pag. · 3 ·

f. iiia

None religiouse by my Learnyng shall make
profession (of) that is commaunded as precept, but
three thinges, that is obedience, chastite, & state
in stedfastnes, that he ne shall that state 5
never more chaunge but for nede on as strength
and Deathes drede, obedience of hir busshop
either of hes Lorde, for who which taketh
thinge in honde, and vowe it god as precept
for to Do it, they be bounde therto & synneth 10
Deadlie in the breche if he it breke will

f. iib. 16 *h . . . d*: probably for *heued*; there is a rust-hole, as in preceding leaf. 19 *Domelick* on an erasure. 20 To the right of *corporall*: *qu* in reverse, offset from the altered *quam* on *f. 1a.*

pag. · 3 · refers probably to the third page of text (*f. 2a*); the translation begins with line 20 of that page, and ends in line *1* of *f. 3b.*

if he it ne vowed not he it may Do
though, and Leave when he wel will: as
of meate of Drinke, fleshe, to forgo
15 *or fishe, all other suche thinges of weringe*
of lyginge of oures of others biddinge
I say many other of suche wise, theis and
whatsoeuer other be all in fre will to do or
f. iiib *to let (vndon) while I will, and when I will,*
excepte they be vowed / but charitie that is
Love and meknes and pacyence fidelitie &
holdinge of the olde ten Commaundementes
5 *shrifte and penaunce, thes and whatsoeuer*
other wch. be some of the olde Law some of
the newe, and be not manes Inventions nor
rule that to man (is) stalde, but be gods heastes
and for that eche man myght them nedly
10 *Holden, and the other all / for theis ruleth*
the harte, of this rulinge is almost that I
write, except in the front of this booke and
in the Last ende / the thinges that I write
here of the owter rule, ye them holdeth all
15 *(my Dere sistren) or Lorde be ithanked, and*
shall thorough his grace the Lenger the

f. iva *better, and thoughe I woulde not that ye*
shoulde vowe them as preceptes to holde, for
as ofte as ye Herafter breke any of them
it woulde to sone hurt yor hart and make
5 *you fall into dispaire, that is in a wan hope*
and an onbyleve, for to be. ffor that that I
write of myne (dere sistren) of owter thinges
in the fore parte of or booke of or service, and
namly in the Last, ye ne shulde not vowe
10 *it, but holde it in hart, and do it as though*
ye it had promised. yf any vnskilled aske you

f. iiia 17 I outside the left ruled margin.
f. iiib 14 owter: w altered from *u*.
f. iva 10 an erasure between first *it* and *olde*; *but* and top of *h* written on the rough surface.

of what order ye be, as some doeth wch
telleth me wch strayneth the gnat & swaloweth
the flie. answered of St Iames wch was gods
appostle & for his great holynes named gods 15
brother, if he thinketh wonder & doubteth
of suche answere, aske him what is order,
and where he finde in holy writ religion
moste openly described & sort like than is
in St Iames canonical epistle / he saieth what 20
is religion wch is righte order. religio munda &c

that is clene religion and without spott is to se to f. ivb
Helpe widowes and fatherles children, and from
the worlde kepe them clene & vnspotted, thus
St Iames Describeth religion in order, the
Later division of his sawe Longeth to recluses 5
for there be ij distinctions to two maner that be
of religiouse, to either longeth his distinction,
as ye maie here, good religiouse be in the
worlde some, namly prelates and true preachers
whiche haue the fore dele (or distinction) 10
of that wch St Iames saieth, that be as he
saieth wch go to helpe widowes & fatherles
Children, the soule is widow wch hathe
Lost her spouse, that is Iesu christ wth any
capitall synne, he is also fatherlesse wch hath 15
thoroughe his synne Lost the father of heaven,
can visit euery one & hele them and helpe
withe foode of holy Lore, this is righte
religion he saieth St Iames /. the Latter
Deale of his sawe longeth to ower religion 20
as I earst saide, whiche kepeth from the world
either other religiouse clene and vnspotted
thus the apostle St Iame describeth religion
neither white nor black not namyth he in his order.

f. 1a R Ecti diligunt te. I þe feaderes ꝛ i þe sunes (M. 2)
IN canticis. spon ꝛ i þe hali gastes nome
sa ad sponsum. her biginneð ancrene
Est rectum gramaticum Rectum. wisse.
5 geometricum. Rectum theologicum.
Et sunt differencie totidem regularum. De recto theolo
gico sermo nobis est. cuius regule due sunt. Vna circa
cordis directionem. Altera uersatur circa exteriorum
rectificationem. Recti diligunt te. Lauerd seið go
10 des spuse to hire deore**wer**ðe spus. þe rihte luuieð þe.
þeo beoð rihte þe luuieð efter riwle. Ant ȝe míne leo
ue sustren habbe**þ** moní dei ícrauet on me **a**fter ri**w**le.
Moníe cunne riwlen beoð. ah twa beoð bimong alle.
Ꝥ ich chulle speoken of þurh ower bone wið godes
15 grace. þe an riwleð þe heorte ꝛ makeð efne ꝛ smeðe wið
ute cnost ꝛ dolc of woh inwit ꝛ of wreiȝende þe segge.
her þu sunegest. oþer þis nis nawt ibet ȝet ase wel as
hit ahte. þeos riwle is eauer inwið ꝛ rihteð þe heorte.
Et hec est caritas quam describit apostolus. de corde puro et

f. 1a. *In the middle of the upper margin* Liber Octauus *in a formal 16th-century hand.*

The text begins with a very large initial R *in blue and red, standing from* 5 *to two line-spaces into the upper margin, ornamented with red line-patterns within, and outside with red and blue, trailing in left margin to* 19 (*the left edge of the ornament now hidden in binding fold*). *The invocation and title is in red, with letters a little finer and larger than the norm. In* 9 *a small red initial* L *touched with blue.*

On this page an ungainly late 14th-century hand began an attempt to modernize the text, chiefly by erasing, here and there, obsolete ƿ, ð *and substituting* w, þ; *and incidentally altering dialectal* e, ea *to* a. *This 'emender' fortunately only looked at recto pages, and tired of the operation after disfiguring* f. 3a. *His substitutes are printed in heavy type. Traces of the original can be seen:* 10 deorewerðe: *the cross-bar of* ð *scraped but visible;* 12 habbeþ: ð *partly visible under* þ; after: e *partly visible under* a; riwle: *tail of* ƿ *visible under* w. 2 *below second* i *of* canticis *a mark or short stroke.* 4 gramaticum, *sic.* 9 *in right margin mark* ×; 9, 10 L)auerd *to* rihte luui(eð *underlined.* 15 heorte *to* ꝛ sme(ðe *underlined with faint strokes.* 16 inwit ꝛ *underlined with red chalk.* 18 inwið ꝛ (*mistaken for* inwit) *doubly underlined with the same.* 19 quam: *left of* m *and bow of* a (*originally* c?) *appear to be in ink of main hand; but* qu *is abnormal,*

consciencia bona ⁊ fide non ficta. þeos riwle is chearite 20
of schir heorte ⁊ cleane inwit ⁊ treowe bileaue. Preten
de inquit psalmista. misericordiam tuam scientibus te per
fidem non fictam.
⁊ iusticiam tuam .id est. uite rectitudinem híís qui recto
sunt corde. Qui .s. omnes uoluntates suas dirigunt
ad regulam diuine uoluntatis. Isti dicuntur boni an 25
(M. 4) tomasice. psalmista. Benefac domine bonis & rectis corde.
istis di
citur ut glorientur testimonio uidelicet bone conscientie.
Gloriamini omnes recti corde. quos scilicet rectificauit

Liber ecclesie sancti Iacobi de Wygemore. quem Iohannes
Purcel dedít | eidem ecclesie ad ínstanciam fratris Walteri de
Lodel' senioris tunc precentoris. | Siquis dictum librum aliena-
uerít a predicta ecclesia — uel titulum hunc maliciose| deleue-
rít: anathema sit. Amen. fiat. fiat. fiat. A M e N.

regula illa supprema rectificans omnia. de qua augustinus. f. 1b
Nichil petendum preter regulam magisteríí. Et apostolus.
Omnes
in eadem regula permaneamus. þe oþer riwle is al wið u
ten ⁊ riwleð þe licome ⁊ licomliche deden. þe teacheð al
hu me schal beoren him wið uten. hu eoten. drinken. 5
werien. síngen. slepen. wakien. Et hec est exercitio corpo
ris que iuxta apostolum modicum ualet. ⁊ est quasi regula
recti mechanici quod geometrio recto continetur. ant þeos
riwle nis nawt bute forte serui þe oþer. þe oþer is as
leafdi. þeos as hire þuften. for al ꝧ me eauer deð of 10

formed by scraping and alteration: it is offset on f. iib. *Above and between* ua *a small faint* e. 21 schir *underlined with red chalk, and* inwit *doubly; in right margin* inwyt ⁙ conscientia *in 16th-century hand.* 24 s.: *read* scilicet. 25, 26 an|tomasice, *sic for* antonomastice.

The note in the bottom margin is in a later hand (*c. 1300*). Lodel' *is probably for* Lodelowe. Liber *has tall red initial* L *rising to* 28; *the other capitals are touched with red, including* A M N *of final* Amen.

f. 1b. 1 supprema, *sic.* 4 licome ⁊ licomliche *underlined with red chalk; in left margin* body & bodely *written with the same, in 16th-century hand.* 6 exercitio: *small* ta *in thin hand interlined, with carets above and below, to follow* ci. 8 ȝeometrio, *sic.*

þe oþer wið uten.' nis bute forte riwlin þe heorte wið
Nu easki ȝe hwet riwle ȝe ancren schu ¶ .ínnen.
len halden. ȝe schulen alles weis wið alle mihte ant
strengðe wel witen þe inre. ⁊ te uttre for hire sake.
15 þe inre is eauer ilich. þe uttre is mislich. for euch
schal halden þe uttre efter ꝥ ha mei best. wið hire
serui þe inre. Nu þenne is hit swa ꝥ alle ancren ma
hen wel halden an riwle. quantum ad puritatem cordis
circa quam uersatur tota religio. ꝥ is alle mahen ⁊ ahen
20 halden a riwle onont purte of heorte. ꝥ is cleane ⁊
schir inwit. consciencia. wið uten weote of sunne ꝥ ne beo
þurh schrift ibet. þis makeð þe leafdi riwle þe riw
leð ⁊ rihteð ⁊ smeðeð þe heorte. ⁊ te inwit of sunne.
for nawt ne makeð hire woh bute sunne ane. Rih
25 ten hire ⁊ smeðin hire is of euch religiun ant of
euch ordre þe goð ⁊ al þe strengðe. þeos riwle is i (M. 6)
maket nawt of monnes fundles.' ah is of godes
heaste. for þi ha is eauer ⁊ an wið ute changunge.
f. 2a ⁊ alle ahen hire in an eauer to halden. Ah alle ne mahe
nawt halden a riwle. ne ne þurue nawt ne ne ahe nawt
halden on a wise þe uttre riwle. quantum scilicet ad obser
uantias corporales. ꝥ is onont licomliche locunges efter
5 þe uttre riwle ꝥ ich þuften cleopede. ⁊ is monnes fundles.
for na þing elles istald bute to seruí þe ínre. þe makeð
feasten wakien. calde ⁊ hearde werien. swucche oþre heard
schipes ꝥ moni fles mei þolien. moni ne mei nawt. for
þi mot þeos changin hire misliche. efter euchanes
10 manere ⁊ efter hire euene. for sum is strong sum un
strong. ⁊ mei ful wel beo cwite ⁊ paie godd mid leas
se. Sum is clergesse sum nawt. ⁊ moten mare wur
chen ⁊ on oðer wise seggen hire bonen. Sum is ald
⁊ eðelich ⁊ is þe leasse dred of. Sum is ȝung ⁊ luuelich

12 *small blue initial* N, *with a few red lines within, and in margin from* 9 *to* 15; *before* .innen. *a red paragraph touched with blue.*
13 halden: ld *altered from* bl (*scribe began* habben, *and left* d *in upright form unusual in vernacular*). 26 goð, *sic for* god.
28 an: n *in rough hand sloping back, on an erasure; as shown by* ⁊ *original had* aa.

f. 2a. 12 moten, *sic for* mot te.

⁊ is neod betere warde. for þi schal euch ancre habben 15
þe uttre riwle efter hire schriftes read. ⁊ hwet se he
bit ⁊ hat hire in obedience þe cnaweð hire manere
⁊ wat hire strengðe. he mei þe uttre riwle changin
efter wisdom as he sẹið ꝥ te inre mahe beo best ihal
Nan ancre bi mi read ne schal makien ¶. den. 20
professiun. ꝥ is bihaten ase heast.ʼ bute þreo þinges. ꝥ
beoþ obedience. chastete. ⁊ stude steaðeluestnesse. ꝥ
ha ne schal ꝥ stude neauer mare changín bute for
nede ane. as strengðe ⁊ deaðes dred. obedience of hire
bischop oðer of his herre. for hwa se nímeð þing 25
on hond ⁊ bihat hit godd as heast forte don hit.ʼ
ha bint hire þerto. ⁊ sunegeð deadliche iþe bruche
ȝef ha hit brekeð willes. ȝef ha hit ne bihat nawt.ʼ
ha hit mei do þah ⁊ leauen hwen ha wel wule. as of mete. f. 2b
(M. 8) of drunch. flesch forgan oðer fisch. alle oþer swucche
þinges. of werunge, of liggunge. of ures. of oþre beoden.
segge swa monie oðer o swucche wise. þeos ⁊ þulliche
oþre beoð alle ifreo wil to don oðer to leten hwil me 5
wule ⁊ hwen me wule bute ha beon bihaten. ah chea
rite ꝥ is luue. ⁊ eadmodnesse ⁊ þolemodnesse. treowe
schipe ⁊ haldunge of þe alde ten heastes. Schrift ⁊ pe
nitence. þeos ⁊ þulliche oþre þe beoð summe of þe al
de lahe summe of þe neowe.ʼ ne beoð nawt monnes 10
fundles ne riwle ꝥ mon stalde.ʼ ah beoð godes heastes.
ant for þi euch mon mot ham nede halden. ⁊ ȝe ouer
alle. for þeos riwleð þe heorte. of hire riwlunge is al
meast ꝥ ich write. bute i þe frumðe of þis boc. ⁊ i þe
leaste ende. þe þinges ꝥ ich write her of þe uttre 15
riwle ȝe ham haldeð alle mine leoue sustren. ure la
uerd beo iþonket. ⁊ schulen þurh his grace se lengre

20 *small red initial* N*; a few blue lines within, and in margin from* 17 *to* 23*; before* .den. *a blue paragraph flourished into right margin, ornamented with red.* 19 sẹið: e *expuncted in paler ink.* 20 Nan ancre, 22 obedience *to* steaðeluest(nesse, 24 deaðes, 27 ⁊ sunegeð deadliche, *underlined with red chalk; written in right margin* (24) *with the same, in 16th-century hand,* deths fear(e)*: the final* e *near edge and rubbed.* 22 beoþ: ð *partly visible under later* þ (*see* f. 1a).

f. 2b. 11 fundles *underlined with red chalk.*

se betere. ant þah nulle ich nawt ꝥ ȝe bihaten ham as
heaste to halden. for as ofte as ȝe þrefter breken ení
20 of ham.· hit walde to swiðe hurten ower heorte ⁊ ma
kien ow swa offearet.· ꝥ ȝe mahten sone ꝥ godd for
beode ow fallen i desesperance. ꝥ is in an unhope ⁊ an
unbileaue forte beon iborhen. for þi ꝥ ich write ow
mine leoue sustren of uttre þinges i þe earste dale.
25 of ower boc of ower seruise. ⁊ nomeliche i þe leaste.· ȝe
ne schule nawt bihaten hit.· ah habbeð hit on heorte
ant doð hit as þah ȝe hit hefden bihaten.

Ȝef ei unweote easkeð ow of hwet ordre ȝe beon.·
f. 3a as summe doð þe telleð me. þe siheð þe gneat ⁊ swolheð
þe flehe.· ondswerieð of seín Iames. þe wes godes apostel.
⁊ for his muchele halinesse icleopet godes broðer. ȝef
him þuncheð wunder ⁊ sullich of swuch ondswere.·
5 easkið him hwet beo ordre. ⁊ hwer he funde in hali
writ religiun openlukest descríueþ ⁊̄ isutelet þen is i
seín iames canonial epistel. he seiþ **what** is Religiun.
hwuch is riht ordre. Religio munda & ímmaculata
apud deum ⁊ patrem hec est. visitare pup. ⁊ viduas in (M. 10)
nes. sua.
10 ⁊ immaculatum se custodire ab hoc seculo. ꝥ is cleane re
ligiun ⁊̄ **wᵗ** ute **w**em is. iseon ⁊ helpen **wydues ⁊̄ fa-**
lese children. ⁊ from þe **w**orld **w**íten him cleane ⁊̄ un
wemmet. þus seín iame descriueþ religiun ⁊̄ ordre. þe
leatere dale of his sahe límpeð to reclusen. for þer
15 beoþ twa dalen to twa manere þe beoð of religiuse. to
eiðer limpeð his dale as ȝe mahen iheren. Gode reli

28 *small blue initial* Ȝ; *red lines within and in margin from* 25 *down into lower margin.*

f. 3a. *On the alterations in this page see* f. 1a. *The same hand added stroke above* ⁊ *in* 6, 11, 12, 13. *Original letters are visible or partly so:* ð *under* þ *in* 7, 13, 15, *and under* wᵗ *in* 11; ƿ *under* w *in* 6, 11 (*all three*), 12 (*both*), 19. 1 þe telleð: þe *is probably error for* ȝe, *or* as ȝe. 6 openlukest . . þen, *sic;* descríueþ: *original probably* descriuet (*mistaken by emender for 3 sg.; cf.* 13); i *has large dot, possibly due to emender.* 7 what: t *is in main hand, but emender added a top above cross-bar.* 9 pup. ⁊ viduas in nes.: *read* pupillos ⁊ viduas in necessitate. 11 *emender omitted* der; *original probably* widewen ⁊ feder (*cf.* 22), *not room for* feader.

giuse beoð i þe world summe. Nomeliche prelaz. ⁊
treowe preachurs þe habbeð þe earre dale of þet
sein iame seide. ꝥ beoð as he seið þe gað to helpen **wy**
dewes ⁊ faderlese children. þe **sow**le is widewe þe haueð 20
forloren hire spus. ꝥ is iesu crist wið eni heaued sunne.
þe is alswa federles þe haueð þurh his sunne forloren
þe feader of heouene. gan iseon þulliche ⁊ elnin ham ⁊
helpen wið fode of hali lare.˙/ þis is riht religiun he seið
sein iame. þe leatere dale of his sahe limpeð to ower 25
religiun as ich ear seide. þe witeð ow from þe worlt ouer
oþre religiuse cleane ⁊unwemmet. þus þe apostle seín
iame þe descriueð religiun nowðer hwit ne blac. ne
nempneð he in his ordre. Ah moni siheð þe gneat ant f. 3b
swolheð þe flehe. ꝥ is. makeð muche strengðe þer as is
þe leaste. Pawel þe earste ancre. antoníe ⁊ arsenie. Ma
karie ⁊ te oþre neren ha religiuse ⁊ of sein iames or
dre? Alswa seinte Sare ⁊ seinte Sicleclice. ⁊ monie oþre 5
swucc hewepmen ba ⁊ wummen wið hare greate mat
ten ⁊ hare hearde héren neren ha of god ordre. ⁊ hweðer
hwite oðer blake as unwise ow easkið þe weneð ꝥ ordre
sitte i þe curtel. Godd wat noðeles ha weren wel baðe.
nawt tah onont claðes.˙/ ah as godes spuse singeð bi hí 10
re seoluen. Nigra sum set formosa. Ich am blac ⁊ tah
hwit ha seið. unseowlich wið uten.˙/ schene wið innen.
O þis wise ondswerieð to þe easkeres of ower ordre.
hweðer hwite oðer blake.˙/ seggeð ȝe beoð ba twa þurh
(M. 12) þe grace of godd ⁊ of seín iames ordre. ꝥ he wrat leatere. 15
Inmaculatum se custodire ab hoc seculo. ꝥ is ꝥ ich seide
ear. from þe worlt witen hím cleane ⁊ unwemmet. her
in is religiun. nawt i þe wide hod ne i þe blake cape.
ne i þe hwite rochet ne i þe greie cuuel. Þer as moníe
beoð igederet to gederes.˙/ þer for anrednesse me schal 20
makie strengðe of annesse of claðes. ⁊ of oþer hwet of
uttre þinges. ꝥ te annesse wið uten bitacni þe annes

20 *space here suggests that original had* wi|dewen ⁊ feaderlese*; a faint* o *between* þe *and* sowle.

f. 3b. 5 Sicleclice, *sic for* Sincletice. 13 boc *crossed out before* ordre.

se of a luue ⁊ of a wil ꝥ ha alle habbeð i meane wið ín
nen. wið hare habit ꝥ is an ꝥ euch haueð swuch as
25 oþer. ⁊ alswa of oðerhwet. ha ȝeiȝeð ꝥ ha habbeð alle
to gederes a luue ⁊ a wil euch alswuch as oþer. loke ꝥ
ha ne lihen. þus hit is i cuuent. ah hwer se wummon
líueð oðer mon bi him ane. hearmite oðer ancre. of
f. 4a þinges wið uten hwer of scandle ne cume nis nawt
muche strengðe. Hercne Michee. Indicabo tibi o homo quid
sit bonum ⁊ quid deus requirat a te. vtique facere iudicium
⁊ iusticiam ⁊ sollicite ambulare cum domino deo tuo. Ich
5 chulle schawi þe mon seið þe hali Michee godes prophete.
Ich chulle schawi þe soðliche hwet is godd. ⁊ hwuch reli
giun ⁊ hwuch ordre. hwuch halinesse godd easkeð of þe.
low þis. Vnderstond hit. Do wel ⁊ dem wac eauer þe seol
uen. ⁊ wið dred ⁊ wið luue ga mid godd ti lauerd. þer
10 as þeose þinges beoð.' þer is riht religiun. þer is soð or
dre. ant do al ꝥ oðer. ⁊ lete þis.' nis bute trichunge ant a
fals gile. Ve uobis scribe ⁊ pharisei ypocrite qui mundatis
quod deforis est calicis ⁊ parapsidis. intus autem pleni
estis omní
spursicia similes sepulcris dealbatis. Al ꝥ gode religiuse
15 doð oþer werieð efter þe uttre riwle.' al to gedere is her
uore. al nis bute ase tole to timbrin her towart. al nís
bute as þuften to serui þe leafdi to riwlín þe heorte. Þis
an Boc is todealet in eahte leasse Bokes.

NV míne leoue sustren. þis boc ich todeale on eah
20 te destinctiuns. ꝥ ȝe cleopieð dalen. ⁊ euch wið u
te monglunge spekeð al bi him seolf of sunderliche (M. 14)
þinges. ⁊ þah euchan riht falleð efter oðer. ⁊ is þe leatere
eauer iteiet to þe earre. Þe earste dale spekeð al of o
wer seruise. Þe oðer is hu ȝe schulen þurh ower fif
25 wittes witen ower heorte ꝥ ordre ⁊ religiun ⁊ sawle lif is

24 swuch: *above* w *a mark* '.

f. 4a. 6 godd, *sic for* god. 14 spursicia, *sic for* spurcitia. 16 tole, *sic.* 17, 18 Þis *to* Bokes *in red, written with finer strokes and slightly enlarged letters.* 19 *large red initial* N *between* 18 *and* 21; *blue line-patterns within, and in margin* 14 *to* 26. 23 *small blue initial* Þ *touched with red.* 24 *small red initial* Þ *touched with blue. In left margin directing letters* N þ þ. 28 hwet, *sic for* wit.

ínne. I þis destinctiun aren chapitres fiue. as fif stuchen
efter fif wittes þe witeð þe heorte as wakemen hwer se
ha beoð treowe. ⁊ spekeð of euch hwet sunderlepes o rawe.
Þe þridde dale is of anes cunnes fuheles þe Dauið i þe f. 4b
sawter eueneð him seolf to as he were ancre. ⁊ hu þe cun
de of þe ilke fuheles beoð ancren iliche. Þe feorðe da
le is of fleschliche fondunges. ⁊ gasteliche baðe. ⁊ confort
aȝeines ham ⁊ of hare saluen. Þe fifte dale is of schrift. 5
Þe Seste dale is of penitence. Þe Seoueðe of schir heor
te. hwi me ah ⁊ hwi me schal iesu crist luuien. ⁊ hwet bi
nimeð us his luue ⁊ let us him to luuien. Þe eahtu
ðe dale is al of þe uttre riwle. earst of mete ⁊ of drunch.
⁊ of oþre þinges ꝥ falleð þer abuten. þrefter of þe 10
þinges þe ȝe mahen underuon ⁊ hwet þinges ȝe ma
hen witen oðer habben. þrefter of ower claðes ⁊ of swuc
che þinges as þer abuten falleð. þrefter of ower werkes.
of doddunge ⁊ of blodletunge. of ower meidnes riwle.
Aleast hu ȝe ham schulen leofliche learen. Her bi 15
gínneð þe earste boc of Vres ⁊ Vreisuns þe gode beoð to
Hwen ȝe earst ariseð.᾽ blescið ow ⁊ .seggen.
seggeð. In nomine patris ⁊ fi. ⁊ s. s. Amen. ant biginneð
(M. 16) anan. Veni creator spiritus. wið up aheuene eh
nen ⁊ honden toward heouene buhinde o cneon 20
forðward up o þe bedde. ant seggeð swa al þe ymne
ut wið þe verset. Emitte spiritum t. ⁊ te vreisun. Deus quí
corda fidelium. her efter scheoiende ow ⁊ claðinde ow
seggeð. Pater noster. ⁊ Credo. Iesu criste fili dei viuí miserere
nobis. Qui de uirgine dignatus es nascí. Miserere n. þis 25 word seg

f. 4b. *Six coloured initials* Þ: 1 *blue*, 3 *red*, 5 *blue*, 6 *blue*, *red*, 8 *blue; each touched with lines of the opposite colour; the first with marginal lines to* 4; *the fourth down to* 10. *Directing letters* þ: 1 *in left margin;* 3, 5, 6 *right. The heading* 15 *to* 17: Her bi *to* beoð to seggen *in red; no paragraph before* .seggen. 17 *very large blue initial* H (*marking beginning of Part I*) *between* 16 *and* 20, *the stem in the margin between* 12 *and* 20; *red line-patterns to right, within. and in margin from* 10 *to* 25. 18 *read* filii ⁊ spiritus sancti. 19 spiritus: spc̄. 22 t.: *read* tuum. 25 n.: *read* nobis.

geð æauer aþet ȝe beon al greiðe. þis word habbeð muchel on us ⁊ i muð ofte euch time ꝥ ȝe mahen sitten ȝe oðer stonden. **H**wen ȝe beoð al greiðe. spren
f. 5a geð ow wið haliweater. ꝥ ȝe schulen eauer habben. ant þenchen o godes flesch ⁊ on his deorewurðe blod ꝥ is abu ue þe hehe weoued. ⁊ falleð adun þer towart wið þeose gretunges. **A**ve principium nostre creationis. **A**ve precium
5 nostre redemptionis. **A**ue viaticum nostre peregrinationis. **A**ve premium nostre expectationis. **A**ue solamen nostre sustentationis. Tu esto nostrum gaudium qui es futurus premí um. sit nostra in te gloria per cuncta semper secula. Mane nobiscum domine noctem obscuram remoue omne delictum ablue.
10 piam medelam tribue. Gloria tibi domine qui natus es de uirgine cum p. ⁊ cetera. Alswa ȝe schule don hwen þe preost halt hit up ed te measse. ant biuore þe confiteor hwen ȝe schule beon ihus let. efter þis falleð o cneon to ower crucifix wið þeose fif gretunges ine munegunge of godes fif wunden. **A**do (M. 18)
15 ramus te christe ⁊ benedicimus tibi quia per sanctam crucem redemisti mundum. Tuam crucem adoramus domine. tuam gloriosam reco limus passionem. miserere nostri qui passus es pro nobis. Salue crux sancta arbor digna cuius robur preciosum mundi tulit talentum. Salue crux que in corpore christi dedicata es. ⁊
20 ex membris eius tanquam margaritis ornata. O crux lignum triumphale mundi uera salus uale inter ligna nullum ta le. fronde flore germíne. Medicina christiana salua sanas egras sana. ⁊ wið þis word beateð on ower breoste quod non

26 æ *in* æauer: a *expuncted, and* e *written partly over it.* 27 time: me *obscured by stain.* 28 *small red initial* H *touched with blue.*

f. 5a. *Six small initials* A: 4 *red, blue;* 5 *red;* 7 *blue, red;* 14 *blue; each touched with lines of the opposite colour; the fourth with curled tail in margin to* 8. *Directing letters in left margin* 4 a.a, 5 a, 6 aa. 5. Aue: u *as* f. 107a. 10 p.: *read* patre.

ualet uis humana sit in tuo nomíne. Hwa se ne con
þeos fíue.' segge þe earste adoramus te. cneolinde fifsiðen. 25
⁊ blescið ow wið euchan of þeose gretunges. ant wið þeo
se wordes. Miserere nostri qui passus es pro nobis.' beateð
ower
heorte. ⁊ cusseð þe eorðe icruchet wið þe þume. þrefter
wendeð ow to ure leafdi onlicnesse ⁊ cneolið wið fif auez. f. 5b
aleast to þe oþre ymagnes. ⁊ to ower relikes luteð oþer
cneolið. nomeliche to þe halhen þe ȝe habbeð to þurh
luue iturnd ower weofdes. swa muche þe reaðere ȝef ei is
Þerefter ananriht ure leafdi uhtsong. ⁊ ¶.ihalhet. 5
seggeð o þis wise. ȝef hit is werc dei.' falleð to þer eorðe.
ȝef hit is halidei.' buhinde sumdeal duneward seggeð.
Pater noster. ⁊ Credo ba stille. Rihteð ow up þrefter ⁊
seggeð.
Domine labia mea aperies. Makieð on ower muð a creoiz wið
þe þume. Ed Deus in adiutorium.' a large creoiz wið þe þu 10
me ⁊ wið þe twa fingres. from buue þe forheaued.' dun to
þe breoste ⁊ falleð to þe eorðe. ȝef hit is wercdei wið gloria
patri. oðer buheð duneward ȝef hit hali dei aþet sicut
erat. þus ed euch gloria patri. ⁊ ed te biginnunge of þe Ve
níte. ⁊ iþe Venite. ed Venite adoremus. ant ed te Aue ma 15
(M. 20) ria. ⁊ hwerse ȝe eauer hereð Maries nome inempnet.
⁊ ed euch pater noster ꝥ falle to ower ures ⁊ to þe credo. ⁊
to þe
collecte ed eauer euch tide. ⁊ ed te leatemeste vérs of eauer
euch ymne. ⁊ ed te leaste vers wið uten an of þe salm.
Benedicite omnia opera domini domino. ed alle þes ilke 20
ȝef hit
is halidei.' buheð sumdel dunewart. ȝef hit is wercdei.' fal
leð to þer eorðe. Ed te biginnunge of eauer euch tide.
wið Deus in adiutorium.' Makieð rode taken as ich ear
tahte. Ed Veni creator buheð oðer cneolið efter ꝥ te

24 in: i *altered from ascender without erasure of top.*

f. 5b. 3 *on edge of right margin a mark or letter like a modern figure 4 in pale red-brown ink* (*offset on* f. 6a). 5 *small red initial* Þ; *blue lines within, and in margin* 2 *to* 8. *Before* .ihalhet. *a red paragraph touched with blue.* 7 .' ⁊ *omitted before* seggeð. 13 is *omitted between* hit hali. 19 ymne: y *has form of wyn* (ƿ) *dotted above.*

25 dei is. wið memento salutis auctor falleð eauer adun. ⁊
ed tis word. Nascendo formam sumpseris:' cusseð þe eor
ðe. ant alswa i þe Te deum laudamus. ed tis word. Non hor
ruisti uirginis uterum. ant ed te messe i þe muchele Credo.
f. 6a ed ex Maria uirgine ⁊ homo factus est.

Euchan segge hire ures as ha haueð iwriten ham. ⁊
euch tide sunderliche ase forð as ȝe mahen seggeð in
his tíme. ear to sone þen to leate. ȝef ȝe ne mahen eauer
5 halde þe tíme. Vhtsong bi niht iwinter. I sumer iþe dah
unge. þis wínter schal biginnen ed te hali rode dei ine
heruest:' ⁊ leasten aþet easter. Prime in winter earliche.
I Sumer bi forð marhen. Pretiosa þrefter. ȝef ȝe habbeð
neode for eani hihðe to speoken:' ȝe muhe seggen hit bi
10 uoren ⁊ efter uhtsong anan ȝef hit swa neodeð. nón eauer
efter mete. ⁊ hwen ȝe slepeð. efter slep hwil ꝥ sumer least
eð bute hwen ȝe feasteð. I winter biuore mete hwen ȝe
al ueasteð. þe sunnedei þah efter mete for ȝe eoteð twí
en. Ed te an salm ȝe schulen stonden ȝef ȝe beoð eise.
15 ⁊ ed te oþer sitten. ⁊ eauer wið gloria patri rungen up ⁊ buh (M. 22)
en. Hwa se mei stonden al on ure leafdi wurðschipe:' ston
de o godes halue. Ed alle þe seoue tiden singeð pater
noster. ⁊
aue Maria ba biuoren ⁊ efter. fidelium anime efter euch ti
de biuore þe pater noster. Ed þreo tiden seggeð Credo
wið pater
20 noster biuoren uhtsong ⁊ efter prime. ⁊ eft from ower com
plie aþet efter pretiosa haldeð Silence.

Efter euensong anan ower placebo euche niht seggeð
hwen ȝe beoð eise. bute hit beo hali niht for feaste of
nihe lesceuns þe cume ine marhen. biuore cumplie oðer
25 efter uhtsong. Dirige wið þreo salmes ⁊ wið þreo lesceuns:'
euche niht sundri. In aniuersaries of ower leoueste freond
seggeð alle nihene. I stude of gloria ed euch psalmes ende.

f. 6a. 2 *small blue initial* E; *red line-ornament within, and in margin from above* 1 *to* 5; *directing* e *in left margin.* 20 *punctuation omitted after* noster. 22 *small red initial* E; *blue line-ornament from* 20 *to* 25 *within, and in margin; directing* e *in left margin.* 25 lesceuns: *MS.* ūns *with* uns *combined.*

Requiem eternam dona eis do. Et lux perpe. luceat e. Ed placebo sitteð.
aþet Magnificat. alswa ed Dirige bute ed te lesceuns. ⁊ f. 6b
ed te Miserere. Ant from laudate al ut. Requiescant in pa
ce i stude of Benedicamus seggeð on ende. Ine marhen oðer
i niht efter þe suffragies of uhtsong seggeð commendací
un. sittinde þe salmes. cneolinde þe ureisuns oðer stond 5
inde. ȝef ȝe þus doð euche niht bute ane sunne niht.
ȝe doð muche betere. In a meldei we seggeð ba. placebo
⁊ dirige efter þe mete graces. I twímel dei efter non. ⁊ ȝe
alswa mote don. Seoue psalmes seggeð sittinde oðer
cneolinde wið þe letaníe. fiftene psalmes seggeð o þis 10
wise. þe earste fiue for ow seolf. ⁊ for alle þe ow god doð
oðer unnen. þe oþre fiue for þe peis of al hali chirche.
þe þridde fiue for alle cristene sawles. Efter þe forme fi
ue. kyrie eleison. christe eleison. kyrie eleison pater noster. Et ne nos. Saluos fac
seruos tuos ⁊ ancillas tuas. Deus meus sperantes in te. 15 Oremus.
(M. 24) Deus cui proprium est. Efter þe oþre fiue alswa. kyrie eleison. christe eleison.
kyrie eleison. pater noster. Et ne nos. Domine fiat pax in uirtute tua. Et
abundancia in tur. t. Oremus. Ecclesie tue quesumus domine preces placatus.
Efter þe þridde fiue þe ȝe schulen seggen wið uten gloria
patri. kyrie eleison. i.i.i. pater noster. Et ne nos. A porta 20 inferi. Erue do.
animas eorum. Oremus. fidelium deus omnium. Seoue salmes ⁊ þus
þeose fiftene seggeð abuten under. for abute swuch tí
me as me singeð measse in alle religiuns. ⁊ ure lauerd
þolede pine up o þe rode. ȝeahen to beo nomeliche i beo
den ⁊ ibonen. ⁊ alswa from prime aþet midmarhen hwen 25

28 *read* domine. Et lux perpetua luceat eis.

f. 6b. 7 In *to* 9 don *not in* M. 9 *small blue initial* S *touched with red lines.* 18 tur. t.: *read* turribus tuis. 23 *in right margin red marks offset from* F *on* f. 7a. 26 *in right margin directing letter* o; *before* þis wise *a blue paragraph touched with red erroneously substituted for* O (*cf.* f. 7b). 21 do.: *read* domine. 26 *after* meassen M *adds 16 lines.*

preostes of þe worlt singeð hare meassen. ¶ þis wise
ȝe mahen ȝef ȝe wulleð seggen ower pater nostres.
Almihti godd. feader. sune. hali geast. as ȝe beoð þreo (M. 26)
f. 7a an godd.' alswa ȝe beoð an mihte. an wisdom. ⁊ an luue.
⁊ þah is mihte iturnd to þe in hali writ nomeliche. þu
deorewurðe feader. to þe wisdom seli sune. to þe luue
hali gast. ȝef me an almihti godd þrile i þreo hades.
5 þes ilke þreo þinges. mihte forte serui þe. wisdom forte
cweme þe. luue ⁊ wil to don hit. mihte ꝥ ich mahe don.
wisdom ꝥ ich cunne don. luue ꝥ ich wulle don aa ꝥ te is
leouest. as þu art ful of euch god.' alswa nis na god wo
ne þer as þeose þreo beoð. mihte ⁊ wisdom ⁊ luue iueiet
10 to gederes. ꝥ tu ȝetti me ham hali þrumnesse iþe wurð
schipe of þe þreo pater nostres. Credo. verset. Benedicamus patrem ⁊ filium·
cum s. s. laudemus ⁊ super exaltemus e. in secula. Oremus. Omnipotens sempiter
ne deus qui dedisti fa. t. in confes. uere fidei eter. gloriam. ag. Alpha ⁊ ω.
hwa se hit haueð. oðer of þe hali þrumnesse segge þe
15 wulle. A iesu þín are. iesu for mine sunnen ahonget o
rode. for þe ilke fif wunden þe þu on hire bleddest heal
mi blodi sawle of alle þe sunnen ꝥ ha is wið iwundet.'
þurh mine fif wittes. i þe munegunge of ham ꝥ hit swa
mote beon deorewurðe lauerd fif pater nostres. verset. Omnis terra adoret
20 te. Et psalmum di. no. t. oremus. Iuste iudex ȝef þu const. oþer of (M. 28)
þe creoiz sum oðer. Deus qui unigeniti tui domini nostri iesu christi
pretioso sanguine uexillum sancte crucis. þis is an of þe beste.
FOR þe seoue ȝiftes of þe hali gast ꝥ ich ham mote hab

28 *red initial* A, *left side prolonged to curl low in bottom margin; blue lines to right, within, and down curl with trailer now cut off at bottom edge.*
f. 7a. 12 *read* spiritu sancto .. eos. 13 *read* famulis tuis in confessione .. eterne [trinitatis *omitted*] gloriam agnoscere. 15 *small blue initial* A *touched with red; directing* a *in left margin.* 20 di. no. t.: *read* dicat nomini tuo. 23 *red initial* F, *with a few blue lines within, and in margin from* 20 *to* 26; *directing* f *in left margin.*

ben. ⁊ for þe seoue tiden ꝥ hali chirche singeð ꝥ ich deale
in ham slepe ich oðer wakie. ⁊ for þe seoue bonen iþe pater 25
noster aȝein þe seoue heaued ⁊ deadliche sunnen. ꝥ tu wite
me wið ham ⁊ alle hare brokes. ⁊ ȝeoue me þe seouene
selie eadínesses þe þu hauest lauerd bihaten þine icorene.
i þin eadi nome seoue pater nostres. verset. Emitte spiritum f. 7b
tuum.
Oremus. Deus cui cor omne patet. Ecclesie tue quesumus
domine.
Exaudi quesumus domine supplicum preces.

FOR þe ten heastes þe ich ibroken habbe. summe
oðer alle. ⁊ me seoluen towart te hwet se beo of 5
oðerhwet untreoweliche iteoheðet. ibote of þeose
bruchen forte sahtní me wið þe deorewurðe lauerd
ten pater nostres. verset. Ego dixi domine miserere mei.
Sana animam
meam quia peccaui tibi. Oremus Deus cui proprium est
misereri.

[I] þe wurðgunge iesu crist of þine tweof apostles. ꝥ ich 10
mote oueral folhin hare lare. ꝥ ich mote habben
(M. 30) þurh hare bonen þe tweolf bohes þe bloweð of chea
rite as seínte pawel writeð. blisfule lauerd tweolf pater
nostres. verset. annuntiauerunt opera dei. Et facta eius
intellexe
runt. Oremus. Exaudi nos deus salutaris noster & aposto- 15
lorum
tuorum nos tuere presidíís.

HIhen þe ȝe luuieð best.ʾ in heore wurðgunge
seggeð oðer leas oðer ma as ow bereð on heor

f. 7b. 4 *large blue initial* F *between* 3 *and* 6, *with tapered stem in margin from* 3 *to* 10; *red line-patterns to right, within, and in margin from* 2 *to* 13. *In left margin,* 4, 10, *directing letters* f j; *the tapered stem of* F, *resembling* I, *occupies place of* I *in* 10, *which was omitted.* 10 tweof *sic* (*probably a genuine form*). 13 tweolfpater: l *altered from* f *and* f *inserted in space, with stroke below to mark word-division.* 17 *large red initial* H *between* 16 *and* 19, *with stem in margin between* 13 *and* 19; *blue line-patterns within, and in margin from* 12 *to* 24; *directing* h *in left margin. The* a *of* Halhen *omitted* (*not painted over*).

te. ⁊ ꝥ uerset efterward wið hare collecte. ¶ or alle
20 þeo þe habbeð eani god ido me. iseid me oðer iun
nen me. ⁊ for alle þe ilke þe wurcheð þe six werkes
of misericorde. mearciable lauerd six pater nostres. verset.
Disper
sit dedit pauperibus. Iusticia eius m. Oremus. Retribuere
dign. ð.
hwa se wule segge þe salm. AD te leuaui. biuore þe
25 pater nostres. ant kyrie eleison. christe eleison. kyrie eleison.

FOR alle þe sawlen þe beoð forð fearen iþe bi
leaue of þe fowr goddspelles þe haldeð al crist
endom up o fowr halues. ꝥ tu þe fowr marheȝeuen
f. 8a ȝeoue ham in heouene. milzfule lauerd fowr pater nostres.
ȝef ȝe seggeð nihene.' as þer beoð nihene englene
weoredes ꝥ godd þurh his mearci hihi ham ut of
pine to hare feolahredden.' ȝe doð ȝet betere. ⁊ her
5 alswa ȝe wulleð seggeð. Deprofundis biuore þe pater
nostres. ⁊ kyrie eleison. iii. verset. A porta inferi. Oremus.
fidelium.

Bi dei sum tíme oder bi niht gederið in ower heorte (M. 32)
alle seke ⁊ sarie ꝥ wa ⁊ pouerte þolieð. þe pinen
þe prisuns þolieð ⁊ habbeð þer ha liggeð wið írn he
10 uie ifeðeret. nomeliche of þe cristene þe beoð in heaðe
nesse. Summe i prisun. summe in ase muche þeowdom
as oxe is oðer asse. habbeð reowðe of þeo þe beoð i
stronge temptatiuns. alle hare sares setteð in ower
heorte. ⁊ sikeð to ure lauerd ꝥ he neome reowðe of
15 ham ⁊ bihalde toward ham wið þe ehe of his are.
ant ȝef ȝe habbeð hwile.' seggeð þe salm. leuauí

19 *before* or alle *a red paragraph, ornamented with blue, mistakenly substituted for* F (*cf.* f. 6b. 26). 23 *read* manet . . dignare domine. 26 *large blue initial* F *between* 25 *and* 27 *with stem in margin extending from* 25 *to low in bottom margin; red line-patterns to right, within, and in margin from* 23 *to bottom edge; directing* f *in left margin.* 25 *second* kyrie *has* p *dotted for* y. 28 marheȝeuen : ȝeuen *crossed out with bold stroke* (*supposed to be identical with* ȝeoue *following*).

f. 8a. 7 *large red initial* B *between* 6 *and* 8; *blue line-patterns to right, within, and in margin from* 3 *to* 13; *directing* b *in left margin;* oder, *sic.* 10 heaðe : h *abnormal with two tail-strokes.*

oculos. Pater noster. verset. Conuertere domine usquequo. Et deprecabilis
esto super s. t. Oremus. Pretende domine famulis & famulabus
I þe measse hwen þe preost heueð up godes licome:
seggeð þis vers stondinde. Ecce salus mundi. uerbum 20
patris. hostia uera. víua caro. deitas integra. uerus homo.
ant þenne falleð adun wið þeose gretunges. AVe
principium nostre creationis. Aue pre. n. r. Aue Viaticum n. pere.
aue premium n. expec. Aue so. n. susten. Tu esto n. g. qui es futurus
pre. sit nostra in te gloria per cuncta s. s. amen. Mane no. 25 domine. Gloria
tibi domine. set quis est locus in me quo ueniat in me deus meus
quo deus ueniat aut maneat in me deus qui fecit celum
⁊ terram. ita ne domine deus meus est quicquam in me quod capiat .te.
Quis michi dabit ut uenias in cor meum & inebries illud. ⁊ f. 8b
unum bonum meum amplectar te? Quis michi es miserere
ut loquar. angusta est tibi domus anime mee. quo ueni
as ad eam dilatetur abs te. ruinosa est refice eam. habet que
offendant oculos tuos. fateor ⁊ scio. set quis mundabit 5
eam? aut cui alteri preter te clamabo? ab ocultis meis
munda me domine ⁊ ab alienis parce famule tue. mí
serere. miserere. Miserere mei deus secundum magnam. ant swa al þe
(M. 34) salm ut wið gloria patri. christe audi nos twien. kyrie eleison.
christe eleison. kyrie eleison. pater noster. Credo. Carnis 10 resurrectionem. Et

18 famulabus: faml' *with irregular flourish out into margin.* 18–23: *for the initial letters or partially written words followed by points read:* 18 seruos tuos; 23 pretium nostre redemptionis . . nostre peregrinationis; 24 nostre expectationis . . solamen nostre sustentationis . . nostrum gaudium; 25 premium . . semper secula . . nobiscum. 19 *large blue initial* I *in margin from* 16/17 *to* 23; *ornamented with red lines from* 13, *with trailer almost to bottom of page; directing* j *in left margin of* 19. 28 .te. *written below* at *of* capiat.

f. 8b. 6 ocultis, *sic.* 8 miserere *written* miseerre.

uitam eter. amen. Saluam fac famulam tuam deus meus speran
tem in te. Doce me facere uoluntatem tuam quia deus meus
es tu. Domine exaudi orationem m. Et cla. meus ad te ue. Oremus.
Concede quesumus omnipotens deus ut quem enigmatice & sub a
15 liena spetie cernimus quo sacramentaliter cibamur
in terris. fatie ad fatiem eum uideamus eo sicuti est
ueraciter ꝛ realiter frui mereamur in celis. per eundem d.
Efter þe measse cos hwen þe preost sacreð. þer for
ȝeoteð al þe world. þer beoð al ut of bodi þer i
20 sperclinde luue bicluppeð ower leofmon þe in to ow
er breostes bur is iliht of heouene. ꝛ haldeð him
heteueste aþet he habbe iȝettet ow al ꝥ ȝe eauer
easkið. þis ureisun biuore þe muchele rode is of
Abute middei hwa se mei .muche strengðe.
25 Ahwa se ne mei þenne.⸗ o sum oðer time þen
che o godes rode. ase muchel as ha eauer con mest
oðer mei. ꝛ of his derue pine. ꝛ biginne þrefter
þe ilke fif gretunges þe beoð iwriten þruppe. ant
f. 9a alswa cneolin to euchan ꝛ blescín as hit seið þer ant
beate þe breoste ꝛ makie a þulli bone.
Adoramus te christe. Tuam crucem. Salue crux que. O
Acrux lignum. aris þenne ꝛ bigin þe antefne.
5 Salua nos christe saluator per uirtutem sancte crucis. wið þe ro
de taken. ꝛ segge stondinde þe salm. Iubilate. wið gloria (M. 36)

11 eter.: *read* eternam. 13 *read* meam . . clamor . . ueniat. 14 *to* 19: *along left ruled margin a line of five curves in red chalk; in outer margin, between* 15 *and* 16, *mark* × *in ink.* 17 d.: *read* dominum. 20 *MS.* sperclinde. 23, 24 *the conclusion* þis ureisun *to* strengðe *written in red with finer strokes and larger letters.* 24 *red initial* A *between* 23 *and* 26; *blue line-patterns to right, within, and in margin from* 22 *down tail to low in bottom margin; directing* a *in left margin. No paragraph before* .muche strengðe.

f. 9a. 1 cneolin . . blescín, *sic for sg.* 3 *large blue initial* A *between* 2 *and* 5 *with tail to* 7; *red line-patterns to right, within, and in margin from above* 1 *to* 9 (*a trailer to* 15); *directing* a *in left margin.*

patri. ꝛ þenne þe antefne segge eauer þus. Salua nos christe saluator per uirtutem sancte c. ꝛ blescín wið qui saluasti petrum
in mare miserere nobis. ꝛ beate þe breoste ꝛ tenne falle adun ꝛ segge christe audi nos. iesu christe. audi nos. kyrie eleison. 10
christe eleison. kyrie eleison. Pater noster. Et ne nos. verset. Protector noster aspice deus.
Et respice in faciem christi tui. Oremus. Deus qui sanctam crucem
as ear. eft biginne adoramus as ear alle fiue. Salua nos christe. þe antefne as ear. þe salm. ad te leuaui. þe antef ne as ear al ut. ꝛ tenne as ear to þe eorðe. christe audi nos 15 twien. ky. iii. pater noster. Et ne nos. verset. protector noster as ear. Ore
mus. ADesto quesumus domine deus noster ꝛ quos sancte crucis le. fa. þridde
chearre riht alswa. ꝛ feorðe chearre ꝛ fifte. nawiht ne changeð bute þe salmes ꝛ te ureisuns. þe forme salm. Iubilate. þe oþer ad te leuaui. þe þridde. Qui confidunt. 20 þe feorðe. Domine non est exaltatum. þe fifte. laudate dominum in sanctis eius.
ꝛ in euch beoð fif uers. þe fif ureisuns beoð. Deus qui sanctam c.
ADesto quesumus d. Deus qui pro nobis fi. t. Deus qui unigeniti. Iuste iu
(M. 38) dex. wið o beata ꝛ intemerata. ant hwa se ne con þeos fif ureisuns. segge eauer an. Ant hwa se þuncheð to long. 25

Leaue þe salmes.

Leafdi seinte Marie for þe ilke muchele blisse ꝥ tu hefdest inwið þe i ꝥ ilke time ꝥ iesu godd godes sune efter þe engles gretunge nom flesch ꝛ blod in þe ꝛ of þe f. 9b underfeng mi gretunge wið þe ilke aue. ꝛ make me telle

8 c.: *read* crucis; blescín, *sic*. 16 ky.: *read* kyrie eleison. 17 le. fa.: *read* letari facis. 22 c.: *read* crucem. 23 d. . fi. t.: *read* domine . . filium tuum. 27 *large red initial* L *with stem between* 24 *and* 28; *blue line-patterns within, and in margin from* 20 *to low in bottom margin; directing* l (*nearly hidden in binding*).

lutel of euch blisse utewið. ah froure me inwið ꝛ ernde
me þeo of heouene. ant ase wis as i þe ilke flesch ꝥ he
5 toc of þe nes neauer sunne. ne i þín as me leueð efter
þe ilke tacunge hwet se biuore were.᷾ clense mi sawle of
fleschliche sunnen. Bigínne þe aue aþet dominus tecum. as me
biginneð antefne. ꝛ tenne þe salm. ꝛ efter þe salm al
ut fifsiðen. ꝛ þus to euch salm. Aue Maria gratia plena
dominus
10 tecum. Magnificat. Aue maria al ut fifsiðen.
Leafdi seinte maria for þe ilke muchele blisse þet
tu hefdest þa þu sehe þe ilke blisfule bearn iboren
of þi cleane bodi to moncunne heale. wið uten eauer
euch bruche. wið ihal meiðhad ꝛ meidenes menske.
15 heal me ꝥ am þurh wil tobroken as ich drede hwet
se beo of dede. ꝛ ȝef me in heouene seon þi blisfule
leor. ꝛ bihalde lanhure meidenes menske.᷾ ȝef ich nam
wurðe forte beon iblisset in hare ferredden. Aue Ma. g.
p. d'. t. AD dominum cum tribularer. aue as ear fiue.
20 Leafdi seinte Marie for þe ilke m. b. ꝥ tu hef.
þa. þ.
sehe þi deore deorewurðe sune efter his derue deað.᷾ ari
sen to blisful lif. his bodi seueualt brihtre þen þe
sunne. ȝef me deien wið him ꝛ arisen in him. worlt
liche deien. gasteliche libben. dealen in his pinen feo
25 lahliche in eorðe . forte beon i blisse his feolahe inheo
uene. for þe ilke muchele blisse ꝥ tu hefdest leafdi
of his blisful ariste efter þi muchele sorhe.᷾ efter mi
sorhe ꝥ ich am in her.᷾ lead me to þi blisse . Aue Ma. g. (M. 40)
f. 10a plena. d'. t. Retribue ser. t. Aue fif siðen.
Leafdi seinte Ma. for þe il. m. b. ꝥ tu h. þa þu sehe
þi brih

f. 9b. 11 *large blue initial* L *with stem in margin between* 8 *and* 12; *red line-patterns within, and in margin from* 5 *to* 15. maria, *sic.* 18, 19 *read* Maria gratia plena dominus tecum. 20 *large red initial* L *with stem in margin between* 16 *and* 21; *blue line-patterns within, and in margin from* 15 *to* 25 (*trailer to below* 28); *read* muchele blisse ꝥ tu hefdest þa þu. 28 *read* Maria gratia.

f. 10a. 1: *read* dominus tecum . . seruo tuo. 2 *large blue*

te blisfule sune ꝥ te giws wenden forte aþrusmin i þruh. se
wurðliche ⁊ se mihtiliche on hali þursdei stihe to his
blisse in to his riche of heouene.· ȝef me warpe wið him 5
al þe worlt under fet. ⁊ stihen nu heorteliche hwen ich
deie gasteliche. o domesdei al licomliche to heouenliche
blissen. Aue Ma. g. p. d'. t. In conuertendo. aue fif
siðen.

Leafdi seinte Marie for þe ilke muchele b. ꝥ fulde al
þe eorðe þa he underueng þe in to unimete blisse. ⁊ wið 10
his blisfule earmes sette þe i trone. ⁊ cwene crune of hea
ued brihtre þen þe sunne. heh heouenliche cwen under
ueng þeos gretunges of me swa on eorðe.· ꝥ ich mote blis
fulliche grete þe in heouene. Aue Ma. g. p. d'. t. AD
te le
uaui. Aue fif siðen. ⁊ þenne ꝥ uerset. Spiritus sanctus 15
superueniet
in te. Et uirtus altissimi ob. tibi. Oremus. Gratiam
tuam. Antefne. Ave regina
celorum. aue domina Angelorum. salue radix sancta ex qua
mundo
lux est orta. vale ualde decora ⁊ pro nobis semper
christum exo
ra. verset. Egredietur uirga de radice iesse. Et flos de
radice eius
ascendet. Oremus. Deus qui uirginalem aulam. Antefne. 20
Gaude dei
genitrix uirgo inmaculata. gaude que gaudium ab angelo
suscepisti. gaude que genuisti eterni luminis claritatem.
Gaude mater. gaude sancta dei genitrix uirgo tu sola mater
innupta te laudat omnis filíí tui creatura genitricem

initial L, *with stem in margin* (*from two line-spaces above* 1 *to below* 2); *red line-patterns within, and in margin from letter-top to* 7; *directing* l *in left margin.* 2 *read* Marie for þe ilke muchele blisse ꝥ tu hefdest. 8 *read* Maria gratia plena dominus tecum. 9 *large red initial* L *with stem in margin from* 7 *to below* 9; *blue line-patterns within, and in margin from letter-top to* 17; *directing* l *nearly hidden in binding.* b.: *read* blisse. 11 of heaued: of *sic.* 14 *read* Maria gratia plena dominus tecum. 15 Spiritus: Sp̂c. 16 ob.: *read* obumbrabit. 17 porta *omitted after* sancta.

25 lucis. sis pro nobis pia interuentrix. verset. Ecce uirgo concipiet ꝛ pa
riet filium. Et uocabitur nomen eius emmanuel. Oremus. Deus
qui de beate marie uirginis utero. Antefne. Gaude uirgo. gaude (M. 42)
dei genitrix. ꝛ gaude gaudium maria omnium fidelium.
f. 10b Gaudeat ecclesia in tuis laudibus assidua. ꝛ pia domina gaude
re fac nos tecum ante dominum. verset. Ecce concipies in utero ꝛ pari
es filium. Et uocabis nomen eius iesum. Oremus. Deus qui salutis eter
ne beate marie uirginitate fecunda hu. ge. Antefne. Alma red
5 emptoris mater que peruia celi porta manes ꝛ stella ma
ris succurre cadenti surgere qui curat populo tuque genu
isti natura mirante tuum sanctum genitorem. uirgo prius ac
posterius gabrielis ab ore sumens illud aue peccatorum misere
re. Her sitteð þe auez. fifti oðer hundret. oðer ma oþer
10 leas efter ꝥ me haueð hwile. On ende ꝥ uerset. Ecce ancil
la domini. fiat michi secundum uerbum tuum. Oremus. O sancta uirgo uirginum.
Hwa se wule mei stutte þruppe ananrihtes. efter
þe forme ureisun. Gratiam tuam. ant segge. þenne hire
tale of auez. efter þe leaste salm. Ad te leuaui. Eauer
15 biuore þe salm biginnen an aue aþet dominus tecum. ꝛ segge
stondinde þe salm. Þe salmes beoð inumene efter þe
fif leattres of ure leafdis nome hwa se nimeð ȝeme.
ant al þis ilke ureisun efter hire fif heste blisses.؍ eor
neð bi fiue. tele i þe antefnes. ꝛ tu schalt finden in ham
20 gretunges fiue. þe ureisuns ꝥ ich nabbe buten ane i
mearket.؍ beoð iwriten ouer al wið ute þe leaste. leo
teð writen on a scrowe hwet se ȝe ne kunnen. Þus
ich biginne mine auez oðerhwiles.

Leafdi swete leafdi swetest alre leafdi. leafdi leouest

f. 10*b*. 3 nomen: nom̄ *with* m̄ *on partly erased* b. 4 hu. ge.: *read* humano generi. 12 þruppe: þ *upon* a *not erased*. 22 *from* Þus *to* f. 11a. 18 frumðe *not in* M. 22 hwet: e *on erasure*. 24 *large red initial* L, *with stem in margin between* 20 *and* 25; *blue line-patterns within, and in margin from* 17 *to* 28.

leafdi. lufsumest leafdi. O pulcherrima mulierum. leaf 25
di seinte Marie deorewurðe. leafdi. leafdi cwen of heoue
ne. leafdi cwen of are. leafdi do me are. leafdi meiden
moder. Meiden godes moder. iesu cristes moder. Meiden
of mílce. moder of grace. O uírgo uirginum Maria mater f. 11a
gratie. mater misericordie. tu nos ab hoste protege & hora mortis
suscipe. per tuum uirgo filium per patrem paraclitum assis pre
sens ad obitum nostrumque muni exitum. Gloria tibi domine qui na.
es de uirgine ꝛ cetera. ant fallen to þer eorðe. ꝛ cussen hire wið þis 5
leaste uers. hwa se is hal iheafdet. ꝛ tenne auez téne ꝛ téne
togederes. þe teoheðe eauer þus forð. Aue Maria. g. p. dominus.
t. benedicta tu in mulieribus. ꝛbe. f. u. t. Spiritus sanctus superueniet in te Et
uirtus altissimi obumbrabit tibi. ideoque & quod nascetur ex te
sanctum uocabitur filius dei. Ecce ancilla domini fiat michi secundum uerbum tu 10
um. ꝛ cusse þe eorðe on ende. oðer degre oðer bench oþer
sumhwet herres. ꝛ biginnen. leafdi swete leafdi as ear
þe forme tene. þe fifti cneolinde up ꝛ dun. þe oþre cneolín
de iriht up stille. buten ed te Aue marie sum semblant
wið þe oðer cneo alutel. þe þridde téne adun ꝛ up o þe 15
elbohen riht to þer eorðe. Þe feorðe: þe elbohen o degre
oðer o bench. ant eauer to þe aue lute wið þe heaued. þe
fifte téne stondinde. ant eft biginne þe turn as i þe frumðe.

(M. 44) Al ꝥ ȝe eauer seggeð of þulliche oþre bonen. as
pater nostres ꝛ auez on ower ahne wise. salmes ꝛ urei 20
suns: ich am wel ipaiet. Euchan segge as best bereð hi

f. 11a. 3 ꝛ *omitted after* patrem. 4 na.: *read* natus. 7, 8 *read* gratia plena . . tecum . . ꝛ benedictus fructus uentris tui. 8 Spiritus: Spc̄. 12 *punctuation omitted after* ear. 13 *small* of *in pale ink interlined above final* e *of* tene. 15 adun ꝛ up: ꝛ *partly erased.* 19 *large blue initial* A *between* 18 *and* 21 *with tail down to* 25; *red line-patterns to right, within, and in margin from* 17 *to* 28; *directing* a *in left margin.*

re on heorte. Verseilunge of sawter. Redunge of englisc
oðer of frensch. halie meditatiuns. ower cneolunges
hwen se ȝe eauer mahen iȝemen. ear mete ⁊ efter. eauer
25 se ȝe mare doð:· se godd ow eche forðre his deorewurðe
grace. ah lokið swa ich bidde ow ꝥ ȝe ne beon neauer
idel. ah wurchen oðer reden. oþer beon i bonen. ⁊ swa
don eauer sumhwet ꝥ god mahe of awakenin. þe ures
f. 11b of þe hali gast ȝef ȝe ham wulleð seggen. seggeð euch
tide of ham biuoren ure leafdi tide. Toward te preos
tes tiden hercnið se forð se ȝe mahen. ah wið him ne
schule ȝe nowðer uerseilín ne singen ꝥ he hit mahe i
5 héren. Ower graces stondinde biuore mete ⁊ efter as ha
beoð iwriten ow. ⁊ wið þe Miserere gað biuoren ower
weoued. ⁊ endið þear þe graces. Bitweone mel þe drín
ken wule:· segge. Benedicite. Potum nostrum filius dei
benedicat.
In nomine patris. ⁊ blesci efterwart. ADiutorium nostrum in
10 nomine dominí. Qui fecit celum ⁊ terram. Sit nomen domini
benedictum.
Ex hoc nunc ⁊ usque in seculum. Benedicamus domino.
Deo gratias.

Hwen se ȝe gað to ower bedd i niht oðer in euen:·
falleð o cneon ⁊ þencheð i hwet ȝe habbeð i þe
dei iwreaðet ure lauerd. ⁊ crieð him ȝeorne merci ⁊ for
15 ȝeuenesse. ȝef ȝe habbeð ei god idon:· þonkið him of
his ȝeoue. wið ute hwam we ne mahen ne wel don ne
wel þenchen. ⁊ seggeð Miserere. ⁊ kyrie eleison. christe eleison.
ky. pater noster.
Et ne nos. verset. Saluas fac an. t. Deus meus sper. in te.
Oremus. Deus

26 lokið swa ich bidde *on an erasure; tops of* dd *visible above* ich, *of* d *between* d-d *of* bidde, *a minim between* bidde *and* ow.

f. 11b. 2 *small blue initial* T *touched with red; directing* t *in right margin.* 12 *large red initial* H *with stem in margin between* 8 *and* 14; *blue line-patterns to right, within, and in margin from* 6 *to* 18. 14 merci : er *expressed by abbreviation.* 15 god : *upright* d *formed by alteration* (? *of* n). 17 christe eleison : *here expressed* xeł; ky. : *read* kyrie eleison. 18 an. t. : *read* ancillas tuas; sper. : *read* sperantes.

cui proprium est. ⁊stondinde. Visita domine habitationem istam.
(M. 46) ant aleast þenne christus vincit ✠ christus regnat ✠ christus ímperat. 20
.✠. wið þreo creoiz wið þe þume up o þe forheaued. ⁊ þenne. Ecce crucem domini fugite partes aduerse. vicit leo de
tribu iuda radix dauið alleluia. A large creoiz as ed Deus in adiutorium. wið ecce crucem domini. ⁊ tenne fowr creoiz o fowr half wið þeose fowre efterwarde clauses. 25
Crux ✠ fugat omne malum. Crux ✠ est reparatio rerum. per crucis hoc signum ✠ fugiat procul omne malignum. ⁊ per idem signum ✠ saluetur quodque benignum.
on ende ow seolf ⁊ o þe bedd baðe. in nomine patris ⁊ f. I bedd f. 12a
se uorð se ȝe mahen ne do ȝe ne ne þenchen na þing
Þe ne con oþer uhtsong oðer ne ℂ.bute slépen.
mei hit seggen.' segge for uhtsong þritti pater nostres.
⁊ Aue Maria efter euch pater noster. ⁊ gloria patri efter euch 5
aue. Aleast oremus hwa se con. Deus cui proprium est. Benedicamus
do. Anime fidelium. for euensong.' twenti. for euch oðer tide.' segge fiftene o þis ilke wise. bute ꝥ ed uhtsong schal seggen earst hwa se con. Domine labia mea aperies. Et os meum. Deus in adiutorium. ant ed Complie.' Conuerte nos deus s. Deus 10
in adiutorium. Ed alle þe oþre tiden. Deus in adiutorium.
Hwa se is unheite.' forkeorue of uhtsong téne. Of euch of þe oþre fiue. þe haluendal of euchan ȝef ha is seccre.
hwa se is ful meoseise.' of al beo ha cwíte. neome hire

20 christus (3): xp̄c x̄ x̄.

f. 12a. 1 f.: *read* filii. 3 *large blue initial* Þ *between* 2 *and* 5, *with tapering stem from above* 1 *to below* 7; *red line-patterns within, and on both sides of stem down to* 8; *directing* þ *in left margin. Before* .bute slépen. *a red paragraph.* 7 do.: *read* domino. 10 s.: *read* salutaris. 12 *large red initial* H *between* 11 *and* 13, *stem in margin between* 9 *and* 13; *blue line-patterns within, and in margin from* 7 *to* 18; *directing* h (*partly visible*) *in left margin.*

15 secnesse nawt ane þolemodliche: ah do swiðe gleadli
che. ⁊ al is hiren þ hali chirche ret oðer singeð. Þah
ȝe ahen of godd þenchen in euch tíme. meast þah
in ower tiden. þ ower þohtes ne beon fleotinde þenne.
ȝef ȝe þurh ȝemeles gluffeð of wordes. oðer misneo
20 með uers: neomeð owe venie dun ed ter eorðe wið þe
hond ane. al fallen adun for muche misneomunge.
⁊ schawið ofte i schrift ower ȝemeles herabuten.

ÞIS is nu þe forme dale þe haueð ispeken hiderto of (M. 48)
ower seruise. hwet se beo nu þerof: þeose riwlen herefter
25 ich walde ha weren of alle as ha beoð of ow þurh go
des grace ihalden. ¶ Her Biginneð þe
oþer dale of þe heorte warde þurh þe
fif wittes.

f. 12b OMNi custodia serua cor tuum quia ex ipso
uita procedit. Wið alles cunnes warde doh
ter seið Salomon wite wel þin heorte. for
sawle lif is in hire ȝef ha is wel iloket. Þe
5 heorte wardeíns beoð þe fif wittes. Sihðe. ⁊ herunge.
Smecchunge. ⁊ Smeallunge. ⁊ euch límes felunge. Ant
we schulen speoken of alle. for hwa se wit þeose wel: he
deð Salomones bode. he wit wel his heorte ⁊ his sawle
heale. Þe heorte is a ful wilde beast. ⁊ makeð moni liht
10 lupe as seínt Gregoire seið. Nichil corde fugatius. Na þing
ne etflid mon sonre þen his ahne heorte. Dauið godes
prophete meande i sum time þ ha wes etsteart him. Cor
meum dereliquit me. þ is. Min heorte is edflohe me. ⁊
eft he blisseð him ⁊ seið þ ha wes icumen hám. Inue
15 nit seruus tuus cor suum. lauerd he seið mín heorte is

16 *small blue initial* Þ *touched with red.* 20 owe, *sic for* ower.
23 *large blue initial* Þ *with tall stem between* 20 *and* 25; *red lines to right within and in margin from* 18 *to below* 28. 26 *to* 28: *after* ihalden. *a red written paragraph;* Her *to* wittes *in red. Except for* iginneð *the letters are larger than normal and the word-spaces increased.*

f. 12b. 1 *very large red initial* O (*marking beginning of Part II*) *between upper margin* (*a line-space above* 1) *and* 5, *ornamented with blue line-patterns round, within, and in margin from present upper edge* (*shaved at top*) *with trails to* 24. 2 Wið: *small blue initial* Þ (*not* V) *touched with red.* 6 *in left margin in red chalk* smack.

icumen aȝeín eft. ich hire habbe ifunden. Hwen se ha
li mon ⁊ se wis ⁊ se war lette hire edstearten: sare
mei an oðer of hire fluht carien. Ant hwer edbrec
ha ut from dauið þe hali king godes prophete? hwer?
Godd wat ed his ehþurl. þurh a sihðe ꝥ he seh þurh 20
(M. 50) a bihaldunge as ȝe schulen efter ihéren. **FOR** þi mí
ne leoue sustren þe leaste ꝥ ȝe eauer mahen luuieð
ower þurles. Alle beon ha lutle. þe parlurs least ⁊
nearewest. þe clað in ham beo twafald. Blac ꝥ clað:
þe cros hwit. wið innen ⁊ wið uten. ꝥ blake clað bi 25
tacneð ꝥ ȝe beoð blake ⁊ unwurð to þe world wiðuten.
ꝥ te soðe sunne haueð utewið forculet ow. ⁊ sẇa wið
ten as ȝe beoð unseowlich imaket ow þurh gleames
of his grace. þe hwite cros límpeð to ow. For þreo crosses f.13a
beoð. read. ⁊ blac. ⁊ hwít. þe reade limpeð to þeo þe beoð for
godes luue wið hare blod schedunge irudet ⁊ ireadet as
þe martirs weren. þe blake cros limpeð to þeo þe maki
eð i þe worlt hare penitence for ladliche sunnen. þe hwite 5
límpeð ariht to hwit meidenhad ⁊ to cleannesse. þet is
muche píne wel forte halden. Píne is ihwer þurh cros
idon to understonden. Þus bitacneð hwit cros þe warde
of hwit chastete. ꝥ is muche pine wel to biwitene. þe bla
ke clað alswa teke þe bitacnunge deð leasse eil to þe eh 10
nen. ⁊ is þiccre aȝeín þe wind ⁊ wurse to seon þurh. ant
halt his heow betere for wind ⁊ for oðerhwet. lokið ꝥ te
parlures beo on eauer euch half feaste ⁊ wel itachet.
⁊ witeð þer ower ehnen leaste þe heorte edfleo ⁊ wende
ut as of dauið. ⁊ ower sawle seccli sone se heo is ute. Ich 15
write muchel for oþre ꝥ nawiht ne rineð ow mine leo
ue sustren. for nabbe ȝe nawt te nome ne ne schulen
habben þurh þe grace of godd of totilde ancres. ne of tol
linde locunges. ne lates ꝥ summe oðerhwiles weilawei:
uncundeliche makieð. for aȝeín cunde hit is ⁊ unmeað 20

21 *small red initial* F *touched with blue; directing* f *in right margin.* 27 swa: w (ƿ) *altered from* ẏ *by placing short bar across top; space at end of line for* u (*omitted*) *filled with a small rough sloping* u. 28 w *erased before* imaket.

f. 13a. 13 parlures beo: beo (*before vowel*) *shows sg. noun understood or omitted* (*either* clað *or* þurl).

sulli wunder ꝥ te deade dotie ⁊ wið cwike worltmen.˙ we
de þurh sunne. Me leoue sire seið sum ⁊ is hit nu se (M. 52)
ouer uuel forte totin utwart? ȝe hit leoue suster. for
uuel þe þer kimeð of.˙ hit is uuel ⁊ ouer uuel to eauer
25 euch ancre. nomeliche to þe ȝunge. ⁊ to þe alde for þi.˙
ꝥ ha to þe ȝungre ȝeoueð uuel forbisne. ⁊ scheld to we
rien ham wið. for ȝef ei edwit ham.˙ þenne seggeð ha
anan. Me sire þeo deð alswa ꝥ is betere þen ich am ⁊ wat
f. 13b betere þen ich hwet ha haueð to donne. leoue ȝunge
ancre ofte a ful haher smið smeoðeð a ful wac cnif.
þe wise folhe i wisdom.˙ ⁊ nawt i folie. an ald ancre mei
do wel.˙ ꝥ te þu dest uuele. ah totín ut wið uten uuel.˙ ne
5 mei ower nowðer. Ním nu ȝeme hwet uuel beo icum
en of totunge. nawt an uuel ne twa.˙ ah al þe wa ꝥ nu
is. ⁊ eauerȝete wes. ⁊ eauer schal iwurðen.˙ al com of sih
ðe. ꝥ hit beo soð.˙ lo her preoue.
Lucifer þurh ꝥ he seh ⁊ biheold on him seolf his
10 ahne feiernesse.˙ leop in to prude. ⁊ bicom of angel eatel
ich deouel. Of eue ure alde moder is iwriten on alre
earst in hire sunne inȝong of hire ehsihðe. Vidit igitur
mulier quod bonum esset lignum ad uescendum. ⁊ pul
crum oculis. aspectu que delectabile.˙ ⁊ tulit de fructu
15 eius ⁊ comedit. deditque uiro suo. ꝥ is. Eue biheold o þe for
boden eappel. ⁊ seh híne feier ⁊ feng to delitin iþe bi
haldunge. ⁊ toc hire lust þer toward. ⁊ nom ⁊ et þrof.˙
⁊ ȝef hire lauerd. low hu hali writ spekeð. ⁊ hu ínwardli
che hit teleð hu sunne bigon. þus eode sunne biuoren
20 ⁊ makede wei to uuel lust. ⁊ com þe dede þrefter ꝥ al
moncun ifeleð. Þes eappel leoue suster bitacneð alle
þe wa ꝥ lust falleð to ⁊ delit of sunne. Hwen þu bihal
dest te mon.˙ þu art in eue poínt. þu lokest o þe eap
pel. hwa se hefde iseid to eue þa ha weorp earst hire ehe

22 Me: *small blue initial* M *touched with red.*

f. 13b. 9 *large red initial* L, *stem in margin between* 5 *and* 9; *blue lines in angle, and in margin from* 3 *to* 16. 12 *between* sunne *and* inȝong *a verb omitted* (*e.g.* nom). 19 eode sunne, *sic for* eode sihðe. 21 *small blue initial* Þ *touched with red.* 22 wa *expuncted* (*dots faint*) *with* ·//. *above; in left margin* þing *marked* ·//. *to replace* wa.

þron. A Eue went te awei þu warpest ehe o þi deað.ꝰ hwet 25
(M. 54) hefde ha iondsweret? Me leoue sire þu hauest woh.
hwerof chalengest tu me.ꝰ þe eappel ꝥ ich loki on.ꝰ is
forbode me to eotene ⁊ nawt to bihalden. þus walde Eue
inohreaðe habben iondsweret. O míne leoue sustren as f. 14a
eue haueð monie dehtren þe folhið hare moder þe
ondswerieð o þisse wise. Me wenest tu seið sum ꝥ ich
wulle leapen on him þah ich loki on him? godd wat
leoue suster mare wunder ilomp. Eue þi moder leop 5
efter hire ehnen. from þe ehe to þe eappel. from þe eap
pel iparais.ꝰ dun to þer eorðe. from þe eorðe to helle. þer
ha lei i prisun fowr þusent ȝer ⁊ mare. heo ⁊ hire were
ba. ⁊ demde al hire ofsprung to leapen al efter hire to
deað wið uten ende. Biginnunge ⁊ rote of al þis ilke 10
reowðe.ꝰ wes aliht sihðe. þus ofte as me seið. of lutel.ꝰ
muchel waxeð. Habbe þenne muche dred euch feble
wummon hwen þeo þe wes riht ta iwraht wið godes
honden.ꝰ wes þurh a sihðe biswiken ⁊ ibroht in to brad
sunne. þet al þe world ouerspreadde. 15

Egressa est dyna filia iacob ut uideret mulieres ali
enigenas. ⁊cetera. A Meiden ạṣ dyna het iacobes doh
ter as hit teleð i Genesy. eode ut to bihalden uncuðe
wummen. ȝet ne seið hit nawt þet ha biheold wepmen.
Ant hwet come wenest tu of ꝥ bihaldunge? ha leas hi 20
re meidenhad ⁊ wes imaket hore. þrefter of þet ilke we
ren trowðen to brokene of hehe patriarches. ⁊ a muchel
burh. forbearnd. ant te king ⁊ his sune ⁊ te burhmen
isleín. þe wummen ilead forð. hire feader ⁊ hire breðren
se noble princes as ha weren.ꝰ utlahen imakede. þus eode 25
ut hire sihðe. Al þullich þe hali gast lette writen o boc
forte warni wummen of hare fol ehnen. ant nim þer
of ȝeme ꝥ tis uuel of dyna com nawt of ꝥ ha seh sichen
(M. 56) emores sune ꝥ ha sunegede wið.ꝰ ah dude of ꝥ ha lette f. 14b

f. 14a. 13 hwen *emended from* hwil*: apparently* il *expuncted* (*dots faint*) *and* en *interlined; later* en *gone over with darker ink, and two darker dots placed above the paler ones.* 16 *large red initial* E *between* 15 *and* 18*; blue line-patterns to right, within, and in margin from* 13 *to* 22 (*a trailer to* 27)*; directing* e *in left margin.* 25 princes: c *abnormal* (*? unfinished tall* s *altered*).

him leggen ehnen on hire. for ꝥ tet he dude hire wes
i þe frumðe sare hire unþonkes.

Alswa Bersabee þurh ꝥ ha unwreah hire idauiðes
5 sihðe.' ha dude him sunegin on hire se hali king
as he wes ⁊ godes prophete. Nu kimeð forð a feble mon.
halt him þah ahelich ȝef he haueð a wid hod ⁊ a lo
ke cape ⁊ wule iseon ȝunge ancres. ⁊ loki nede ase stan
hire wlite him liki.' þe naueð nawt hire leor forbearnd
10 i þe sunne. ⁊ seið ha mei baldeliche iseon hali men.
ȝe swucche as he is for his wide sleuen. Me surquide sire
ne herest tu ꝥ dauið godes ahne deorling bi hwam
he seolf seide. Inueni uirum secundum cor meum. Ich habbe
ifunden qð he mon efter mín heorte. þes þe godd
15 seolf seide bi þis deorewurðe sahe king ⁊ prophete icuret
of alle.' þes þurh an ehe wurp to a wummon as ha
wesch hire.' lette ut his heorte ⁊ forȝet him seoluen.
swa ꝥ he dude þreo utnume heaued ⁊ deadliche sun
nen o Bersabees spusbruche. þe leafdi ꝥ he lokede on.'
20 treisun ⁊ monslaht on his treowe cniht. vrie hire la
uerd. ⁊ tu a sunful mon art se swiðe hardi to keasten
cang ehnen up o ȝung wummon. ȝe míne leoue
sustren ȝef ei is anewil to seon ow.' ne wene ȝe þer
neauer god.' ah leueð him þe leasse. Nulle ich þet
25 nan iseo ow bute he habbe of ower meistre spetiale
leaue. for alle þe þreo sunnen ꝥ ich spec of least. ⁊ al
ꝥ uuel of dína ꝥ ich spec of herre. al com nawt for
þi ꝥ te wummen lokeden cangliche o wepmen.' ah |
f. 15a traisun inwið þe gale heorte. nawt ane euch fleschlich
hondlunge.' ah ȝetten euch gal word.' is ladlich vilainíe.
⁊ godes grome wurðe þah hit ne weoxe forðre bitweone
mon ⁊ ancre. Nu þurh riht godes wrake geað hit forð

f. 14b. 4 *large blue initial* A *between* 3 *and* 6, *red line-patterns to right, within, and in margin from* 3 *to* 10. 8 *after* stan *in right margin* (h *on outer ruling*) hu *in darker ink*. 28 *after* ah *two leaves lost*.

f. 15a. *This folio appears to have been at one time folded back to the left down the centre* (*some letters near the fold are rubbed*); *its contents as far as the verso* 11 (seoluen) *are not in* M. *There is a hole near right edge* (*approx. level with* 17); *between hole and text are two stitched tears sloping down towards edge from level of* 14 *and* 16.

re ⁊ forðre ⁊ bikimeð ofte ⁊ ear me least wene in to þet 5
fule sunne. we hit habbeð weilawei iherd of inohe. Ne
leue na mon ancre þe let in monnes ehe to schawin
hire seoluen. Ouer al ꝥ ȝe habbeð iwriten in ower riw
le of þinges wið uten.˙/ þis point þis article of wel to beo
bitunde.˙/ ich wulle beo best ihalden. To wummon þe wil 10
neð hit.˙/ openið ow o godes half. ȝef ha ne spekeð nawt
þrof.˙/ leoteð swa iwurðen. bute ȝef ȝe dreden ꝥ heo þrefter
beo iscandlet. Of hire ahne suster haueð sum ibeon i
temptet. In toward ower weoued ne beode ȝe namon for
te bihalden. ah ȝef his deuotiun bit hit ⁊ haueð grant.˙/ 15
draheð ow wel ínward. ⁊ te ueil adun toward ower breo
ste. ant sone doð þe clað aȝeín ⁊ festnið heteueste. ȝef
he lokeð toward bed oðer easkeð hwer ȝe liggeð.˙/ ondswe
rieð lihtliche. Sire þerof wel mei duhen ⁊ haldeð ow stille.
ȝef bischp kimeð to seon ow.˙/ hihið sone towart him. 20
ah sweteliche bisecheð hím ȝef he bit to seon ow.˙/ ꝥ ȝe
moten þer onont halden ow towart him.˙/ as ȝe habbeð
idon ⁊ doð to alle oþre. ȝef he wule allegate habben a
sihðe.˙/ lokið ꝥ hit beo ful scheort. þe ueil anan adun. ⁊
draheð ow behinden. An ancre wearnde eadmodliche 25
seín martin hire sihðe. ant he þeruore dude hire þe
menske ꝥ he neauer ne dude to nan oþer. Ant heruore
hire word is aþet cume þis dei iboren in hali chirche.
for as we redeð of hire. hwa se wule hire windowes witen f. 15b
wel wið þe uuele.˙/ ha mot ec wið þe gode. Hwen se ȝe
moten to eani mon eawiht biteachen.˙/ þe hond ne cume
nawt ut. ne ower ut ne his ín. Ant ȝef hit mot cumen
ín.˙/ ne ríne nowðer oþer. Heo is siker seið hali writ.˙/ þe 5
feor from grunen draheð hire. ⁊ þeo þe luueð peril.˙/ i peril
ha schal fallen. Qui caret laqueis securus est. ⁊ qui amat
periculum.˙/ incidet in illud. þe deofles grune is ofte itild.
þer me least weneð. Nis nan ꝥ nis dredful. ꝥ ha nís
ilecchet. for godd nule wite nan ꝥ is se fol hardi. þet 10
(M. 64) ha ne wit wearliche wið him hire seoluen. Þis is nu
of þis wit inoh iseid ed tis chearre to warnin þen

20 bischp, *sic*. 24 *MS*. anan·adun *with point as separator*.

seli. we schulen þah sone her efter speoken her of ma
Spellunge ⁊ smechunge beoð i muð baðe ¶.re.
15 as sihðe is iþe ehe. ah we schulen leten smechun
ge aþet we speoken of ower mete. ⁊ speoken nu of
spellunge. ⁊ þrefter of herunge. of ba imeane sum
chearre as ha gað togederes. ON alre earst hwen
ȝe schulen to ower parlurs þurl.' witeð ed ower mei
20 den hwa hit beo ꝥ beo icumen. for swuch hit mei beon
ꝥ ȝe schule essinieien ow. hwen ȝe alles moten forð.'
crossið ful ȝeome muð. ehnen ⁊ earen. ⁊ te breoste
mid al. ⁊ gað forð mid godes dred. To preost on earst
Confiteor. ⁊ þrefter Benedicite. ꝥ he ah to seggen. hercnið
25 hise wordes ⁊ haldeð ow al stille. ꝥ hwen he parteð
from ow.' ꝥ he ne cunne ower god.' ne ower uuel now
ðer. ne ne cunne ow nowðer lastin ne preisin. Sum
is se wel ilearet oðer se wis iwordet. ꝥ ha walde he wiste
f. 16a hit þe sit ⁊ spekeð toward hire. ⁊ ȝelt him word aȝeín
word. ⁊ forwurðeð meistre þe schulde beon ancre. ⁊ lea
reð him ꝥ is icumen hire forte learen. walde bi hire
tale beon sone wið wise icuððet ⁊ icnawen. Icnawen
5 ha is. for þurh ꝥ ilke ꝥ ha weneð to beo wis ihalden.'
he understont ꝥ ha is sot. for ha hunteð efter pris.' ⁊ (M. 66)
kecheð lastunge. for ed te alre leaste hwen he is awei
iwent.' þeos ancre he wule seggen is of muche speche.
Eue heold i parais long tale wið þe neddre. talde him
10 al þe lesceun ꝥ godd hefde ired hire. ⁊ Adam of þe eap
pel. ⁊ swa þe feond þurh hire word understod anan
riht hire wacnesse. ⁊ ifond wei toward hire of hire for
lorenesse. Vre leafdi seinte Marie dude al on oþer wise.
Ne talde ha þen engel na tale. ah easkede him scheort
15 liche þing ꝥ ha ne cuðe. ȝe mine leoue sustren folhið
ure leafdi.' ⁊ nawt te cakele eue. for þi ancre hwet se

f. 15b. 14 *large red initial* S *between* 13 *and* 16, *with tail to* 19; *blue line-patterns to right, within, and in margin from above* 11, *trailing to* 26. *Before* .re. *a red paragraph touched with blue.* 18 *small blue initial* O *touched with red; directing* o *in right margin.* 21 essinieien: *sic clearly; probably* essinien *written for* essuinien/essunien (*the forms natural to this text*) *with dittography of* ie.

f. 16a. 5 is *crossed out and expuncted before* weneð.

ha beo. hu muchel se ha eauer cunne.' halde hire stille.
nabbe ha nawt henne cunde. þe hen hwen ha haueð
ileid.' ne con bute cakelin. ah hwet biȝet ha þrof?
kimeð þe kaue ananriht ⁊ reaueð hire hire eairen. 20
⁊ fret of ꝥ schulde forð bringe cwike briddes. Al riht al
swa þe caue deouel bereð awei from cakelinde ancres
⁊ forswolheð al þe god ꝥ ha istreonet habbeð. ꝥ schul
de as briddes beoren ham up towart heouene.' ȝef hit
nere icakelet. þe wrecche poure peoddere mare nurð 25
he makeð to ȝeien his sape.' þen þe riche mercer al
his deorewurðe ware as is iseid her efter. To sum gas
telich mon ꝥ ȝe beoð trusti upon as ȝe mahe beon o
lut.' god is ꝥ ȝe easki read ⁊ salue ꝥ he teache ow to f. 16b
ȝeines fondunges. ⁊ i schrift schawið him ȝef he wu
le iheren ower greaste ⁊ ower ladlukeste sunnen. for
þi ꝥ him areowe ow. ⁊ þurh þe areownesse inward
luker crie crist mearci for ow ⁊ habbe ow in his bo 5
nen. Set multi ueniunt ad uos in uestimentis ouium
intrinsecus autem sunt lupi rapaces. Ah witeð ow ant
beoð warre he seið ure lauerd. for monie cumeð to
ow ischrud mid lombes fleos. ⁊ beoð wedde wulues.
worltliche leueð lut. religiuse ȝet leas. ne wilni ȝe 10
(M. 68) nawt to muchel hare cuððunge. Eue wið ute dred
spec wið þe neddre. Vre leafdi wes offearet of gabri
eles speche. Vre freres prechurs ⁊ ure freres meonurs
beoð of swuch ordre ꝥ al folc mahte wundrin ȝef ei
of ham wende ehe towart te wude lehe. for þi ed 15
euch time ꝥ eani of ham þurh chearite kimeð
ow to learen ⁊ to frourin i godd. ȝef he is preost
seggeð. ear þen he parti.' mea culpa. Ich schriue me
to godd almihti ⁊ to þe. ꝥ ich as ich drede riht repen
tant neauer nes of mine greaste sunnen ꝥ ich habbe 20
ischawet to mine schrift feaderes. Ant tah minen
tente beo to beten ham her inne.' ich hit do se poure
liche. ⁊ sunegi in oðre deihwamliche seoððen ich
wes nest ischríuen. ⁊ ꝥ 'wes þenne ⁊ of þe ⁊ nempnin.

f. 16b. 6 *a hand drawn in left margin pointing to this line.* 13 Vre *to* f. 17a. 2 for þe *not in* M. meonurs: s *written above as flourish from* r.

25 Ich habbe þus isunget. ⁊ segge o hwucche wise as hit
is iwriten ow in ower schriftes boc towart te ende
þrof. ⁊ aleast Seggeð. þis ⁊ muche mare. Confiteor.
⁊ bide him underuo þe spetiale in his god. ⁊ þonke
f. 17a him of his inturn ⁊ bisech him aleast greten þe
⁊ te. ant ꝥ ha bidden for þe. Wið uten witnesse
of wummon oðer of wepmon þe ow mahe iheren
ne speoke ȝe wið namon ofte ne longe. ⁊ tah hit
5 beo of schrift.· allegate i þe ilke hus. oðer þer he mahe
iseon toward ow sitte þe þridde. bute ȝef þe ilke þrid
de ọþẹr stude trukie. Þis nis nawt for ow leoue sustren
iseid.· ne for oþre swucche. nawt for þi þe treowe is
ofte mistrowet. ⁊ te saclese bilohen. as iosep i Genesy.
10 of þe gale leafdi for wone of witnesse. Me leueð þe
uuele sone. ⁊ te unwreaste bliðeliche liheð o þe go
de. Sum unseli haueð hwen ha seide ha schraf hi
re.· ischriuen hire al towundre. for þi ahen þe gode
habben eauer witnesse. for twa acheisuns nomeli
15 che. þe an is ꝥ te ondfule ne mahe lihen on ham.·
swa ꝥ te witnesse ne pruuíe ham false. Þe oþer is
forte ȝeouen þe oþre forbisne. ⁊ reaui þe uuele an
cre þe ilke unseli gile ꝥ ich of seide. Vt þurh þe
chirche þurl ne halde ȝe tale wið namon.· ah beo
20 reð þer to wurðmunt for þe hali sacrement ꝥ ȝe
seoð þerþurh. ⁊ neomeð oðerhwile to ower wum
men þe huses þurl. to oþre.· þe parlur. Speoken ne
ahe ȝe bute ed tes twa þurles. Silence eauer ed te
mete. ȝef oðre religiuse as ȝe witen doð hit.· ȝe ah
25 en ouer alle. ȝef ei haueð deore gẹast.· do hire meid
nes as in hire stude to gleadien hire feire. ⁊ heo
schal habbe leaue forte unsperren hire þurl eanes (M. 70)
oðer twien. ⁊ makie sines toward hire of a glead
f. 17b chere. Summes curteisie is iturnt hire to uuel. Vnder
semblant of god is ofte ihulet sunne. Ancre ⁊ huses

f. 17a. 2 Wið: *small red initial* Ƿ (*not* V) *touched with blue.*
7 oþer *expuncted with faint dots; in left margin faint back-sloping* opðer, *written in pencil by someone who did not understand* oþer stude.
18 *small blue initial* V *touched with red.* 23 *small red initial* S *touched with blue.* 27 *MS.* unsperren.

leafdi ah muchel to beon bitweonen. Euche fridei of
þe ȝer haldeð silence bute hit beo duble feaste. Ant
tenne haldeð hit sum oðer dei i þe wike. I þe aduenz 5
⁊ i þe umbriwiken.ʾ weodnesdei ⁊ fridei. I þe lenten.ʾ
þreo dahes. ⁊ al þe swiíng wike aðet non. ⁊ froṃ
ṇoṇ efteṛ ṃeṭe ạđeṭ euen. to ower wummen ȝe ma
hen þah seggen wið lut word hwet se ȝe wulleð. ȝef
eani god mon is of feorren icumen.ʾ hercnið his 10
speche ⁊ ondswerieð wið lut word to his easkunges.
Muche fol were þe mahte to his bihoue hweðer
se he walde grinden greot oþer hweate. ȝef he grunde
þe greot ⁊ lette þe hweate. Hweate is hali speche as
seint Anselme seið. Heo grint greot þe chafleð. þe 15
twa cheken beoð þe twa grindel stanes. þe tunge is
þe cleappe. lokið leoue sustren ꝥ ower cheken ne
grinden neauer bute sawle fode. ne ower eare nedrín
ke neauer bute sawle heale. ⁊ nawt ane ower eare.ʾ
ah ower ehþurhsperreð to aȝeines idel speche. to ow 20
ne cume na tale.ʾ ne tidinge of þe worlde. Ȝe ne
schule for na þing wearien ne swerien. bute ȝef ȝe
seggen witerliche oðer sikerliche.ʾ oðer o sum swuch
wise. Ne preachi ȝe to namon. ne mon ne easki ow
cunsail ne ne telle ow. readeð wummen ane. Seint 25
pawel forbeot wummen to preachin. Mulieres non
permitto docere. Na wepmon ne chastie ȝe. ne edwiten
his him unþeaw bute he beo þe ouer cuðre. Halie al
de ancres hit mahe don summes weis. ah hit nis nawt f. 18a
siker þing.ʾ ne ne limpeð nawt to ȝunge. Hit is hare
(M. 72) meoster þe beoð ouer oþre iset ⁊ habbeð ham to

f. 17b. 7, 8 efter: n *altered to* r. *In pencil,* from *to* aðet *expuncted, and in right margin, rubbed,* on easter, *joined by line to first* non. *MS. error apparently due to reading* aðet non on e(a)ster euen *as* aðet non non efter euen, *and supplying* ⁊ from *and* mete aðet *in attempt to make sense.* 12 *small blue initial* M, *red lines within, and in margin from* 9 *to* 16. 20 *MS.* ehþurhsperreð *for* ehþurl sperreð; *over* e *a tick corresponding to mark* × *in left margin.* 21 *small red initial* Ȝ *touched with blue; directing* ȝ *in right margin.* 25 Seint: Seinte *with final* e *erased, as* ff. 63b. 8, 64b. 10 (pawel *elsewhere preceded by* seinte).

f. 18a. 1 *second* hit: t *dotted above.*

witene as hali chirche larewes. Ancre naueð forte
5 hire ane ⁊ hire meidnes. Halde euch hire ahne
meoster. ⁊ nawt ne reauí oþres. Moní weneð to do
wel.' þe deð al to wundre. for as ich seide ear. Vnder
semblant of god is ofte ihulet sunne. þurh swuch
chastíement haueð sum ancre arearet bitweonen
10 hire ⁊ hire preost.' oðer a falsinde luue oðera mu
che weorre. Seneca. ad summam uolo uos esse. rari
loquas.' tuncque pauciloquas. ꝥ is þe ende of þe tale seið
Seneke þe wise. Ich chulle ꝥ ȝe speoken seldene ant
þenne lutel. Moní punt hire word forte leote ma
15 ut. as me deð weater ed mulne. Swa duden iobes
freond þe weren icumen to frourin hím. seten stille
seoue niht. ah þa ha hefden alles bigunnen to speo
kene.' þa ne cuðen ha neauer stutten hare cleappe. Gregorius.
Censura silencíí.' nutritura est uerbi. Swa hit is of mo
20 nie as sein Gregoire seið. Silence is wordes fostrilt
⁊ bringeð forð chaffle. On oðer half as he seið. Iuge
silentium cogit celestia meditari. long silence ⁊
wel iwist.' nedeð þe þohtes up towart heouene. Al
swa as ȝe mahe seon weater hwen me punt hit.'
25 ⁊ stoppeð hit biuore wel ꝥ hit ne mahe duneward.'
þenne is hit inedd aȝeín.' forte climben uppart.
ant ȝe al þisses weis pundeð ower wordes. forstop
pið ower þohtes. as ȝe wulleð ꝥ ha clímben ant
f. 18b hehin toward heouene. ⁊ nawt ne fallen duneward.' ⁊ to
fleoten ȝont te worlt.' as deð muchel chaffle. Hwen ȝe
nede moten.' a lute wiht lowsið up ower muðes flod
ȝeten as me deð ed mulne ⁊ leoteð adun sone. Ma (M. 74)
5 sleað word þen sweord. Mors ⁊ uita in manibus lingue.
lif ⁊ deað seið Salomon is i tunge honden. Qui custo

4, 5 naueð forte | hire ane: *the MS. now reads* naueð forte loken bute hire; *in a different, slightly larger, hand* loken *added at end of* 4 (ken *projecting into right margin*), bute *at the beginning of* 5 (b *in left margin*, ute *on an erasure*); ane *expuncted. The main hand probably wrote* forte | wite hire ane, *mistakenly omitting* bute *after* wite. 5 *in outer left margin, in pencil,* bute. 7 wel.': l.' *written thickly on erasure.* 11 *Small blue initial* S *touched with red.*

f. 18b. 4 *small red initial* M *touched with blue.* 8 patens:

dit os suum custodit animam suam. Hwa se witeð wel
his muð:' he witeð he seið his sawle. Sicut urbs patens
⁊ absque murorum ambitu. sic ⁊ cetera. Qui murum silencíí
non habet:' patet inimici iaculis ciuitas mentis. hwa 10
se ne wiðhalt his wordes seið Salomon þe wise. he
is as þe burh wið ute wal ꝥ ferde mei in ouer al. þe
feond of helle mid his ferd wend þurh ut te tutel
þe is eauer open:' in to þe heorte. I vitas patrum hit te
leð ꝥ an hali mon seide þa me preisede ane breðren 15
ꝥ he hefde iherd of muche speche. Boni utique sunt
set habitatio eorum non habet ianuam. quicumque
uult intrat ⁊ asinum soluit. Gode qð he ha beoð
ah hare wununge naueð na ȝete. hare muð mea
ðeleð eauer. hwa se eauer wule mei gan ín ⁊ leaden 20
forð hare asse. ꝥ is hare unwise sawle. for þi seið seín
iame. Si quis putat se religiosum esse non refrenans
linguam suam set seducens cor suum:' huius uana est
religio. ꝥ is ȝef ení weneð ꝥ he beo religius. ⁊ ne
bridli nawt his tunge:' his religiun is fals. he gi 25
leð his heorte. he seið swiðe wel ne bridleð nawt
his tunge. Bridel nis nawt ane i þe horses muð:'
ah sit sum up o þe ehnen. ⁊ geað abute þe earen
for alle þreo is muche neod ꝥ ha beon ibridlet. Ah i f. 19a
þe muð sit tet irn. ⁊ o þe lihte tunge. for þear is
meast neod hald hwen þe tunge is o rune ⁊ ifole to
Ofte we þencheð hwen we foð on to ¶.eornen
speoken:' forte speoke lutel ⁊ wel isette wordes. ah þe 5
tunge is slubbri for ha wadeð i wete. ⁊ slit lihtliche
forð from lut word in to monie. ant tenne as Salo
mon seið. In multiloquio non deerit peccatum. Ne mei
nawt mu̦lche speche ne ginne hit neauer se wel:' beo
wið ute sunne. for from soð hit slit to fals. ut of 10

h-*shaped* n *and* s *combined.* 13 tutel *resembles* tittel: *bar of second* t *extended to left, or second stroke of* u *crossed in error* (*this stroke is not stem of* t *according to norm of main hand; cf.* f. 22a. 2). 22 religiosum: o *altered from* u. *In bottom right-hand corner catchword at end of second gathering:* for alle (*small*).

f. 19a. 4 *small red initial* O; *blue lines within, and in margin from* 1 *to* 19; *directing* o *in left margin. Before* .eornen. *a blue paragraph, with tail into right margin, ornamented with red.*

god in to sum uuel. from [meosure in to unimete.
⁊ of a drope waxeð in to a muche flod þe adrencheð
þe sawle. for wið þe fleotinde word tofleoteð þe heor (M. 76)
te. swa ꝥ longe þrefter ne mei ha beon riht igederet
15 to gederes. Et os nostrum tanto est deo longinqum.' quanto
mundo proximum. tanto que minus exauditur in
prece.' quanto amplius ⟨co⟩inquinatur in locutione. þis beoð
seint gregoires word in his dyaloge. Ase neh as u
re muð is to worldlich speche.' ase feor he is godd
20 hwen he spekeð toward him ⁊ bit him eani bone.
for þi is ꝥ we ȝeiȝeð up on him ofte. ⁊ he firseð him
awei frommard ure steuene. ne nule nawt iheren
hire. for ha stinkeð to him al of þe worldes meaðel
unge ⁊ of hire chafle. hwa se wule þenne ꝥ godes
25 eare beo neh hire tunge.' firsi hire from þe world
elles ha mei longe ȝeiȝen.' ear godd hire ihere. ⁊
seið þurh ysaie. Cum extenderitis manus uestras.' auer
tam oculos meos a uobis. ⁊ cum multiplicaueritis orationes.'
f. 19b non exaudiam uos. ꝥ is. þah ȝe makien monifalde ower
bonen toward me. ȝe þe pleieð wið þe world.' nule ich
ow nawt iheren. ah ich wulle turne me awei hwen ȝe
heoueð toward me hehe ower honden. VRe deore
5 wurðe leafdi seinte Marie þe ah to alle wummen to
beo forbisne.' wes of se lutel speche. ꝥ nohwer in hali writ
ne finde we ꝥ ha spec bute fowr siðen. ah for se selt spe
che hire wordes weren heuie ⁊ hefden muche mihte.
Bernardus ad Mariam. In sempiterno dei uerbo facti sumus
10 omnes ⁊ ecce morimur. in tuo breui responso refitiendi
sumus ut ad uitam reuocemur. Responde uerbum ⁊ sus
cipe uerbum. profer tuum ⁊ concipe díuínum. Hire forme
wordes ꝥ we redeð of weren þa ha ondswerede gabriel
þen engel. ant teo weren se mihtie. ꝥ wið ꝥ ha seide.
15 Ecce ancilla domini fiat michi secundum uerbum tuum. Ed
tis word
godes sune ⁊ soð godd bicom mon. ⁊ te lauerd ꝥ al þe

15 longinqum, *sic.* 17 ⟨co⟩ *interlined with caret.*

f. 19b. 4 *small blue initial* V *ornamented with red; directing* v *in right margin.*

world ne mahte nawt bifon.' bitunde him inwið hi
re meidnes wombe. Hire oþre wordes weren þa ⟨ha⟩ com ⁊
grette elyzabeth hire mehe. ant hwet mihte wes icud
(M. 78) ed þeose wordes.' hwet.' ꝥ a child bigon to pleien toȝei 20
nes ham. ꝥ wes sein iuhan in his moder wombe. Idem.
Vox eius iohannem exultare fecit in utero. ꝥ þridde time
ꝥ ha spec ꝥ ha spec wes ed te neoces. ant ter ꝥurh hi
re bisocne wes weater iwent to wíne. þe feorðe time
wes þa ha hefde ímíst hire sune.' ⁊ eft him ifunde. ⁊ 25
hu muche wunder folhede þeose wordes? ꝥ godd al
mihti beah to mon. to marie ⁊ to ioseph. to a smið
⁊ to a wummon. ⁊ folhede ham ase heoren hwider se
ha walden. Neomeð nu her ȝeme ⁊ leornið ȝeorne her f. 20a
bi. hu seltsene speche haueð muche strengðe. **V**ir lin
guosus non dirigetur in terra. feole iwordet mon seið þe
salm wruhte ne schal neauer leaden riht lif on eorðe. for
þi he seið elleshwer. Dixi custodiam uias meas ut non 5
delinquam in lingua mea .ywallage. ant is as þah he
seide. Ich chulle wite mine weies wið mí tunge warde. wi
te ich wel mí tunge.' ich mei wel halden þe wei toward
heouene. for as ysaie seið. Cultus iusticie.' silentium. þe
tilunge of rihtwisnesse.' ꝥ is silence. Silence tileð hire. 10
⁊ heo itilet bringeð forð sawles eche fode. for ha is un
deadlich as Salomon witneð. Iusticia inmortalis est.
for þi feieð ysaie hope ⁊ silence baðe to gederes. ⁊ seið in
ham schal stonden gastelich strengðe. In Silentio ⁊ spe.'
erit fortitudo uestra. ꝥ is. i silence ⁊ in hope schal beon ow 15
er strengðe. Neomeð ȝeme hu wel he seið. for hwa se is
muche stille. ⁊ halt silence longe.' ha mei hopien siker
liche ꝥ hwen ha spekeð toward godd.' ꝥ he hire ihere. ha
mei ec hopien ꝥ ha schal singen þurh hire silence swe
teliche in heouene. þis is nu þe reisun of þe ueiunge 20
hwi ysaie ueieð hope ⁊ silence ⁊ cupleð ba togederes.
teke ꝥ he seið i þe ilke auctorite. ꝥ i silence ⁊ in hope

18 ha *interlined with caret.* 22 ꝥ (*large*) *for* þe. 23 ꝥ ha spec *repeated in error.*

f. 20a. 2 *small red initial* V *touched with blue.* 6 ywallage *sic, with* ƿ *erroneously for* þ. *Holes in right margin opposite* 9/10 *and* 13/14. *In* ff. 20 *to* 24 (*slight trace still in* f. 25) *the tops of the outer side-edges are damaged.*

schal beon ure strengðe i godes strengðe toȝein þe deof
les turnes ⁊ his fondunges. Ah lokið þurh hwet reisun.
25 Hope is a swete spice inwið þe heorte ꝥ sweteð al ꝥ bitter (M. 80)
ꝥ te bodi drinkeð. Ah hwa se cheoweð spice.' ha schal tunen
hire muð. ꝥ te swote breað ⁊ te strengðe ꝥrof leaue wið ín
nen. Ah heo þe openeð hire muð wið muche meaðelunge.
f. 20b ⁊ brekeð silence.' ha spit hope al ut. ⁊ te swotnesse þrof mid
worltliche wordes. ⁊ leoseð aȝeín þe feond gastelich strengðe.
for hwet makeð us stronge i godes seruise ⁊ ine fondunges
forte drehe derf. to wreastli stealewurðliche toȝeín þe deofles
5 swenges.' bute hope of heh mede. hope halt te heorte hal hwet
se þe flesch drehe. as me seið. ȝef hope nere heorte to breke.
A iesu þin are hu stont ham þe beoð þer as alle wa ⁊ weane
is wið uten hope of utcume ⁊ heorte ne mei bersten? for
þi as ȝe wulleð halden inwið ow hope ⁊ te swete breað of
10 hire. þe ȝeueð sawle mihte.' wið muð itunet cheoweð hi
re inwið ower heorte. ne blawe ȝe hire nawt ut wið mea
ðelinde muðes. wið ȝeoniende tuteles. Non habeatis linguam
uel aures prurientes. lokið seið sein ierome ꝥ ȝe nabben
ȝicchinde nowðer tunge ne earen. ꝥ is to seggen. ꝥ ow ne
15 luste nowðer speoken.' ne hercni worltlich speche. Hiderto
is iseid of ower silence. ⁊ hu ower speche schal beo seltsene.
Contrariorum eadem est disciplina. of silence ⁊ of speche nis bu
te a lare. ⁊ for þi i writunge ha eorneð ba to gederes. Nu
we schulen sumhwet speoken of ower herunge aȝeín u
20 uel speche. ꝥ ȝe þer toȝeines.' tunen ower earen. ⁊ ȝef
ned is.' spearren ower þurles.

FOR al uuel speche míne leoue sustren stoppið ower
earen. ⁊ habbeð wleatunge of þe muð þe speoweð
ut atter. De omni uerbo otioso ⁊ cetera. Vuel speche is þreofald. (M. 82)
25 attri. ful. ⁊ idel. Idel speche is uuel. ful speche is wurse. Attri
is þe wurste. Idel is ⁊ unnet.' al ꝥ god ne kimeð of. ⁊ of

f. 20b. 22 *large blue initial* F *between* 21 *and* 24, *with tapering stem in margin from* 23 *to below* 28*; red line-patterns within, and in margin from* 20 *to bottom of page.*

þulli speche seið ure lauerd schal euch word beon iriken
et. ⁊ iȝeue reisun hwi þe an hit seide. ⁊ te oðer hit lustne
de. ant þis is þah ꝥ leaste uuel of þe þreo uueles. Hwet hu f. 21a
þenne schal me ȝelde reisun of þe wurse? hwet hu of þe
wurste? þ is of attri ⁊ of ful speche? nawt ane ꝥ hit
spekeð:

ah ꝥ hit hercneð. ful speche is as of leccherie. ⁊ of oðre
fulðen ꝥ unweschene muðes speokeð oðerhwiles. þeose 5
beoð alle ischrapede ut of ancre riwle. þe swuch fulðe
spit ut ín eani ancre earen: me
schulde dutten his mud.
nawt wið scharpe sneateres:
ah wið hearde fustes. . Attri speche is 10
heresie. þweartouer leasunge. bacbitunge. ⁊ fikelunge.
þeos beoð þe wurste. Heresie godd haue þonc ne rix
leð nawt in englelond. leasunge is se uuel þing. þet
seint austin seið. ꝥ forte schilde þi feader from deað: ne
schuldest tu nawt lihen. Godd seolf seið ꝥ he is soð. ⁊ 15
hwet is mare aȝeín soð þen is leas? Diabolus mendax
est ⁊ pater eius. þe deouel is leas ⁊ leasunge feader. þe ilke
þenne þe stureð hire tunge i leasunge: ha makeð of
hire tunge cradel to þe deofles bearn ⁊ rockeð hit ȝeorn
liche as his nurrice. 20

BAcbitunge. ⁊ fikelunge. ⁊ eggunge to don uuel:
ne beoð nawt monnes speche: ah beoð þe deofles
bleas ⁊ his ahne steuene. ȝef ha ahen to beo feor alle
worltliche men: hwet hu ahen ancren heatien ham ⁊
schunien ꝥ ha ham ne iheren? iheren ich segge. for 25
hwa se spekeð ham: nis ha nawt ancre. Salomon. Si
mordet serpens in silentio: nichil minus eo habet qui
detrahit in occulto. þe neddre seið Salomon stingeð
al stille. ant þeo þe spekeð bihinden ꝥ ha nalde biuoren: f. 21b
nis nawiht betere. Herst tu hu Salomon eueneð bacbitere

f. 21a. 7 *to* 10: *large hole divides the lines as shown.* 8 mud, *sic.*
10 *small red initial* A *touched with blue; directing* a *in left margin.*
21 *red initial* B *between* 20 *and* 23; *blue line-patterns to right, within, and in margin from* 20 *to* 28; *directing* b *in left margin. A tear on left edge (between* 13 *and* 14) *with holes for lost stitches; from ruled margin at* 21 *to right edge a tear stitched with green silk.*

to stinginde neddre. Swa hit is witerliche ha is neddre
cundel ⁊ bereð þeo þe uuel spekeð.' atter i þe tunge. (M. 84)

5 Þe fikelere blent mon ⁊ put him preon i þe ehe ꝥ he
wið fikeleð. .GG'. ADulator ei cum quo sermonem conse
rit. quasi clauum in oculo figit.
þe bacbitere cheoweð ofte
monnes flesch i fridei ⁊ bea
10 keð wið his blake bile o cwike charoínes as þe ꝥ is
þes deofles corbin of helle. Salomon. Noli esse in conuí
uíís eorum. ⁊ cetera. qui conferunt carnes ad uescendum
⁊ cetera.
ȝef he walde pilewin ⁊ toteoren wið his bile rotet stín
kinde flesch as is reauenes cunde. ꝥ is. walde he seggen
15 uuel bi nan oþer. bute bi þeo þe rotieð ⁊ stinkeð al i
fulðe of hare sunne.' hit were leasse wunder. ah lihteð
up o cwic flesch. tolímeð ⁊ tolukeð hit. ꝥ is. misseið bi
swuch ꝥ is cwic íne godd.' he is to ȝiuer reuen ⁊ to bald
mid alle. On oðer half neomeð nu ȝeme of hwucche
20 twa meosters þes twa menestraws seruið hare lauerd
þe deouel of helle. ful hit is to seggen.' ah fulre forte
beon hit. ⁊ swa hit is allegate. Ne uideatur hec moralitas
minus decens. recolat in esdra quod melchia hedificauit
portam stercoris. Melchia enim corus domino interpretatur
filius rechab
25 .id est. mollis patris. Nam uentus aquilo dissipat pluuias.
⁊ fa
ties tristis linguam detrahentem. ha beoð þes deofles gong
men ⁊ beoð aa in his gong hus. Þe fikeleres meoster
is to hulie þe gong þurl. ꝥ he deð as ofte as he wið
f. 22a his fikelunge ⁊ wið his preisunge wrið mon his sunne.
ꝥ stinkeð na þing fulre. ant he hit huleð ⁊ lideð swa.' ꝥ

f. 21b. 5 *large blue initial* Þ *between* 4 *and* 7, *with tapered stem in margin from* 2 *to* 11, *ornamented with red within, and in margin from* 1 *to* 17; *directing* þ *in left margin.* 6 GG*us*: *read* Gregorius. 7–9 *the hole* (*see recto*) *divides words as shown. The stitched tear intrudes between* 20 *and* 21; *the beginning of* 21 *is set in.* 24 corus domino, *sic* (*MS.* corus dn̄o).

f. 22a. 2 huleð: u *has top bar* (*probably dittographic after* hit); *the down-strokes are not those of* t; *cf.* f. 18b. 13.

he hit nawt ne stinkeð. Þe bacbitere unlideð hit ꝛ openeð
swa ꝥ fulðe ꝥ hit stinkeð wide. Þus ha beoð aa bisie i þis
fule meoster. ꝛ eiðer wið oþer striueð her abuten. þulli 5
che men stinkeð of hare stinkinde meoster. ꝛ bringeð
euch stude o stench ꝥ ha to nahið. Vre lauerd schilde ꝥ te
breað of hare stinkinde þrote ne nahi ow neauer. Oþer
spechen fuleð. ah þeose attrið baðe þe earen ꝛ te heorte.
ꝥ ȝe bet icnawen ham. ȝef ei kimeð toward ow.· low 10
(M. 86) her hare molden. Fikeleres beoð þreo cunnes. þe forme
beoð uuele inoh. þe oþre þah beoð wurse. Þe þridde þah
beoð wurst. Ve illis qui ponunt puluillos ꝛ cetera. Ve illis qui
dant bonum malum. ꝛ malum bonum. ponentes lu
cem tenebras. ꝛ ten. lu. hoc scilicet detractatoribus ꝛ adulato 15
ribus peruenit. Þe forme ȝef a mon is god.· preiseð him
biuoren him seolf ꝛ makeð him inohreaðe ȝet betere
þen he beo. ꝛ ȝef he seið wel oðer deð wel.· heueð hit to
hehe up wið ouerherunge. Þe oðer ȝef a mon is uuel. ꝛ
seið ꝛ deð se muche mis ꝥ hit beo se open sunne. þet 20
he hit ne mahe nanes weis allunge wiðseggen. he
þah biuore þe mon seolf makeð his uuel leasse. Nis
hit nawt nu he seið se ouer uuel as me hit makeð
nart tu nawt te ane i þis þis þing þe forme ne þe
leaste. þu hauest monie feren. let iwurðe god mon 25
ne geast tu nawt te ane. Moní deð muche wurse. þe
þridde cunne of fikelere is wurst as ich seide. for he
preiseð þe uuele ꝛ his uuele dede. as þe þe seið to þe
cniht. þe robbeð his poure men. A Sire as þu dest wel. f. 22b
for eauer me schal þene cheorl peolkin ꝛ pilien. for
he is as þe wiðin þe spruteð ut þe betere ꝥ me hine crop
peð ofte.· laudatur peccator in desideriís anime sue ꝛ iniquus
benedicitur. Augus. Adulantium lingue alligant hominem 5
in peccatis. þus þes false fikeleres ablendeð þe ham her
nið. as ich ear seide. ꝛ wriheð hare fulðe ꝥ ha hit ne
mahe stínken. ꝛ ꝥ is hare muchel unselhðe. for ȝef
ha hit stunken.· ham walde wleatie þer wið. ꝛ eornen

15 ten. lu.: *read* tenebras lucem. 23 *second* hit: h *thick and clumsy*. 24 te ane *mistaken addition, from* 26; þis þis, *sic*.
f. 22b. 5 *read* Augustinus. 6 her, *sic for* herc.

10 to schrift ⁊ speowen hit ut þer ⁊ schunien hit þrefter. Clemens. Homicidarum tria esse genera dixit beatus petrus. ⁊ eorum parem penam esse uoluit. Qui corporaliter occidit. ⁊ qui detrahit fratri. ⁊ qui inuidet. Bacbiteres þe biteð bi hinde bac oþre.· beoð of twa maneres. ah þe leatere is
15 wurse. þe earre kimeð al openliche ⁊ seið uuel bi an oþ er. ⁊ speoweð ut his atter se muchel se him eauer to muð kimeð. ⁊ culcheð al ut somet ꝥ te attri heorte sent (M. 88) up to þe tunge. Ah þe leatere kimeð forð al on oþer wi se. wurse feond þen þe oðer is. ⁊ under freondes huckel
20 warpeð adun ꝥ heaued. feð on forte siken ear he eawt segge. ⁊ makeð drupi chere. bisampleð longe abuten.· forte beo bet ileuet. hwen hit alles kimeð forð.· þenne is hit ȝeolow atter. weila ha seið wa is me ꝥ he oðer heo habbeð swuch word icaht. Inoh ich wes abuten ah ne
25 healp me nawt to don her of bote. ȝare is ꝥ ich wiste þrof.· ah þah þurh me ne schulde hit beon neauer mare íuppet. ah nu hit is þurh oþre swa wide ibroht forð. ꝥ ich ne mei hit nawt wiðsaken. Vuel me seið ꝥ hit is.·
f. 23a ant ȝet hit is wurse. Sorhful ich am ⁊ sari ꝥ ich hit schal seggen. ah for soðe swa hit is ⁊ ꝥ is mu chel sorhe. for i feole oðer þing he oðer heo is swiðe to herien. ah onont þis þing wa is me þer
5 uore ne mei ham namon werien. þis beoð þe deofles neddren þe Salomon spekeð of. Vre lauerd þurh his grace halde ower earen feor hare attrie tungen. ne leue ow neauer stinken ꝥ fule put ꝥ ha unwreoð as þe fikele res wreoð. ⁊ hulieð as ich seide. Vnwreon hit to ham seol
10 uen þeo þe hit to limpeð. ⁊ hulien hit to oþre ꝥ is a muche þeaw. nawt to þeo þe hit schulden smeallen ⁊ heatien ꝥ fulðe. NV mine leoue sustren from al u

f. 22b. 13 *small red initial* B *touched with blue; directing* b *in right margin.*

f. 23a. 2, 3 *a tear, avoided by scribe, divides words as shown; now drawn together with green silk, but holes of older stitching can be seen. Two tears proceed from damaged outside edge (see* f. 20a)*: the upper intrudes at* 3 (oðer *stops short of it); it is stitched with yellow silk, the smaller tear below with green.* 9 to: t *altered from* e. 12 *small blue initial* N *touched with red; directing* N *in left margin.*

uel speche ꝥ is þus þreouald. Idel. ful. ⁊ attri.' haldeð
feor ower eare. Me seið up on ancren ꝥ euch meast
haueð an ald cwene to feden hire earen. A mea 15
ðelilt þe meaðeleð hire alle þe talen of þe lond. a ri
kelot þe cakeleð al ꝥ ha sið ⁊ hereð. swa ꝥ me seið i bisa
he. From mulne ⁊ from chepinge. from smiððe ⁊ from
(M. 90) ancre hus me tidinge bringeð. Wat crist þis is a sari sa
he. ꝥ ancre hus ꝥ schulde beon anlukest stude of alle.' 20
schal beon ifeiet to þe ilke þreo studen.' ꝥ meast is in of
chaffle.' Ah ase cwite as ȝe beoð of þullich leoue sustren.'
weren alle oþre ure lauerd hit uðe. NV ich habbe
sunderlepes ispeken of þes þreo limen. of ehe. of muð.
of eare. Of eare is al þis leaste to ancre bihoue. for lef 25
lich þing nis hit nawt ꝥ ancre beore swuch muð. ah
muchel me mei dreden to swucche muðes sumcheare.'
ꝥ ha beie hire eare. Of sihðe. of speche. Of hercnunge.'
is iseid sunderlepes of euchan o rawe. Cume we nu eft a f. 23b
ȝein ⁊ speoken of alle imeane

Zelatus sum syon zelo magno in propheta za
charia. Vnderstond ancre hwas spuse þu art
⁊ hu he is gelus of alle þine lates. Ego sum deus zelotes. 5
in exodo. Ich am he seið bi him seolf þe geluse godd. ze
latus sum ⁊ cetera. Ich am gelus of þe syon mi leofmon
wið muche gelusie. þuhte him nawt inoh iseid. ꝥ he
is gelus of þe.' bute he seide þer to.' wið muche gelusie.
Auris zeli audit omnia. seið Salomon þe wise. Vbi a 10
mor.' ibi oculus. Wite þe nu ful wel. his eare is eauer to
ward te ⁊ he hereð al. His ehe aa bihalt te. ȝef þu ma
kest ei semblant. eani luue lates toward unþeawes.
Zelatus sum syon. Syon ꝥ is schawere. he cleopeð þe

15 *before* earen: ehnen *crossed out.* 23 *small red initial* N *touched with blue.*

f. 23b. 2 *tear* (*see recto*) *above* magn)o in propheta. 3 *long tear* (*see recto*) *intrudes as far as inner ruled margin; the large blue initial* Z *is set in* (*about three letter-spaces*)*; its red ornament* (*on both sides*) *stops short of the tear on the left.* 3 *to* 16*: underlinings in light brown:* 3 *all but* Z*;* 4 charia. V(nder*;* 7 Ich *to end;* 8 wið muche ge(lusie*;* 11 his eare is eauer*;* 12 ward *to* hereð*;* 16 Ostend(e. *In left margin corresponding four marks* ×, *approx. opposite* 3, 7, 12, 16.

15 his schawere. swa his ꝥ nan oþres. for þi he seið in can
ticis. Ostende michi fatiem tuam. Schaw þi neb to me he seið
⁊ to nan oþer. bihald me ȝef þu wult habbe briht sih
ðe wið þine heorte ehnen. bihald inward þer ich am
⁊ ne sech þu me nawt wið ute þin heorte. Ich am woh
20 ere scheomeful. ne nule ich nohwer bicluppe mi leof
mon bute i stude dearne. O þulli wise ure lauerd spekeð
to his spuse. Ne þunche hire neauer wunder ȝef ha
nis muchel ane.' þah he hire schunie. ⁊ swa ane ꝥ ha (M. 92)
putte euch worldlich þrung. ⁊ euch nurð eorðlich.'
25 ut of hire heorte.' for heo is godes chambre. Nurð ne
kimeð in heorte bute of sum þing ꝥ me haueð oðer
isehen oðer iherd. ismaht oðer ismeallet. ⁊ utewið i
felet. Ant ꝥ witeð to soðe ꝥ eauer se þes wittes beoð ma
f. 24a re isprengde utward.' se ha leasse wendeð inward. Eauer se
recluse toteð mare utward.' se ha haueð leasse leome of
ure lauerd inward. ant alswa of þe oþre. Qui exteriori oculo
negligenter utitur.' iusto dei iudicio interiori cecatur.
5 lo hwet sein gregoire seið. Hwa se ȝemelesliche wit hire
uttre ehnen.' þurh godes rihtwise dom ha ablindeð iþe
ínre. ꝥ ha ne mei iseo godd mid gastelich sihðe. ne
þurh swuch sihðe icnawen. ⁊ þurh þe cnawleachunge
ouer alle þing luuien. for efter ꝥ me cnaweð his mu
10 chele godnesse.' ⁊ efter ꝥ me feleð his swote swetnesse.'
efter ꝥ me luueð him mare oðer leasse. FOR þí mí
ne leoue sustren beoð wið ute blinde. as wes þe hali ia
cob ⁊ tobie þe gode. Ant godd wule as he ȝef ham.' ȝeo
uen ow liht wið ínnen. him to seon ⁊ cnawen. ⁊ þurh þe
15 cnawlechunge ouer alle þing him luuien. þenne schu
le ȝe iseon hu al þe world is nawt. hu hire froure
is fals. þurh ꝥ sihðe ȝe schule seon alle þe
deofles wiheles hu he biwrencheð wrecches. ȝe schulen

f. 24a. 4 *before* interiori *a word blurred by stain and partly crossed out:* teriori *is crossed out, before it a confusion of* ex *and* ín. *Scribe apparently wrote* exteriori *erroneously* (*after* 3), *altered* ex *to* ín, *then dissatisfied wrote* interiori *in full.* 11 *small red initial* F *touched with blue.* 16, 17 *a tear* (*now stitched with green silk*) *from ruled margin inwards; the lines stop short of it by about four and eleven letter-spaces respectively, at* froure *and* alle þe.

iseon in ow seolf hwet beo ȝet to beten of ower ahne
sunnen. ȝe schulen bihalde sum cheare toward te píne 20
of helle. ꝥ ow uggi wið ham. ⁊ fleo þe swiðere ham from
mard. ȝe schulen gasteliche iseon þe blissen of heouene.
þe ontenden ower heorte to hihín ham toward. ȝe
schulen as i schawere iseon ure leafdi wið hire meidnes.
(M. 94) al þe englene weoret. al þe halhene hird. ⁊ him ouer 25
ham alle þe blisseð ham alle.· ⁊ is hare alre crune. Þis
sihðe leoue sustren schal frourin ow mareþen mahte
ei worltlich sihðe. Hali men witen wel þe habbeð
hit ifondet. ꝥ euch eorðlich gleadunge is unwurð her f. 24b
toȝeínes. Manna absconditum est ⁊ cetera. Nomen nouum
quod

nemo scit nisi qui accipit. Hit is a dearne healewi seið seínt
iuhan euuangeliste i þe apocalipse. hit is a dearne hea
lewi ꝥ na mon ne cnaweð ꝥ naueð hit ismecchet. Þis 5
smech ⁊ tis cnawunge kimeð of gastelich sihðe. of gas
telich herunge. of gastelich speche. ꝥ ha schulen hab
ben þe forgað for godes luue worldliche herunges.
eorðliche spechen. fleschliche sihðen. Videamus enim
quasi per

speculum in enígmate. Ant efter ꝥ sihðe ꝥ is nu dosc 10
her.· ȝe schulen habbe þruppe þe brihte sihðe of godes
neb ꝥ alle gleadunge is of i þe blisse of heouene mu
che biuore þe oþre. for þe rihtwise godd hit haueð
swa idemet. ꝥ euchanes mede þer.· ondswerie aȝein
þe swinc. ⁊ aȝeines þe ennu. ꝥ ha her for his luue 15
eadmodliche þolieð. for þi hit is semlich ꝥ anc
ren þeos twa marheȝeouen habben
biuoren oþre. swiftnesse. ⁊ leome of a briht sihðe. swift
nes aȝeines ꝥ ha beoð nu swa bipinnet. leome of
briht sihðe. aȝeines ꝥ ha her þeostrið nu ham seol 20
uen. ne nulleð nowðer iseo mon.· ne of mon beon ise
hene. Alle þeo in heouene schule beon ase swifte.· as is

28 *small hole between* þe *and* habbeð.

f. 24b. 4 *MS.* euu*u*angeliste. 4, 5 hit is *to* ismecchet. þis *underlined; mark* × *in left margin.* 16, 17 *a tear* (*see recto*) *causes writing to begin at* eadmodliche *five, and at* anc|ren *thirteen letter-spaces within ruled margin.*

nu monnes þoht. as is þe sunne gleam þe smít from
est:· in to wést. as þe ehe openeð. ah ancres bisperret
25 her:· schulen beo þer ȝef ei mei lihtre ba ⁊ swiftre. ⁊
i se wide schakeles. as me seið pleien in heouene lar
ge lesewen. ꝥ te bodi schal beon hwer se eauer þe gast
wule:· in an hondhwile. þis is nu þe an marhe (M. 96)
f. 25a ȝeoue ꝥ ich seide ancren schulden habben biuoren oþre.
þe oðer is of sihðe. Gregorius enim quod nesciunt ubi
scientem omnia
sciunt. Alle þeo in heouene seoð i godd alle þing. ant
ancren schule brihtluker for hare blindfellunge her:·
5 iseon ⁊ understonde þer:· godes dearne runes ⁊ his der
ue domes. þe ne kepeð nu to witen of þinges wið uten:·
wið eare ne wið ehe. FOR þi mine leoue sustren
ȝef ei mon bit to seon ow:· easkið him hwet god þer
of mahte lihten. for moni uuel ich iseo þrin. ⁊ nane
10 biheue. ȝef he is meadles:· leueð him þe wurse. ȝef ei
wurðeð swa awed ꝥ he warpe hond forð toward te
þurl clað:· swiftliche ananriht schutteð al ꝥ þurl to
⁊ leoteð him iwurðen. Alswa. Sone se eauer eani feleð
in to ei luðer speche ꝥ falle toward ful luue:· sperreð
15 þe þurl ananriht:· ne ondswerie ȝe him nawiht.
ah wendeð awei wið þis uers. ꝥ he hit mahe iheren.
Declinate a me maligni ⁊ scrutabor mandata dei mei.
Narrauerunt michi iniqui fabulationes domine sed non
ut lex t.
ant gað biuoren ower weoued wið þe miserere. Ne
20 chastie ȝe na swuch mon neauer on oþer wise. for in
wið þe chastiement he mahte ondswerie swa:· ⁊ blawen
se liðeliche:· ꝥ sum sperke mahte acwikien. Na wohlech
nis se culuert as o pleinte wise. As hwa se þus seide. Ich
nalde forte þolie deað:· þenche fulðe toward te. ⁊ swer
25 eð deope aðes. ah þah ich hefde isworen hit luuien ich
mot te. hwa is wurse þen me? Moni slep hit binimeð
me. nu me is wa ꝥ tu hit wast. ah forȝef me nu þet

24 *MS.* bisperret. 28 *hole between* in *and* an.

f. 25a. 7 *small blue initial* F *touched with red.* 12 *first* þurl, *probably for* þurh þe. 14 *MS.* sperreð. 18 t. : *read* tua. 22 *MS.* sperke.

ich habbe hit itald te. þah ich schule wurðe wod·/ ne schalt tu neauer mare witen hu me stonde. Ha hit for f. 25b ȝeueð him for he spekeð se feire. speokeð þenne of oðer hwet. ah eauer is þe ehe to þe wude lehe. Eauer is þe (M. 98) heorte i þe earre speche. ȝet hwen he is forðe·/ ha went in hire þoht ofte swucche wordes. hwen ha schulde oðer 5 hwet ȝeornliche ȝemen. He eft secheð his point forte breoke foreward. swereð he mot nede. ant swa waxeð ꝥ wa se lengre se wurse. for na feondschipe nis se uuel·/ as is fals freondschipe. feond þe þuncheð freond·/ is sweoke ouer alle. for þi mine leoue sustren ne ȝeoue 10 ȝe to swuch mon nan inȝong to speokene. for as hali writ seið. hare speche spreat ase cancre. ah for alle ond sweres wendeð ow frommard him alswa as ich seide·/ þruppe. Sawuín ow seoluen. ne maten him betere·/ ne mahe ȝe o nane wise. 15

Lokið nu hu propreliche þe leafdi i canticis godes deore spuse leareð ow bi hire sahe hu ȝe schule seg gen. En dilectus meus loquitur michi. Surge propera amica mea.

⁊ cetera. low ha seið hercne. Ich ihere mi leof speoken. he cleo

peð me ich mot gan. ant ȝe gan ananriht to ower 20 deore leofmon. ⁊ meaneð ow to his earen þe luueliche cleopeð ow to him wið þes wordes. Surge propera amica mea. columba mea. formosa mea ⁊ veni. Ostende mihi fatiem tuam. Sonet uox tua in auribus meis. ꝥ is. Aris up. hihe þe heonewart. ⁊ cum to me mi leofmon. Mi 25 culure. mi feire. ⁊ mi schene spuse. Ostende michi fa. tuam. Schaw to me þi leoue neb·/ ⁊ ti lufsume leor. went te from oþre. Sonet vox tua in auribus meis. Sei hwa

f. 25b. 3 l *erased between* þe *and* ehe. 14 maten: e *altered from* i. 16 *large red initial* L *with stem in margin between* 12 *and* 17; *blue line-patterns in angle, and in margin from* 8 *to* 23. *In* 16 *to* 28 *several underlinings:* 16 Lokið nu hu; 19, 20 Ich ihere mi leof speoken he c . . . peð me ich mot g; 24 *to* 26 is. Aris *to* schene spuse; 27, 28 Schaw *to* from, *and* Sei hwa. *Corresponding marks* × *in left margin* (16, 20, 26), *and scribbled side-lines from level of* 27 *downwards.* 26 fa.: *read* faciem.

f. 26a haueð ido þe. hwa haueð ihurt mi deore. Sing i míne
earen. for þi ꝥ tu ne wilnest bute to seo mi wlite. ne
speoke bute to me.· þi steuene is me swete.· ⁊ ti wlite
schene. Vnde ⁊ subditur. Vox tua dulcis. ⁊ fa. t. decora. þis beoð
5 nu twa þinges þe beoð iluuet swiðe. swete speche ant
schene wlite hwa se ham haueð togederes. Swucche
cheoseð iesu crist to leofmon ⁊ to spuse. ȝef þu wult
swuch beon.· ne schaw þu na mon þi wlite. ne ne leo (M. 100)
te bliðeliche here þi speche. ah turn ham ba to iesu crist
10 to þi deorewurðe spus as he bit þruppe. as þu wult ꝥ
ti speche þunche him swete. ⁊ ti wlite schene. ⁊ habben
him to leofmon ꝥ is þusent fald schenre þen þe sunne.

Hercnið nu ȝeornliche mine leoue sustren
Hal an oðer speche ⁊ frommard tis earre.
15 Hercnið nu hu iesu crist spekeð as o wreaððe.
⁊ seið as o grím hoker. ⁊ o scarn to þe ancre.
þe schulde beon his leofmon. ⁊ secheð þah gealunge
utward ⁊ froure. wið ehe oðer wið tunge. In canticis.
Si ignoras te o pulcra inter mulieres.· egredere ⁊ abi
20 post uestigia gregum tuorum ⁊ pasce edos tuos iuxta
tabernacula pastorum. þis beoð þe wordes. ȝef þu ne
cnawest te seolf þu feier bimong wummen.· wend
ut ⁊ ga efter gate heorden. ⁊ lesewe þine tichnes bi
heordemenne hulen of Ris ⁊ of leaues. þis is a cruel
25 word. a grím word mid alle. ꝥ ure lauerd seið as o gro
me ⁊ o scarn. to totinde ⁊ to hercwile ⁊ to speokele an
cres. hit is bileppet ⁊ ihud.· ah ich hit wulle unualden.
ȝef þu ne cnawest te seolf he seið ure lauerd. neomeð
f. 26b nu gode ȝeme. ꝥ is ȝef þu nast hwas spuse þu art. ꝥ tu
art cwen of heouene. ȝef þu art me treowe as spuse ah
to beonne. ȝef þu þis hauest forȝeten ⁊ telest her to lu

f. 26a. *A side-scribble on outer ruled margin right from* 1 *to* 3. 1 *to* 4 *as far as* schene. Vnde *is in intention underlined, though the hasty strokes do not cover all the words.* 4 Vnde: *erroneous emendation to* vide; fa. t.: *read* facies tua. 13 *large blue initial* H *between* 13 *and* 15, *with stem rising in margin to* 9; *red line-patterns within, and in margin from* 5 *to* 19; *directing* h *in left margin.* 21 *to* 24: ȝef þu *to* of leau(es *underlined; side-scribbles beside outer ruled margin to right of* 21–23, 26–28.

tel.' wend ut ⁊ ga he seið. hwider? ut of þis hehschipe.
of þis muchele menske ⁊ folhe heorde of geat he seið. 5
hwet beoð heorde of geat? ꝥ beoð flesches lustes þe stín
keð ase geat doð biuoren ure lauerd. ȝef þu hauest forȝe
te nu þi wurðfule leafdischipe.' ga ⁊ folhe þeos geat. fol
he flesches lustes. Nu kimeð þrefter. ⁊ lesewe þine tich
nes. ꝥ is as ich seide. fed tíne ehnen wið ut totunge. þi 10
tunge wið chaflunge. þine earen wið spellunge. þi
nease wið smeallunge. þi flesch wið softe felunge.
þeose fif wittes.' he cleopeð tichnes. for alswa as of a
ticchen ꝥ haueð swete flesch.' kimeð a stinkinde gat
(M. 102) oðer a ful bucke.' al riht alswa of a ȝung swete locun 15
ge. oðer of a swote herunge. oðer of a softe felunge.' wax
eð a stincínde lust ⁊ a ful sunne. Hweðer ei totilde ancre
fondede eauer þis þe beakeð eauer utward as untohe
brid i cage? Hweðer þe cat of helle cahte eauer towart hi
re. ⁊ lahte wið cleaures hire heorte heued? ȝe soðes ⁊ 20
droh ut al þe bodi efter. wið clokes of crokede ⁊ kene fon
dunges. ⁊ makede hire to leosen baðe godd ⁊ mon wið
brad scheome ⁊ sunne. ⁊ bireafde hire ed an cleap þe eor
ðe ⁊ ec þe heouene. Inoh sari lure. to wraðerheale bea
kede eauer swa ut ancre. Egredere he seið o grome. Ga 25
ut as dude dyna iacobes dohter to himmere heile. hire
to wraðer heale. ꝥ is to seggen. leaf me ⁊ micunfort.'
ꝥ is inwið þi breoste. ⁊ ga sech wið uten þe worldes fra
kele froure þe schal endin eauer i sar ⁊ i sorhe. tac þerto ⁊ f. 27a
leaf me hwen þe swa is leouere. for ne schalt tu nanesweis
þes ilke twa cunforz. min ⁊ te worldes. þe ioie of þe hali
gast. ⁊ ec flesches froure habbe to gederes. Cheos nu an of
þes twa.' for þe oðer þu most léten. O pulcra inter mulier 5
es. ȝef þu ne cnawest te seolf þu feier bimong wummen
seið ure lauerd. þu feier bimong wummen. ȝe nu her.'
do þer to ꝥ schalt. ⁊ tu wel wulle elles hwer beo feier.'
nawt ane bimong wummen.' ah bimong engles. þu mí
wurðli spuse seið ure lauerd. schalt tu folhín geat o feld. 10

f. 26b. 4 hwider *written on an erasure.* 1 *to* 8*: scribbled line within left ruled margins.* 10 *after* tich|nes *an omission;* as ich *for* as þah he. 17 stincínde, *sic.* 20 heued, *sic.* 26 himmere heile, *sic.*

ꝥ beoð flesches lustes. feld is willes breade. Schalt tu o
þis wise folhi geat ȝont te feld? þe schuldest iþin heor
te bur biseche me cosses. as mi leofmon ꝥ seið to me i ꝥ
luue boc. Osculetur me osculo oris sui. ꝥ is. Cusse me mí
15 leofmon wið þe coss of his muð muðene swetest. þis
coss leoue sustren is a swetnesse ⁊ a delit of heorte swa
unimete swete.· ꝥ euch worldes sauur is bitter þer toȝeí
nes. Ah ure lauerd wið þis coss ne cusseð na sawle. þe lu
ueð ei þing buten him ⁊ te ilke þinges for him þe hel
20 peð him to habben. Ant tu þenne godes spuse ꝥ maht
heren herbiuoren hu sweteliche þi spus spekeð. ⁊ cleo
peð þe to him se luueliche. þrefter hu he went te lof. ⁊ (M 104)
spekeð swiðe grimliche ȝef þu ut wendest. Hald te i þi
chambre. ne fed tu nawt wið uten þine gate tichnes.·
25 ah hald wið innen þin hercnunge. þi speche ant ti
sihðe. ⁊ tun feaste hare ȝeten. muð. ⁊ ehe. ⁊ eare.· for
nawt ha beoð bilokene ínwið wah oðer wal þe þes
ȝeten openið.· bute aȝeín godes sonde.· ⁊ líueneð of
f. 27b sawle. Omni custodia custodi cor tuum. Ouer alle þing
þenne as Salomon þe leareð. ⁊ ich seide feor biuoren i þe
frumðe of þis dale. mine leoue sustren witeð ower heor
te. þe heorte is wel iloket.· ȝef muð. ⁊ ehe. ⁊ eare. wisliche
5 beon ilokene. for heo as ich seide þer.· beoð þe heorte war
deíns. ant ȝef þe wardeins wendeð ut.· þe ham bið bi
wist uuele. þis beoð nu þe þreo wittes ꝥ ich habbe ispe
ken of. Speoke we nu scheortliche of þe twa oþre. þah nis
nawt speche þe muðes wit. ah is smechunge þah ba
10 beon i muðe.

Smeal of nease is þe feorðe of þe fif wittes. Of þis
wit seið seínt austin. De odoribus non satago nimis.
Cum assunt non respuo. cum absunt non requiro. Of
smealles
he seið ne fondi ich nawt mucheles. ȝef ha beoð neh.·
15 o godes half. ȝef feor.· me ne recche. Vre lauerd þah þurh
ysaie. þreateð ham wið helle stench. þe habbeð delit her

f. 27a. 14, 15: Cusse *to* swetest *underlined; mark* × *in right margin.*
f. 27b. 11 *large red initial* S *with tail to* 16; *blue line-patterns within, and in margin from* 8, *trailing to* 22.

i fleschliche smealles. Erit pro suaui odore fetor. Þer toȝeí
nes ha schulen habben heouenliche smealles.˞ þe hab
beð her of irnes swat. oðer of heren ꝥ ha beoreð. oðer
of swati hettren. oðer of þicke eir in hire hus. ⁊ muh 20
linde þinges. stench oðerhwiles ⁊ strong breað i nease.
Þerof beoð iwarnet míne leoue sustren. ꝥ oðerhwile þe
(M. 106) feond makeð sum þing to stinken ꝥ ȝe schulden noti
en. for þi ꝥ he walde ꝥ ȝe hit schulden schunien. oþer
hwile þe wiheleare of sum dearne þing ꝥ ȝe ne mahe 25
nawt iseon. as dust of dearne sedes makeð a swote
smeal cumen as þah hit were of heouene. for ȝe schul
den wenen ꝥ godd for ower hali lif sende ow his elne.
ant leote wel to ow seolf.˞ ⁊ leapen in to prude. Smeal þe f. 28a
kimeð o godes half froureð þe heorte.˞ mare þen þe nea
se. þeos ⁊ oþre truiles ꝥ he bitruileð monie.˞ schulen
beon ibroht to nawt. wið haliweater. ⁊ wið þe hali ro
de taken. Hwa se þohte hu godd seolf wes i þis wit ider 5
uet.˞ ha walde þe derf þrof þuldeliche þolien.

I þe munt of caluarie þer ure lauerd hongede.˞ wes þe
cwalm stowe. þer leien ofte licomes irotet buuen eor
ðe. ⁊ stunken swiðe stronge. he as he hongede mahte
habben hare breað. wið al his oðer wa.˞ riht amidden 10
his nease. Alswa as he wes ideruet in alle his oþre
wittes. In his sihðe þa he seh his deorewurðe moder tea
res. ⁊ seín iuhanes euuangeliste. ⁊ te oðre Maries. ⁊ þa he
biheold hu his deore deciples fluhen alle from him ant
leafden him ane. He weop him seolue þrien wið his feire 15
ehnen. he þolede al þuldeliche ꝥ me him blindfeallede.
hwen his ehnen weren þus ischendlac iblintfeallet. forte
ȝeoue þe ancre þe brihte sihðe of heouene.˞ þah þu þi
ne ehnen for his luue. ⁊ i munegunge þrof blintfealli
A on eorðe to beoren him feolahreadden.˞ nis na muche 20
mid þe muð me gurde him. sum ¶.wunder.

22 *blue initial* Þ *ornamented with a few red lines from* 19 *to* 26.

f. 28a. 7 *red initial* I *in margin from* 5 *to* 10, *ornamented with a few blue lines from* 3 *to* 12. 11 *small blue initial* A *touched with red; directing* a *in left margin.* 13 *MS.* euuuangeliste. 21 *red initial* A *with long tail to* 24; *blue line-ornament, the elaboration of the tail trailing to* 28; *before* .wunder. *a blue paragraph flourished out to right and ornamented with red.*

cheare inohreaðe as me tobeot his cheken. ⁊ spitte
him o scarne. ⁊ an ancre is for a word ut of hire witte.
Hwen he þolede þuldeliche ꝥ te giws dutten as ha
25 buffeteden him. his deorewurðe muð wið hare
dreori fustes. ⁊ tu for þe luue of him. ⁊ for þin ahne
muchele biheue.' þi tutelinde muð dute wið þíne
lippen. Teke ꝥ he smahte galle on his tunge. forte
f. 28b learen ancre. ꝥ ha ne grucchi neauer mare for na mete (M. 108)
ne for na drunch ne beo hit swa unorne. ȝef ha hit
mei eoten.' eote ⁊ þonki godd ȝeorne. ȝef ha ne mei
nawt.' beo sari ꝥ ha mot sechen estfulre. Ah ear þen ꝥ
5 biddunge areare eani scandle.' ear deie martir in hire
meoseise. Deað me ah forte fleon ase forð as me mei.'
wið ute sunne. ah me schal ear deien þen me do eani
heaued sunne. ant nis hit muche sunne to makien ꝥ
me segge. estful is þeos ancre. muchel is ꝥ ha bid. ȝet
10 is wurse ȝef me seið ꝥ ha is grucchilt ⁊ fulitohe dan
gerus. ⁊ erueð forte paien. were ha imid te world.'
ha moste beo sum chearre ipaiet inohreaðe mid leas
se ⁊ mid wurse. Muchel hofles hit is. cumen in to an
cre hus. in to godes prisun willes ⁊ waldes to stude of
15 meoseise forte sechen eise þrin. ⁊ meistrie ⁊ leafdischi
pe. mare þen ha mahte habben inohreaðe ihaued i
i þe worlde. þen⟨c⟩ ancre hwet tu sohtest þa þu forsoke
þe world i þi biclusunge. biwepen þine ahne ⁊ oþres
sunnen. ⁊ forleosen alle þe blissen of þis lif. forte clup
20 pen blisfulliche þi blisfule leofmon i þe eche lif of heo
uene. O seið seín ierome. Quomodo obscuratum est aurum
optimum ⁊ cetera. O weilawei weilawei. hu is gold iþeostret
hu is feherest heow biturnd ⁊ forweolewet. þe apost
le spekeð to swucche grimliche as o wreaððe. Quis
25 uos fascinauit ⁊ cetera. vt cum spiritu ceperitis.' carne
consumma
mini. Me hwuch unseli gast haueð swa bimalscret

f. 28b. 16, 17 ihaued i i þe, *sic*. 17 þen⟨c⟩: c *interlined with caret. In left margin a hand with middle finger pointing to* 19. 21 seín ierome, *for* ieremie. 21 quomodo obs(curatum; 22 optimum ⁊ cetera. O weilawei weila(wei; 26 hwuch *to* bima(lscret; 27 ow. ꝥ ȝe i *underlined; marks* × *in left margin opposite* 22, 26.

ow. ꝥ ȝe i gast bigunnen. ⁊ i flesch wulleð endin. þe
gastelich lif bigunnen i þe hali gast.' beoð bicume
ne al fleschliche. al fleschliche iwurðen lahinde. lihte f. 29a
ilatet. ane hwile lihte iwordet. an oðer luðere iwordet
estfule. ⁊ sarcurne. ⁊ grucchildes. meanildes. ant ȝet ꝥ
wurse is cursildes. ⁊ chidildes bittre ⁊ attrie wið heorte
to bollen. Bihofde nawt ꝥ swuch were leafdi of castel. Ho 5
ker ⁊ hofles þing is ꝥ a smiret ancre ⁊ ancre biburiet
for hwet is ancre hus bute hire burinesse? ⁊ heo schal beo
greattre ibollen. leafdiluker leoten of þen a leafdi of há
mes. ȝef ha makeð hire wrað aȝeines gult of sunne.
ȝef ha setteð hire wordes swa efne ꝥ ha ne þunche ouer 10
sturet. ne nawt ilead ouer skile.' ah inwardliche ⁊ soðli
che wið uten hihðe ⁊ hehschipe in a softe steuene. Filia
fatua in deminoratione erit. þis is Salomones sahe. ꝥ
hit limpe to ei of ow.' godd ne leue neauer. Cang dohter
iwurð as mone i wonunge. þrieð as þe cangun se 15
lengre se wurse. ȝe as ȝe wulleð waxen ⁊ nawt wenden
hindward.' sikerliche ȝe moten rowen aȝein stream
wið muchel swinc breoken forð.' ⁊ gasteliche earmðes.
stealewurðliche sturien. ⁊ swa ȝe moten alle. for alle we
beoð i þis stream. i þe worldes wode weater þe bereð a 20
dun monie. Sone se we eauer wergið ⁊ resteð us i slaw
ðe.' ure bat geað hindward. ⁊ we beoð þe cang doh
ter þe gað woniende. þe wlecche þe godd speoweð as
is iwriten her efter. þe bigunnen i gast. ⁊ i flesch en
dið. Nain ai ah as iob seið. þe delueð efter golt 25
hord. eauer se he mare nahheð hit.' se his heortes
gleadschipe makeð him mare lusti. ⁊ mare fersch
to diggín. ⁊ deluen deoppre ⁊ deoppre.' aðet he hit finde.
Ower heorte nis nawt on eorðe. for þi ne þurue ȝe f. 29b
nawt deluen dunewardes. ah heouen uppart þe heor
te. for ꝥ is þe uprowunge aȝeín þis worldes stream.'

f. 28b. 21 O *to* f. 29b. 25 ideruet *not in* M.

f. 29a. *Between* 13 *and* 16 *a hand drawn in right margin pointing at* 13. 18 earmðes, *sic for* earmes. 23 speoweðas *close but not joined; small stroke below and between* ða *to indicate word-division.* 25 sei)ð. þe delueð efter g(olt *underlined; mark* × *in right margin; scribbled side-line beyond ends of* 25 *to* 28.

driuen hire aȝeinward to deluen þe golthord ꝥ up
5 is in heouene. Ant hwet is ꝥ deluunge? ȝeornful sech
inde þoht. hwer hit beo hwuch hit beo. hu me hit ma
he ifinden. þis is þe deluunge. beon bisiliche ⁊ ȝeornful
liche eauer her abuten. wið anewil ȝirnunge. wið heate
of hungri heorte.' waden up of unþeawes. creopen ut
10 of flesch. breoken up ouer hire. astihen up on ow seolf
wið heh þoht toward heouene. swa muchel þe neode
luker ꝥ ower feble tendre flesch heardes ne mei þo
lien. Nu þenne þer aȝeín ȝeoueð godd ower heorte.
i softnesse. i swetnesse. in alles cunnes meoknesse. ⁊ sof
15 test eadmodnesse. nawt nu granin ⁊ peonsin. þrefter
hehi steuene. wreaðen hire unweneliche. sinetin hire
wordes. wrenchen aweiward. wenden þe schuldre. keaste
þe heaued swa ꝥ godd heateð hire ⁊ mon hire scarneð.
Nai nai ripe wordes. lates ripe ⁊ werkes bilimpeð to an
20 cre. Hwen wordes beoð eadmodliche ⁊ soðfestliche iseide.'
nawt fulitoheliche ne babanliche.' þenne habbeð
ha burðerne to beo riht understonden. Nu is þis al i
seid ꝥ ȝe efter iesu crist þe me gurde ine muð ⁊ galle
ȝef to drinken. wið muðes sunne witen ow. ⁊ þolieð sum
25 derf i ꝥ wit as he wes þrin ideruet. IN his eare he (M. 108)
hefde þe heouenliche lauerd al þe edwit ⁊ te upbrud
al þe scarn ⁊ al þe scheome ꝥ eare mahte iheren. ant
he seið bi him seolf us forte learen. Et factus sum sicut
f. 30a homo non audiens ⁊ non habens in ore suo redargutiones.
Ich heold
me he seið stille as dumbe ⁊ deaf deð ꝥ naueð nan ond
swere. þah me him mis do oðer mis segge. þis is þi leofmon
nes sahe. ⁊ tu seli ancre þe art his leoue spuse leorne hit
5 ȝeorne of him ꝥ tu hit cunne ⁊ mahe soðliche seggen.
NV ich habbe ispeken of ower fowr wittes. ⁊ of godes
froure. hu he þurh hise froureð ow as ofte as ȝe in ower

f. 29b. 11, 12 neode|luker: er *altered from* ee *without erasure.* *Between* 17 *and* 20 *a hand drawn in left margin pointing at* 19. 25 *small blue initial* I *touched with red.*

f. 30a. 6 *red initial* N *ornamented with a few blue lines* (*in margin from* 3 *to* 9); *directing* N *in left margin.* 7 froure, *sic for* fowre.

feleð eani weane. Nu hercnið of þe fifte ꝥ is meast neod
(M. 110) elne. for þe pine is meast þrín. ꝥ is i felunge ant te licun
ge alswa ȝef hit swa turneð. 10

Þe fifte wit is felunge. þis ilke an wit is in alle þe oþre.
⁊ ȝont al þe licome. ⁊ for þi hit is neod to habben
best warde. Vre lauerd wiste hit wel. ⁊ for þi he walde meast
i ꝥ wit þolien al forte frourin us ȝef we þolieð wa þrin.
⁊ forte wenden us frommard te licunge ꝥ flesches lust eas 15
keð. nomeliche i felunge mare þen ín oþre. Vre lauerd
i þis wit nefde nawt in a stude:· ah hefde ouer al píne. nawt
ane ȝond al his bodi:· ah hefde ȝet inwið his seli sawle.
in hire he felde þe stiche of sari sorhe ⁊ sorhful ꝥ dude
him sike sare. þis stiche wes þreouald. þe ase þreo speren 20
smat him to þe heorte. þe an wes his modres wop ⁊ te oþre
maries. þe flowen o teares. þe oðer ꝥ his ahne deore decip
les ne lefden him namare ne ne heolden for godd. for þi ꝥ
he ne healp him seolf in his muchele pine. ⁊ fluhen alle
from him ⁊ leafden him as fremede. þe þridde wes ꝥ mu 25
chele sar ⁊ te ofþunchunge ꝥ he hefde inwið him of hare
forlorenesse þe drohen him to deaðe. ꝥ he seh onont ham
al his swinc forloren ꝥ he swonc on eorðe. þeos ilke
þreo stichen weren in his sawle. In his licome euch lim as f. 30b
seint austin seið þolede sundri pine. ⁊ deide ȝond al his
bodi. as he ear ȝond al his bodi deaðes swat sweatte. ⁊
her seið sein Beornard. ꝥ he ne weop nawt ane wið eh
nen:· ah dude as wið alle his limen. Quasi inquit membris 5
omnibus fleuisse uidetur. for se ful of angosse wes ꝥ ilke ned
(M. 112) swat ꝥ lihte of his licome aȝein þe angoisuse deað ꝥ
he schulde þolien:· ꝥ hit þuhte read blod. factus est sudor
eius quasi gutte sanguinis decurrentis in terram. On oðer
half swa largeliche. ⁊ swa swiðe fleaw ꝥ ilke blodi swat:· 10
of his blisfule bodi:· ꝥ te streames urnen dun to þer
eorðe. Swuch grure hefde his monliche flesch aȝein

11 *large blue initial* Þ *between* 10 *and* 13, *with tapered stem in margin* 8 *to* 18; *red line-patterns within, and in margin with elaboration of tail down to* 26; *directing* þ *in left margin. The* e *of* Þe *is partly overlaid by bow of* Þ. 16 *small red initial* V *touched with blue.*
f. 30b. 5 *MS.* Qu*a*Si. 6 angosse, *sic.*

þe derue pinen ꝥ hit schulde drehen.ʼ ꝥ nes na feorlich
wunder. for eauer se flesch is cwickre.ʼ se þe reopunge
15 þrof ⁊ te hurt is sarre. Alutel hurt i þe ehe. deracð ma
re þen deð a muchel i þe hele. for þe flesch is deaddre.
Euch monnes flesch is dead flesch aȝein ꝥ wes godes
flesch. as ꝥ te wes ínumen of þe tendre meiden. ⁊ na
þing neauer nes þrín.ʼ ꝥ hit adeadede. ah eauer wes iliche
20 cwic of ꝥ cwike godd head þe wunede þrínne. for þi in
his flesch wes þe pine sarre.ʼ þen eauer eaní mon in his
flesch þolede. þet his flesch wes cwic ouer alle flesches.ʼ
lo hwuc an essample. A mon for uuel ꝥ he haueð. ne let
him nawt blod o þe seke halue.ʼ ah deð o þe hale to heale
25 þe seke. ah in al þe world þe wes o þe feure. nes bimong
al moncun an hal dale ifunden þe mahte beon ilete
blod.ʼ bute godes bodi ane þe lette him blod o rode. nawt
o þe earm ane.ʼ ah dude o fif halue. forte healen mon
f. 31a cun of þe secnesse ꝥ te fif wittes hefden awakenet. þus
lo þe hale half ⁊ te cwike dale droh ꝥ uuele blod ut.ʼ
frommard te unhale. ⁊ healde swa þe seke. Þurh blod is
in hali writ sunne bitacnet. þe reisuns hwi beoð efter
5 sutelliche ischawet. ah þerof neomeð ȝeme mine leoue
sustren. ꝥ ower deorewurðe spus þe luuewurðe lauerd. þe
healent of heouene iesu godd godes sune. þe wealdent
of al þe world. þa he wes þus ilete blod.ʼ understondeð
ꝥ dei hwuch wes his diete. i þe ilke blodletunge se ba (M. 114)
10 leful ⁊ se bitter. þe ilke ꝥ he bledde fore.ʼ ⟨ne⟩ brohten
⟨ha⟩ him
to present. ne wín. ne ale. ne weater. ȝet þa he seide. Si
cio. ⁊ meande as he bledde of þurst o þe rode.ʼ ah duden
bitter galle. Hwer wes eauer iȝeuen to eani blodleten
se poure pitance? ant tah ne gruchede he nawt. ah un
15 derueng hit eadmodliche forte learen hise. Ant ȝet he
dude mare us to forbisne. dude his deore muð þer to
⁊ smahte þrof.ʼ þah he hit notie ne mahte. Hwa i s þen
ne efter þis ⁊ ancre hure ⁊ hure þe gruccheð ȝef ha
naueð nawt oðer mete oðer drunch efter hire eise? ⁊
20 siker hwa se gruccheð ha offreð ȝet ure lauerd þis luðe

f. 31a. 10 ⟨ne⟩ brohten ⟨ha⟩: ne, ha *interlined, the latter with caret.*

re pitance. as duden þa þe giws. ⁊ is giwes fére to beo
den him in his þurst drunch of sur galle. His þurst
nis bute ȝirnunge of ure sawle heale. ⁊ grucchunge
of bitter ⁊ of sur heorte:' is him surre ⁊ bittrure nu:'
þen wes þa þe galle. ant tu his deore spuse ne beo þu 25
nawt giwes make forte birlin him swa:' ah ber him
feolahreadden. ⁊ drinc wið him bliðeliche al þet ti
flesch þuncheð sur oðer bitter. ꝥ is pine ⁊ wone ant
alle meoseises. ant he hit wule þe ȝelden as his treowe fe f. 31b
re:' wið healewi of heouene. ÞVS wes iesu crist þe almih
ti godd in alle his fif wittes derfliche ipinet. ⁊ nomeliche
i þis leaste. ꝥ is ifelunge for his flesch wes alcwic as is þe
tendre ehe. ant ȝe witen þis wit. ꝥ is flesches felunge ouer 5
alle þe oþre. Godes honden weren ineilet o rode. þurh
(M. 116) þe ilke neiles ich halsi ow ancres. nawt ow ah do oþre
for hit nis na neod mine leoue sustren. Haldeþ ower
honden inwið ower þurles. Hondlunge oðer ei felun
ge bitweone mon ⁊ ancre. is þing swa uncumelich. ⁊ 10
dede se scheomelich ⁊ se naket sunne. to al þe world se
eatelich ⁊ se muche scandle:' ꝥ nis na neod to speoken
ne writen þer toȝeínes. for al wið ute writunge ꝥ ful
is to etscene. Godd hit wat as me were muche deale leo
uere ꝥ ich isehe ow alle þreo mine leoue sustren wummen 15
me leouest hongin on a gibet. forte wiðbuhe sunne:' þen
ich sehe an of ow ȝeouen anlepi cos eani mon on eorðe swa
as ich meane. Ich am stille of ꝥ mare. nawt ane mong
lin honden. ah putten hond utward bute hit beo for
nede:' is wohunge efter grome. ⁊ tollunge of his eorre. 20
hire seolf bihalden hire ahne hwite honden:' deð hearm
moni ancre. þe haueð ham to feire as þeo þe beoð for
idlet. ha schulden schrapien euche dei þe eorðe up of ha
re put ꝥ ha schulien rotien in. Godd hit wat ꝥ put
deð muche god moni ancre. for as Salomon seið. Me 25
morare nouissima tua ⁊ in eternum non peccabis. þeo

f. 31b. 2 *red initial* Þ *with no blue ornament; directing* þ *in right margin.* 20 *in left margin* (*in different hand*) /.godes, *marked* (*with* /. *above*) *to precede* grome. 24 schulien, *sic* (*by anticipation of* rotien) *for* schulen.

þe haueð eauer hire deað as biuoren hire ehnen ꝥ
te put munegeð. Ȝef ꝥ ha þencheð wel o þe dom of
f. 32a domesdei. þer þe engles schule cwakien. ⁊ te eche ⁊ te eate
liche pinen of helle. ⁊ ouer al ⁊ al o iesu cristes passiun.ʹ
hu he wes ipinet as is sumdeal iseid in alle his fif wittes.ʹ
lihtliche nule ha nawt folhi flesches licunge efter willes
5 lust. ne drahen in toward hire nan heaued sunne wið
hire fif wittes. Þis is nu inoh iseid of þe fif wittes. þe
beoð ase wardein wið uten of þe heorte. ꝥ sawle lif is
ínne. as we seiden þruppe on earst ꝥ Salomon seide.
Omni custodia custodi cor tuum quoniam ex ipso uita pro
10 cedit. Nu beoð crist haue þonc þe twa dalen ouercumen.
Ga we nu wið his help up o þe þe þridde.

MINe leoue sustren (M. 118)
alswa as ȝe miteð wel
ower wittes utewið.ʹ alswa
15 ouer alle þing lokið ꝥ ȝe beon inwið
Softe. ⁊ Milde. ⁊ eadmode. swete ⁊ swote iheortet. ⁊ þole
mode aȝein woh of word ꝥ me seið ow. ⁊ werc þet me
misdeð ow.ʹ leste ȝe al leosen. Aȝein bittre ancres dauið
seið þis uers. Similis factus sum pellicano solitudinis.
20 ⁊ cetera. Ich am he seið as pellican þe wuneð bi him ane.
Pellican is a fuhel se weamod ⁊ se wreaðful.ʹ ꝥ hit sleað
ofte o grome his ahne briddes hwen ha doð him teone.
ant þenne sone þrefter hit wurð swiðe sari. ⁊ makeð
swiðe muche man. ⁊ smít him seolf wið his bile ꝥ he
25 sloh ear his briddes wið.ʹ ⁊ draheð blod of his breoste.
⁊ wið ꝥ blod acwikeð eft his briddes isleine. þis fuhel
pellican is þe weamode ancre. hire briddes beoð hire
gode werkes ꝥ ha sleað ofte wið bile of scharp wreððe.
f. 32b Ah hwen ha swa haueð idon.ʹ do as deð þe pellican. ofþun
che hit swiðe sone. ⁊ wið hire ahne bile beaki hire breoste.
ꝥ is wið schrift of hire muð ꝥ ha sunegede wið. ⁊ sloh hi
re gode werkes. drahe ꝥ blod of sunne ut of hire breoste.
5 ꝥ is of þe heorte ꝥ sawle lif is ínne. ant swa schulen eft

f. 32a. 11 þe þe, *sic.* 12 *Very large blue initial* M (*marking the beginning of Part III*) *between* 12 *and* 16, *with specially elaborate red ornament within, and in margin trailing to below* 28; *directing* M *in left margin.*

acwikien hire isleine briddes. ꝥ beoð hire gode werkes.
Blod bitacneð sunne. for alswa as a mon bibled is gris
lich ⁊ eatelich i monnes ehe·/ alswa is þe sunfule biuo
re godes ehe. On oðer half na mon ne mei iuggi wel
blod ear hit beo icolet. Alswa is of sunne. Hwil þe heor 10
te walleð inwið of wreaððe·/ nis þer na riht dom. oðer
hwil þe lust is hát toward eani sunne·/ ne maht tu
nawt te hwiles deme wel hwet hit is. ne hwet ter wule
cumen of. Ah let lust ouergan·/ ⁊ hit te wule likin. let
ꝥ háte acolin as deð þe wule iuggi blod. ⁊ tu schalt 15
demen ariht þe sunne ful ⁊ ladlich·/ ꝥ te þuhte feier.
(M. 120) ⁊ vuel se muchel cumen þrof ʒef þu hit hefdest idon
hwil ꝥ hate leaste·/ ꝥ tu schalt deme wod te seolf þa þu
þer toward þohtest. þis isof euch sunne soð hwi blod
hit bitacneð. ⁊ nomeliche of wreaððe. Impedit ira a 20
nimum ne possit cernere uerum. Wreaððe hit seið hwil
hit least ablindeð swa þe heorte·/ þet ha ne mei soð icna
wen. Maga quedam est transformans naturam humanam.
Wreaððe is a forschuppilt as me teleð i spelles. for ha rea
ueð mon his wit ⁊ changeð al his chere. ⁊ forschuppeð 25
him from mon·/ in to beastes cunde. Wummon wrað
is wuluene. Mon·/ wulf. oðer liun. oðer unicorne. hwil
ꝥ eauer wreaððe is i wummone heorte. Versaili. segge
hire Vres. Auez. Pater nostres. ne deð ha bute þeoteð. Na f. 33a
ueð ha bute as þeo ꝥ is iwent to wuluene i godes eh
nen·/ wuluene steuene in his lihte earen. Ira furor bre
uis est. wreaððe is a wodschipe. wrað mon nis he wod?
hu lokeð he hu spekeð he. hu feareð his heorte inwið? 5
Hwucche beoð utewið alle hi se lates? he ne cnaweð na
mon hu is he mon þenne. Est enim homo animal man
suetum natura. Mon cundelich is milde. Sone se he
leoseð mildheortnesse·/ he leoseð monnes cunde. ant
wreaððe þe forschuppilt forschuppeð him in to beast as 10
ich ear seide. Ant hwet ʒef eni ancre iesu cristes spuse
is forschuppet into wuluene. nis ꝥ muche sorhe? nis

f. 33a. 6 hi se *for* hise: i *altered from* a, *with erasure leaving space.*
11 ich: c *altered from* s *with partial erasure of top.* 16 *small red initial* L *touched with blue.*

þer bute sone forwarpe ꝥ ruhe fel abute þe heorte. ⁊
wið softe sahtnesse makien hire smeðe ⁊ softe as is cun
15 deliche wummone hude. for wið ꝥ wuluene fel na þing
ꝥ ha deð nis gode licwurðe. Lo her aȝeines wreaððe
monie remedies. frouren a muche floc ⁊ misliche boten.
ȝef me misseið þe.' þench ꝥ tu art eorðe. ne totret me
eorðe. ne bispit me eorðe? þah me dude swa bi þe.' me (M. 122)
20 dude þe eorðe rihte. ȝef þu berkest aȝeín.' þu art hun
des cunnes. ȝef þu stingest aȝeín.' þu art neddre cund
el. ⁊ nawt cristes spuse. þench dude he swa.' Qui tanquam
ouis ad occisionem ductus est ⁊ non aperuit os suum.
Efter alle þe schendfule pinen ꝥ he þolede oþe longe
25 friniht. me leadde him ine marhen to hongin o wea
ritreo. ⁊ driuen þurh his fowr limen irnene neiles.
ah namare þen a schep as þe hali writ seið.' cwich
ne cweð he neauer.

f. 33b Þench ȝet on oþer half. hwet is word bute wind. To
wac ha is istrengðet ꝥ a windes puf a word mei afel
len ⁊ warpen in to sunne. ant hwa nule þunche wund
er of ancre windfeallet? On oðer half ȝetten. ne schaw
5 eð ha ꝥ ha is dust ⁊ unstable þing. þe wið a lute wor
des wind is anan toblawen? þe ilke puf of his muð
ȝef þu hit wurpe under þe.' hit schulde beore þe upp
art toward te blisse of heouene. ah nu is muche wun
der of ure muchele meadschipe. Vnderstondeð þis word.
10 Seint Andrew mahte þolien ꝥ te hearde rode heue him
toward heouene. ⁊ luueliche biclupte hire. Sein lorenz
alswa þolede ꝥ te gridil heue him uppardes wið bear
ninde gleden. Seinte stefne ꝥ te stanes ꝥ me sende him
⁊ underueng ham gleadliche. ⁊ bed for ham þe ham sen
15 den him wið hommen ifalden. ⁊ we ne mahe nawt
þolien ꝥ te wind of a word beore us towart heouene.
ah beoð wode aȝeines ham. þe we schulden þonkin
as þe ilke þe seruið us of muche seruise. þah hit beo
hare unþonkes. Impius uíuít pio uelit nolit. Al ꝥ te

f. 33b. 1 *large blue initial* Þ *between* 1 *and* 3, *with tapered stem in margin from below upper edge to curl at* 8; *red line-patterns within, and about, stem trailing to* 17. 13 *after* him *an omission.*

unwreaste ⁊ te uuele deð for uuel:· al is þe gode to 20
(M. 124) god. al is his bihéue. ⁊ timbrunge toward blisse. let
him ⁊ ꝥ gleadliche breide þi crune. Þench hu þe hali
mon i vitas patrum custe ⁊ blescede þe oþres hond þe hef
de him ihearmet. ⁊ seide se inwardliche cussinde hire
ȝeorne. iblescet beo eauer þeos hond. for ha haueð itim 25
bret me þe blissen of heouene. Ant tu segge alswa bi
hond þe misdeð þe. ⁊ bi þe muð alswa þe ewt misseið
þe. Iblescet beo þi muð sei. for þu makest lome þrof to
timbrí mí crune. wel me is for mí god. ⁊ wa þah for þín f. 34a
uuel. for þu dest me freame ⁊ hearmest te seoluen. ȝef
ei mon oðer wummon misseide oðer misdude ow mine
leoue sustren:· swa ȝe schulden seggen. Ah nu is muche
wunder ȝef we wel bihaldeð. hu godes halhen þoleden 5
wunden on hare bodi. ⁊ we beoð wode ȝef a wind blawe
alutel toward us. ⁊ te wind ne wundeð nawt bute þe eir
ane. for nowðer ne mei þe wind. ꝥ is ꝥ word ꝥ me seið.
ne wundi þe i þi flesch:· ne fule þi sawle þah hit puffe up
o þe bute þe seolf hit makie. Bernardus. Quid irrita 10
ris quid inflammaris ad uerbi flatum. qui nec carnem uulne
rat:· nec inquinat mentem. wel þu maht underȝeoten þet
ter wes lute fur of chearite ꝥ leiteð al of ure lauerdes lu
ue. lute fur wes þer ꝥ a puf acwencte. for þear as mu
che fur is:· hit waxeð wið winde. Aȝeín misdede oðer 15
mis sahe:· lo her on ende þe beste remedie. ⁊ cunneð þis
essample. A mon þe leie i prisun oðer ahte muche ran
cun. ne o nane wise ne schulde ut bute hit were to hon
gin ear he hefde his rancun fulleliche ipaiet:· nalde he
cunne god þonc a mon þe duste uppon him of peo 20
nehes a bigurdel forte reimin him wið ⁊ lesen him
of pine. þah he wurpe hit ful hearde aȝeines his heor
(M. 126) te:· al þe hurd were forȝeten for þe gleadnesse. O þis
ilke wise we beoð alle i prisun her. ⁊ ahen godd greate

In left margin a hand pointing to 20.

f. 34a. *A straight-sided depression* (*about* $\frac{7}{10}$ *in. wide*) *descends from the upper edge nearly to line* 1 *on this folio and the next* (*with a corresponding stain in upper margin of* f. 33b); *a clip or marker was probably attached for a long time.* 15 *small red initial* A *touched with blue.*

25 deattes of sunne. for þi we ȝeiȝeð to him i þe pater noster.
Et dimitte nobis debita nostra. lauerd we seggeð forȝef us
ure deattes. alswa as we forȝeoueð ure deatturs. woh ꝥ
me deð us. oðer of word oðer of werc. ꝥ is ura rancun
f. 34b ꝥ we schulde reimín us wið. ⁊ cwitin ure deattes toward ure
lauerd. ꝥ beoð ure sunnen. for wið ute cwitance up of þis
prisun nis nan inumen ꝥ nis anan ahonget. oðer i purga
toire.' oþer i þe pine of helle. ant ure lauerd seolf seið. Di
5 mittite ⁊ dimittetur uobis. forȝef.' ⁊ ich forȝeoue þe. as þah
he seide. þu art endeattet toward me swiðe wið sunnen.
ah wult tu god foreward. al ꝥ eauer ei mon misseið þe
oþer misdeð þe.' ich wulle neomen onward þe deatte þe
þu ahest me. Nu þenne þah a word culle ful hearde
10 up o þe breoste. ⁊ as þe þuncheð on earst hurte þin
heorte.' þench as þe prisun walde þe þe oðer hurte sare.'
wið þe bigurdel. ⁊ underueng hit gleadliche forte a
cwiti þe wið. ⁊ þonke þe þe hit sent te. þah godd ne
cunne him neauer þonc of his sonde. he hearmeð hím
15 ⁊ freameð þe ȝef þu hit const þolien. for asdauið
seið swiðe wel wið alle. Godd deð in his tresor þe unwrea
ste ⁊ te uuele. forte hure wið ham as me deð wið ger
sum þeo þe wel fehteð. Ponens in thesauris abyssos.
Glosa. crudeles quibus donat milites suos.

20 Eft up on oðer half pellican þis fuhel haueð an
oðer cunde. ꝥ hit is aa leane. for þi as ich seide. da
uið eueneð him þer to in ancre persone. In ancre steue
ne. Similis factus sum pellicano solitudinis. Ich am pel
lican ilich þe wuneð bi him ane. Ant ancre ah þus
25 to seggen. ⁊ beon ilich pellican onond ꝥ hit is leane.
Iudith clausa in cubiculo ieiunabat omnibus diebus
uíte sue ⁊ cetera. Iudith bitund inne as hit teleð in hire
boc.' leadde swiðe heard lif. feaste ⁊ werede hére. Iudith
f. 35a bitund ínne.' bitacneð bitund ancre þe ah to leaden heard
lif as dude þe leafdi iudith efter hire euene. nawt ase swin **(M. 128)**

28 ura, *sic for* ure.

f. 34b. 20 *large blue initial* E *between* 19 *and* 22, *with red line-patterns within, and margin from* 17 *to* 23. 27, 28 Iudith bitund inne *and* b)oc *to* Iudit(h *underlined; mark* × *in left margin.*

ipund isti to feattin ⁊ to greatin aȝein þe cul of þe axe.
Twa cunnes ancren beoð ꝥ ure lauerd speked of. ⁊
seið i þe godspel. of false ⁊ of treowe. Vulpes foueas 5
habent ⁊ uolucres celi nidos. ꝥ is foxes habbeð hare ho
len. ⁊ briddes of heouene habbeð hare nestes. þe fox
es beoð false ancres. ase fox is beast falsest. þeose
habbeð he seið holen þe holieð inward eorðe wið eorð
liche unþeawes. ⁊ draheð in to hare hole al ꝥ ha mah 10
en reopen ⁊ rínnen. Þus beoð gederinde ancres of
godd i þe godspel to uoxes ieuenet. fox ec is a frech
beast ⁊ freotewil mid alle. ⁊ te false ancre draheð in
to hire hole. ⁊ fret ase fox deð baðe gés ⁊ hennen.
habbeð efter þe uox a simple semblant sum chearre. 15
⁊ beoð þah ful of gile. Makieð ham oþre þen ha beoð
ase uox þe is ypocrite. weneð forte gili godd as ha bi
dweolieð simple men.: ⁊ gilið meast ham seoluen. Geal
strið as þe uox deð. ⁊ ȝelpeð of hare god hwer se ha
durren ⁊ mahen. chafflið of idel. ⁊ se swiðe worltliche i 20
wurðeð ꝥ on ende hare nome stinkeð as fox þer he
geað forð. for ȝef ha doð uuele: me seið bi ham wurse.
Þeos eoden in to ancre hus: as dude Saul in to hole.
nawt as dauið þe gode. Ba ha wenden in to hole Sa
ul ⁊ dauið. as hit teleð i regum. ah Saul wende þider 25
in: forte don his fulðe þrín. as deð bimong monie:
sum unseli ancre. went in to hole of ancre hus to bi
fule ꝥ stude. ⁊ don dearnluker þrín fleschliche fulðen:
þen ha mahten ȝef ha weren amidde þe worlde. for hwa ha f. 35b
(M. 130) ueð mare eise to don hire cweadschipes þen þe false ancre?
Þus wende Saul in to hole to bidon ꝥ stude. Ah dauið
wende þider in: ane forte huden him from Saul ꝥ him
heatede. ⁊ sohte to sleanne. Swa deð þe gode ancre. 5

f. 35a. 4 *red initial* T; *blue lines within, and in margin from* 1 *trailing to* 13; *directing* t *in left margin* (*nearly hidden in binding*). 4 *to* 8 *transverse slit* (*stitched with green silk*) *crosses text avoided by the writing as shown.* 23 *blue initial* Þ *with curled stem to* 26; *ornamented with red lines from* 18 *to below* 28; *directing* þ *in left margin* (*nearly hidden*).

f. 35b. 4 *to* 8: *the slit* (*see recto*) *crosses text as shown, dividing* 7 hud-en, 8 ho-le.

þeṣ Saul þ is þe feond heateð ⁊ hunteð efter. ha
deð hire in to hud en hire from hise kene clokes.
ha hud hire in hire ho le ba from worltliche men.·
⁊ worltliche sunnen. ⁊ for þi ha is gasteliche dauið. þ
10 is strong toȝein þe feond. ⁊ hire leor lufsum to ure la
uerdes ehnen. for swa muchel seið þis word. dauið. on e
breische ledene. þe false ancre is Saul efter þ his no
me seið. Saul abutens siue abusio. for Saul on ebreisch.·
is mis notunge on englisch. ant te false ancre misno
15 teð ancre nome ⁊ al þ ha wurcheð. þe gode ancre is
Iudith as we ear seiden. þ is bitund as heo wes. ⁊ alswa
as heo dude.· feasteð. wakeð. swinkeð. ⁊ wereð hearde.
Ha is of þe briddes þ ure lauerd spekeð of efter þe uox
es þe wið hare lustes ne holieð nawt duneward.· ase
20 doð þe uoxes. þ beoð false ancres. ah habbeð on heh
ase brid of heouene iset hare nestes. þ is hare reste.
Treowe ancres beoð briddes icleopede. for ha leaueð þe eor
ðe. þ is þe luue of alle worltliche þinges. ⁊ þurh ȝirn
unge of heorte to heouenliche þinges.· fleoð uppart
25 toward heouene. ⁊ tah ha fleon hehe wið heh lif ⁊ ha
li.· haldeð þah þe heaued lah þurh milde eadmodnes
se. as brid fleonninde buheð þ heaued. leoteð al noht
wurð þ ha wel wurcheð. ⁊ seggeð as ure lauerd learde
f. 36a alle hise. Cum omnia benefeceritis.· dicite. Seruí inutiles
sumus. Hwen ȝe al habbeð wel idon.· he seið ure lauerd. seg
geð þ ȝe beoð unnete þrealles. fleoð hehe ⁊ haldeð þah
þ heaued eauer lahe. þe wengen þe uppard beoreð ham.·
5 þ beoð gode þeawes. þ ha moten sturien in to gode wer
kes. as brid hwen hit fleo wule.· stureð hise wengen. þe
treowe ancres ȝetten þe we to briddes euenið. nawt we (M. 132)
þah ah deð godd.· ha spreadeð hare wengen ⁊ makieð
creoiz of ham seolf as brid deð hwen hit flið, þet is i
10 þoht of heorte ⁊ i bitternesse of flesch beoreð godes rode.

16, 17, Iudith as we ear . . . as heo dude *to* wereð h(earde *underlined; mark* × *in left margin.*

f. 36a. *Between* 5 *and* 6 *a slit from right edge (about* ⅜ *in.) stitched with green silk.* 6 wengen: d *altered to* g *without erasure of upper stroke.*

Þeo briddes fleoð wel þe habbeð lutel flesch as þe pellican haueð ⁊ feole fiðeren. þe strucoín for his muchele flesch. ⁊ oþre swucche fuheles makieð a semblant to fleon.' ⁊ beateð þe wengen. ah þe uet eauer draheð to þer eorðe. Alswa fleschlich
ancre þe liueð i flesches lustes ⁊ folheð hire eise.' þe heuínes 15
se of hire flesch ⁊ flesches unþeawes bineomeð hire hire fluht. ⁊ tah ha makie semblant ⁊ muche nurð wið wengen.' oþres nawt hiren. ꝥ is leote of as þah ha fluhe. ⁊ were an hali ancre. hwa se ȝeorne bihalt.' lahheð hire to bismere. for hire uét eauer as doð þe strucoins. ꝥ beoð hire lustes.' 20
draheð to þere orðe. Þeos ne beoð nawt ilihc þe leane fuhel pellican. ne ne fleoð nawt on heh.' ah beoð eorð briddes. ⁊ nisteð on eorðe. ah godd cleopeð þe gode ancres.' briddes of heouene as ich ear seide. Vulpes foueas habent. ⁊ uolucres celi nidos. foxes habbeð hare holen. ⁊ briddes 25
of heouene habbeð hare nestes. treowe ancres beoð a riht briddes of heouene. þe fleoð on heh ⁊ sitteð singin de murie o þe grene bohes. ꝥ is þencheð uppart of þe blisse of heouene þe neauer ne faleweð.' ah is aa grene. ⁊ f. 36b
sitteð o þis grene singinde murie. ꝥ is resteð ham i þulli þoht. ant ase þeo þe singeð habbeð murhðe of heorte. Brid tah oðer hwile forte sechen his mete for þe flesches neode lihteð to þer eorðe. ah hwil hit sit on eorðe.' hit nis 5
neauer siker.' ah biwent him ofte ⁊ bilokeð him aa. ȝeorn liche abuten. alswa þe gode ancre. ne fleo ha neauer se hehe.' ha mot lihten oðerhwiles dun to þer eorðe.' of hire bodi. Eoten. drinken. slepen. wurchen. speoken. héren of ꝥ hire neodeð to of eorðliche þinges. ah þenne as þe brid deð 10
(M. 134) ha mot wel biseon hire. bilokin hire on euch half. þet ha nohwer ne misneome leste ha beo icaht þurh sum of þe deofles grunen. oðer ihurt summes weis þe hwil ha
Þeos briddes habbeð nestes he seið ⸿.sit se lahe.

11 *red initial* Þ *with tapered stem in margin from* 9 *to* 14; *blue lines within, and in margin from* 6 *trailing to* 18; *directing* þ *in left margin.* 12 strucoín, 20 strucoins, *sic for* strucion(s). 21 ilihc, *sic.*

f. 36b. 14 *large blue initial* Þ *with tapered stem in margin from* 12 *to* 18; *red lines within, and about stem with tail (one trailer descending to bottom edge). Before* .sit se lahe. *a red paragraph, with flourish into right margin, ornamented with blue.*

15 ure lauerd. Volucres celi nidos. Nest is heard utewið of
prikinde þornes. inwið nesche ⁊ softe. swa schal ancre
utewið þolien heard on hire flesch ⁊ prikiende pinen. swa
wisliche þah ha schal swenche ꝥ flesch.' ꝥ ha mahe seggen
wið þe psalmwruhte. fortitudinem meam ad te custodiam.
20 ꝥ is. Ich chulle wite mí strengðe lauerd to þine bihoue.
for þi beo flesches pine efter euchanes euene. ꝥ nest beo
heard wið uten.' ⁊ softe ⁊ swete þe heorte wiðínnen. þeo þe
beoð of bitter oðer of heard heorte. ⁊ nesche to hare flesch.'
ha makieð frommard hare nest. softe wið uten.' ⁊ þorni
25 wið ínnen. Þis beoð þe weamode ⁊ te estfule ancres. bittre
wið ínnen as ꝥ swete schulde beon. ⁊ estfule wiðuten as
ꝥ hearde schulde beon. þeos i þulli nest mahen habben
uuel rest hwen ha ham wel biþencheð. for leate ha
f. 37a schulen bringe forþ briddes of swuch nest. ꝥ beoð gode wer
kes þe fleon toward heouene. Iob cleopeð nest þe ancre hus.
⁊ seið as he were ancre. In nidulo meo moriar. ꝥ is. ich chulle
deien i mí nest. beon ase dead þrín. for ꝥ is ancres rihte. ⁊
5 wunien aðet deað þrín. ꝥ ich nulle neauer slakien hwil þe
sawle is i þe buc.' to drehen heard wiðuten alswa as nest
is. ⁊ softe beo wiðínnen. Of dumbe beastes leorne wisdom
⁊ lare. Þe earn deð in his nest a deorewurðe ʒímstan acha
te hatte. for nan attri þing ne mei þe stan nahhín. ne
10 hwil he is i þe nest.' hearmin his briddes. þis deorewurðe
stan ꝥ is iesu crist ase stan treowe. ⁊ ful of alle mihtes ouer
alle ʒimstanes. he is þe achate ꝥ atter of sunne ne nah
hede neauer. do him i þi nest. ꝥ is i þin heorte. þench hwuch
pine he þolede on his flesch wiðuten. hu swote he wes iheor **(M. 136)**
15 tet. hu softe wiðínnen. ⁊ swa þu schalt driuen ut euch at
ter of þin heorte. ⁊ bitternesse of þi bodi. for iþulli þoht ne
beo hit neauer se bitter pine ꝥ tu þolie for þe luue of hím.'
þe droh mare for þe.' schal þunche þe swote. Þes stan as ich
seide afleieð attrie þinges. Habbe þu þes stan inwið þi breos
20 te þer godes nest is.' ne þearf þu noht dreden þe attri ned

f. 37a. 2 *a scribble in the right margin.* 2 *to* 4: Iob cleop . . est þe ancre hus . . . In nidulo meo moriar *to* deien in mi nest *underlined.* 7 *small blue initial* O *touched with red.* 8 *MS.* acha . . 18 *third* þe: þ *clumsy, on erasure.*

dre of helle. Þine briddes ꝥ beoð þine gode werkes.: beoð al
Hwa se ne mei þes ȝimstan hab ¶.sker of his atter.
ben ne halden i þe nest of hire heorte.: lanhure i þe nest
of hire ancre hus.: habbe his iliche. ꝥ is þe crucifix bihal
de ofte þron. ⁊ cusse þe wunde studen i swote munegunge 25
of þe soðe wunden þe he o þe soðe rode þuldeliche þolede.
Se uorð se ha mei beo iudith. ꝥ is libben hearde. beon i
cnawen ofte to godd his muchele godlec toward hire. ⁊
hire fawtes toward him ꝥ ha him ȝelt hit uuele. criehím f. 37b
ȝeorne þrof mearci ⁊ are. ⁊ schríue hire ilome. Þenne is ha
iudith þe sloh oloferne. for iudith on ebreisch.: is schrift
on englisch. ꝥ sleað gasteliche þen deouel of helle. Iudith.:
Confessio. for þi seið ancre to euch preost.: Confiteor on al 5
re earst. ⁊ schriueð hire ofte.: forte beo iudith ⁊ slean olo
ferne. ꝥ is þe deofles strengðe. for ase muchel seið þis no
me oloferne.: as stínkinde in helle. Secundum nominis
ethimolo
giam olofernus olens in inferno secundum interpretationem
infir
mans uitulum saginatum. On ebreische ledene oloferne 10
is þe feond þe makeð feble ⁊ unstrong feat kealf ⁊ to
wilde. ꝥ is ꝥ flesch þe awildgeð sone se hit eauer featteð
þurh eise ⁊ þurh este. Incrassatus est dilectus ⁊ recalcitrauít.
Mi leof is ifeatteð he seið ure lauerd. ⁊ smít me wið his
(M. 138) héle. Sone se flesch haueð his wil.: hit regibeð anan ase 15
feat meare ⁊ idel. þis featte kealf haueð þe feond streng
ðe to unstrengen ⁊ buhen toward sunne. for swa muche
seið þis nome oloferne. Ah ancre schal beo Iudith þurh
heard lif ⁊ þurh soð schrift. ⁊ slean as dude iudith þes
uuel oloferne. temie ful wel hire flesch sone se ha ifel 20
eð ꝥ hit awilgeð to swiðe.: mid feasten. mid wecchen. wið
hére. wið heard swinc. wið hearde disceplines. wisliche

22 *red initial* H *with stem in margin between* 19 *and* 23*; blue line-patterns within, and in margin from* 16 *to below* 28*; directing* h *in left margin (nearly hidden). Before* .sker of his atter. *a blue paragraph touched with red.*

f. 37b. 3, 4 iudith *to* deouel *underlined; a scribble in outer left margin.* 9 olofern*us*. 14 ifeatteð, *sic.* 14, 15 Mi leof is ifeatteð he seið *and* héle *underlined; scribble in left margin and mark* ×.

þah ⁊ wearliche. Habete inquit sal in uobis. Item. In omni
sacrifitio offeretis michi sal. ꝥ is ín euch sacrefise he seið
25 ure lauerd offrið me salt eauer. Veaste. wecche ⁊ oþre
swucche as ich nempnede nu.· beoð mi sacrefises. Salt
bitacneð wisdom. for salt ȝeueð mete smech. ⁊ wisdom
ȝeueð sauur al ꝥ we wel wurcheð. wið ute salt of wis
f. 38a dom þuncheð godd smechles alle ure deden. On oþer
half wið ute salt.· flesch gedereð wurmes. stinkeð swiðe
fule ⁊ forroteð sone. alswa wið ute wisdom flesch as wurm
forfret hire ⁊ wasteð hire seoluen. forfeareð as þing þe
5 forroteð sleað hire on ende. Ah þulli sacrefise stinkeð

Þah þe flesch beo ure fa.· hit is us ihá ❡ .ure lauerd.
ten ꝥ we halden hit up. wa we moten don hit as hit
is wel ofte wurðe.· ah nawt fordon mid alle. for hu wac
se hit eauer beo.· þenne is hit swa icuplet. ⁊ se feste ifeiet
10 to ure deorewurðe gast godes ahne furme.· ꝥ we mahten
sone slean ꝥ an wið ꝥ oþer. Augustinus. Natura mentis huma
ne que ad ymaginem dei creata est. ⁊ síne peccato est. solus
deus maior est. Ant tis is an of þe measte wundres on
eorðe. ꝥ te heste þing under godd. ꝥ is monnes sawle
15 as seint Austin witneð. schal beo se feste ifeiet to flesch
ꝥ nis bute fen ⁊ a ful eorðe. ⁊ þurh ꝥ ilke limunge lu
uíen hit se swiðe.· ꝥ ha forte cwemen hit in his fule
cunde. geað ut of hire hehe heouenliche cunde. ⁊ forte
paien hire.· wreaðeð hire schuppere þe scheop hire efter
20 him seolf. ꝥ is king ⁊ keiser of eorðe ⁊ of heouene. wun (M. 140)
der ouer wunder ⁊ hokerlich wunder. ꝥ se unimete
lah þíng. fere nichil. for neh nawt seið seint austin.
schal drahen in to sunne.· se unimete heh þing. ase saw
le is. ꝥ seint awstín cleopeð fere summum. ꝥ is for neh
25 hest þing wið ute godd. Ah godd nalde nawt ꝥ ha lupe
i prude. ne wilnede to climben. ⁊ feolle as dude lucifer
for he wes bute charge. ⁊ teide for þi a clot of heui eorðe

f. 38a. 6 *large blue initial* Þ *betewen* 5 *and* 8, *tapering stem in margin from* 3 *to* 11; *red line-ornament within, and in margin from* 1 *to* 13; *directing* þ *in left margin* (*only bow now visible*); *before* .ure lauerd. *red paragraph with blue lines, flourished into margin.* 21 *first* wunder: r *altered from* s. 28 oþer to þe oþer, *sic.*

to hire as me deð þe cubbel to þe ku.ʹ oþer to þe oþer
beast ꝥ is to recchinde.ʹ ⁊ renginde abuten. þis is ꝥ iob f. 38b
seide. Qui
fecisti uentis. id est. spiritibus pondus. lauerd he seið þu
hauest íma
ket foðer to feðerín wið þe sawlen. ꝥ is ꝥ heuie flesch þet
draheð hire duneward. Ah þurh þe hehschipe of hire hit
schal wurðe ful liht. lihtre þen þe wind is ⁊ brihtre þen þe 5
sunne. ȝef hit folheð hire her. ne ne draheð hire toswiðe
in to hire lahe cunde. leoue sustren for his luue ꝥ ha is
ilich to.ʹ beoreð hire menske. ne leote ȝe nawt þe lahe
flesch meistrin hire to swiðe. ha is her in uncuððe iput
in a prisun. bitund in a cwalm hus. ne nís nawt edscéne 10
of hwuch dignete ha is. hu heh is hire cunde. ne hwuch
ha schal þunche ȝet in hire ahne riche. ꝥ flesch
is her ed háme. as eorðe þe is in eorðe. ⁊ is for þi cointe ⁊
couer. as me seið ꝥ curre is kene on his ahne mixne.
Ha haueð to muche meistrie weilawei o monie. Ah ancre 15
as ich habbe iseid ah to beon al gastelich ȝef ha wule
wel fleon as brid ꝥ haueð lutel flesch ⁊ feole fiðeren. nawt
ane ȝet tis.ʹ ah teke ꝥ ha temeð wel hire fulitohe flesch
⁊ strengeð ⁊ deð menske þe wurðfule sawle.ʹ teke þis ha
mot ȝet þurh hire forbisne. ⁊ þurh hire hali beoden 20
ȝeouen strengðe oþre. ⁊ up halden ham ꝥ ha ne fallen
(M. 142) i þe dunge of sunne. Ant for þi dauið anan efter ꝥ he
haueð ieuenet ancre to pellican.ʹ he eueneð hire to
nihtfuhel þe is under euesunges. Similis factus sum
pellicano solitudinis factus sum sicut nicticorax in domi 25
cilio. Þe nihtfuhel i þe euesunges bitacneð recluses.ʹ
þe wunieð for þi under chirche euesunges. ꝥ ha un
derstonden ꝥ ha ahen to beon of se hali lif. ꝥ al hali
chirche. ꝥ is cristene folc leonie ⁊ wreoðie up on ham. ant heo f. 39a
halden hire up.ʹ wið hare lif halínesse ⁊ hare eadie bonen.
for þi is ancre ancre icleopet. ⁊ under chirche iancret as
ancre under schipes bord forte halden ꝥ schip. ꝥ uþen ant

f. 38b. 12 cunde *crossed out between* ahne *and* riche. 17 nawt *small and cramped at line end (projecting into margin).* 26 *small red initial* Þ *touched with blue.*

5 stormes hit ne ouerwarpen. Alswa al hali chirche ꝥ is schip i
cleopet. schal ancrin o þe ancre. ꝥ heo hit swa halde ꝥ te deof
les puffes. ꝥ beoð temptatiuns. ne hit ouerwarpen. Euch ancre
haueð þis o foreward. ba þurh nome of ancre. ⁊ þurh þet
ha wuneð under þe chirche to understiprín hire ȝef ha wal
10 de fallen. ȝef ha brekeð foreward.' loki hwam ha lihe. ⁊ hu
continuelement.' for ha ne stureð neauer.' ancre wununge ⁊
hire nome ȝeieð eauer þis foreward ȝet hwen ha slepeð.
ON oðer half þe nihtfuhel flið bi niht ⁊ biȝet i þeoster
nesse his fode. alswa schal ancre fleon wið contempla-tiun. ꝥ is
15 wið heh þoht. ⁊ wið hali bonen bi niht toward heouene.
⁊ biȝeote biniht hire sawle fode. Bi niht ah ancre to beon
waker ⁊ bisiliche abuten gastelich biȝete. for þi kimeð a
nan þrefter. Vigilaui ⁊ factus sum sicut passer solitarius
in tecto. Vigilaui. Ich wes waker seið dauið in ancre persone.
20 ⁊ ilich spearewe under rof ane. Vigilaui. Ich wes waker. for
ꝥ is ancre rihte muchel forte wakien. Ecclesiasticus. Vigilia ho **(M. 144)**
nestatis tabefatiet carnes. Na þing ne awealdeð wilde flesch
ne ne makeð hit tomre.' þen muche wecche. wecche is in hali
writ i feole studen i preiset. Vigilate ⁊ orate ne intretis in
25 temptationem. Alswa as ȝe nulleð nawt fallen in to fondun
ge he seið ure lauerd. wakieð ⁊ ibiddeð ow ꝥ schal don ow
stonden. Eft he seið. Beatus quem inuenerit uigilantem. Eadi is
þe ilke ꝥ hwen ure lauerd kímeð.' ifint wakiende. ⁊ he hím
f. 39b seolf sum chearre. pernoctauit in oratione. wakede i beoden al niht.
ant swa he tahte us wecche. nawt ane wið his lare.' ah dude
wið his dede. EAhte þinges nomeliche leaðieð us to wa

f. 39a. 11 *in left margin an arrow combined with abbreviation for* Nota bene, *apparently calling attention to* continuelement. 13 *small red initial* O, *blue lines within, and in margin from* 10 *to* 16*; directing* o *in left margin (faint).* 26, 28*: the last eight lines of this page are unusually crowded;* ⁊ *is probably omitted after* ibiddeð ow*; and* he *after* kímeð.'.

f. 39b. 3 *small blue initial* E *touched with red.*

·i·
kien eauer i sum god ⁊ beo wurchinde. þis scheorte lif. þis
·ii· iii iiii
stronge wei. Vre god ꝥ is se þunne. Vre sunnen þe beoð se 5
v.
monie. deað ꝥ we beoð siker of. ⁊ unsiker hwenne. ꝥ sterke
vi
dom of domesdei ⁊ se nearow mid alle. ꝥ euch idel word
bið þer ibroht forð. ⁊ idele þohtes þe neren ear her ibette.
Dominus in euuangelio. de omni uerbo otioso ⁊ cetera.
Item. ⁊ capilli de ca
pite non peribunt. id est. cogitatio non euadet inpunita. 10
Anselmus.
Quid faties in illa die quando exigetur a te omne tempus
inpensum qualiter sit a te expensum. ⁊ usque ad minimam
cogitationem. loke nu hwet beo of unwreaste willes ⁊ sunfu
le werkes. ȝet þe seoueðe þing þe munegeð us to wakien.'
·vii
ꝥ is þe Sorhe of helle. þer bihald þreo þing. þe unta 15
leliche pinen. þe echnesse of euchan. þe unimete bitter
·viii
nesse. Þe eahtuðe þing. hu muchel is þe mede iþe blis
se of heouene.' world buten ende. Hwa se wakeð her wel
ane hondhwile. hwa se haueð þeos eahte þing ofte ín
hire heorte.' ha wule schaken of hire slép of uuel slawðe. 20
I þe stille niht hwen me ne sið nawiht. nowðer ne ne hereð
(M. 146) ꝥ lette þe bone.' þe heorte is ofte se schir. for naþing nis
witnesse of þing ꝥ me þenne deð.' bute godes engel þe is
i swuch time bisiliche abuten to eggin us to gode. for þer
nis nawt forloren as is bi dei ofte. Hercnið nu leoue sust 25
ren hu hit is uuel to uppín. ⁊ hu god þing hit is to heo
len goddede. ⁊ fleo bi niht as nihtfuhel. ⁊ gederin bi þeos
tre. ꝥ is i priuite. ⁊ dearnliche sawle fode. Oratio hester
placuit regi assuero. ꝥ is. hesteres bone þe cwen wes þe king f. 40a
assuer licwurðe ⁊ icweme. Hester on ebreisch.' ꝥ is ihud on
englisch. ⁊ is to understonden ꝥ bone ⁊ oðer goddede þet is

9 *MS.* euuuangelio. 15 Sorhe: S *has form* ꙍ. 28 *very small red initial* O *touched with blue.*

f. 40 a. 1 hesteres *to* wes þe k(ing *underlined; in right margin mark* ×, *side-scribble at ends of* 1, 2.

idon on hudles. is assuer icweme. ꝥ is þe king of heouene.
5 for assuer on ebreisch.ˊ is eadi on englisch. ꝥ is ure lauerd
þe is
eadi ouer alle. Dauið spekeð to ancre þe wes iwunet in
hudles wel forte wurchen. ⁊ seoððen o sum wise uppeð hit
⁊ schaweð. Vt quid auertis manum tuam ⁊ dexteram tuam de
medio sinu tuo in finem. ꝥ is. hwi drahest tu ut þin
10 hond. ⁊ ʒet ti riht hond of midde þi bosum? In finem.
on ende. Riht hond is god werc. Bosum is priuíte. ⁊ is as
þah he
seide. þe riht hond ꝥ tu heolde ancre i þi bosum. ꝥ is þi gode
werc ꝥ tu hefdest idon priuement as þing is dearne ibosum.
hwi drahest tu hit ut in finem. on ende? ꝥ is ꝥ tí mede endi se
15 sone. þi mede ꝥ were endeles ʒef þi goddede ihole were. hwi
openest tu hit ⁊ nimest se scheort mede? hure ꝥ is agan ín
an hondhwile. Amen dico uobis receperunt mercedem suam.
þu ha
uest iuppet þi god he seið ure lauerd. witerliche þu hauest
underuo þi mede. Sein gregoire awundreð him. ⁊ seið þet
20 men beoð wode þe trochið swa uuele. magna uerecundia est
grandia agere ⁊ laudibus inhiare. vnde celum mereri potest. (M. 148)
nummum
transitoríí fauoris querit. Muchel meadschipe hit is he seið
don wel.ˊ ⁊ wilni word þrof. don hwer þurh he buð þe kíne
dom of heouene.ˊ ⁊ sullen hit for a windes puf of wordes
25 hereword of monnes herunge. for þi mine leoue sustren
haldeð ower rihthond inwið ower bosum. leste mede ende
les neome scheort ende. we redeð ín hali writ ꝥ moyseseṣ
hond godes prophete. sone se he hefde idrahen hire ut of his
f. 40b bosum.ˊ bisemde o þe spitel uuel ⁊ þuhte lepruse. þurh hwet
is bitacnet ꝥ goddede idrahe forð. nis nawt ane forloren
þurh ꝥ uppinge.ˊ ah þuncheð ʒet eatelich biuore godes

13 puement (*of* priuement) *crossed out with two thin strokes; above in scratchy hand* darnliche: *probably due to a purist, and derived from* dearnliche f. 39b. 28 *and* dearne *in this line* (*in left margin a faint* ×); *cf.* f. 52a. 20 uerecundia, *sic* (*as* L *and some others*) for uecordia.
21 nummum: *MS.* numum. 26 *small hole above* w *of* inwið.
27 y *and last* s *of* moyseses *expuncted with pale dots* (*apparently to correct name to post-medieval form*).

ehe :· as spitel uuel is eatelich biuore monnes sihðe. lo a feor
li god word ꝥ te hali iob seið. Reposita est hec spes mea 5
in sinu
meo. I mi bosum he seið is al min hope ihalden. as þah he
seide. hwet god se ich do were hit ut of bosum iuppet ⁊ idra
he forð :· al min hope were edslopen. Ah for þi ꝥ ich hit heo
le ⁊ hude as i bosum :· ich hopie to mede. for þi ȝef ei deð ea
ní god :· ne drahe ha hit nawt utward ne ȝelpe nawiht þrof :· 10
for wið a lutel puf. wið a wordes wind hit mei beon al to
VRe lauerd i Iohel meaneð him swiðe of ℂ.weauet.
þeo þe forleoseð ⁊ spilleð al hare god þurh wilnunge of
hereword :· ⁊ seið þeos wordes. Decorticauit ficum meam
nudans
spoliauit eam ⁊ proiecit. Albi facti sunt rami eius. Allas seið 15
ure lauerd. þeos þe schaweð hire god :· haueð bipilet mi fier.
irend al þe rinde of. despuilet hire steort naket. ⁊ iwarpen
awei. ⁊ te grene bohes beoð fordruhede ⁊ forwurðen to drue
hwite rondes. þis word is dosc. ah neomeð nu ȝeme hu ich
(M. 150) hit wulle brihtín. Fier is a cunne streo þe bereð swete frut 20
ꝥ me cleopeð figes. Þenne is þe fier bipilet ⁊ te rinde írend
of :· hwen goddede is íuppet. þenne is þe lif ut. þenne adeadeð
þe treo hwen þe rinde is awei. no nowðer ne bereð hit frut :·
ne greneð þrefter ilufsume leaues. ah druhieð þe bohes :·
⁊ wurðeð hwite rondes. to na þing betere þen to fures fode. 25
þe boh hwen hit adeadeð :· hit hwiteð utewið ⁊ adruheð ín
wið ⁊ warpeð his rinde. alswa goddede þe wule adeadin :·
forwarpeð his rinde. ꝥ is unhuleð him. þe rinde þe wrið
hit :· is þe treoes warde. ⁊ wit hit i strengðe. ⁊ i cwicnesse. f. 41a
Alswa
þe hulunge is þe goddedes lif. ⁊ halt hit i strengðe. ah hwen
þe rinde is offe :· þenne as þe boh deð hwiteð hit utewið þurh
worltlich hereword :· ⁊ adruheð inwið ⁊ leoseð þe swetnesse of
godes grace. þe makede hit grene. ⁊ licwurðe godd to bihal 5

f. 40b. 12 *blue initial* V *with red line-patterns to right, within, and in margin from* 8 *to* 21; *before* .weauet. *a red paragraph scribbled with blue.* 15 *to* 19: *side-scribble to right over the ornament of* V (*drawing attention to translation*); *mark* × *in outer margin* (16). 23 no nowðer, *sic for* ne nowðer.

den. for grene ouer alle heowes froureð meast ehnen. Hwen
hit is swa adruhet:' þenne nis hit to nawt se god:' as to þe fur
of helle. for þe earste bipilunge hwer of al þis uuel is:' nís
bute of prude. Ant nis þis muche reowðe ꝥ te fier þe schulde
10 wið hire swete frut. ꝥ is goddede. fede godd gasteliche þe
lauerd
of heouene schal adruhien rindeles þurh ꝥ hit is unhulet
⁊ wurðen buten ende helle fures fode. Ant nis ha to unseli
þe wið þe wurð of heouene buð hire helle? Vre lauerd iþe
godspel seolf eueneð heoueriche to gold hord. þe hwa se
15 hit fínt:' as he seið hudeð hit. Quem qui ínuenit homo ab
scondit. Golthord is goddede þe is to heouene ieuenet. for
me hit buð þerwið. ant þis golthord bute hit beo þe betere
ihud ⁊ iholen:' hit is forlore sone. for as seín geegoire seið.
Depredari desiderat qui thesaurum puplice portat in uia. þe
20 bereð tresor openliche i wei ꝥ is al ful of reaueres ⁊ of þeoues:'
him luste leosen hit ⁊ beon irobbet. þis world nis bute a wei
to heouene oðer to helle. ⁊ is al biset of hellene mucheres:'
þe robbið alle þe golthordes ꝥ ha mahen underȝeoten ꝥ **(M. 152)**
mon oðer wummon iþis wei openeð. for ase muchel wurð
25 is as hwa se seide. ⁊ ȝeide as he eode. Ich beore golthord.
Ich beo
re golthord. lowr hit her read gold. hwit seoluerinoh:' ant
deorewurðe stanes. A Sapere þe ne bereð bute sape ⁊ nelden:'
ȝeiȝeð hehe ꝥ he bereð. A riche mercer geað forð al stille
f. 41b freínið hwet itidde of ezechie þe gode king. for þi ꝥ he
schawde
þe celles of his aromaz. his muchele þinges. his deorewurðe
tresor. Nis hit nawt for nawt iwriten iþe hali godspel of þe
þreo kinges. þe comen to offrin iesu crist þe deore þreo lakes.
5 procidentes adorauerunt eum. ⁊ apertis thesauris suis
obtulerunt ⁊ cetera.
ꝥ tet ha walden offrin him:' ha heolden eauer ihud aðet ha co
men biuoren him. þa earst ha unduden þe presenz ꝥ ha bé
ren. for þi mine leouesustren bi niht as þe nihtfuhel ꝥ an
cre is to ieuenet beoð ȝeorne sturiende. Niht ich cleopie prí

f. 41a. 18 geegoire, *sic*. 28 *stop omitted at end of page.*
f. 41b. 7 earst: r *from* s *without erasure.*

uite. þis niht ȝe mahen habben euch time of þe dei. ꝥ al þe 10
god ꝥ ȝe eauer doð. beo idon as bi niht ⁊ bi þeosternesse. ut of
monnes ehe. ut of monnes eare. þus i niht beoð fleonnín
de. ⁊ sechinde ower sawle heouenliche fode. þenne ne beo ȝe
nawt ane.·ʹ pellicanus solitudinis.·ʹ ah beoð ec Nicticorax in do
Vigilauí ⁊ factus sum sicut passer solitarius ¶.micilio. 15
in tecto. ȝet is ancre ieuenet her to spearewe ꝥ is ane un
der rof as ancre. Spearewe is a chiterinde brid. chitereð
aa. ant
chirmeð. ah for þi ꝥ moni ancre haueð ꝥ ilke unþeaw. da
uið ne eueneð hire nawt to spearewe þe haueð fére.·ʹ ah deð
to spearewe ane. Sicut passer solitarius. Ich am he seið bi 20
ancre
as spearewe ꝥ is ane. for swa ah ancre hire ane in anlich stu
de as ha is chirmín ⁊ chiterin eauer hire bonen. ⁊ underston
deð leofliche mine leoue sustren ꝥ ich write of anlich lif
(M. 154) forte frourin ancren ⁊ ow ouer alle. Hu god is to beon
ane.·ʹ is ba i þe alde lahe ⁊ i þe neowe isutelet. for i baðe me 25
ifint ꝥ godd his dearne runes ⁊ heouenliche priuitez schaw
de his leoueste freond. nawt i monne floc.·ʹ ah dude þer ha
weren ane bi ham seoluen. ant heo ham seolf alswa as
ofte as ha walden þenchen schirliche of godd ⁊ makien f. 42a
cleane bonen. ⁊ beon in heorte gasteliche ihehet toward heo
ueue.·ʹ aa me ifínt ꝥ ha fluhen monne sturbunge. ⁊ wenden
bi ham ane. ⁊ þer godd edeawde ham ⁊ schawde him seolf to
ham. ⁊ ȝef ham hare bonen. for þi ꝥ ich seide ꝥ me ifint tis 5
ba i þe alde testament ⁊ ec i þe neowe.·ʹ ich chulle of ba twa
EGressus est ysaac in agrum ad ¶.schawín forbisne.
meditandum quod ei fuisse creditur consuetudínarium. Ysaac
þe patriarche forte þenche deopliche.·ʹ sohte anlich stude
⁊ wen
de bi him ane. as genesys teleð. ⁊ swa he imette wið þe eadi 10

f. 41b. 15 *red initial* V *ornamented with blue* (*in margin from* 14 *to* 20); *before* micilio. *a blue paragraph with red tails.* 24 *small blue initial* H *touched with red; directing* h *in right margin.*

f. 42a. 7 *small red initial* E *touched with blue lines; directing* e *in left margin; before* .schawín forbisne. *a blue paragraph touched with red.*

rebecca. þ is wið godes grace. Rebecca enim interpretatur multum dedit.
Et quicquid habet meriti preuentrix gratia donat. Alswa þe eadi iacob
þa ure lauerd schawde him his deorewurðe nebscheft ⁊ ȝef
him his blesceunge. ⁊ wende his nome betere. he wes iflohe
15 men ⁊ wes him al ane. neauerȝete imonne floc ne cahte he
swuch biȝete. Bi Moysen ⁊ bi helye godes deorewurðe freond
is sutel ⁊ edscene hwuch baret ⁊ hu dredful lif is eauer
imong þrung. ⁊ hu godd his priuitez schaweð to þeo þebeoð
priuement ham ane. Me schal leoue sustren þeose estoires tel
20 len ow. for ha weren to longe to writen ham hére. ⁊ þenne schu
le ȝe al þis brihte understonden. Set ⁊ Ieremias solus sedet. þe (M. 156)
eadi Ieremie seið he sit ane. ⁊ seið þe reisun for hwi. Quia commi
natione tua replesti me. Vre lauerd hefde ifullet him of his
þreatunge. Godes þreatunge is wontreaðe ⁊ weane i licome ⁊
25 i sawle. worlt buten ende. þe were of þis þreatunge as he wes
wel ifullet.' nere þer nan empti stude i þe heorte to underfon
fleschliche lahtren. for þi he bed wealle of teares. Quis dabit
michi fontem lacrimarum ? þ ha ne adruhede neauer namare
f. 42b þen wealle forte biwepe slei folc. þ is meast al þe world þet is
gasteliche islein mid deadliche sunnen. Vt lugeant inter
fectos populi mei. ant to þis wop lokið nu he bit anlich stu
de. Quis michi dabit diuersorium uiatorum in solitudine ut ⁊ cetera.
5 þe hali prophete forte schawi witerliche. þ hwa se wule biwep
en hire ahne ⁊ oþres sunnen as ancre ah to donne. ⁊ hwa
se wule ifinden ed te nearewe domesmon mearci ⁊ are.' a þing
þ let him meast. is beowiste þ is wununge bimong men.
⁊ þ swiðest furðreð hit.' þ is anlich stude mon oþer wum

12 *small blue initial* A *touched with red.* 21 ⁊ Ieremias solus sedet *underlined; scribble down right ruled margin from* 21 *to* 28; *mark* × *to right of* 24.

f. 42b. 1 *to* 5 *scribble* (*continued from recto*) *down left margin.* 2 lugeant, *sic for* lugeam. 4 Quis: Q*ui*S.

mon eiðer to beon ane. ȝet spekeð ieremie of anlich stu 10
de mare. Sedebit solitarius ⁊ tacebit. Me schal sitten he seið
him ane ⁊ beo stille. Of þis stilnesse he spekeð þer bíuoren
lutel. Bonum est prestolari cum silentio salutare deí. Beatus
qui portauerit iugum domini ab adholescencia sua. God hit
is i si
lence ikepen godes grace. ⁊ ꝥ me beore godes ȝeoc anan from 15
his ȝuheðe. ant þenne kimeð þrefter. Sedebit solitarius ⁊ tace
bit. quia leuabit se supra se. Hwa se swa wule don: ha schal
sitten
ane. ⁊ halden hire stille. ⁊ swa heouen hire seolf buuen hire
seoluen. ꝥ is wið heh lif hehi toward heouene: ouer hire
cunde. teke þis hwet oðer god cume of þis anlich sittunge ꝥ 20
Ieremie spekeð of. ant of þis seli stilðe kimeð anan efter. Da
bit percuscienti se maxillam ⁊ saturabitur obprobrííis. Ha
wule
he seið þe swa líueð aȝeines þe smitere beode forð þe cheke.
(M. 158) ⁊ beo þurhfullet wið schentfule wordes. Her beoð iþeos
word twa eadi þeawes to noti swiðe ȝeorne. þe limpeð ariht 25
to ancre þolemodnesse i þe earre half. i þe leatere eadmod
nesse of milde ⁊ meoke heorte. for þolemod is þe þuldeli
cheabereð woh ꝥ me him deð. Eadmod is þe þolie mei þet
me him mis segge. þeos þe ich habbe inempnet her: weren of f. 43a
þealde testament. cume we nu to þe neowe. Seín íuhan
baptiste bi hwam ure lauerd seide. Inter natos mulierum non
surrexit maior iohanne baptista. ꝥ bimong wiues sunen ne
aras neauer herre. he kenneð us openliche bi his ahne dede. ꝥ 5
anlich stude is baðe ⁊ siker ⁊ bihéue. for þah þe engel gabriel
hefde his burde ibocket. al wére he ifullet of þe hali gast anan
inwið his moder wombe. al were he þurh miracle of bereget
iboren. ⁊ in his iborenesse unspende his feader tunge in to
prophe

11 *to* 24: *underlining strokes marking all or most of* 11 Sedebit solitarius, 14 God hit, 15 *all*, 16 his ȝuheðe, 17 Hwa *to end*, 18 *all*, 19 seoluen *to* heouene, 20 cunde. teke, 24 ⁊ beo þurhfullet; *four marks* × *in left margin*. 22 percuscienti, *sic* (sc *for* c/t=ts *as in vernacular spelling*).

f. 43a. 2 *small red initial* S *touched with blue;* s *in right margin*. 6 baðe ⁊, *sic*. 8 bereget, *sic* (cf. *T. Coll. Hom.* 133 barrage).

10 cie.˞ for al þis ne durst hæ ȝet wunie bimong men.˞ se dredful
lif he seh þrín þah hit nere of nawt elles bute of speche ane.
ant for þi hwet dude he ? ȝung of ȝeres fleh awei ín to wilder
nesse. leste he wið speche sulde his cleane lif. for swa is in his
ymne. ANtra deserti teneris sub annis cí. tur. f. pe. ne leui saltem
15 maculare uí. fa. posses. He hefde as hit þuncheð iherd ysaie
þe meande him ⁊ seide. Ve michi quia homo pollutis labíís ego sum.
wumme wa is me he seið þe hali prophete. for ich am a mon of
sulede líppen. ⁊ seið þe acheisun hweruore. Quia in medio populi
polluta labia habentis ego habito. ⁊ ꝥ is for þi he seið ꝥ ich wu
20 nie bimong men þe suleð hare lippen mid misliche spechen.
lo hu godes prophete seið he wes isulet þurh beowiste bimong (M. 160)
monne. Swa hit is sikerliche. Beo neauer se briht or. Metal. gold.
seoluer. Irn. stel. ꝥ hit ne schal drahe rust of an oþer ꝥ is irustet.
for hwon ꝥ ha longe liggen togedere. for þi fleh sein iuhan þe
25 feolahschipe of fule men.˞ leste he were ifulet. Ah ȝet forte scha
win us ꝥ me ne mei þe uuele fleon bute me fleo þe gode.˞ he
fleh his hali cun icoren of ure lauerd. ⁊ wende in to anli stude
⁊ wunede i þe wildernesse. ant hwet biȝet he þer ? he biȝet ꝥ
f. 43b he wes godes baptiste. O þe muchele hehnesse ꝥ he heold
i fulluht under hise honden þe lauerd of heouene. þe
halt up al þe world wið his anes mihte. þer þe hali tri
nite. þrumnesse on englisch schawde hire al to him. þe
5 feader in his steuene. þe hali gast i culure heow. þe sune
in his honden. In anlich lif he biȝet þreo preminences. prí
uilegie of preachur. merite of martirdom. Meidenes me
de. þeos þreo manere men habbeð in heouene wið ouer
fullet mede crune up o crune. ⁊ te eadi iuhan in anlich

10 hæ: **ha** *emended to* he *without erasure.* 13 sulde, 20 suleð: *blending of* fulen, sulien (*probably linguistic*). 14, 15 *abbreviations for* cíuium t*ur*mas fugiens petisti *and* uitam famine.

f. 43b. 6 p*r*eminences *for* preeminences.

stude as he wes alle þeose þreo estaz ofearnede him ane. 10
VRe leoue leafdi ne leadde ha anlich lif? ne fond te en
gel hire in anli stude al ane? nes ha nowher ute.' ah wes
biloken feste. for swa we ifindeð. Ingressus angelus ad eam
dixit. Aue Maria gratia plena d'. t. b. tu in ml. ꝥ is. þe
engel wende in to hire. þenne wes heo ínne in anli stude 15
hire ane. Engel to mon i þrung ne eadewede neauer ofte.
On oðer half þurh ꝥ nohwer in hali writ nis iwriten
of hire speche bute fowr siðen as is iseid þruppe.' sutel
prufunge hit is ꝥ ha wes muchel ane þe heold swa silen
Hwet seche ich oþer.' of godd ane were inoh forbisne .ce. 20
to alle. þe wende him self in to anli stude. ⁊ feaste þeras
he wes ane i wildernesse forte schawin þerbi. ꝥ bimong
(M. 162) monne þrung ne mei nan makien riht penitence. Þer
in anli stude him hungrede hit seið ancre to froure. ꝥ is
meoseise. Þer he þolede ꝥ te feond fondede him feoleweis. 25
ah he ouercom hím. alswa forte schawin ꝥ te feond fondeð
muchel þeo þe leadeð anlich lif.' for onde ꝥ he haueð to
ham. ah he is þer ouercumen. for ure lauerd seolf þer stont
bi ham i fehte. ⁊ bealdeð ham hu ha schulen stonden strong f. 44a
liche aȝeín.' ⁊ ȝeueð ham of his strengðe. he as hali writ seið
ꝥ na nurð ne þrung of folc.' ne mahte letten him of his
beoden. ne desturbin his godḍhe þah noðeleatere hwen he
walde beon ibeoden.' he fleh nawt ane oþre men.' ah dude ȝet 5
his halie deorewurðe apostles ⁊ wende ane up on hulles us
to forbisne. ꝥ we schule turne bi us seolf ⁊ climben wið hím
on hulles. ꝥ is þenchen hehe ⁊ leauen lahe under us alle
eorðliche þohtes hwiles we beoð ibonen. Pawle ⁊ Antonie. hy
larium. ⁊ Benedict. Sincletice. ⁊ Sare. ⁊ oþre swucche monie 10

11 *red initial* V *ornamented with blue lines; corner of directing* v *in left margin (rest cropped).* 14 *read* dominus tecum benedicta tu in mulieribus. 19 silence: silen *with* .ce. *below* en. 20 *no paragraph before* .ce.; *blue initial* H, *with short stem, red line-patterns within, and in margin from* 15 *to* 25. *Water-stains running down inner margin from* 7 *to* 25, *and branching at top towards middle of* 5, *affect right-hand ends of text on this page, and left on next.*

f. 44a. f. 44 *has a large bay in outer edge (from about* 6 *to* 27*); a small slit below inner end of* 28, *with holes for lost stitches; for stains see preceding page.* 4 *MS.* god'ḍhe *intended to emend* goddhe *to* god.' he. 9, 10 hy|larium *sic for* hilariun.

men ⁊ wummen baðe. fondeden witerliche. ⁊ underȝeten soðliche þe biȝete of anlich lif. as þeo þe duden wið godd al ꝥ ha walden. Seín ierome nu leate seið bi him seoluen. Quotiens inter homines fui :· minor homo recessi. As ofte 15 as ich eauer wes he seið bimong men :· ich wende from ham leasse mon þen ich ear wes. for þi seið þe wise ecclesiasticus. Ne oblecte ris in turbis. assidua est enim commissio. ꝥ is. ne þunche þe nea uer god imong monne floc :· for þer is eauer sunne. Ne seide þe steuene to arseníe of heouene. Arseni fuge homines 20 ⁊ saluaberis. Arseni flih men ⁊ tu schalt beon iborhen. ⁊ eft hit com ⁊ seide. Arseni fuge. tace. quiesce. ꝥ is. arseni flih. beo stille. ⁊ wune studeuestliche i sum stude ut of monne.

NV ȝe habbeð iherd mine leoue sustren forbisne of þe al de lahe ⁊ ek of þe neowe. hwi ȝe ahen anlich lif swiðe to lu 25 uien. Efter þe forbisnes hereð nu reisuns hwi me ah to fleo **(M. 164)** þe world. eahte ed te leaste. Ich ham segge scheortliche neom eð þe betere ȝeme. Þe forme is sikernesse. ȝef a wod líun urne ȝont te strete. nalde þe wise bitunen hire sone ? ant f. 44b Seínte peter seið. ꝥ helle líun rengeð ⁊ reccheð eauer abuten. forte sechen inȝong sawle to forswolhen. ⁊ bid us beo wakere ⁊ bisie in hali beoden leste he us lecche. Sobríí estote ⁊ uigila te in orationibus. quia aduersarius uester diabolus tanquam leo rugiens 5 circuit querens quem deuoret. þis is seínte petres word ꝥ ich ear seide. for þi beoð ancren wise þe habbeð wel bitund ham aȝein helle líun forte beo þe sikerure. Þe oþer reisun is. þe bere a deore licur. a deorewurðe wét as bas me is. in a feble uetles. healewi ibruchel gles. nalde ha gan

17, 18 ne þunche *to end of* 18 *underlined; in right margin mark* × *and* Eccl' (*small*). 22 ut of monne, *sic; omission, if any, probably early; the versions vary.* 23 *red initial* N*; blue lines in margin from* 19 *to* 27 (*rest obliterated by stain*)*; directing* N *in left margin.* 27 *small blue initial* Þ *touched with red; directing* þ *in left margin.*

f. 44b. 1 helle líun *marked with curved stroke above;* sei)ð *to* reccheð e(auer *underlined.* 2 forte *to* for(swolhen *underlined; mark* × *in left margin.* 4 rugiens: ns *as* f. 18b. 8. 7 aȝ)ein helle líun for(te *underlined; small red initial* Þ *touched with blue; directing* þ *in right margin.*

ut of þrung bute ha fol were? Habemus thesaurum istum 10
in uasıs fictilibus dicit apostolus. þis bruchele uetles. ꝥ is wummone
flesch. þah noðeleatere þe basme þe healewi. is meidenhad ꝥ is
þrin. oðer eft meiðlure. chaste cleannesse. þis bruchele uetles
bruchel as is eani gles. for beo hit eanes tobroken.ˀ ibet ne bið
hit neauer. ibet ne hal as hit wes ear.ˀ namare þene gles. AH 15
ȝet hit brekeð mid leasse þen bruchel gles do. for gles ne to
brekeð nawt bute sum þing hit rine. ⁊ hit onont meiðlure
mei leosen his halnesse wið a stinkinde wil swa uorð hit
mei gan ⁊ leaste se longe. ah þis manere bruche mei beon
ibet eft ase hal allunge as hit wes eauer halest þurh medeci 20
ne of schrift ⁊ bireowsunge. Nu þe preoue herof. Sein iuhan
euuangeliste nefde he brud ibroht ham? nefde he iþoht þa
ȝef godd nefde ilet hím meiðhad toforleosen? seoððen þah
(M. 166) nes he meiden neauer þe unhalre. ah wes meiden bitaht mei
den to witene. Virginem uirgini commendauit. Nu as ich 25
segge. þis deorewurðe healewi i bruchel uetles is meiðhad
⁊ cleannesse in ower bruchele flesch bruchelure þen
eani gles. ꝥ ȝef ȝe weren i worldes þrung.ˀ wið alutel hur
lunge ȝe mahten al leosen. as þe wrecches i þe world þe hur f. 45a
lið to gederes ⁊ breokeð hare uetles ⁊ cleannesse schedeð.
for þi ure lauerd cleopeð þus. In mundo pressuram in me au
tem pacem habebitis. leaueð þe world ⁊ cumeð to me. for
þer ȝe schulen beon i þrung. ah reste ⁊ peis is in me. 5

Þe þridde reisun of þe worldes fluht is. þe biȝete of heouene.
þe heouene is swiðe heh. hwa se wule biȝeoten hit ⁊ area
chen þer to.ˀ hire is lutel inoh forte warpen al þe world un
der hire fotes. for þi alle þe halhen makeden of al þe world
as a scheomel to hare uet to areache þe heouene. Apoca- 10
lypsis.

13 eft, *sic for* efter. 14 as is, *sic for* is as; 15 ibet *from* 14: *errors not peculiar to this MS.* 22 *MS.* euuuangeliste. 25 *line ends with* s *begun, crossed by line-filling flourish.*

f. 45a. 6 *large blue initial* Þ *between* 5 *and* 8, *with tapering stem in margin between* 3 *and* 12; *red line-patterns within, and in margin from* 1 *to* 14; *directing* þ *in left margin.*

Vidi mulierem amictam sole ⁊ luna sub pedibus eius. þis is
seín iuhanes word euuangeliste i þe apocalipse. Ich iseh a
wummon ischrud mid te sunne. ⁊ under hire uet þe mone.
þe mone woneð ⁊ waxeð. ne nis neauer studeuest. ⁊ bitacneð
15 for þi worltliche þinges þe beoð as þe mone eauer ichange.
þes mone mot te wummon halden under hire uét. ꝥ is
worldliche þinges totreoden ⁊ forhohien. þe wule heouene a
reachen ⁊ beo þer ischrud mið te soðe Sunne.

Þe feorðe reisun is preoue of noblesce ⁊ of largesce. Noble
20 men ⁊ gentile ne beoreð nanes packes. ne ne feareð itrus
set wið trussews ne wið purses. hit is beggilde riht to beore (M. 168)
bagge on bac. burgeise to beore purs.ꝰ nawt godes spuse þe
is leafdi of heouene. Trussen ⁊ purses. baggen ⁊ packes beoð
worltliche þinges. alle eorðliche weolen ⁊ worltliche rentes.

25 Þe fifte reisun is. Noble men ⁊ wummen makieð large
relef. ah hwa mei makie largere þen þe oðer þeo þe seið
wið seinte peter. Ecce nos reliquimus omnia ⁊ secuti
sumus te.
Lauerd forte folhi þe.ꝰ we habbeð al forleauet. Nis þis
large re

f. 45b lef? nis þis muche laue? Mine leoue sustren kínge ⁊ keisers
habbeð hare liueneð of ower large relef ꝥ ȝe ileauet hab
beð. lauerd forte folhi þe seið seinte peter we habbeð al for
leauet. as þah he seide. we wulleð folhi þe i þe muchele gen
5 terise of þi largesce. þu leafdest to oþre men alle richesces.
⁊ makedest of al relef ⁊ lauese large. we wulleð folhi þe. we
wulleð don alswa. leauen al as þu dudest. folhi þe on eorðe i
ꝥ ⁊ in oþerhwet. forte folhi ec ín to þe blisse of heouene. ⁊
ȝet tear ouer al folhi þe hwiderward se þu eauer wendest
10 as nane ne mahen bute ane meidnes. Hií secuntur agnum

12 *MS.* euuuangeliste. apocalipse. Ich iseh a *underlined; mark* × *in right margin.* 18 mið te, *sic* (mid *half altered to* wið). 19 *large red initial* Þ *between* 18 *and* 21, *the stem between* 16 *and* 23, *ornamented with a few blue lines* (*in margin from* 13 *to* 24); *directing* þ *to left.* 20 nanes packes, *sic.* 25 *large blue initial* Þ *between* 24 *and* 26; *the stem from* 23 *has long tail into lower margin; red line-patterns within and down stem, trailing to bottom edge.*

f. 45b. 1 kínge, *sic.* 6 lauese, *sic for* laue se. 8 þe *probably omitted between* folhi ec.

quocumque ierit. utroque scilicet. pede. id est. integritate cordis ⁊ corporis.

Þe Seste reisun is hwi ȝe habbeð þe world iflohen. famí liarite. muche cunredden. forte beo priue wið ure lauerd. for þus he seið bi osee. Ducam te in solitudinem ⁊ ibi lo quar ad cor tuum. Ich chulle leade þe he seið to his leof 15 mon in to anli stude. ⁊ ter ich chulle luueliche speoke to þin heorte. for me is lað preasse. Ego dominus ⁊ ciuitatem non

(M. 170) Þe Seoueðe reisun is forte beo þe brihtre ℂ.ingredior. ⁊ brihtluker seon in heouene godes brihte nebscheft for ȝe beoð iflohe þe world ⁊ hudeð ow for hire her. ȝet ter 20 teken ꝥ ȝe beon swifte as þe sunne gleam. for ȝe beoð wið iesu crist bitund as i sepulcre. bibarret as he wes o þe deo re rode as is iseid þruppe.

Þe eahtuðe reisun is. to habben cwic bone. ⁊ lokið ȝeor ne hweruore. þe eadmode cwen hester bitacneð ancre. 25 for hire nome seið ihud on englische ledene as me ret in hire boc. ha wes þe king assuer ouer al icwene. ⁊ þurh hi re bone arudde of deað al hire folc þe wes to deað idemet. þis nome assuer is ispealet eadi as is ear iseid. ⁊ bitacneð f. 46a godd eadi ouer alle. He ȝetteð hester þe cwen. ꝥ is þe treowe ancre ꝥ is riht hester. ꝥ is riht ihud. he héreð ant ȝet teð hire alle hire bénen. ⁊ sawueð þurh ham muche folc. Mo ni⟨e⟩ schulde beo forloren.˙ þe beoð þurh þe ancre benen 5 iborh

12 *large red initial* Þ *between* 11 *and* 14, *stem in margin from* 9 *to* 15; *blue line-patterns within* (*smeared*), *and in margin from* 7 *to* 15. 14 bi osee. Ducam *underlined; mark* × *in left margin.* 16 *to* 18 *a scribble down left margin.* 18 *large blue initial* Þ *between* 17 *and* 20, *stem in margin* 15 *to* 21; *red line-patterns within and along stem. Before* .ingredior. *a red paragraph with blue tails.* 23 rode *to* þruppe *written slightly larger and expanded.* 24 *large red initial* Þ *between* 23 *and* 26; *tapered stem from* 21 *to curled tail low in bottom margin; blue line-patterns within, and along stem* (*the elaboration of the tail now cut off at bottom edge*). 25 cwen hester bitacneð *underlined; mark* × *in left margin; side-scribble* 25 *to* 28. 27 king *interlined* (*small*) *above* cwen *crossed out* (*correction probably immediate:* g *and* e *below have run together*).

f. 46a. 3 *a hole between* ant *and* ȝet.

en. as weren þurh hesteres. forhwon ꝥ ha beo hester. ⁊ halde
hire as heo dude Mardochees dohter. Mardo
che is ispealet. amare conterens inpudentem ꝥ is bitter
liche totreodinde þene scheomelese. Scheomeles is þe mon
10 þe seið eani untu oðer deð biuoren ancre. ȝef eani þah
swa do:' ⁊ heo breoke bitterliche his untohe word. oðerhis
fol dede. totreoden ham ananriht wið unwurð tellunge.
þenne is ha hester Mardochees dohter. bitterliche breokín
de þene scheomelese. Bitterluker ne betere ne mei ha hím
15 neauer breoken. þen is itaht þruppe wið Narrauerunt michi
oðer mid tis uers. Declinate a me maligni ⁊ scru. m. dei
mei. ⁊ wende inward anan toward hire weouede ant
halde hire ed hame. as hester þe ihudde. Semei i Regum
hefde deað ofseruet. ah he criede mearci. ant Salomon
20 forȝef hit him. þah þurh swuch a foreward. ꝥ he ed hame **(M. 172)**
heolde him i ierusalem as he wunede ⁊ hudde him in his hu
se. ȝef he ohwider wende ut:' swuch wes þe foreward. ꝥ he
were eft al ful ⁊ to deað idemet. he þah brec foreward þurh
his unselhðe. his þrealles edfluhen hím ⁊ edbreken him
25 ut. ⁊ he folhede ham ⁊ ⟨wende⟩ ut efter ham. hwet wult tu ma
re wes sone forwreiet. to þe king Salomon. ⁊ for þe foreward
tobroken wes fordemet to deaðe. Vnderstondeð ȝeorne þis
míne leoue sustren. Semey bitacneð þe utwarde ancre.
f. 46b nawt hester þe ihudde. for Semey seið audiens. ꝥ is herín
de on ure ledene. ꝥ is þe recluse þe haueð asse earen. lon
ge to here feor. ꝥ is hercninde efter utrunes. Semeís
stude wes ierusalem ꝥ he schulde in huden him ȝef he walde
5 libben. þis word ierusalem spealeð sihðe of peis ⁊ bitacneð
ancre hus. for þrinne ne þearf ha seon bute peis ane.
Ne beo neauer Semei. ꝥ is þe recluse swa swiðe
forgult toward te soðe Salomon. ꝥ is ure lauerd:'
halde hire ed hame i ierusalem. ꝥ ha nawiht nute of þe

7, 8 *a curved slit stitched with green silk separates* dohter . . . Mardo *and* inpudentem . . . þis. 12 totreoden, *sic for sg.* 16 *abbreviation for* scrutabor mandata. 23 ful, *cf.* f. 83b. 28. 25 ⟨wende⟩ *interlined above* brec (*not crossed out*); *probably main hand, though* p *is sloped to right to avoid* ⁊.

f. 46b. 3 *hole between* lon|ge *and* to here. 7, 8 *slit* (*see recto*) *separates* 7 beo . . . neauer, 8 forgult . . . toward.

worldes baret.' Salomon ȝetteð hire bliðeliche his are. 10
ah ȝef ha entremeateð híre of þinges wið uten mare
þen ha þurfte. ⁊ hire heorte beo utewið. þah a clot of eor
ðe ꝥ is hire licome beo inwið þe fowr wahes.' ha is iwend
wið Semei ut of ierusalem alswa as he dude efter his þrealles.
Þeos þrealles beoð þe eðele fif wittes. þe schulden beon et 15
hame ⁊ seruin hare leafdi. þenne ha seruið wel þe ancre
hare leafdi.' hwen ha notieð ham wel in hare sawle neode.
hwen þe ehe is oþe boc. oþer o sum oðer god. þe eare to
godes word. þe muð in hali bonen. ȝef ha wit ham uue
le ⁊ let ham þurh ȝemeles etfleon hire seruise. ⁊ folhi 20
ham utwart wið hire heorte as hit bitímeð eauer meast
(M. 174) ꝥ gan þe wittes ut.' þe heorte geað ut efter. ha brekeð Sa
lomon foreward wið þe unseli Semey.' ⁊ is to deað idemet.
FOR þi mine leoue sustren ne beo ȝe nawt Semey.' ah
beoð hester þe ihudde. ⁊ ȝe schule beon ihehet iþe blisse 25
of heouene. for þe nome of hester ne seið nawtaneab
scondita. ꝥ is nawt ane ihud.' ah deð þerteken. Eleuata
in populis. ꝥ is i folc ihehet. ant swa wes hester as hire no
me cwiddeð ihehet to cwen of a poure meiden. Iþis word f. 47a
hester

beoð hudunge ⁊ hehnesse ifeiet to gederes. ⁊ nawt ane heh
nesse.' ah hehnesse ouer folc. forte schawin witerliche ꝥ teo
þe hudeð ham ariht in hare ancre hus.' ha schulen beon
in heouene ouer oþres cunnes folc wurðliche ihehet. Ba 5
hesteres nome. ⁊ hire hehunge pruuieð ꝥ ich segge. On
oðer half understondeð. ȝe beoð i ierusalem. ȝe beoð iflohe to
chirche grið. for nes ower nan ꝥ nere sum chearre godes
þeof. Me weiteð ow ꝥ wite ȝe ful ȝeorne wið uten as me deð
þeoues þe beoð ibroke to chirche. Haldeð ow feaste ínne. 10
nawt te bodi ane.' for ꝥ is þe unwurðest. ah ower fif wittes. ⁊
te heorte ouer al ⁊ al þer þe sawle lif is. for beo ha bitrept
utewið.' nis þer bute leade forð toward te gealforke. ꝥ is þe
wearitreo of helle. Beoð ofdred of euch mon alswa as þe

19 word: *long-tailed* r *blotted.* 24 *blue initial* F *with tapered tail in margin from* 23 *to* 28; *red line-patterns within, and in margin from* 22 *down into bottom margin.*

f. 47a. 14 *to* 16: curved slit *stitched with green silk from end of* 14 *inwards to* ow *in* 16: *top stitch cuts bottom of* þ *in* þe (*end of* 14); 15 *ends short;* 16 ow *widely separated from* his.

15 þeof is. leste he drahe ow utwart. ꝥ is biswike wið
sunne. ⁊ weiti forte warpen up on ow his
cleches. Bisecheð ȝeornliche godd as þeof ibroke to chirche.
ꝥ he wite ⁊ wardi ow wið alle þe ow weitið. chiterið ower
beoden aa. as spearewe deð ane. for þis an word is iseid of
20 anlich lif. of anlich stude. þer me mei beon hester ihud
ut of þe world. ⁊ do betere þen i þrung euch gastelich biȝete.
for þi eueneð dauið ancre to pellican. ꝥ leat anlich lif ⁊ to
Spearewe haueð ȝet acunde. ꝥ is bi ℂ spearewe ane. (M. 176)
heue ancre þah me hit heatie. ꝥ is þe fallinde uuel. for mu
25 che neod is ꝥ ancre of hali lif ⁊ of heh habbe fallinde uuel
ꝥ uuel ne segge ich nawt ꝥ me swa nempneð.' ah fallinde
uuel ich cleopie. licomes secnesse. oðer temptatiuns of
flesches fondunges. hwer þurh hire þunche ꝥ ha falle du
f. 47b neward of hali hehnesse. ha walde awilgin elles oðer to wel
leo
ten of.' ⁊ swa to noht iwurðen. þe flesch walde awilgín ⁊ bicu
men to fulitohen toward hire leafdi ȝef hit nere ibeaten.' ⁊
makie sec þe sawle ȝef secnesse hit ne temede wið uuel oðer
5 Þe licome ne þe gast ȝef hare nowðer nere ℂ. wið sunne.
sec as hit timeð seldene.' orhel walde awakenin. ꝥ is
þe measte
dredfule secnesse of alle. ȝef godd fondeð ancre wið ei uuel
utewið. oðer þe feond ínwið wið gasteliche unþeawes. ase
Prude. Wreaððe. Onde oðer wið flesches lustes.' ha haueð ꝥ
10 fallinde uuel. ꝥ me seið is spearewe uuel. godd hit wule for
þi ꝥ ha beo eauer eadmod. ⁊ wið lah haldung of hire
seoluen. falle to þer eorðe leste ha falle i prude.
NV we hurteð leoue sustren to þe feorðe dale ꝥ ich seide

19, 20 *hole in ruled margin right.* 19 *before* ane *is omitted* ꝥ is (*probably also in* 23). 23 *red initial* S *ornamented with a few blue lines within, and in margin from* 21 *to* 26; *before* spearewe ane. *a blue paragraph with tail into right margin curling above* 21; *red lines and scribbled red tails.* 26 *red stroke on ruled margin right is offset from ornament of* F *on preceding page.*

f. 47b. 2 hire seoluen *omitted after* leo|ten of. 5 *blue initial* Þ *with tapered stem in margin from* 3 *to* 8; *red lines within, and in margin from* 1 *to* 11. *Before* .wið sunne. *a red paragraph with tail into right margin, touched with blue.* 13 *small red initial* N; *a few hasty blue lines within, and from* 11 *to* 15.

schulde beon of feole fondunges. for þer beoð uttre ⁊ inre. ⁊
eiðer moniualde. Salue ich bihet to teachen toȝei 15
nes ham ⁊ bote. ⁊ hu hwa se haueð ham:·
mei gederín of þis dale cunfort ⁊ froure toȝeines ham
alle. þet ich þurh þe lare of þe hali gast mote halden
foreward:· he hit ȝetti me þurh ower bonen.

20

(M. 178) NE wene nan of heh lif
ꝥ ha ne beo itemptet. mare
beoð þe gode þe beoð iclumben hehe:· itemp
tet þen þe wake. ant ꝥ is reisun. for se þe
hul is herre:· se þe wind is mare þron. Se 25
þe hul is herre of hali lif ⁊ of heh:· se þe feondes puffes þe
windes of fondunges beoð strengre þron ⁊ mare. ȝef ei
ancre is þe ne ueleð nane fondunges:· swiðe drede iꝥ puínt
ꝥ ha beo ouer muchel ⁊ ouer swiðe ifondet. for swa seín f. 48a
gregoi
re seið. Tunc maxime inpugnaris cum te inpugnari non
sentis. Sec mon haueð estaz swiðe dredfule. ꝥ an is hwen he
ne feleð nawt his ahne secnesse. ⁊ for þi ne secheð nawt leche
ne lechecreft. ne easkeð namon read. ⁊ asteorueð ferliche 5
ear me least wéne. þis is þe ancre þe nat nawt hwet is fond
unge. to þeos spekeð þe engel i þe apocalipse. Dicis
quia diues
sum ⁊ nullius egeo. ⁊ nescis quia miser es ⁊ nudus. ⁊ pauper
⁊ cecus.
þu seist þe nis neod na medecine. ah þu art blind iheortet
ne ne sist nawt hu þu art poure ⁊ naket of halínesse ant 10
gastelich wrecche. ꝥ oþer dredfule estat ꝥ te seke haueð is al

14 *to* 16 *slit (see recto) from* schulde *inwards to* ham *in* 16. 20 *left blank but for head of* N (*pierced by hole on margin*). 21 *very large blue initial* N (*marking beginning of Part IV*) *standing from* 25 *up to* 19; *elaborate red line-patterns to right, within, and in margin from* 15 *downwards* (*last trailer cut off at present bottom edge*).

f. 48a. 3 twa (tpa) *interlined* (*probably by main hand*), *with prolonged tail of* p *serving as caret between* haueð estaz. 9 *hole touching outer ruled margin right; beyond it mark* ×. 9 *to* 12: *side-scribble to right; many words underlined:* 9 *all;* 10 *all to* halinesse; 11 gastelich wrecche.

frommard þis. ꝥ is hwen he feleð se muchel angoise. ꝥ he ne
mei þolien ꝥ me hondli his sar ne ꝥ me him heale. þis is
sum ancre þe feleð se swiðe hire fondunges. ⁊ is se sare ofdred
15 ꝥ na gastelich cunfort ne mei hire gleadien ne makien to
understonden ꝥ ha mahen ⁊ schulen þurh ham þe betere
beon iborhen. Ne teleð hit iþe godspel ꝥ te hali gast leadde
ure lauerd seolf in to anlich stude. to leaden anlich lif forte
beon itemptet of þe unwine of helle. Ductus est iesus in desertum
20 a spiritu ut temptaretur a diabolo. ah his temptatiun þe ne mahte
sunegin.᾽ wes ane wið uten. UNderstondeð þenne on alre
earst leoue sustren. ꝥ twa cunne temptatiuns. twa cunne fondun **(M. 180)**
ges beoð. uttre ⁊ ínre. ant ba beoð feoleualde. Vttre fondun
ge is hwer of kímeð licunge oþer mislicunge wið uten oðer
25 wið innen. mislicunge wið uten.᾽ ase secnesse. meoseise. scheome.
vnhap. ⁊ euch licomlich derf ꝥ te flesch eileð. wiðinnen.᾽ heorte
sar. grome. ⁊ wreaððe. Alswa onont ꝥ ha is píne. licunge wið
uten licomes heale. mete. drunch. clað ínoh ⁊ euch flesches
f. 48b eise. onont swucche þínges. licunge wið innen.᾽ as sum fals glead
schipe. oðer of monne hereword. oðer ȝef me is iluuet mare
þen an oþer. mare iolhnet. mare idon god oðer menske.
Þis dale of þis temptatiun ꝥ is uttre icleopet.᾽ is swikelure
5 þen þe oðer half. Ba beoð a temptatium⁊ eiðer wiðinnen.᾽

16 mahen ⁊ schulen, *sic for sg.* 21 *small red initial* U *touched with blue: directing* v *on right edge.* 23 *half directing* v *on right edge (rest cropped); but coloured initial of* Vttre *not inserted, though reckoned as blue in the alternation; the* V *abnormal for this hand, probably later correction.* 26 mislicunge *omitted before* wiðinnen. 27 *small red initial* A *touched with blue;* píne, *sic for* i píne *or* ipínet*: the enumerative passage seems to have been misunderstood and mis-punctuated early in the tradition; in spite of initial* A, ⁊ wreaððe alswa onont ꝥ ha is ipinet *probably belong together (one of the 'interior' pains is resentment of the 'exterior' just named).*

f. 48b. 5 temptatium⁊, *sic with last stroke of* m *cancelled by superior dot and* ⁊ *in contact.*

⁊ wið uten baðe of hire twa dalen. ah ha is uttre icleopet.
for ha is eauer oðer i þing wið uten.·/ oðer of þing wið u
ten. ant te uttre þing is þe fondunge. Þeos fondunge ki
með oðerwhile of godd.·/ of mon oðerhwiles. Of godd.·/ as of
freondes deað. secnesse oðer on ham oðer oþe seoluen. po 10
uerte. mishapnunge. ⁊ oþre swucche. Heale alswa ⁊ eise. Of
mon.·/ as mislich woh. oðer of word oðer of werc. oþe oðer o
þíne. alswa hereword oðer goddede. þeos cumeð alswa of
godd. ah nawt as doð þe oþre. wið uten euch middel. Ah
wið alle he fondeð mon hu he him drede ⁊ luuíe. Inre fon 15
dunges beoð misliche unþeawes. oðer lust towart ham. oðer
þohtes swikele þe þencheð þah gode. Þeos inre fondunge
kímeð. of þe feond. of þe world. of ure flesch oðerhwile.
To þe
uttre temptatiun is neod patience. ꝥ is þolemodnesse. To þe
inre is neod wisdom ⁊ gasteliche strengðe. We schulen 20
nu speo
ken of þe uttre. ⁊ teachen þeo þe habbeð hire hu ha mahen
wið godes grace ifinde remedie. ꝥ is eine aȝeines hire to fro

(M. 182) Beatus uir qui suffert temptationem ℂ.urín ham seoluen.
quoniam cum probatus fuerit accipiet coronam uite
quam repro
misit deus diligentibus se. Eadi is ⁊ seli. þe haueð i 25
temptatíun
þolemodnesse. for hwen ha is ipruet hit seið ha schal beon
icrunet mid te crune of lif þe godd haueð bihaten his
leoue icorene. Hwen ha is ipruuet hit seið. wel is hit iseid.
for alswa pruueð godd his leoue icorene.·/ as þe goltsmið fon f. 49a
deð ꝥ gold i þe fure. ꝥ false gold forwurðeð þrín. ꝥ gode kí
með ut brihtre. Secnesse is a brune hat forte þolien.
ah na þing
neclenseð gold.·/ as hit deð þe sawle. Secnesse ꝥ godd send
nawt ꝥ sum lecheð þurh hire ahne dusischipe. deð þeose 5

8, 9 *hole*[t] *ouching outer ruled margin left.* 17 þencheð, *sic for* þuncheð. 23 *large red initial* B *between* 22 *and* 25; *blue line-patterns within, and in margin fron* 21 *down into bottom margin; before* .urin *blue paragraph touched with red.* 26 ipruet, *sic.*

f. 49a. 4 *small red initial* S *touched with blue lines.*

·i· ·ii·
six þinges. wescheð þe sunnen þe beoð ear iwrahte. wardeð
·iii· ·iii·
toȝein þeo þe weren towardes. Pruueð pacience. Halt in ead
·v·
modnesse. Muchleð þe mede. Eueneð to martir þene þole
mode. þus is secnesse sawlene heale. Salue of hire wunden.
10 Scheld ꝥ ha ne kecche ma:· as godd sið ꝥ ha schulde ȝef sec
nesse hit ne lette. Secnesse makeð mon to understonden
hwet he is. to cnawen hím seoluen. ant as god meister beat
forte leorni wel. hu mihti is godd. hu frakel is þe wọrldes blisse.
Secnesse is þi goldsmið þe iþe blisse of heouene ouergul
15 deð þi crune. se þe secnesse is mare se þe goldsmið is bisgre.
⁊ se hit lengre least:· se he brihteð hire swiðere. to beo mar
tirs euening þurh a hwilinde wa. hwet is mare grace to þeo
þe hefde ofearnet þe pinen of helle world abuten
ende. Nalde me tellen hím alre monne dusegest þe
20 forseke a buffet for a speres wunde ? a nelde pricchunge for an (M. 184)
bihefdunge ? a beatunge for an hongunge on helle weari
treo aa. on ecnesse ? Godd hit wat leoue sustren al þe wa of
þis world is ieuenet to helle alre leaste píne. al nis bute
bal plohe. al nis nawt swa muchel as is alutel deawes
25 drope. toȝeines þe brade sea ⁊ alle worldes weattres. þe
mei þenne edstearten ꝥ ilke grisliche wa. þe eateliche pínen
þurh secnesse ꝥ agead þurh ei uuel ꝥ her is seliliche mei
ha seggen. ON oðer half leornið moniualde frouren
f. 49b aȝein þe uttre fondunge þe kimeð of monnes uuel. for þeos
þe ich habbe iseid of is of godes sonde. Hwa se eauer mis
seið þe oðer misdeð þe:· nim ȝeme ⁊ understond ꝥ he is þi
vile þe lorimers habbeþ. ⁊ fileð al þi rust awei ⁊ ti ruhe
5 of sunne. for he fret him seoluen weilawei as þe file deð.
ah he makeð smeðe ⁊ brihteð þi sawle. ON oðer wise
þench hwa se eauer hearmeð þe. oðer eni wa deð þe. scheo
me. grome. teone:· he is godes ȝerde. for swa he seið

8 *numeral* vi *omitted over* Eueneð. 10 *a tear from right edge inwards with holes for lost stitches.* 13 wọrldes, *sic.* 17 *to* 20: *slit, with holes for lost stitches, passes through* 18 *and* 19 *as shown.* 27 agead, *sic.* 28 *small blue initial* O *touched with red.*

f. 49b. 6 *small red initial* O *touched with blue; directing* o *in right margin.* 8 teone *has greatly extended* N.

þurh sein iuhanes muð i þe apocalipse. Ego quos amo
arguo ⁊ castigo. Ne beat he nan bute hwam se he luueð 10
⁊ halt for his dohter. namare þen þu waldest beaten a fre
mede child þah hit al gulte. ah nawt ne leote he wel of ꝥ
is godes ȝerde. for as þe feader hwen he haueð inoh ibeaten
his child ⁊ haueð hit ituht wel. warpeð þe ȝerde i þe fur.
for ha nis noht namare.' alswa þe feder of heouene hwen 15
he haueð ibeaten wið an unwreast mon oþer an unwrest
wummon his leoue child for his god.' he warpeð þe
ȝerde ꝥ is þe unwreste in to þe fur of helle. for þi
he seið elleshwer. Michi uindictam ego retribuam. ꝥ is.
(M. 186) min is þe wrake. ich chulle ȝelden. as þah he seiðe. Ne wreo 20
ke ȝe nawt ow seoluen. ne grucchi ȝe ne wearien hwen
me gulteð wið ow.' ah þencheð anan ꝥ he is ower feadres
ȝerde. ⁊ ꝥ he wule ȝelden him ȝerde seruise. ant nis þet
child fulitohen ꝥ scratleð aȝeín ⁊ bit up o þe ȝerde? þet
deboneire child hwen hit is ibeaten. ȝef þe feader hat hit.' 25
hit cusseð þe ȝerde. ant ȝe don alswa mine leoue sustren.
for swa hat ower feader. ꝥ ȝe cussen nawd wið muð. ah wið
luue of heorte. þeo þe he ow wið beateð. Diligite ínimícos
uestros. benefacite híís qui oderunt uos. ⁊ orate pro perse- f. 50a
quentibus
⁊ calumpniantibus uos. Þis is godes heste ꝥ him is muchel
leoure þen ꝥ tu eote gruttene bred. oðer weredest hearde hé
re. luuieð ower uamen he seið ⁊ doð god ȝef ȝe mahen to
þeo ꝥ ow weorrið. ȝef ȝe elles ne mahen biddeð ȝeorne for 5
þeo ꝥ ow eni eil doð oðer misseggeð. ant te apostle leareð.
Ne ȝelde ȝe neauer uuel for uuel.' ah doð god eauer aȝein
uuel. as dude ure lauerd seolf ⁊ alle his hali halhen. ȝef ȝe
þus haldeð godes heaste.' þenne beo ȝe his hende child ant
cusseð þe ȝerde þe he haueð ow wið iþorschen. Nu seið o 10
þerhile sum. his sawle oðer hiren ich chulle wel luuien.
his bodi o nane wise. Ah ꝥ nis nawt to seggen. Þe sawle ⁊

10 *slit from left edge* (*see recto*). 13 haueð: u *rubbed, second stroke touched up*. 17 *to* 19: *slit* (*see recto*) *divides* 18 þe/fur, 19 ego/retribuam; 17 his *has ill-formed elongated* s *avoiding stitching holes*. 19 uindictam, *sic*. 27 nawd, *sic*.

f. 50a. 1 benefacite: bnfacite. 11 o|þerhile, *sic for* -hwile.

te licome nis bute a mon. ⁊ ba ham tit a dom. wult tu
dealen o twa þe godd haueð to an isompnet? he forbeot
15 hit ⁊ seið. Quod deus coníunxit homo non separet. Ne
wurðe nan
se wod ꝥ he todeale þe þing þe godd haueð iueiet
Þencheð ȝet þisses weis. ꝥ child ȝef hit spurneð o sum
þing oðer hurteð:· me beat ꝥ hit hurte on. ⁊ ꝥ child is
wel ipaiet. forȝeteð al his hurt ⁊ stilleð hise teares. for þi
20 frourið ow seoluen. letabitur iustus cum uiderit uindictam
Godd schal o domesdei don as þah he seide. Dohter hurte (M. 188)
þes þe. dude he þe spurnen i wreaððe oðer in ⟨h⟩eorte sar. í
scheome oðer in eani teone. loke dohter loke he seið hu he
hit schal abuggen. Ant þer ȝe schule seon bunkin hím
25 wið þes deofles betles ꝥ wa bið him þes líues. ȝe schulen
beo wel ipaiet þrof. for ower wil ⁊ godes wil schal swa beon
iueiet:· ꝥ ȝe schulen wullen al ꝥ he eauer wule. ⁊ he al ꝥ
ȝe wulleð. Ouer alle oþre þohtes in alle ower passíuns
f. 50b þencheð eauer inwardliche up o godes pinen. ꝥ te worldes
wealdent walde for his þrealles þolien swucche schendlakes.
hokeres. buffez. Spatlunge. Blindfeallunge. þornene cru
nunge. ꝥ set him i þe heaued swa:· ꝥ te blodi strundes stri
5 ken adun ⁊ leaueden dun to þer eorðe. his swete bodi ibun
den naket to þe hearde pilar ⁊ ibeate swa:· ꝥ tet deorewurðe
blod ron on euche halue. ꝥ attri drunch ꝥ me him ȝef
þa him þurste o rode. hare heafde sturunge up on hím
þa heo on hokerunge gredden se lude. lo her þe healde
10 oþre. lo hu he healeð nu ⁊ helpeð him seoluen. turneð
þruppe þer ich spec. hu he wes ipinet in alle his fif wíttes.
⁊ eueneð al ower wa. secnesse ⁊ oðerhwet. woh of word oðer
of werc. ⁊ al ꝥ mon mei þolien:· to ꝥ tet he þolede. ant ȝe
schulen lihtliche iseon hu lutel hit reacheð. nomeliche
15 ȝef ȝe þencheð ꝥ he wes al ladles ⁊ ꝥ he droh al þis nawt
for him seoluen:· for he ne agulte neauer. ȝef ȝe þolieð wa:·

17 *large blue initial* Þ *between* 16 *and* 19; *tapered stem in margin from* 14 *to* 23; *red line-patterns to right, within, and in margin from* 11 *to* 28; *directing* þ *in left margin.* 22 ⟨h⟩eorte: h *interlined with caret.* 28 *small red initial* O *touched with blue; directing* o *in left margin.*

f. 50b. 6 deorewurðe: *above* u *a mark* ' *offset from* ⟨e⟩ f. 51a. 6.

ȝe habbeð wurse ofseruet. ⁊ al þ ȝe þolieð al is for ow seol
Gað nu þenne gleadluker bi strong wei ⁊ bi ¶ .uen.
swincful toward te muchele feaste of heouene. þer as
(M. 190) ower gleade freond ower cume ikepeð. þenne dusie worl 20
des men gað bi grene wei toward te wearitreo ⁊ te deað
of helle. Betere is ga sec to heouene þen hal to helle. to murh
ðe wið meoseise.' þen to wa wið eise. Salomon. Via impiorum
complantata est lapidibus. id est. duris afflictionibus. Nawt for þi
witerliche. wrecche worltliche men buggeð deorre helle þen 25
ȝe doð þe heouene. a þing to soðe wite ȝe. amís word þet
ȝe þolieð. a deies longunge. a secnesse of a stunde. ȝef
me chapede ed ow an of þeos o domesdei. þ is þe mede þe
ariseð þrof.' ȝe hit nalden sullen for al þe world of golde. For f. 51a
þ schal beon ower song biuoren ure lauerd. letati sumus pro diebus
quibus nos humiliasti. annis quibus uidimus mala. þ is. wel is us
for þe dahes þ tu lahedest us wið oðer monne wohes. ⁊ wel is
us nu lauerd for þe ilke ȝeres þ we weren seke ín. ⁊ sehen sar 5
⁊ sorhe. Euch worltlich wa hit is godes sonde. Heh monnes
messager me schal hehliche underuon ⁊ makien him
glead chére. nomeliche ȝef he is priue wið his lauerd. ⁊ hwa
wes mare priue wið þe king of heouene hwil he her wunede.
þen wes þes sondesmon. þ is worldes weane þe ne com nea 10
uer from him aðet his liues ende. þes messager hwet teleð
he ow.' he froureð ow o þis wise. Godd as he luuede me.' he
send me to his leoue freond. Mi cume ⁊ mi wununge
þah hit þunche attri.' hit is halwende. Nere þ þing grís
lich hwas schadewe ȝe ne mahte nawt wið uter hurt felen? 15

18 *small blue initial* G *with a few red lines from* 16 *to* 20; *before* .uen. (*of* seoluen) *a red paragraph touched with blue.* 21 wearitreo: *first* e *formed by adding bow to upright stroke.*

f. 51a. 3 *to* 5: *mark* × *in right margin, side-scribble from* 3 *to* 5; *underlined* 3 wel is us; 4 wo)hes ⁊ we(l; 5 wer)en seke ín . . . sehen sar (*line passes through last two words*). 4 *mark* ′ *above* w *of* wið. 6 *above* o *of* sorhe *a small* e. 15 uter *sic for* uten.

hwet walde ȝe seggen bi ꝥ eisfule wiht ꝥ hit of come ? wite
ȝe to soðe ꝥ al þe wa of þis world nis bute schadewe of þe wa
of helle. Ich am þe schadewe seið þes messager. ꝥ is worldes
weane. nedlunge ȝe moten oðer underuo me:· oðer ꝥ grisli
20 che wa ꝥ ich am of schadewe. Hwa se underueð me (M. 192) gleadliche
⁊ makeð me feier chére:· mi lauerd send hire word. ꝥ ha is cwi
te of ꝥ þing ꝥ ich am of schadewe. Þus spekeð godes messa
ger. for þi seíð seín iame. Omne gaudium existimate fratres
cum in temptationes uarias incideritis. Alle blisse haldeð hit
25 to fallen i misliche of þeose fondunges:· þe uttre beoð ihá
ten. ant seinte pawel. Omnis disciplina in presenti uidetur esse
non gaudíí:· set meroris. postmodum uero fructum ⁊ cetera. Alle þe
ilke fondunges þe we beoð nu ibeaten wið:· þuncheð wop:· nawt
f. 51b wunne. ah ha wendeð efterward to weole ⁊ to eche blisse.

Þe ínre fondunge is twaualt. alswa as is þe uttre. for þe (M. 194) uttre
is inaduersite ⁊ i prosperite. licunge þe limpeð to sunne. þis
ich segge for þi ꝥ sum licunge is ⁊ sum mislicunge þe ofear
5 neð muche mede. as licunge i godes luue. ⁊ mislicunge for
sunne. Nu as ich segge þe ínre fondunge is twauald. flesch
lich ⁊ gastelich. fleschlich:· as of leccherie. of glutunie. of slaw
ðe. Gastelich:· as of prude. of onde. ⁊ of wreaððe. alswa of ȝiscun
ge. þus beoð þe inre fondunges þe seouen heaued sunnen.
10 ⁊ hare fule cundles. flesches fondunge mei beon ieuenet to
fot wunde. Gastelich fondunge ꝥ is mare dred of. mei beon
for þe peril icleopet breost wunde. ah us þuncheð greattre
flesliche temptatiuns for þi ꝥ heo beoð eð fele. Þe oþre þah we

19, 20 *bottom of the ornament of* G *on preceding page offset at end of the lines.* 24 *to* 28: *marks* × *in right margin* (24, 27); *underlined* 24, 25 Alle *to* fondunges, 27, 28 Alle þe *to end.*

f. 51b. 1 *underlined, stroke passing through top of* Þ. *After* blisse: M. 192, 11 *to* 194, 13 *not in A.* 2 *large red initial* Þ, *straight stem standing in margin from above* 6 *to above* 1; *blue line-ornament from upper edge (cut off) to* 8. 6 Nu *marked with* ″, *and* ″ *in left margin.*

habben ham :' ofte nute we hit nawt. ⁊ beoð þah greate ⁊ gris
liche i godes ehe. ⁊ beoð muchel for þí to drede þe mare. for 15
þe oþre þe me feleð wel. secheð leche ⁊ salue. Þe gasteliche
(M. 196) hurtes ne þuncheð nawt sare. ne ne saluið ham wið schrift
ne wið penitence. ⁊ draheð to eche deað ear me least wene.

Hali men ⁊ wummen beoð of alle fondunges swiðest ofte
itemptet. ⁊ ham to goderheale. for þurh þe feht toȝei 20
nes ham :' ha biȝeoteð þe blisfule kempene crune. lo þah
hu ha meaneð ham i Ieremie. Persecutores nostri uelociores
aquilis celi. super montes persecuti sunt nos. in deserto insidi
ati sunt nobis. ꝥ is. Vre wiðeriwines swiftre þen earnes up o
þe hulles. ha clumben efter us. ⁊ þer fuhten wið us. ⁊ ȝet 25
i þe wildernesse ha spieden us to sleanne. Vre wiðeriwines
beoð þreo. þe feond. þe worlt. ure ahne flesch as ich ear
seide. lihtliche ne mei me nawt oðerhwile icnawen hwuch
of þeos þreo him weorreð. for euch helpeð oþer. þah þe f. 52a
feond proprement eggeð to atternesse. as to prude. to ouerhohe.
to onde ⁊ to wreaððe. ⁊ to hare attri cundles þe her efter
beoð inempnet. Þe flesch sput proprement toward swetnes
se. eise ⁊ softnesse. Þe world bit mon ȝiscin worldes weole 5
⁊ wurðschipe. ⁊ oþre swucche giuegauen þe bidweolieð
cang men to luuien a schadewe. þeos wiðeriwines hit
seið folhið us on hulles. ⁊ weitið i wildernesse hu ha us

15 þí*: thick stroke on* i. 19 *large blue initial* H *between* 18 *and* 21, *stem rising in margin to* 16; *red line-patterns within, and in margin from* 13 *to* 26. 24 *to* 26*: from* Vre wiðeriwines *to* sleanne. Vre *underlined* (*strokes fall short of line-ends*)*; mark* × *in left margin* (25).

f. 52a. 2 *and* 4*: above* proprement (*crossed out*) *is interlined in darker ink and different hand* (*?simulating the original*) ouneliche. *There seems to be no other record in later English of this word, whether derived from* (*rare*) *OE.* agenlic, *or similarly formed. The emendation* (*? and invention*) *had the same motive as that seen in* darnliche, f. 40a*; but if due to the same purist, he took more care here to imitate the main hand. The natural native word here is* cundeliche (*cf.* M kundeliche *for first* proprement) *which resembles* ouneliche *and may have suggested it. In* 2 *there is an erasure affecting bottom of* þre(o 1 *and* pre *of* proprement*; on this* oun *shows black; no erasure in* 4.

mahen hearmín. Hul ꝥ is heh lif. þer þe deoflesasawz
10 ofte beoð strengest. Wildernesse is anlich lif of ancre wu
nunge. for alswa as i wildernes beoð alle wilde beastes ant
nulleð nawt þolien monne nahunge. ah fleoð hwen
ha heom ihéreð.' alswa schulen ancres ouer alle oþre wum
men beo wilde o þisse wise. ⁊ þenne beoð ha ouer oþre leo
15 ue to ure lauerd. ⁊ swetest him þuncheð ham. for of all fles
ches is wilde deores fleschs leouest ⁊ swetest. Bi þis wil
dernesse wende ure lauerdes folc as exode teleð toward te
eadi lond of ierusalem ꝥ he ham hefde bihaten. Ant ȝe míne
leoue sustren wendeð bi þe ilke wei toward te hehe ierusalem. **(M 198)**
20 þe kinedom ꝥ he haueð bihaten his icorene. gað þah ful
warliche. for i þis wildernesse beoð uuele beastes monie. Líun
of prude. Neddre of attri onde. Vnicorne of wreaððe. Beore
of dead slawðe. Vox of ȝisceunge. Suhe of ȝiuernesse. Scorpi
un wið þe teil of stinginde leccherie. ꝥ is galnesse. Her
25 beoð nu o rawe itald þe seouen heaued sunnen.

Þe líun of prude haueð swiðe monie hwelpes. ant ich
chulle nempni summe. Vana gloria. ꝥ is hwa se let wel
of ei þing ꝥ ha deð oðer seið. oðer haueð wlite oðer wit.
f. 52b god acoíntance. oðer word mare þen an oþer. Cun oðer
meistrie. ⁊ hire wil forðre. ant hwet is wlite wurð her.'
gold ring i suhe nease. acointance i religiun. wa deð hit
ofte. al is uana gloria. þe let eawiht wel of. ⁊ walde habben
5 word þrof. ⁊ is wel ipaiet ȝef ha is ipreiset. mispaiet ȝef
ha nis itald swuch as ha walde. An oþer is indignatio. ꝥ
is þe þuncheð hokerlich of ei þing ꝥ ha sið bi oðer oþer
hereð. ⁊ forhoheð chastiement. oþer ei lahres lare. Þe þrid
de hwelp is ypocresis. þe makeð hire betere þen ha is. Þe feor
10 ðe is presumtio. Þe nímeð mare on hond þen ha mei ouercu
men. oðer entremeteð hire of þíng ꝥ to hire ne falleð
oðer is to ouertrusti up o godes grace. oðer on hire seoluen.
to bald up on ei mon ꝥ is fleschlich as heo is ⁊ mei beon

16 fleschs, *sic; a small blue initial* B *with red lines and scribbles.* 26 *large red initial* Þ *between* 25 *and* 28 (e *of* Þe *almost covered*), *straight stem standing from below* 28 *to* 23; *blue lines within, and in margin from* 20 *to foot; directing* þ *in left margin. In bottom margin a slit with holes for lost stitches from under* of *to left edge.* 28 oðer *to* f. 52 b. 5 þrof *not in* M.

itemptet. Þe fifte hwelp hatte inobedience. nawt ane þe
ne buheð. oðer grucchinde deð. oðer targeð to longe. þet 15
child þe ne buheð ealdren. Vnderling his prelat. parosch
ien his preost. Meiden hire dame. Euch lahre his herre. Þe
seste is loquacite. þe fedeð þis hwelp þe is of muche speche.
ʒelpeð. demeð oþre. liheð oðerhwile. gabbeð. upbreideð. chí
deð. fikeleð. stureð lahtre. Þe Seoueðe is blasphemie. þis 20
hwelpes nurrice is. þe swereð greate aþes oðer bitterliche
curseð. oðer misseið bi godd oðer bi his halhen. for ei þing
ꝥ he þoleð. sið oðer hereð. Þe eahtuðe is ínpatience. þis
hwelp fet þe nis þolemod aʒein alle wohes ⁊ in alle uue
les. Þe Niheðe is contumace. ant þis fet hwa se is anewil i 25
þing ꝥ ha haueð undernume to donne. beo hit god beo
hit uuel. ꝥ na wisure read ne mei bringen hire ut of
hire riote. þe teoheðe is Contentio. ꝥ is strif to ouercumen
ꝥ te oþer þunche underneoðen awarpen ⁊ crauant. ant heo **f. 53a**
me⟨i⟩stre of þe mot. ⁊ crenge ase champíun þe haueð biʒete
þe place. I þis unþeaw is upbrud. ⁊ edwitunge of al ꝥ uuel
ꝥ ha mei bi þe oðer ofþenchen. ant eauer se hit biteð bíttru
re:⁊ se hire likeð betere. þah hit were of þing þe wes biuore 5
ʒare amendet. Her imong beoð oðerhwiles nawt ane
bittre wordes:⁊ ah beoð fule stinkinde scheomelese ⁊ schent
fule. sum chearre mid great sware. monie ⁊ prude wordes wið
warínesses ⁊ bileasunges. Her to falleð euenunge of ham
seolf. of hare cun. of sahe oðer of dede. Þis is among nun 10
nen. ⁊ gað wið swuch muð seoððen ear schrift ham habbe
iweschen to herie godd wið loftsong. oðer biddeð him pri
uee bonen. Me þinges amansede nuten ha ꝥ hare song ant
hare bonen to godd stinkeð fulre to him ⁊ to alle his halh
en:⁊ þen ei rotet dogge. Þe ealleofte hwelp is ifed wið supersti 15
ciuns. wið semblanz ⁊ wið sínes. as beoren on heh ꝥ heaued.
crenge wið swire. lokín o siden. bihalden on hokere. winche

f. 52b. 14, 15 nawt *to* longe: *an addition* (*not in* M) *defining* inobedience*;* ah þe *probably omitted after* buheð. *Slit in bottom right-hand margin, under end of* ouercumen (*see recto*). 28 þe teoheðe *to* f. 53a. 26 fingres *not in* M.

f. 53a. 2 me⟨i⟩stre: ⟨i⟩ *interlined with caret. In right margin, pointing to* 11, *a hand drawn so that part of an earlier* Nota (*opposite* 12) *serves as the end of its unfinished forefinger.*

mid ehe. binde seode mid te muð. wið hond oðer wið hea
ued makie scuter signe. warpe schonke ouer schench. sitten
20 oðer gan stif as ha istaket wére. luue lokin o mon. speo
ken as an ínnocent. ⁊ wlispín for þen anes. Her to falleð
of ueil of heaued clað. of euch oðer clað. to ouegart ace
munge oðer in heowunge. oðer ipinchunge. gurdlesant
gurdunge o dameiseles wise. scleaterunge mid smirles
25 fule fluðrunges. heowin hér. litien leor. pinchin bruhen
oðer bencín ham uppart wið wéte fingres. Monie oþre
þer beoð þe cumeð of weole of wunne. of heh cun. of fei (M. 200)
er clað. of wit. of wlite. of strengðe. Of heh cun waxeð
f. 53b prude. ⁊ of hali þeawes·⁄ monie ma hwelpes þen ich habbe
inempnet·⁄ haueð þe líun of prude. ah abute þeose studieð
wel swiðe. for ich ga lihtliche ouer. ne do bute nempni ham
ah ȝe eauer ihwer se ich ga swiðere uorð·⁄ leaueð þer lengest.
5 for þer ich feðeri on a word téne oðer tweolue. Hwa se
eauer haueð eani unþeaw of þeo þe ich her nempnede.
oðer ham iliche·⁄ ha haueð prude sikerliche hu se eauer
hire curtel beo ischapet oðer iheowet. heo is þe líunes
make ꝥ ich habbe ispeken of. ⁊ fet hire wode hwelpes
10 Þe néddre of attri onde ¶ .ínwið hire breoste.
haueð seoue hwelpes. Ingratitudo. þis cundel bret
hwa se nis icnawen goddede. ah teleð lutel þrof. oðer
forȝet mid alle. goddede ich segge nawt ane ꝥ ⟨mon⟩
deð him·⁄ ah ꝥ godd deð him. oðer haueð idon him.
15 oðer him oðer hire. mare þen ha understont ȝef ha
hire wel biþohte. Of þis unþeaw me nimeð to ⟨lutel⟩
ȝeme. ⁊ is þah of alle an laðest godd ⁊ meast aȝeín his
grace. Þe oðer cundel is Rancor siue odíum. ꝥ is heatun
ge oðer great heorte. Þe bret hit i breoste·⁄ al is attri to
20 godd ꝥ he eauer wurcheð. Þe þridde cundel is ofþun
chunge of oþres god. Þe feorðe·⁄ gleadschipe of his uuel.
Þe fifte wreiunge. Þe Seste bacbitunge. Þe Seoueðe up

22 ouegart, *sic for* ouergart. 28 cun, *sic* (*from* 27) *for* lif.

f. 53b. 10 *large blue initial* Þ *between* 8 *and* 15, *ornamented with red line-patterns within, and in margin from* 5 *to* 21. *Before* .ínwið hire breoste. *a red paragraph.* 13 mon *interlined above* godd *crossed out.* 16 lutel *interlined above* muchel *crossed out.*

brud oðer scarnunge. Þe eahtuðe is suspitio. ꝥ is mis
ortrowunge bi mon oðer bi wummon wið uten witer
tacne. þenchen. þis semblant ha makeð. þis ha seið oðer 25
deð me forte gremien. hokerín oðer hearmin. ⁊ ꝥ hwen
þe oþer neauer þideward ne þencheð. Herto falleð fals
dom ꝥ godd forbeot swiðe. as þenchen oðer seggen. ȝe
ne luueð ha me nawt. Herof ha wreide me. lo nu ha speokeð f. 54a
of me þe twa. þe þreo. oðer þe ma þe sitteð togederes. swuch
ha is ⁊ swuch ⁊ for uuel ha hit dude. Iþulli þoht we beoð
ofte bichearret. for ofte is god ꝥ þuncheð uuel. ⁊ for þí
beoð aldei monnes domes false. Herto limpeð alswa luðe 5
re neowe fundles ⁊ leasunges ladliche þurh nið ⁊ þurh
onde. Þe Niheðe cundel is sawunge of unsibsumnesse of
wreaððe ⁊ of descorde. þeo þe saweð þis deofles sed.· ha is of
godd amanset. Þe teoheðe is luðer stilðe. þe deofles silence.
ꝥ te an nule for onde speoken o þe oþer. ant þis spece is al 10
swa cundel of wreaððe. for hare teames beoð imengt ofte to
gederes. Hwer as ei of þeos wes.· þer wes þe cundel oðer þe
alde moder of þe attri neddre of onde.

Þe Vnicorne of wreaððe þe bereð on his nease þe þorn
ꝥ he asneaseð wið al ꝥ he areacheð.· haueð six hwel 15
pes. Þe earste is chast oðer strif. Þe oðer is wodschipe.
Bihald te ehnen ⁊ te neb hwen wod wreaððe is imunt.
Bihald hire contenemenz. loke on hire lates. hercne huþe
muð geað. ⁊ tu maht demen hire wel ut of hire witte.
Þe þridde is schentful upbrud. Þe feorðe is wariunge. 20
(M. 202) Þe fifte is dunt. Þe seste is wil ꝥ him uuel tidde. oðer
on him seolf. oðer on his freond. oðer on his ahte. Þe
seoueðe hwelp is. don for wreaððe mis. oðer leauen wel
to don. forgan mete oðer drunch. wreoken hi
re wið teares ȝef ha elles ne mei. ⁊ wið weariunges 25
hire heaued spillen o grome. oðer on oþer wise hearmin

23 Þe eahtuðe *to* f. 54a. 12 gederes *not in* M. 27 þideward, *sic.* f. 54a. 14 *large red initial* Þ *between* 11 *and* 17, *ornamented with blue within, and in margin from* 7 *to* 21; *directing* þ *in left margin.* 14 þorn, *sic.* 20 wariunge: warnunge *with second stroke of* n *erased.* 17 *to* 19, *and* 22 Þe *to* 28 seoluen, *not in* M. 23 *to* 25 *long slit from binding to* teares, *with holes for lost stitches, avoided by writing as shown.*

hire i sawle ꝛ i bodi baðe. þeos is homicide ꝛ morðre of
hire seoluen. Þe Beore of heuí slawðe haueð þeose
f. 54b hwelpes. Torpor is þe forme. ꝥ is wlech heorte. vnlust to eni
þíng. þe schulde leitin al o lei i luue of ure lauerd. Þe oþer
is pusillanimitas. ꝥ is to poure heorte ꝛ to earh mid alle
ei heh þing to underneomen in hope of godes help.· ant i
5 trust on his grace. nawt of hire strengðe. Þe þridde is cordis
grauitas. þis haueð hwa se wurcheð god. ꝛ deð hit tah mid
a dead ꝛ mid an heuí heorte. Þe feorðe is ydelnesse hwa
se stut mid alle. Þe fifte is heorte grucchunge. Þe seste
is a dead sorhe for lure of ei worltlich þing. oþer for ení
10 unþonc bute for sunne ane. Þe Seoueðe is ȝemelesschi
pe oðer to seggen oðer to don. oðer to biseon biuoren.·
oðer to þenchen efter. oðer to miswiten ení þing ꝥ ha
haueð to ȝemen. Þe eahtuðe is unhope. þis leaste beore
hwelp is grimmest of alle. for hit to cheoweð ꝛ tofret go
15 des milde milce ꝛ his muchele mearci. ꝛ his unimete grace.
Þe Vox of ȝisceunge haueð þeose hwelpes. Triccherie.
ꝛ gile. Þeofðe. Reaflac. wite. ꝛ herrure strengðe. false
witnesse oðer að. dearne symonie. Gauel. Oker. festschipe.
prinschipe of ȝeoue oðer of lane. þis is icluht heorte.
20 vnþeaw gode laðest. þe ȝef us al him seoluen. Monslaht
oðerhwile. Þis unþeaw is to uox for moni reisun ieuen
et. Twa ich chulle seggen. Muche gile is i vox. ꝛ swa is i
ȝisceunge of worltlich biȝete. An oðer. þe Vox awuri
eð al a floc þah he ne mahe buten an frechli
25 che swolhen. Alswa ȝisceð aȝiscere ꝥ tet moni
þusent mahten bi flutten. ah þah his heorte berste.
ne mei he bruken on him seolf bute a monnes dale.
Al ꝥ mon wilneð mare oðer wummon. þen ha mei
f. 55a rihtliche leade ꝥ lif bi. euch efter ꝥ ha is.· al is ȝisceunge (M. 204)

28 *small blue initial* Þ *descending into bottom margin, ornamented with red lines and tail.*

f. 54b. 1,2 vnlust *to* þíng *not in* M. 16 *large red initial* Þ *between* 13 *and* 21, *ornamented within with blue line-patterns, and in margin from* 10 *to bottom margin; the bow nearly covers* e. 23 worltlich: w (ƿ) *has bow on either side, and small tick above right bow; scribe probably began* eorð *and immediately altered* e *to* ƿ. 23 *to* 25 *slit (see recto) avoided by writing at end of* 24 *and in* 25 *as shown.*

⁊ rote of deadlich sunne. ꝥ is riht religiun ꝥ euch efter
his stat borhi ed tis frakele worlde se lutel se ha least
mei. of mete. of clað. of ahte. of alle hire þinges. Notið
ꝥ ich segge. Euch efter his stat. for ꝥ word is ifeðeret. ȝe 5
mote makien ꝥ wite ȝe i moni word muche strengðe.
þenchen longe þerabuten. ⁊ bi ꝥ ilke an word under
stonden monie þe limpeð þer to. for ȝef ich schulde
writen al.' hwenne come ich to ende?

Þe Suhe of ȝiuernesse haueð gris þus inempnet. To 10
earliche hatte ꝥ an. þet oþer to esteliche. ꝥ þridde to
frechliche. ꝥ feorðe hatte to muche. ꝥ fifte to ofte. I drunch
mare þen i mete beoð þeos gris iferhet. Ich speoke scheort
liche of ham. for nam ich nawt ofdred mine leoue sustren

Þe Scorpiun of leccherie. ꝥ is ℭ .leste ȝe ham feden. 15
of galnesse. haueð swucche cundles. ꝥ in a wel itohe
muð hare summes nome ne sit nawt forte nempnín.
for þe nome ane mahte hurten alle wel itohene earen.
⁊ sulen cleane heorten. þeo þah me mei nempnín wel.'
hwas nomen me icnaweð wel. ⁊ beoð mare hearm is to 20
monie al to cuðe. Horedom. Eawbruche. Meiðlure. ⁊ Incest.
ꝥ is bituhe sibbe fleschliche oðer gasteliche. ꝥ is o feole i
dealet. ful wil to ꝥ fulðe wið skiles ȝettunge. helpen oþ
re þiderward. beo weote ⁊ witnesse þrof. hunti þrefter
wið wohunge. wið toggunge. oðer wið eni tollunge. wið 25
gigge lahtre. hore ehe. Eanie lihte lates. wið ȝeoue. wið
(M. 206) tollinde word. oðer wið luue speche. Cos. Vnhende grap
unge ꝥ mei beon heaued sunne. luuíe tide oðer stude
forte cumen i swuch keast. ⁊ oþre foreridles þe me mot ne f. 55b
de forbuhen. þe i þe muchele fulðe nule fenniliche fallen.
as seínt austín seið. Omissis occasionibus que solent adi
tum aperire peccatis.' potest consciencia esse incolimis. ꝥ is.
hwa se

f. 55a. 2 *hole immediately after* efter. 10 *large blue initial* Þ *between* 9 *and* 12 *ornamented with red lines within, and in margin from* 4 *to* 13, *the bow cuts the* e *of* þe; *directing* þ *in left margin.* 15 *large red initial* Þ *between* 13 *and* 19; *blue pattern within, and blue lines in margin from its top to* 23. *Blue paragraph, touched with red, before* .leste.

f. 55b. 2 *hole avoided by writing before* de. 4 incolimis, *sic.*

5 wule hire inwit witen hal ⁊ fére.' ha mot fleon þe forerid
les þe weren iwunet ofte to openín þe inȝong ⁊ leoten
ín sunne. Ich ne dear nempnín þe uncundeliche cund
les of þis deofles scorpiun attri iteilet. Ah sari mei ha
beon þe bute fere oðer wið.' haueð swa ifed cundel of
10 hire galnesse. ꝥ ich ne mei speoken of for scheome ne
ne dear for drede. leste sum leorni mare uuel þen ha
con ⁊ beo þrof itemptet. Ah þenche on hire ahne awea
riede fundles ín hire galnesse. for hu se hit eauer is
icwenct wakinde ⁊ willes wið flesches licunge bute
15 ane i wedlac.' hit geað to deadlich sunne. I ȝuheðe me
deð wundres. Culche hit i schrift ut utterliche as ha hit
dude. þe feleð hire schuldi oðer ha is idemet þurh ꝥ
fule brune cwench.' to ꝥ eche brune of helle. Þe Scorpíu
nes cundel þe ha bret in hire bosum.' schake hit ut
20 wið schrift ⁊ wið deadbote slea. ȝe þe of swucches nute
nawt. ne þurue ȝe nawt wundrin ow ne þenchen hwet
ich meane. ah ȝeldeð graces godd ꝥ ȝe swuch unclean
nesse nabbeð ifondet. ⁊ habbeð reowðe of ham þe i
swuch beoð ifallen. INoh is etscene hwi ich habbe í
25 euenet prude to líun.' onde to neddre. ⁊ of þeo alle þe
oþre. wið ute þis leaste. ꝥ is hwi galnesse beo to scorpi
un ieuenet. Ah lo her þe skile þrof sutel ⁊ etscene.
Scorpiun is a cunnes wurm. þe haueð neb as me seið
f. 56a sumdeal ilich wummon.' ⁊ neddre is bihínden. Makeð fei
er semblant. ⁊ fikeð mid te heaueð.' ⁊ stingeð mid te teile.
þis is leccherie. þis is þe deofles beast ꝥ he leat to chepínge.
⁊ to euch gederunge. ⁊ chepeð forte sullen. ⁊ biswikeð mo
5 níe. þurh ꝥ ha ne bihaldeð nawt bute þe feire neb.' oðer
ꝥ feire heaued. ꝥ heaued is þe biginnunge of galnesse
sunne. ⁊ te licunge hwil hit least þe þuncheð swiðe swote. (M. 208)
Þe teil ꝥ is þe ende þrof. is sar ofþunchunge. ⁊ stingeð her
wið atter of bitter bireowsunge. ⁊ of deadbote. ant selili
10 che mahen ha seggen þe þe teil swuch ifindeð. for ꝥ atter
ageað. ah ȝef hit ne suheð her.' þe teil ⁊ te attri ende is þe

20 wið deadbote *and* slea *marked for transposition with* ″ *above* de *and* sl; ȝe‸þe *to* 24 ifallen *not in* M. 24 *small red initial* I *with blue line-ornament.*

eche pine of helle. Ant nís he fol chapmon þe hwen he
wule buggen hors oðer oxe. ȝef he nule bihalden bute
ꝥ heaued ane? for þi hwen þe deouel beodeð forð þis
beast. beot hit to sullen ⁊ bit ti sawle þeruore·˙ he hut eauer 15
þe teil·˙ ⁊ schaweð forð þe heaued. Ah þu ga al abuten. ⁊
schaw þe ende forð mid al. hu þe teil stingeð. ant swiðe
flih þer frommard ear þu beo iattret.

ÞVS mine leoue sustren i þe wildernesse þer ȝe gað·˙
ín. wið godes folc toward ierusalemes lond. ꝥ is þe 20
riche of heouene·˙ beoð þulliche beastes. þulliche wurmes.
ne nat ich na sunne ꝥ ne mei beon ilead oðer to an of
ham seouene·˙ oðer to hare streones. Vnsteaðeluest bileaue
aȝein godes lare. nis hit te spece of prude inobedience?
Herto falleð sygaldren. false teolunges. lefunge o swefne. o 25
Nore. ⁊ on alle wicchecreftes. Neomunge of husel in eaní
heaued sunne. oðer ei oþer sacrement. nis hit te spece of
prude ꝥ ich cleopede presumptio. ȝef me wat hwuch sunne
hit .is.

ȝef me hit nat nawt·˙ þenne is hit ȝemeles under acci f. 56b
die. ꝥ ich slawðe cleopede. Þe ne warneð oðer of his uuel
oðer of his biȝete. Nis hit slaw ȝemeles oðer attri on
de? teoheði mis. edhalden cwide. fundles oðer lane. oðer
þerwið mis fearen. Nis hit spece of ȝisceunge. ⁊ anes 5
cunnes þeofðe? Edhalden oðres hure ouer his rihte terme
Nis hit strong reaflac hwa se ȝelden hit mei þe is under
ȝisceunge? ȝef me ȝemeð wurse ei þing ileanet. oðer
bitaht to witene. þen he wene þe ah hit. Nis hit oðer
triccherie. oðer ȝemeles of slawðe? Alswa is dusi heast 10
oðer folliche ipliht trowðe. longe beon unbischpet.
(M. 210) falsliche gan to schrift. oðer to longe abiden. ne teache
pater noster godchild ne Credo. Þeos ⁊ alle þulliche
beoð ilead
to slawðe. ꝥ is þe feorðe moder of þe seoue sunnen. Þe
dronc drunch oðer ei þing dude. hwer þurh na child 15
ne schulde beon on hire istreonet. oðer ꝥ istreonede

f. 56a. 2 heaueð, *sic.* 19 *large blue initial* Þ *between* 18 *and* 21, *red line-pattern within, and in margin from* 12 *to bottom line; directing* þ *in left margin.* 28 .is. *written below* hit.

schulde forwurðen. Nis þis strong monslaht of galnes
se awakenet? Alle sunnen sunderliche bi hare nomeli
che nomen ne mahte namon rikenín. Ah i þeo þe ich
20 habbe iseid.' alle oþre beoð bilokene. Ant nis ich wene
namon þe ne mei understonden him of his sunne no
meliche under sum of þe ilke imeane þe beoð her iwri
tene. Of þeose seoue beastes ⁊ of hare streones i wilder
nesse of anlich lif. is iseid herto. þe alle þe forfearinde
25 fondið to fordonne. Þe liun of prude sleað alle þe prude.
alle þe beoð hehe ⁊ ouerhohe iheortet. Þe attri neddre.' þe
ontfule ⁊ te luðere iþonket. Wreaðfule.' þe Vnicorne.
Alswa of þe oþre o rawe. to godd ha beoð isleíne. Ah
f. 57a ha libbeð to þe feond. ⁊ beoð alle in his hond. ⁊ seruið
him in his curt euch of þe meoster þe him to falleð.

Þe prude beoð his bemeres. draheð wínd inward wið
worltlich hereword. ⁊ eft wið idel ȝelp puffeð hit ut
5 ward as þe bemeres doð. makieð noise ⁊ lud dream to
schawin hare orhel. ah ȝef ha wel þohten of godes beme
res of þe englene bemen þe schulen o fowr half þe world
biuore þe grurefule dom grisliche blawen. Ariseð deade
ariseð cumeð to drihtines dom forte beon idemet. þear
10 na prud bemere ne schal beon iborhen. ȝef ha þohten þis
wel.' ha walden inohreaðe i þe deofles seruise dimluker
bemín. Of þeose bemeres seið Ieremie. Onager solitarius in
desiderio anime sue attraxit uentum amoris suí. Of þe
wind drahinde ín for luue of hereword seið as ich seide.

15 Summe iuglurs beoð þe ne cunnen seruin of nan
oþer gleo bute makien chéres. wrenche þe muð
mis. schulen wið ehnen. Of þis meoster seruið þe unselí (M. 212)
ontfule i þe deofles curt. to bringen o lahtre hare ondfu
le lauerd. ȝef ei seið wel oðer deð wel.' ne mahen ha nanes
20 weis lokin þider wið riht ehe of god heorte. ah winkið o ꝥ

f. 56b. 6 *MS.* terme. 19, 20 *stain between lines, touching* e *of* nomen, *and* d *of* iseid *below.* 24 forfearinde, *sic, probably for* forð-.
f. 57a. 3 *large blue initial* Þ *between* 2 *and* 5, *ornamented with red line-patterns within, and in margin from top of page to* 11; *directing* þ (*now nearly hidden*) *in left margin.* 14 Ieremie *omitted after* seið. 15 *large red initial* S *between* 14 *and* 17 *with red tail to* 20, *blue line-patterns within, and in margin from* 11 *to* 20.

half ⁊ bihaldeð o luft ȝef þer is eawt to edwiten. oðer lad liche þiderward schuleð mið eiðer. Hwen ha ihereð ꝥ god.' skleatteð þe earen adun. ah þe luft aȝein ꝥ uuel.' is eauer wid open. þenne he wrencheð þe muð.' hwen he turneð god to uuel. ⁊ ȝef hit is sumdel uuel. þurh mare lastun 25 ge wrencheð hit to wurse. þeos beoð forecwidderes hare ahne prophetes. þeos bodieð biuoren hu þe eateliche deof len schulen ȝet ageasten ham wið hare grennunge. ⁊ hu ha schulen ham seolf grennin ⁊ niuelín ⁊ makien f. 57b sur semblant for þe muchele angoise i þe pine of helle. Ah for þi ha beoð þe leasse to meanen ꝥ ha biuoren hond leornið hare meoster to makien grím chére.

Þe wreaðfule biuore þe feond skirmeð mid cniues. ⁊ 5 is his cnif warpere. ⁊ pleieð mid sweordes. bereð ham bi þe scharp ord up on his tunge. Sweord ⁊ cnif eiðer beoð scharpe ⁊ keoruinde word ꝥ he warpeð from hím ⁊ skirmeð toward oþre. ⁊ he bodeð hu þe deoflen schulen pleien wið him mid hare scharpe eawles. skirmi wið him 10 abuten ⁊ dusten ase pilche clut euch toward oðer.' ant wið helle sweordes asneasen him þurh ut. ꝥ beoð kene ant eateliche ant keoruinde pínen.

Þe slawe lið ⁊ slepeð o þe deofles bearm as his deore deorling. ⁊ te deouel leið his tutel dun to his eare. ⁊ 15 tuteleð him al ꝥ he wule. for swa hit is sikerliche to hwam se is idel of god.' meaðeleð þe feond ȝeorne. ⁊ te idele un derueð luueliche his lare. Idel ⁊ ȝemeles is þes deofles (M. 214) bearnes slep. ah he schal o domesdei grimliche abreiden wið þe dredfule dream of þe englene bemen. ⁊ in helle 20 wontreaðe echeliche wakien. Surgite aíunt mortui surgite ⁊ ueníte ad iudicium saluatoris.

Þe ȝiscere is his eskibah. feareð abuten esken. ⁊ bisi liche stureð him to rukelin to gederes muchele ⁊ monie ruken. blaweð þrín ⁊ blent him seolf. peaðereð 25

f. 57a. 22 mið, *sic*. 23 luft, *sic*.

f. 57b. 5, 14, 23: *large initial* Þ *in three shapes (blue, red, blue) with line ornaments (red, blue, red) from high in top margin to deep in bottom margin. The first bow cuts* e *of* Þe 5; *the second the* t *of* tuteleð 16; *the blue wash of third bow passes partly over* e *of* Þe 23, l *of* liche 24. *In left margin (now shaved) traces visible of bow of directing* þ *opposite* 5, 14.

⁊ makeð þrín figures of augrím. as þes rikeneres doð
þe habbeð muche to rikenín. Þis is al þe canges blisse
⁊ te feond bihalt tis gomen ⁊ laheð ꝥ he bersteð. Wel un
f. 58a derstont euch wis mon ꝥ gold ba ⁊ seoluer. ⁊ euch eorðlich
ahte. nis bute eorðe ⁊ ahte esken þe ablendeð euch mon
þe ham in blaweð. ꝥ is þe bolheð him þurh ham in heor
te prude. Ant al ꝥ he rukeleð ⁊ gedereð to gederes. ⁊ et
5 halt of ei þing ꝥ nis bute esken mare þen hit neodeð.'
schal in helle wurðen him tadden ⁊ neddren. ⁊ ba as ysa
ie seið. schulen beon of wurmes.' his cuuertur ⁊ his hwí
tel. þe nalde þerwið neodfule feden ne schruden. Subter
te sternetur tinea ⁊ operimentum tuum uermis.

10 Þe ȝiuere glutun is þe feondes manciple. ah he stikeð
eauer iceler oðer icuchene. his heorte is i þe dissches.
his þoht al i þe neppes. his lif i þe tunne. his sawle i þe
crohhe. Kimeð biuoren his lauerd bismuddet ⁊ bismulret.
a disch in his an hond. a scale in his oðer. Meaðeleð mís
15 wordes. wigleð as fordrunke mon þe haueð imunt to
fallen. bihalt his greate wombe. ⁊ te deouel lahheð. þeo
se þreatið þus godd þurh ysaie. Serui mei comedent
⁊ uos esurietis ⁊ cetera. Míne men schulen eoten ⁊ ow schal ea
uer hungrin. ⁊ ȝe schule beon feode world buten ende. (M. 216)
20 Quantum glorificauít se ⁊ in deliciís fuit.' tantum
date illi tormentum ⁊ luctum. In apocalipsi. Contra unum
poculum quod miscuit miscete ei duo. ȝef þe kealche
cuppe wallinde bres to drinken. ȝeot in his wide þrote ꝥ
he swelte inwið. aȝeín an ȝef him twa. þullich is godes
25 dom aȝeín ȝiuere ⁊ druncwile iþe apocalipse.

Þe lecchurs i þe deofles curt habbeð riht hare ahne no
me. for iþes muchele curz þeo me cleopeð lecchurs

f. 58a. 2 *second* ahte *false repetition.* 10 *large red initial* Þ, *ornamented with blue, between* 9 *and* 12*; in margin tapered stem from* 7 *to* 15. 18 *to* 22: Mine *to* ea 18, Qua)ntum *to* delic(iís 20, In apocalipsi. Cont(ra 21, poculum *to* duo 22, *underlined; marks* × *in right margin opposite* 18 *and* 20/21*; scribble at ends of* 20 *to* 23. 19 feode (*with* n *altered to upright* d) *for* feo[ndes fo]de. 20, 21 *narrow hole from left margin to* 21 *after* illi*;* Quantum *is set in as shown.* 26 *large blue initial* Þ, *ornamented with red, between* 25 *and* 28*; tapered stem into lower margin.*

þe habbeð swa forlore scheome ꝥ heom nís nawiht of
scheome. ah secheð hu ha mahen meast vilaínie wurch f. 58b
en. Þe lecchur i þe deofles curt bifuleð him seoluen fulli
che ⁊ his feolahes alle. stinkeð of ꝥ fulðe ⁊ paieð wel his
lauerd wið ꝥ stinkinde breað betere þen he schulde wið ea
ní swote rechles. Hu he stinke to godd: I vitas patrum þe 5
engel hit schawde þe heold his nease þa þer com þe pru
de lecchur ridínde. ⁊ nawt for ꝥ rotede lich ꝥ he healp
þe hali earmite to biburien. Of alle oþre þenne hab
beð þeos þe fuleste meoster i þe feondes curt. þe swa bí
doð ham seoluen. Ant he schal bidon ham. pinin ham 10
wið eche stench iþe put of helle. NV ȝe habbeð ane
dale iherd mine leoue sustren of þeo þe ⟨me⟩ cleopeð þe
seoue modersunnen. ⁊ of hare teames. ⁊ of hwucche
meosters þes ilke men seruið i þe feondes curt. þe hab
beð iwiuet o þeose seouen haggen. ⁊ hwi ha beoð swiðe 15
to heatien ⁊ to schunien. ȝe beoð ful feor from ham u
re lauerd beo iþoncket. ah ꝥ fule breað of þis leaste
unþeaw. ꝥ is of leccherie. stinkeð se swiðe feor. for þe
feond hit saweð ⁊ to blaweð ouer al. ꝥ ich am sumdel
ofdred leste hit leape sum chearre in to ower 20
heortes nease. Stench stiheð uppart ⁊ ȝe beoð
(M. 218) hehe iclumben þer þe wind is muchel of stronge temp
tatiuns. Vre lauerd ȝeoue ow strengðe wel to wiðstonden.
SVm weneð ꝥ ha schule stronglukest beon ifon
det iþe forme tweofmoneð ꝥ ha bigon ancre 25
lif. ⁊ i þe oþer þrefter. ant hwen ha efter feole ȝer
feleð ham stronge: wundreð hire swiðe. ⁊ is ofdred
leste godd habbe hire al forwarpen. Nai nawt nis
hit swa. I þe forme ȝeres nis bute balplohe to moníe f. 59a
men of ordre. Ah neomeð ȝeme hu hit feareð bi a for
bisne. Hwen a wis mon neowliche haueð wif ilead ham:
hi nimeð ȝeme al softeliche of hire maneres. þah he seo bi

f. 58b. 11 *small blue initial* N *ornamented with red lines.* 12 ⟨me⟩ *interlined with caret.* 20, 21*: hole* (*see* f. 58) *occupies end of* 20, *and a space between* ȝe *and* beoð 21. 24 *large red initial* S *between* 23 (*overlying lower part of* tatiuns) *and* 26, *with long tail into bottom margin, and blue line-patterns within, and in margin from* 20 *to below* tail. 25 tweofmoneð, *sic.*

5 hire ꝥ him mis paieð.' he let ȝet íwurðen. makeð hire fei
re chere. ⁊ is umben euches weis ꝥ ha hím luuie ínward
liche in hire heorte. Hwen he understont wel ꝥ hire luue
is treoweliche toward hím ifestnet.' þenne mei he siker
liche chastien hire openliche of hire unþeawes.' ꝥ he
10 ear forber as he ham nawt nuste. Makeð hím swiðe
sturne. ⁊ went te grimme toð to forte fondín ȝetten
ȝef he mahte hire luue toward him unfestnín. Alest
hwen he understont ꝥ ha is al wel ituht. ne for þing
ꝥ he deð hire. ne luueð him þe leasse.' ah mare ⁊ ma
15 re ȝef ha mei.' from deie to deie.' þenne schaweð he hi
re ꝥ he hire luueð sweteliche. ⁊ deð al ꝥ ha wule as þeo
ꝥ he wel icnaweð. þenne is al ꝥ wa.' iwurðe to wunne.
Ȝef iesu crist ower spus deð alswa bi ow mine leoue
sustren. ne þunche ow neauer wunder. I þe frumðe nis
20 þer buten olhnunge forte drahen in luue. Ah Sone
se he eauer understont ꝥ he beo wel acóintet.' he wule
forbeoren ow leasse. Efter þe spreoue on ende.' þenne is
þe muchele ioie. Al o þis ilke wise þa he walde his
folc leaden ut of þeowdom. ut of pharaones hond.'
25 ut of egypte.' he dude for ham al ꝥ ha walden. Mirac
les feole ⁊ feire. druhede þe reade sea. ⁊ makede ham (M. 220)
freo wei þurh hire. ⁊ þer ha eoden drufot. adrencte
pharaon ⁊ hare fan alle. Iþe desert forðre þa he hefde
f. 59b ilead ham feor i þe wildernesse.' he lette ham þolien
wa ínoh. hunger. þurst. ⁊ muche swínc. ⁊ weorren mu
chele ⁊ monie. On ende he ȝef ham reste. ⁊ alle weole ⁊
wunne. al hare heorte wil. ⁊ flesches eise ⁊ este. Terram
5 fluentem lacte ⁊ melle. þus ure lauerd speareð on earst
þe ȝunge ⁊ te feble. ⁊ draheð ham ut of þis world.'
swoteliche ⁊ wið liste. Sone se he sið ham heardin.'
he let weorre awakenín ⁊ teacheð ham to fehten ⁊
weane to þolien. On ende efter long swinc.' he ȝeueð
10 ham swote reste. her ich segge i þis world ear ha cu
men to heouene. ⁊ þuncheð þenne swa god.' þe reste

f. 59a. 6 ę *erased before* í *of* ínward.

f. 59b. *In left margin faint lines resembling letters (made at time of ruling?) opposite* 5, 6, 10, 13/14.

efter þe swinc. þe muchele eise efter þe muchele meos
eise þuncheð se swote. NV beoð i þe sawter under
þe twa temptatiuns ꝥ ich ear seide. ꝥ beoð þe uttre. ⁊
te inre þe temeð alle þe oþre.' fowr dalen todealet 15
þus. Fondunge liht ⁊ dearne. Fondunge liht ⁊ open
lich. Fondunge strong ⁊ dearne. fondunge strong ⁊
openlich. as is þer understonden. Non timebis a
timore nocturno. A sagitta uolante in die. a ne
gotio perambulante in tenebris. ab incursu ⁊ demo 20
nio meridiano. Of fondunge liht ⁊ dearne.' seið
iob þeose wordes. lapides excauant aque. ⁊ alliuio
ne paulatim terra consumitur. lutle dropen þurlið þe
flínt þe ofte falleð þron. ⁊ lihte dearne fondunges
þe me nis war of.' falsið a treowe heorte. Of þe lihte 25
openliche bi hwam he seið alswa. lucebit post eum se
mita. Nis nawt se muche dute. of strong temptatiun
ꝥ is þah dearne.' is ec ꝥ Iob meaneð. Insidiati sunt michi
⁊ preualuerunt. ⁊ non erat qui adíuuaret. ꝥ is. Míne f. 60a
fan weitið me wið triccherie ⁊ wið treisun. ⁊ ha streng
den up o me ⁊ nes hwa me hulpe. ysaias. Veniet malum
super te ⁊ nescies ortum eius. Wa schal cumen on þe. ⁊ tu
ne schalt witen hweonne. Of þe feorðe fondunge ꝥ is 5
strong ⁊ openlich.' he makeð his man of his fan þe há
li iob ⁊ seið. Quasi rupto muro ⁊ aperta ianua irruerunt
super me. ꝥ is ha þreasten in up o me as þah þe wal we
(M. 222) re tobroken ⁊ te ȝeten opene. Þe forme ⁊ te þridde fon
dunge of þeose fowre beoð al meast under þe ínre. Þe 10
oþer ⁊ te feorðe falleð under þe uttre. ⁊ beoð al meast
fleschliche ⁊ eð for þi to felen. Þe oþre twa beoð gasteli
che of gasteliche unþeawes. ⁊ beoð ihud ofte. ⁊ dearne
hwen ha derueð meast. ⁊ beoð muche for þi þe mare to

13 *small red initial* N *ornamented with blue lines.* 22 iob, *and* 23, 24 lutle dropen *to* falleð þron *underlined, and mark* × *in left margin* 23/24. 22, 23 alliuio|ne, *sic for* alluuione.

f. 60a. *On this page the markings* (*concerned with the translation of Latin texts*) *are: scribbles in right margin at ends of* 1 *to* 6*; marks* × *opposite ends of* 1, 3/4, 7/8, 18*; underlinings in* 7 *to* 9 *of* iob *and* Quasi *to* opene*;* 18, 19 Vnholde *to* nawt nuste. ȝ(et. 7 *MS.* Qua*Si*. 8 þreasten: *second* e *altered from* i.

15 dreden. Moní þ ne weneð nawt bret in hire breoste
sum liunes hwelp. sum neddre cundel þe forfret þe
sawle. of hwucche Osee seið. Alieni comederunt robur
eius ⁊ ipse nescíuít. þ is. Vnholde forfreten þe strengðe
of his sawle ⁊ he hit nawt nuste. ȝet is meast dred of
20 hwen þe sweoke of helle eggeð to a þing þ þuncheð
swiðe god mid alle. ⁊ is þah sawle bone. ⁊ wei to deadlich
sunne. Swa he deð as ofte as he ne mei wið open uuel
cuðen his strengðe. Na he seið ne mei ich nawt makien
þeos to sungín þurh ȝiuernesse.ˀ ant ich chulle as þe
25 wreastleare wrenchen hire þiderward as ha meast dreai
eð. ⁊ warpen hire o þ half ⁊ breiden ferliche adun ear
ha least wene. ⁊ eggeð hire toward se muchel abstinen
ce.ˀ þ ha is þe unstrengre i godes seruise. ⁊ to leaden se
f.60b heard lif. ⁊ pinín swa þ licome.ˀ þ te sawle asteorue.
He bihalt an oþer þ he ne mei nanesweis makien
luðere iþoncket. se luueful. ⁊ se reowðful is heorte. hire
Ich chulle makien hire he seið to reowðful mid alle.
5 Ich schal don hire se muchel þ ha schal luuien ahte.
þenchen leasse of godd. ⁊ leosen hire fame. ⁊ put þenne
a þulli þonc in hire softe heorte. Seinte Marie naueð
þe mon oðer þe wummon meoseise. ⁊ namon nule
don ham nawt. Me walde me ȝef ich bede. ⁊ swa ich
10 mahte helpen ham ⁊ don on ham ealmesse. bringeð
hire on to gederin. ⁊ ȝeouen al earst to poure. forðre
to oðer freond. Aleast makien feaste ⁊ wurðen al world
lich. forschuppet of ancre to husewif of halle. Godd
wat swuch feaste makeð sum hore. weneð þ ha wel do.ˀ
15 as dusie ⁊ adotede doð hire to understonden. flatrið hi
re of freolec. herieð ⁊ heoueð up þe ealmesse þ ha deð (M. 224)
hu wide ha is icnawen. ant heo let wel of ⁊ leapeð in orhel.
Sum seið inohreaðe þ ha gedereð hord. swa þet hire
hus mei ⁊ heo ba beon irobbet. Reowðe ouer reowðe. Þus
20 þe traitre of helle makeð him treowe readesmon. Ne
leue ȝe hím neauer. Dauið cleopeð him demonium
meridianum. briht schininde deouel. Ant seínte pawel.ˀ

f. 60b. 3 heorte. hire *marked for transposition with two strokes above each* h.

angelum lucis. ꝥ is. engel of liht. for swuch ofte he mak
eð him ⁊ schaweð him to moníe. Na sihðe ꝥ ȝe seoð.·
ne i swefne ne waken.· ne telle ȝe bute dweole. for nis 25
hit bute his gile. he haueð wise men of hali ⁊ of heh
lif ofte swa bichearret. as þe ꝥ he com to i wummone
liche i þe wildernesse. seide ha wes igan o dweole as meos
eise þing efter herbearhe. Ant te oþer hali mon ꝥ he ma f. 61a
kede iléuen ꝥ he wes engel. bi his feader.· ꝥ he wes þe deo
uel. ⁊ makede him to slean his feader. swa ofte þerbiuor
en he heafde iseid him eauer soð. forte biswiken him sari
liche on ende. Alswa of þe hali mon ꝥ he makede cumen 5
ham forte dealen his feader feh.· to neodfule ⁊ to poure. se
longe ꝥ he deadliche sunegede o wummon. ⁊ swa feol in to
unhope.· ⁊ deide ín heaued sunne. Of mon þe spekeð wið
ow þulliche talen hereð. hu ȝe schulen witen ow wið þes
deofles wiltes.· ꝥ he ow ne bichearre. Sum of ow sumchear 10
re he makede to leuen. ꝥ hit were fikelunge ȝef ha spe
ke feire. ⁊ ȝef ha eadmodliche meande hire neode. ȝef
ha þonckede mon of his goddede. ⁊ wes mare ouerhohe
forte acwenchen chearite.· þen rihtwisnesse. Sum he is
umben to makien se swiðe fleon monne froure.· ꝥ ha 15
falleð i deadlich sar. ꝥ is accidie. oðer in to deop þoht
swa ꝥ ha dotie. Sum heateð swa sunne.· ꝥ ha haueð ouer
hohe of oþre þe falleð. þe schulde wepen for hire. ⁊ sare
dreden for aswuch onont hire seoluen. ⁊ seggen as þe ha
li mon þe seac ⁊ weop ⁊ seide. þa me him talde þe fal of 20
(M. 226) an of his breðren. Ille hodie. ego cras. weilawei strongli
che wes he itemptet ear he swa feolle. as he feol to dei.· ich
mei qð he alswa fallen to marhen.

NV míne leoue sustren monie temptatiuns ich hab
be ow inempnet under þe seoue sunnen. nawt þah 25
þe þusent fald ꝥ me is wið itemptet. Ne mahte ich wene
ham namon nomeliche nempnin. Ah i þeo þe beoð iseid.·
alle beoð bilokene. lut beoð i þis world oðer nan mid
alle. ꝥ ne beo wið hare sum oðerhwile ítemptet. He f. 61b

f. 61a. 24 *large blue initial* N *between* 23 *and* 26, *ornamented with red line-patterns within, and in margin from* 20, *with trails deep into bottom margin; in left margin directing* N.

haueð se monie buistes ful of his letuaires þe luðere
leche of helle. þe forsakeð an:· he beot an oðer forð anan
riht. þe þridde. þe feorðe. ⁊ swa eauer forð aþet he cume o
5 swuch:· ꝥ me on ende underuo. ⁊ he þenne wið ꝥ birleð
him ilome. þencheð her of þe tale of his ampoiles.
Héreð nu as ich bihet aȝeín alle fondunges moni
cunne froure. ⁊ wið godes grace þrefter þe Salue.

Siker beo of fondunge hwa se eauer stont in heh
10 lif. Ant þis is þe earste froure. for eauer se herre tur:·
se haueð mare windes. ȝe beoð tur ow seoluen mine
leoue sustren. ah ne drede ȝe nawt hwil ȝe beoð se treo
weliche ⁊ se feste ilimet wið lím of anred luue euch (M. 228)
of ow to oþer. for na deofles puf ne þurue ȝe dreden
15 bute ꝥ lím falsi. ꝥ is to seggen. bute luue bitweonen
ow þurh þe feond wursi. Sone se ei unlimeð hire:· ha
bið sone iswipt forð:· bute ȝef þe oþre halden hire:·
ha bið sone ikeast adun as þe lowse stan is from þe
tures cop:· in to þe deope dich of sum suti sunne.

20 NV an oðer elne. Muchel ah to frourin ow hwen
ȝe beoð itemptet. Þe tur nis nawt asailet ne castel
ne cite. hwen ha beoð iwunnen. Alswa þe helle weor
rur ne asaileð nan wið fondunge. þe he haueð in
his hond:· ah deð þeo þe he naueð nawt. for þi leoue
25 sustren hwa se nis nawt asailet:· ha mei sare beon of
dred leste ha beo biwunnen.

Þe þridde cunfort is. ꝥ ure lauerd seolf iþe pater noster tea
cheð us to bidden. Et ne nos índucas in temptationem.
f. 62a ꝥ is. lauerd feader ne suffre þu nawt þe feond ꝥ he leade us
allunge in to fondunge. lo neomeð ȝeme. he nule nawt
ꝥ we bidden ꝥ we ne beon nawt ifondet:· for ꝥ is ure purga
toire. ure cleansing fur. Ah ꝥ we ne beon nawt allunge i
5 broht þrín wið consens of heorte. wið skiles ȝettunge.

f. 61b. 9 *large red initial* S *between* 8 *and* 11, *with tail to* 15, *ornamented with blue within, and in margin from* 6 *to* 17. 20 *large blue initial* N *between* 19 *and* 22, *with red pattern within, and red lines in margin from* 17 *to* 22; *the bow partly hides* v *of* Nv. 27 *large red initial* Þ *between* 26 *and* 28, *with tapered stem from* 24 *to curled tail deep in bottom margin; blue pattern within, and in margin from* 23 *to present bottom edge; the* e *of* þe *almost covered.*

Þe feorðe froure is sikernesse of godes help iþe fehtunge
aȝeín as seinte pawel witneð. Fidelis est deus qui non sínít
nos temptari ultra quam pati possumus. set ⁊ cetera. Godd
he seið is
treowe nule he neauer suffrín ꝥ te deouel tempti us ouer
ꝥ he sið wel ꝥ we mahen þolien. Ah i þe temptatiun he ha 10
ueð iset to þe feond a mearke as þah he seide. Tempte
hire swa feor.' ah ne schalt tu gan na forðre. ant swa feor
he ȝeueð hire strengðe to wið stonden. þe feond ne mei
M. 230) nawt forðre gan a pricke. ANt þis is þe fifte fro
ure. ꝥ he ne mei na þing don us.' bute bi godes leaue. 15
ꝥ wes wel ischawet as þe godspel teleð. þa þe deoflen þet
ure lauerd weorp ut of a mon.' bisohten ⁊ seiden. Si eicitis
nos hínc.' mittite nos in porcos. ȝef þu heonne dríuest
us.' do us i þeos swín her. þe eoden þer an heorde. Ant he
ȝettede ham. lo hu ha ne mahten nawt fule swin swen 20
chen wið uten his leaue. Ant te swín ananriht urnen
an urn to þe sea.' to adrenchen ham seoluen. Seinte Ma
rie swa he stonc to þe swín. ꝥ ham wes leoure to adren
chen ham seoluen.' þen forte beoren him. ant an unseli
sunful godes ilicnesse bereð him in his breoste. ant ne 25
nimeð neauer ȝeme. Al ꝥ he dude iob.' eauerhe nom leue
þrof ed ure lauerd. Þe tale i dyaloge lokið ꝥ ȝe cunnen.
hu þe hali mon wes iwunet to seggen to þe deofles neddre.
Si licenciam accepisti.' ego non prohibeo. ȝef þu hauest f. 62b
leaue do sting ȝef þu maht. ⁊ bead forð his cheke. ah he
nefde þa nan bute to offearen hím ȝef bileaue him tru
kede. ⁊ hwen godd ȝeueð him leaue on his leoue children
hwi is hit bute for hare muchele biheue þah hit ham 5
Þe Seste confort is ꝥ ure lauerd hwen ℂ.greuí sare.
he þoleð ꝥ we beon itemptet.' he pleieð wið us as þe

f. 62a. 6 *large blue initial* þ *between* 5 *and* 8, *the bow nearly covering following* e; *tapering stem from* 3 *ending in tail* 13; *red lines within, and in margin line-patterns from above* 1 *to* 15; *directing* þ *in left margin.* 8, 9, 10 Godd *to* þolien *underlined. In the right margin a hand drawn with forefinger pointing between* 7 *and* 8, *and to its right a mark* ×; *another hand pointing to* mei 13. 14 *a small red initial* A *touched with blue lines.*

f. 62b. 6 *large blue initial* þ *between* 5 *and* 8, *stem in margin between*

moder wið hire ȝunge deorling. flið from him ⁊ hut
híre. ⁊ let him sitten ane. ⁊ lokin ȝeorne abuten cleo
10 pien dame dame. ⁊ wepen ane hwile. ⁊ þenne wið spred
de earmes leapeð lahhinde forð. cluppeð ⁊ cusseð ⁊ wi
peð his ehnen. Swa ure lauerd let us ane iwurðen oðer
hwile. ⁊ wiðdraheð his grace. his cunfort ⁊ his elne. þet
we ne findeð swetnesse i na þing ꝥ we wel doð. ne sauur (M. 232)
15 of heorte. ⁊ þah i ꝥ ilke point ne luueð us ure lauerd
neauer þe leasse. ah deð hit for muche luue. Ant ꝥ un
derstod wel dauið þa he seide. Non me derelinquas
usque quaque. Allunge qð he lauerd ne leaf þu me nawt. lo
hu he walde ꝥ he leafde him.' ah nawt allunge. Ant six
20 acheisuns notið. hwi godd for ure god wiðdraheð
him oðerhwiles. AN is ꝥ we ne pruden. AN oðer ꝥ we
cnawen ure ahne feblesce. Vre muchele unstrengðe ⁊
ure wacnesse. Ant þis is a swiðe muche god as seint
gregoire seið. Magna perfectio est sue inperfectionis cog
25 nitio. ꝥ is. muche godnesse hit is to cnawen wel his
wrecchehead ⁊ his wacnesse. Ecclesiasticus. Intemptatus
qualia scit.
Hwet wat he seið Salomon þe ꝥ is unfondet. ⁊ seint
austín bereð seín⟨t⟩ gregoíre witnesse. wið þeose wordes.
f. 63a Melior est animus cui propria est infirmitas nota.' quam
qui scrutatur celorum fastigia ⁊ terrarum fundamenta.
Betere is
þe þe truddeð ⁊ ofsecheð wel ut his ahne feblesce.' þen
þe þe meteð hu heh is þe heouene.' ⁊ hu deop þe eorðe.
5 Hwen twa beoreð a burðerne. ⁊ te oþer leaueð hit.' þenne
mei þe þe up haldeð hít felen hu hit weieð. Alswa leoue
suster hwil ꝥ godd wið þe bereð þi temptatiun.' nast tu
neauer hu heui hit is. ⁊ for þi ed sum chearre he leaueð
þeane. ꝥ tu understonde þin ahne feblesce ⁊ his help cleo
10 pie. ⁊ ȝeie lude efter him ȝef he is to longe. Hald hit

3 *and* 9; *red lines within, and in margin from above* 1 *to* 13; *a blue paragraph before* .greuí. *In left margin a hand with forefinger pointing to* he þoleð 7. 19 *above* A *of* Ant *two strokes, and in left margin* Nota *and two strokes.* 26, 27 Ecclesiasticus *to* unfondet *underlined with mark* × *in left margin.* 28 sein⟨t⟩: t *interlined with caret.*

wel þe hwile up ne derue hit te se sare. Hwa se is siker
of sucurs ꝥ him schal cume sone. ⁊ ȝelt tah up his cas
tel to his wiðeriwines: swiðe he is to edwiten. Þencheð
her of þe tale hu þe hali mon in his fondunge seh bi
west toȝeines hím se muche ferd of deoflen. ⁊ forleas 15
for muche dred þe strengðe of his bileaue. aþet te oðre
seiden him. Bihald qð he bi esten. Plures nobiscum sunt
(M. 234) quam cum illis we habbeð ma þen heo beoð to help on ure
halue. for þe þridde þing is ꝥ tu neauer ne beo al siker.
for sikernesse streoneð ȝemeles ⁊ ouerhohe. ⁊ ba þeose 20
streoníð inobedience. Þe feorðe acheisun is hwi ure lauerd
hut hím: ꝥ tu seche him ȝeornluker. ⁊ cleopie ⁊ wepe efter
him as deð þe lutel baban efter his moder. Þrefter is
þe fifte. ꝥ tu his ȝeíncume underuo þe gleadluker. Þe
Seste ꝥ tu þrefter þe wisluker wite him. hwen þu ha 25
uest icaht him ⁊ festluker halde. ⁊ segge wið his leof
mon. Tenuí eum nec dimittam. þeose six reisuns beoð
under þe seste froure þe ȝe mahen habben mine leo
ue sustren aȝeines fondunge. f. 63b

Þe Seoueðe confort is. ꝥ alle þe hali halhen weren
wodeliche itemptet. Nim of þe heste on alre earst.
To seinte peter seide ure lauerd. Ecce sathan expetiuit
uos ut cribraret sicut triticum ⁊ cetera. lo qð he sathan is 5
ȝeorne abuten forte ridli þe ut of mine icorene. Ah
ich habbe for þe bisoht ꝥ ti bileaue allunge ne tru
kie. Seint pawel hefde as he teleð him seolf flesches
pricunge. Datus est michi stimulus carnis mee. ⁊ bed ure
lauerd
ȝeorne ꝥ he dude hit from hím. ant he nalde ah seide. 10
Sufficit tibi gratia mea. Virtus in infirmitate perficitur. ꝥ is

26 *in right margin a mark* × *and below in 16th-century hand* cantic^s^.
16, 17 oðre seiden, *sic for sg.* 27 Tenuí *to* dimittam *underlined.*
f. 63b. 2 *large red initial* Þ *between* 1 *and* 4, *with tapered stem from high in top margin, ending at* 11 *in curled tail; blue line-patterns within, and in margin from letter-top to* 18. 7 *to* 12: *in left margin downward scribble, overlying the ornament of initial* Þ; *a mark* × *opposite* 9. *Blue marks, offset from ornament of* f. 64, *in right margin at ends of* 10 *and* 12. 8 Seinte *with final* e *erased* (*cf.* f. 17b. 25).

mi grace schal wite þe ꝥ tu ne beo ouercumen. Beo strong
in unstrengðe ꝥ is muche mihte. Alle þe oþre beoð i
crunet þurh feht of fondunge. Seínte Sare nes ha
15 fulle þreottene ȝer itemptet of hire flesch? Ah for þi ꝥ
ha wiste ꝥ i þe muchele angoise aras þe muchele me
de:' nalde ha neauer eanes bisechen ure lauerd ꝥ he allun
ge deliurede hire þrof:' ah þis wes hire bone. Domine da
michi uirtutem resistendi. Lauerd ȝef me strengðe forte
20 wiðstonden. Efter þreottene ȝer com þe acursede gast
þe hefde hire itemptet blac ase blamon ⁊ bigon to gre (M. 236)
den. Sare þu hauest me ouercumen. ant heo hím ond
swerede. þu lihest qð ha ful þing. nawt ich ah ha
ueð iesu crist mi lauerd. lo þe sweoke hu he walde ma
25 kien hire aleast to leapen in to prude. ah ha wes wel
war þrof ⁊ turnde al þe meistrie to godes strengðe.
Sein Beneit. Seínt Antonie. ⁊ te oþre wel ȝe wíten
hu ha weren itemptet. ⁊ þurh þe temptatiuns:' ipru
f. 64a uede to treowe champiuns. ⁊ swa wið rihte ofse⟨r⟩ueden
Ant þis is þe eahtuðe elne ¶.kempene crune.
þet alswa as þe goltsmið cleanseð ꝥ gold iþe fur:'
alswa deð godd te sawle i fur of fondunge.

5 Þe Niheðe confort is. ꝥ ȝef þe feond wið fondunge
greueð þe sare:' þu greuest him hwen þu edstondest
hundret siðe sarre. for þreo reisuns nomeliche. þe an is
ꝥ he forleoseð as origene seið his strengðe forte temptin:'
eauer mare þer onuuen of swuch manere sunne. þe oþ
10 er is ꝥ he forðluker echeð his píne. Þe þridde fret his
heorte of sar grome ⁊ of teone. ꝥ he unþonc hise téð
i þe temptatiun ꝥ tu stondest aȝeín:' muchleð þí mede.
ant for píne ꝥ he wende forte drahe þe toward:' breideð
þe crune of blisse. ⁊ nawt ane an ne twa:' ah ase feole
15 siðen as þu ouerkimest hím:' ase feole crunen. ꝥ is to seg
gen. ase feole mensken of misliche murhðen. for swa
seín Beornard seið. Quotiens uíncis:' totiens coronabe

f. 64a. 1 ofse⟨r⟩ueden: r *with caret interlined in paler ink.* 2 *small blue initial* A *touched with red lines; directing* a *in left margin; a blue paragraph before* .kempene. 5 *large red initial* Þ *between* 4 *and* 6, *with tapered and curled stem in margin,* 3 *to* 9; *blue line-patterns within, and in margin from* 2 Ant *to* 15; *directing* þ *in left margin.*

ris. Þe tale i vitas patrum witneð þis ilke:˙ of þe deciple þe
set biuoren his meistre. ant his meistre warð o slepe
hwil ꝥ he learde hím. ⁊ slepte aðet mid niht. þa he a 20
wakede:˙ art tu qð he ȝet her:˙ ga ⁊ slep swiðe. Þe hali
mon his meistre warð eft o slep sone as þe þe hefde
þerbiuoren ibeon imuche wecche. ⁊ seh aswiðe feier
stude. ⁊ iset forð atrone. ⁊ þron seoue crunen. ⁊ com a
(M. 238) steuene ⁊ seide. þis sege ⁊ þeose crunen haueð þin deci 25
ple þis ilke niht ofsaruet. Ant te hali mon abreaid
⁊ cleopede him to hím. Sei qð he hu stod te hwil þu
as ich slepte sete biuore me? Ich þohte qð he ofte ꝥ
ich walde awakenín þe. ⁊ for þu sleptest swote:˙ ne mah f. 64b
ich for reowðe. Ant þenne þohte ich gan awei to slepen
for me luste. ⁊ nalde bute leaue. Hu ofte qð his meister
ouercome þu þi þoht þus? Seoue siðen seide he. þa under
stond his meister wel hwet weren þe seoue crunen. Seo 5
ue cunne blissen ꝥ his deciple hefde in eucha chearre of
seruet. ꝥ he wiðseide þe feond:˙ ⁊ ouercom him seoluen.

Al þus leoue sustren i wreastlunge of temptatíun ariseð
þe biȝete. Nemo coronabitur nisi qui legittime certauerit.
Ne schal nan beon icrunet seið seínt pawel. bute hwa se 10
strongliche ⁊ treoweliche fehteð aȝein þe world. aȝeín
him seolf. aȝeín þe feond of helle. Þeo fehteð treoweliche:˙
þe hu se ha eauer beoð íweorret wið þeos þreo wiðeriwines
nomeliche of þe flesch. hwuch se eauer þe lust beo. se hit
meadluker is:˙ wrínnið aȝeín festluker. ⁊ wiðseggeð þe 15
grant þrof wið anewile heorte ne prokie hit se swiðe. þeo
þe þus doð beoð iesu cristes feolahes. for ha doð as he dude:˙
honginde o rode. Cum gustasset acetum:˙ noluit bibere. ꝥ is.
he smahte ꝥ bittre drunch. ⁊ wiðdroh him anan. ⁊ nalde
hit nawt drínken þah he ofþurst were. Heo is þe swa deð 20
wið godd on his rode. þah hire þurste i þe lust. ⁊ te deouel

26 ofsaruet, *sic, from* ofearnet *by alteration of* e, n.

f. 64b. 1 mah: te *omitted.* 8 *blue initial* A *between* 7 *and* 9, *with tail in margin down to* 13, *ornamented with red lines and tendrils on the tail down to* 16. 9 legittime, *sic.* 10 seínt, *with final* e *erased* (*cf.* f. 17b. 25). 10, 11 *to left of tail, mark* × *and downward scribble; underlining with hasty strokes of* Ne schal nan beon icrunet seið . . . el. bute hwa . . . strongliche ⁊ treowliche.

beot hire his healewi to drínken.˙ Vnderstonde ⁊ þenche þah
ꝥ ter is galle under. Ant tah hit beo a píne.˙ betere is forte þo
lien þurst.˙ þen to beon iattret. let lust ouergan.˙ ⁊ hit te wu
25 le eft likin. Hwil þe ȝicchunge least hit þuncheð god to
gnuddín. ah þrefter me feleð hit bitterliche smeorten. wei
lawei. ⁊ moni an is for muchel heate se swiðe ofþurst mid (M. 240)
alle. ꝥ hwil ha drinkeð ꝥ drunch ne beo hit ne se bitter.˙ ne
f. 65a feleð ha hit neauer. ah gluccheð in ȝiuerliche. ne nimeð nea
uer ȝeme. Hwen hit is al ouer.˙ spit ⁊ schakeð ꝥ heaued. feð
on forte niuelín. ⁊ makien grim chere. ah to leate þenne.
Speowen hit anan ut wið schrift to þe preoste. for leaue
5 hit inwið; hit wule deað breden. for þi mine leoue sustren
beoð biuoren warre. ⁊ efter þe frouren þe beoð her iwritene
aȝeín alle fondunges secheð þeose saluen.

Aȝein alle temptatiuns. ⁊ nomeliche aȝein fleschliche.˙
Saluen beoð ⁊ bote under godes grace. Halie meditatiuns
10 inwarde ⁊ meadlese. ⁊ angoisuse bonen. Hardi bileaue. re
dunge. Veasten. wecchen. ⁊ licomliche swinkes. Oþres froure
forte speoke toward i þe ilke stunde ꝥ hire stont stronge.
Eadmodnesse. freolec of heorte. ⁊ alle gode þeawes beoð ar
mes i þis feht. ⁊ anrednesse of luue ouer alle þe oþre. Þe
15 his wepnen warpeð awei.˙ him luste beon iwundet.

Hali meditatiuns beoð bicluppet in a uers ꝥ wes ȝare
itaht ow mine leoue sustren. Mors tua. mors christi. Nota
culpe gaudia celi. Iudicíí terror. figantur mente fideli. ꝥ
is. þench ofte wið sar of þine sunnen. þench of helle wa
20 of heoueriches wunnen. þench of þin ahne deað of godes
deað o rode. þe grímme dom of domesdei.˙ munneð ofte
ofte i mode. Þench hu fals is þe worlt. hwucche beoð hire
meden. þench hwet tu ahest godd for his goddeden. Euchan (M. 242)
of þeose word walde a long hwile forte beo wel iopenet.
AH ȝef
25 ich hihi forðward.˙ demeori ȝe þe lengre. A word ich segge.
Ef

f. 65a. 3, 4 *an omission between* þenne . . . [þenne] speowen. 8 *small red initial* A *touched with blue lines; directing* a *in left margin.* 16 *small blue initial* H, *stem in margin between* 15, 17, *ornamented with red lines from* 12 *to* 21. 17, 19 *above* M *of* Mors *and* þ *of* þench ″; *in right margin* (17 *and* 19) ″Nota. 21, 22 ofte ofte, *sic.*

ter ower sunnen. hwen se ȝe þencheð of helle wa ⁊ of heoue
riches wunnen. understondeð ꝥ godd walde o sum wise scha
wín ham to men i þis world bi worltliche pinen ⁊ worltliche
wunnen. ⁊ schaweð ham forð as schadewe. for na lickre f. 65b
ne beoð ha to þe wunne of heouene. Ne to þe wa of helle
þen is schadewe to ꝥ þing ꝥ hit is of schadewe. ȝe beoð
ouer þis worldes sea.' up o þe brugge of heouene. lokið
ꝥ ȝe ne beon nawt þe hors eschif iliche þe schuncheð 5
for a schadewe. ⁊ falleð adun i þe weater of þe hehe brug
ge. To childene ha beoð þe fleoð a peínture þe þuncheð
ham grislich ⁊ grureful to bihalden. Wa ⁊ wunne i þis
world al nis bute peíntunge. al nis bute schadewe.

Nawt ane hali meditatiuns as of ure lauerd. ⁊ of alle 10
his werkes. ⁊ of alle his wordes. of þe deore leafdi ⁊ of al
le hali halhen. ah oþres þohtes sum chearre i meadlese
fondunges habbeð iholpen. fowr cunne nomeliche
to þeo þe beoð of flesches fondunges meadlese asailet
Dredfule. wunderfule gleadfule. ⁊ sorhfule. willes wið 15
ute neod areret iþe heorte. as þenchen hwet tu wald
est don ȝef þu sehe openliche stonde biuore þe. ⁊ ȝeoni
ende wide up o þe.' þen deouel of helle. as he deð dearn
liche i þe fondunge. ȝef me ȝeide fur fur. ꝥ te chirche
bearnde. ȝef þu herdest burgurs breoke þine wahes. 20
þeos ⁊ oþre þulliche dredfule þohtes. wunderfule ant
gleadfule.' as ȝef þu sehe iesu crist. ⁊ herdest him easki
þe hwet te were leouest efter þi saluatiun. ⁊ þine leo
ueste freond of þing o þisse líue. ⁊ beode þe cheosen wið
ꝥ tu wiðstode. ȝef þu sehe al witerliche heouene ware 25
(M. 244) ⁊ helle ware i þe temptatiun bihalde þe ane. ȝef me
come ⁊ talde þe ꝥ mon ꝥ te is leouest þurh sum mira
cle as þurh steuene of heouene. were icoren to pape.
⁊ alle oþre swucche. wunderfule ⁊ sorhfule. as ȝef þu her f. 66a
dest seggen ꝥ mon ꝥ te is leouest were ferliche adrenct.
isleín oþer imurðret. ꝥ tine sustren weren in hare
hus forbearnde. þulliche þohtes ofte i fleschliche saw
len wrencheð ut sonre fleschliche temptatiuns.' þen sum 5

f. 65b. 2 helle: lle *on partial erasure of* ou. 24 freond, *for gen.*
10 *small red initial* N; *blue lines within, and in margin from* 6 *to* 13.

of þe oþre earre. Inwarde ⁊ meadlese. ⁊ ancrefule bonen
biwinneð sone sucurs ⁊ help ed ure lauerd. aȝeines flesch
es fondunges ne beon ha neauer se ancrefule ne se fulito
hene.' þe deouel of helle duteð ham swiðe. for teke ꝥ ha
10 draheð adun sucurs aȝein hím. ⁊ godes hond of heoue
ne.' ha doð him twa hearmes. bindeð him ⁊ bearneð. lo
her preoue of baðe. Publius an hali mon wes in his bonen.
⁊ com þe feond fleonninde bi þe lufte. ⁊ schulde al on
toward te west half of þe worlt. þurh Iulienes heast
15 þe empereur. ⁊ warð ibunden heteueste wið þe hali mon
ne bonen þe oftoken hím as ha fluhen uppard toward
heouene. ꝥ he ne mahte hider ne þider ten dahes fulle.
Nabbe ȝe alswa of Ruffin þe deouel beliales broðer in
ower englische boc of seinte Margarete. Of ꝥ oðer me
20 redeð ꝥ he gredde lude to seín Bartholomew þe muchel
wes ibenen. Incendunt me orationes tue. Bartholomew wa
me. Þine beoden forbearneð me. Hwa se mei þurh godes
ȝeoue i beoden habbe teares.' ha mei don wið godd al þet
ha eauer wule. for swa we redeð. Oratio lenit. lacrima
cogit. hec
25 ungit. illa pungit. Eadi bone softeð ⁊ paieð ure lauerd.
ah teares doð him strengðe. Beoden smirieð him wið
softe olhnunge. ah teares prikieð him ne ne ȝeoueð
him neauer pes ear þen he ȝetti ham al ꝥ ha easkið. **(M. 246)**
f. 66b hwen me asaleð burhes oðer castel.' þeo wið innen
healdeð scaldinde weater ut. ⁊ werieð swa þe walles.
ant ȝe don alswa as ofte as þe feond asaileð ower
castel ⁊ te sawle burh.' wið ínwarde bonen warpeð ut
5 up on him scaldinde teares. ꝥ Dauið segge bi þe. Con
tribulasti capita draconum in aquis. þu hauest forscal
det te drake heaueð wið wallinde weater. ꝥ is wið hate
teares. þear as þis weater is.' sikerliche þe feond flið les
te he beo forscaldet. Eft an oþer. Castel þe haueð dich a
10 buten. ⁊ weater beo i þe dich.' þe castel is wel carles aȝeín
es his unwines. Castel is euch god mon ꝥ te deouel weor

f. 66a. 19 ꝥ oðer me*: a second* ꝥ *probably omitted after* oðer.

f. 66b. 1 asaleð, *sic. Red ornament of* H, f. 67, *has offset in red marks in right margin between* 3 *and* 10. 7 heaueð, *sic.*

reð. ah habbe ȝe deop dich of deop eadmodnesse·⁄ ⁊ wéte
teares þerto·⁄ ȝe beoð strong castel. Þe weorrur of helle
mei longe asailin ow ⁊ leosen his hwile. Eft me seið ⁊
soð hit is. ꝥ a muche wínd alið wið alute reín. ant te 15
sunne þrefter schineð þe schenre. Alswa a muche temp
tatiun. ꝥ is þe feondes bleas. afealleð wið a softe reín
of ane lut wordes teares. ⁊ soðe sunne schineð þrefter
schenre to þe sawle. þus beoð teares gode wið inwarde
bonen. ant ȝef ȝe understondeð ich habbe iseid of ham 20
her fowr muchele efficaces for hwi ha beoð to luuien.
In alle ower neoden sendeð cwicliche anan þes sonde
toward houene. for as Salomon seið. Oratio humilian
tis se penetrat nubes. ⁊ cetera. ꝥ is. þe eadmodies bone þur
leð þe weolcne. ant ter seið seint austin. Magna est 25
uirtus pure conscientie que ad deum intrat. ⁊ mandata peragit
ubi caro peruenire nequit. O muchel is þe mihte of schir
⁊ cleane bone þe flið up ⁊ kimeð ín biuoren almihti
godd. ⁊ deð þe ernde se wel. ꝥ godd haueð o liues boc f. 67a
iwriten al ꝥ ha seið. as sein Beornard witneð. edhalt
hire wið him seolf. ⁊ sent adun his engel to don al þet
ha easkeð. Nule ich her of bone segge namare.

Hardi bileaue bringeð þe deouel o fluht ananrihtes. 5
(M. 248) þet wítneð seín Iame. Resistite diabolo ⁊ fugiet a uobis.
Edstont ane þe feond·⁄ ⁊ he deð him o fluhte. Edstond·⁄
þurh hwet strengðe? Seinte peter teacheð. Cui resisti
te fortes in fide. Stondeð aȝeín him wið stronge bileaue.
beoð hardi of godes help. ⁊ witeð hu he is wac. þe na 10
strengðe naueð on us bute of us seoluen. ne mei he
bute schawin forð sumhwet of his eapeware. ⁊ olhnín
oðer þreatin ꝥ me bugge þrof. Hweðer se he deð·⁄ scarn
ið hím. lahheð þe alde eape lude to bismere þurh treo
we bileaue. ⁊ he halt him ischent ⁊ deð him o fluht swi 15
ðe. Sancti per fidem uícerunt regna. ꝥ is. þe hali halhen al

18 wordes, *only in* A; te *omitted after* ⁊. 23 houene, *sic.* 23 *to* 25 *underlining with hasty strokes of* Salomon *and* is. þe *to* weolcne; 24 *in left margin mark* ×.

f. 67a. 5 *small blue initial* H *between* 4 *and* 6, *stem in margin* 3 *to* 5; *red line-patterns within, and in margin from* 1 *to* 15 (*directing* h *hidden in binding fold*). 16, 17 halhen al|hen alle *error for* halhen alle.

hen alle ouercomen þurh bileaue þe deofles rixlunge. ꝥ nis bute sunne. for ne rixleð he i nan.' bute þurh sunne ane. Neomeð nu gode ȝeme hu alle þe seouene 20 deadliche sunnen muhen beon afleiet þurh treowe bileaue. On earst nu of prude.

Hwa halt him muchel as þe prude deð. hwen he bihalt hu lutel þe muchele lauerd makede him ín wið a poure meidenes breoste. Hwa is ontful þe bi 25 halt wið ehnen of bileaue. hu iesu godd nawt for his god.' ah for oþres god. dude. ⁊ seide. ⁊ þolede.' al ꝥ he þo lede. þe ontfule ne kepte nawt ꝥ eani dealde of his god. ant godd almihti ȝet efter al ꝥ oþer lihte dun to helle. f. 67b forte sechen feolahes. ⁊ to deale wið ham þe god ꝥ he hefde. Lo nu hu frommard beoð ontfule ure lauerd. þe an cre þe wearnde an oþer a cwaer to lane. for ha hefde heoneward hire bileaue ehe. Hwa halt wreaððe (M. 250) 5 þe bihalt ꝥ godd lihte on eorðe.' to makien þrofald sahte bitweone mon ⁊ mon. bitweone godd ⁊ mon. bi tweone mon ⁊ engel. ant efter his ariste þa he com ⁊ schawde him.' þis wes his gretunge to his deore deciples. Pax uobis. Sahtnesse beo bitweonen ow. Neomeð nu 10 ȝeorne ȝeme. Hwen leof freond went from oþer. þe leaste wordes ꝥ he seið þeo schulen beo best edhalden. vre lauerdes leaste wordes þa he steah to heouene ⁊ leaf de his leoue freond in uncuðe þeode.' weren of swote luue ⁊ of sahtnesse. Pacem relinquo uobis. pacem meam 15 do uobis. ꝥ is. Sahtnesse ich do imong ow. Sahtnesse ich leaue wið ow. þis wes his druerie ꝥ he leafde ant ȝef ham in his departunge. In hoc cognoscetis quoð dicipuli mei sitis.' si dilectionem adinuicem habue ritis. Lokið nu ȝeorne. For his deorewurðe luue hwuch 20 a mearke he leide up on his icorene þa he steah to heo

22 *large red initial* H *between* 21, 24; *stem in margin between* 18, 24; *blue line-patterns within, and in margin from* 18 *to* 28; *directing* h *close to stitching of binding.* 24 *small blue initial* H *touched with red.* 25 iesu, *sic.*

f. 67b. 3 for, *sic, probably for* feor. 4 *small red initial* H *touched with blue lines.* 5 þrofald *sic.* 17, 18 quoð dicipuli, *sic: Vulgate* cognoscent omnes quia discipuli mei estis.

uene. IN hoc cognoscetis quod ⁊ cetera. Bi ꝥ ȝe schulen
icnaw
en qð he ꝥ ȝe beoð mine deciples.' ȝef swete luue ⁊ saht
nesse is eauer ow bitweonen. Godd hit wite ⁊ he hit wat.
me were leouere ꝥ ȝe weren alle o þe spitel uuel.' þen ȝe
weren ontfule oðer feol iheortet. for iesu is al luue. ⁊ i 25
luue he resteð him ⁊ haueð his wununge. In pace factus
est locus eius. Ibi confregit potencias. ar. s. gladium. ⁊ bellum.
ꝥ is.
iSahtnesse is godes stude. ant hwer se sahte is ⁊ luue.'
þear he bringeð to nawt al þes deofles strengðe. þer he f. 68a
brekeð his bohe hit seið. ꝥ beoð dearne. fondunges ꝥ he
scheot of feor. ⁊ his sweord baðe. ꝥ beoð temptatiuns keor
uínde of neh ⁊ kene. Neomeð nu ȝeorne ȝeme bi
moni forbisne hu god is anrednesse of luue.' ⁊ annes 5
se of heorte. For nis þing under sunne ꝥ me is leouere.'
ne se leof ꝥ ȝe habben. Nute ȝe þer men fehteð i þes
stronge ferdes. þe ilke þe haldeð ham feaste to gederes.'
(M. 252) ne muhe beo descumfit o neauer nane wise. Alswa hit is in
gastelich feht aȝeines þe deouel. Al his entente is forte 10
tweamen heorten. forte bineomen luue ꝥ halt men to
gederes. for hwen luue alið.' þenne beoð ha isundret. ⁊
te deouel deð him bitweonen ananriht ⁊ sleað on euche
halue. Dumbe beastes habbeð þis ilke warschipe. þet
hwen ha beoð asailet of wulf oðer of líun.' ha þrungeð 15
to gederes al þe floc feste. ⁊ makieð scheld of ham seolf
euch of heom to oþer. ⁊ beoð þe hwile sikere. ȝef eaní un
seli went ut.' hit is sone awuriet. Þe þridde. þer an geað
hím ane in a slubbrí wei.' he slit ⁊ falleð sone. þer monie
gað to gederes. ⁊ euch halt oþres hond.' ȝef eaní feð to slí 20
den.' þe oðer híne breid up ear he ful falle. ȝef ha wergið
euchan halt him bi oþer. fondunge is sliddrunge. þurh
wergunge beoð bitacnet þe unþeawes under slawðe. þe
beoð itemptet þruppe. þis is ꝥ sein gregoire seið. Cum nos

27 ar. s.: *read* arcum scutum.

f. 68a. 4 *small blue initial* N *touched with red lines* (*directing* n *hidden in binding fold*). *In right margin a hand, between* 7 *and* 10, *pointing towards* 6 leouere; *another between* 14 *and* 18 *pointing to* 14 þet. 24 itemptet, *sic for* inempnet.

25 nobis per orationis opem coniungimus. per lubricum inced-
entes :' quasi
adinuicem manus teneamus. vt tanto quisque amplius robo-
retur
quanto alteri ínnititur. Alswa i strong wind ⁊ swifte weattres
þe
me mot ouerwaden :' of monie euch halt oðer. þe isundrede
f. 68b is iswipt forð ⁊ forfeareð eauer. To wel we witen hu þe wei
of þis world is slubbri. hu þe wínd ⁊ te stream of fondun
ge aren stronge. Muche neod is ꝥ euch halde wið bisie
bonen ⁊ wið luue oþres honden. for as Salomon seið. Ve
5 soli quia cum ceciderit :' non habet subleuantem. Wa eauer
þe ane. for hwen he falleð :' naueð he hwa him areare.
Nan nis ane þe haueð godd to fére. ant ꝥ is euch ꝥ soð
luue haueð in his heorte. Þe Seoueðe forbisne is þis ȝef
ȝe riht telleð. Dust ⁊ greot as ȝe seoð. for hit is isundret
10 ⁊ nan ne halt to oþer :' a lutel windes puf to driueð (M. 254)
hit al to nawt. Þear hit is in a clot ilimet to gederes :'
hit lið al stille. An hondful of ȝerden beoð earueð to
breoken hwil ha beoð togederes. Euchan itweamet :' liht
liche bersteð. A treo þe wule fallen :' undersete hit wið an
15 oþer :' ⁊ hit stont feste. tweam ham :' ⁊ ba falleð. Nu ȝe hab
beð nihene. þus i þinges utewið neomeð forbisne. Hu
god is annesse of luue. ⁊ sometreadnesse ꝥ halt þe go
de somet ꝥ nan ne mei forwurðen. Ant þis wule iwiss
habben þe rihte bileaue. Bihald ȝeorne ⁊ understont
20 iesu cristes deorewurðe wordes ⁊ werkes. þe iluue weren
alle ⁊ i swetnesse. Ouer alle þing ich walde ꝥ ancren leor
neden wel þis lesceunes lare. for monie mare hearm is
beoð Samsones foxes. þe hefden þe neb euchan iwend
frommard oþer. ⁊ weren bi þe teiles iteiet to gederes. as
25 Iudicum teleð. ant in euchanes teil a blease bearninde.
Of þeose foxes ich spec feor þruppe. ah nawt o þisse wise.
Neomeð gode ȝeme hwet þis beo to seggen. Meturneð
þe neb bliðeliche towart þíng ꝥ me luueð. ⁊ frommard
f. 69a þing ꝥ me heateð. Þeo þenne habbeð þe nebbes wrongwen

f. 68b. 18 iwiss (*with final flourish*); *cf.* ff. 78b. 28, 106a. 14. L *has* et certe hanc habere wlt recta fides.

de euch frommard oðer:· hwen nan ne luueð oþer. ah bí
þe teiles ha beoð somet. ⁊ beoreð þes deofles bleasen þe bru
ne of galnesse. On an oðer wise. teil bitacneð ende. In ha
re ende ha schulen beon ibunden to gederes as weren 5
Samsones foxes bi þe teiles. ⁊ iset bleasen þrin. ꝥ is ꝥ fur
Al þis is iseid mine leoue sustren. ꝥ ower leoue ¶ .of helle.
nebbes beon eauer iwent somet wið luueful semblant:· ⁊
wið swote chére. ꝥ ȝe beon aa wið annesse of an heorte ⁊
of a wil ilimet togederes. as hit iwriten is bi ure lauerdes 10
deore deciples. Multitudinis credentium erat cor unum
⁊ anima una. Pax uobis. þis wes godes gretunge to his
deore deciples. Grið beo bimong ow. ȝe beoð þe ancren of
englond swa feole togederes. twenti nuðe oðer ma. godd
i god ow mutli:· ꝥ meast grið is among. Meast annesse ⁊ 15
anrednesse. ⁊ sometreadnesse of anred lif efter a riwle.
Swa ꝥ alle teoð an. alle iturnt anesweis:· ⁊ nan frommard
oðer. efter ꝥ word is. for þi ȝe gað wel forð ⁊ spedeð in ow
er wei:· for euch is wiðward oþer ín an manere of liflade.
as þah ȝe weren an cuuent of lundene ⁊ of oxnefort. of 20
schreobsburi:· oðer of chester. þear as alle beoð an wið
an imeane manere. ant wið uten singularite. ꝥ isanful
frommardschipe. lah þíng i religiun. for hit to warpeð
annesse ⁊ manere imeane:· ꝥ ah to beon in ordre. þis
nu þenne ꝥ ȝe beoð alle as an cuuent. is ower hehe fa 25
me. þis is godd icweme. þis is nunan wide cuð. swa þet
ower cuuent biginneð to spreaden toward englondes
ende. Ȝe beoð as þe moderhus ꝥ heo beoð of istreonet.
ȝe beoð ase wealle. ȝef þe wealle woreð:· þe strunden wo f. 69b
rið alswa. A weila ȝef ȝe worið ne bide ich hit neauer.
ȝef ei is imong ow þe geað i singularite. ⁊ ne folheð
nawt þe cuuent. ah went ut of þe floc ꝥ is as in a cloistre.
ꝥ iesu is heh príur ouer. went ut as a teowi schep ⁊ mea 5
peð hire ane in to breres teilac. in to wulues muð toward

f. 69a. 7 *small red initial* A *with curled tail down to* 12, *blue line-ornament within, and along tail down to* 17; *directing* a *in left margin; blue paragraph before* .of helle. *On right margin of* 9, 10 *a scribble with mark* × *to the right.* 9 *to* 12 *from* ꝥ ȝe beon *to* P(ax *underlined. With* Pax *begins a passage not in* M, *ending* f. 69b. 11. 15 mutli, *sic.* 17 nan: nam *with last stroke partly erased.*

te þrote of helle. ȝef ei swuch is imong ow·˙ godd turne
híre in to floc. wende hire in to cuuent. ⁊ leue ow þe
beoð þrín. swa halden ow þrín·˙ ꝥ godd þe hehe priur
10 neome ow on ende þeonne up·˙ ín to þe cloistre of heo
uene. Hwil ȝe haldeð ow in an·˙ offearen ow mei þe feond
ȝef he haueð leaue. ah hearmín nawt mid alle. ꝥ he wat **(M. 256)**
ful wel. ⁊ is for þi umben deies ⁊ nihtes. to unlímín ow wið
wreaððe oðer wið luðer onde. ant sent mon oþer wum
15 mon. þe telle þe an bi þe oþer sum suhinde sahe þet
suster ne schulde nawt segge bi suster. Ower nan ich
forbeode ow ne leue þe deofles sondes mon. ah lokið ꝥ
euch of ow icnawe wel hwen he spekeð i þe Vuele mon
nes tunge. ⁊ segge ananrihtes. Vre meistre haueð iwri
20 ten us as in heast to halden. ꝥ we tellen him al ꝥ euch
of oþer hereð. ant for þi loke þe ꝥ tu na þing ne telle
me·˙ ꝥ ich ne muhe him tellen. þe mei don þe amende
ment. ⁊ con swaliches don hit. ꝥ ich ⁊ tu baðe ȝef we beoð
i þe soð·˙ schule beon unblamet. Euch noðele warni oþ
25 er þurh ful siker sondesmon sweteliche ⁊ luueliche
as hire leoue suster of þing ꝥ ha misnimeð ȝef ha
hit wat to soðe. ⁊ makie hwa se bereð ꝥ word. recordín
hit ofte biuoren hire ear ha ga·˙ hu ha wule seggen. ꝥ
f. 70a ha ne segge hit oðerweis·˙ ne cluti þerto mare. for a lute
clut mei ladlechin swiðe·˙ a muchel hal péce. þeo þe ed hi
re suster þis luue salue underueð·˙ þoncki hire ȝeorne.
⁊ segge wið þe salmwruhte. Corripiet me iustus in misericordia.
5 ⁊ increpabit me. oleum aú. pec. non inp. c. m. Ant þrefter
wið Salomon. Meliora sunt uulnera corripientis·˙ quam
oscula blandientis. ȝef ha ne luuede me·˙ nalde ha nawt
warní me i misericorde. leouere me beoð hire wunden·˙ þen

f. 69b. *With* 10, 11 heouene *ends passage not in* M. 19 *to* 24 *from* ⁊ segge *to* beon unblamet *not in* M. 24 noðele, *sic for* noðeles.

f. 70a. *A cockling and staining of the vellum proceeds from upper edge, entering at* 1 h(it *and* þ)er, *in V-shaped patch with point in* 9 cosses. 5 *read* autem peccatoris non inpinguet caput meum. 7 *in right margin*: + *above* þreaȝendes *written in pale brown ink by 16th-century hand imitating Anglo-Saxon letters* (þ, r, ȝ, s); 8 *above* hire *in pale ink a small* ×: *an attempt to replace* hire *by English for* corripientis. 8, 9 leouere me beoð h *and* fikiende cosses. þus *underlined*;

fikiende cosses. Þus ondswerie eauer. ⁊ ȝef hit is oðerweis
þen þe oðer understont:' sende hire word aȝeín þrof:' 10
luueliche ⁊ softe. ⁊ te oþer leue ananriht. for ꝥ ich chul
le alswa. ꝥ euch of ow luuíe oþer as hire seoluen. ȝef
þe feond bitweonen ow to blaweð eani wreaððe. oþer
great heorte ꝥ iesu crist forbeode. ear ha beo iset wel:'
nawt ane to neomen godes flesch ⁊ his blod:' ne wur 15
ðe nan se witles. ah ȝet ꝥ is leasse. ꝥ ha eanes ne bihal
de þeron. ne loki i ful wreaððe toward him þe lihte to
mon in eorðe of heouene. to makien þreouald sahte.
as is iseid þruppe. Sende eiðer þenne oþer word ꝥ ha
(M. 258) haueð imaket hire as þah ha were biuoren hire:' ead 20
modliche Venie. ant þeo þe ear ofdraheð þus luue of hí
re suster. ⁊ ofgeað sahte. ⁊ nimeð þe gult toward hire
þah þe oþer hit habbe mare:' ha schal beo mi deore
wurðe ⁊ mi deore dohter. for ha is godes dohter. he hím
seolf hit seið. Beati pacifici quoniam filíí dei uocabuntur. 25
þus prude. ⁊ onde, ⁊ wreaððe. beoð ihwer afleiet hwer se
soð luue is ⁊ treowe bileaue:' to godes milde werkes:' ⁊ luue
fule wordes. Ga we nu forðre to þe oþre on a reawe.

Hwa mei beo for scheome slummi. sloggi. ⁊ slaw:' þe f. 70b
bihalt hu swiðe bisi ure lauerd wes on eorðe. per-
transiit bene
fatiendo ⁊ sanando omnes. Efter al ꝥ oðer bihaldeð hu he
i þe euen of his lif swong o þe hearde rode. Oþre habbeð
reste. fleoð liht i chambre. hudeð ham hwen ha beoð ile 5
te blod on an earm eðre. Ant he o munt caluaire:'
steah ȝet o rode herre. ne ne swong neauer mon se swiðe
ne se sare as he dude ꝥ ilke dei ꝥ he bledde o fif half bro
kes of ful brade wunden ⁊ deope. wið uten þe eþren capi
tale þe bledden on his heaued under þe kene þornene 10
crune. ⁊ wið uten þe ilke reowfule garces of þe luðere
scurgunge ȝont al his leofliche lich. nawt ane o þe
schonken. Toȝeines slawe ⁊ sleperes:' is swiðe openliche his
earliche ariste from deaðe to líue.

× *in margin.* 12 luuíe, *sic* (*as also* G), *probably correct.*

f. 70b. 1 *large red initial* H *standing up into top margin, ornamented with a few blue lines from top edge to* 4.

15 Aȝeínes ȝisceunge is his muchele pouerte þe weox eauer up on him se lengre se mare. for þa he wes iboren earst. þe ꝥ wrahte þe eorðe. ne fond nawt on eorðe swa muche place as his lutle licome mahte beon ileid up on. Swa nearow wes ꝥ stude. ꝥ unneaðe his moder ⁊
20 iosep seten þrín. ant swa ha leiden him on heh up in a crecche wið clutes biwrabbet as ꝥ godspel seið. Pan (M. 260) nis eum inuoluít. þus feire he wes ischrud þe heouenliche schuppent þe schrudeð þe sunne. Her efter þe poure mei den of heouene fostrede him ⁊ fedde wið hire lutle milc
25 as meiden deh to habben. þis wes muche pouerte. ah mare com þrefter. for lanhure þeȝet he hefde fode as feol to hím. ⁊ i stude of ín.· his cradel herbearhede him. Seoððen as he meande him.· nefde he hwer he mahte his heaued
f. 71a huden. filius hominis non habet ubi capud suum reclinet. Þus poure he wes of ín. of mete he wes se neodful.· ꝥ þa he hefde i ierusalem o palmsunnedei al dei ipreachet. ⁊ hit neoleche de niht.· he lokede abuten hit seið i þe godspel. ȝef ei walde
5 cleopien him to mete oþer to herbearhe.· ah nes þer nan. ant swa he wende ut of þe muchele burh.· in to Bethaníe. to Marie hus ⁊ to marthen. þer as he eode mid his decip les sum chearre. ha breken þe eares bi þe wei. ⁊ gnuddeden þe curnles ut bitweonen hare honden ⁊ eten for hunger.
10 ⁊ weren þeruore swiðe icalenget. ah alre meast pouerte com ȝet her efter. For steort naket he wes despuilet o þe rode. Þa he meande him ofþurst.· weater ne mahte he habben. ȝet ꝥ meast wunder is of al þe brade eorðe ne moste he habben a greot forte deien up on. Þe rode hefde a fot oðer
15 lute mare. ⁊ ꝥ wes to his pine. Hwen þe worldes wealdent walde beo þus poure. unbileuet he is þe luueð to muchel ant ȝisceð worldes weole ant wunne.

15 *large blue initial* A *between* 14 *and* 17, *with curled tail in margin down to* 21, *ornamented with red line-patterns to right, within, and in margin from* 11; *the elaboration of the tail* (*shaved at left edge*) *descends deep into bottom margin.* 21 crecche: checche *with first* h *altered to* r *without erasure of top and bow.*

f. 71a. 9 bitweonen: *first* n *altered from* r. 14 greot, *sic* (*probably for* grot).

Aȝeín glutunie is his poure pitance ꝥ he hefde o ro
de. Twa manere men habbeð neode to eote wel
(M. 262) Swinkinde ⁊ blodletene. þe dei ꝥ he wes baðe i sar swinc 20
⁊ ilete blod as ich nest seide. nes his pitance o rode bute a
spunge of galle. Loke nu hwa gruccheð ȝef ha þencheð
wel heron mistrum mel of unsauuree metes. of poure
pitance. Of na mon ne of na wummon ne schule ȝe
makie na man. ne pleaínín ow of na wone. bute to 25
sum treowe freond ꝥ hit mei amendín. ⁊ godín ham
oðer ow. ant ꝥ beo priueiliche iseid as under seel of schrift
ꝥ ȝe ne beon iblamet. ȝef ȝe of ei þing habbeð wone.'
⁊ sum freond ȝeorne freiní ow ȝef ȝe ei wone habbeð. ȝef f. 71b
ȝe hopieð god of hím.' ondswerieð o þis wise. lauerd godd for
ȝelde þe. Ich drede mare ich habbe þen ich were wurðe. ant
leasse wone ich þolie þen me neod wére. ȝef he easkeð ȝe
ornluker.' þonkið him ȝeorne. ⁊ seggeð. Ich ne dear nawt 5
lihen o me seoluen.' wone ich habbe ase riht is. Hwuch an
cre kímeð in to ancre hus to habben hire eise. Ah Nu
þu wult hit alles witen.' Vre lauerd te forȝelde. þis is nu an
þing ꝥ ich hefde neode to. ⁊ þus bid ure riwle ꝥ we schaw
ín to gode freond as oþre godes poure doð hare meosei 10
se wið milde eadmodnesse. ne nawt ne schule we forsa
ken þe grace of godes sonde.' ah þonkin him ȝeorne leste
he wreaðe him wið us ⁊ wiðdrahe his large hond ⁊ þrefter
wið to muche wone abeate ure prude. ant nis hit mu
chel hofles hwen godd beot his hond forð puttinde hi 15
re aȝeín segge. Ne kepe ich hit nawt haue þe seolf. Ich
wulle fondin ȝef ich mei libben her buten. þurh þis
ich habbe iherd þof swuch ꝥ nom uuel ende.

Aȝeín leccherie is his iborenesse of ꝥ cleane meiden
⁊ al his cleane lif ꝥ he leadde on eorðe. ⁊ alle þe 20

18 *large red initial* A *with curled tail down to* 25*; blue line-patterns to right, within, and in margin, and along tail* (*trailing deep into bottom margin*)*; directing* a *in left margin. The bottom right-hand corner of this folio is greasy and partly transparent; the initial* A *on reverse is visible and part of the writing, especially at the ends of* 25 *to* 28 *on this side.* 24 Of na *to end of paragraph not in* M.

f. 71b. 18 þof, *sic for* of. 19 *large blue initial* A *between* 18 *and* 21*; red line-patterns to right, within, and in margin from* 17 *to* 26.

hine fuleden. Þus lo þe articles. ꝥ beoð as þah me seide.
þe liðes of ure bileaue onont godes monhead hwa se
inwardliche bihalt ham.· fehteð toȝein þe feond þe
fondeð us wið þeose deadliche sunnen. For þi seið sein
25 te peter. christo in carne passo ⁊ uos eadem cogitatione
armeminí. Armið ow he seið wið þoht up o iesu crist
þe in ure flesch wes ipínet. Ant seinte pawel. Recogi
tate qualem aput semet ipsum sustinuit contradictionem ut
f. 72a non fatiget. Þencheð þencheð seið seínte pawel hwen ȝe
wergið i feht aȝeínes þe deouel.· hu ure lauerd seolf wiðseide
his fleschliche wil.· ⁊ wiðseggeð ower. Nondum enim usque
ad sanguinem restitistis. Ȝet nabbe ȝe nawt wiðstonden
5 aþet te schedunge of ower blod. þe ilke blisfule bodi þet
com of þe meiden ⁊ deide o þe rode niht ⁊ dei bi ow. nis bu
te a wah bitweonen. ⁊ euche dei he kimeð forð ⁊ schaweð him
to ow fleschliche ⁊ licomliche ínwið þe measse. biwrixlet
þah on oþres lite under breades furme. for in his ahne
10 ure ehnen ne mahten nawt þe brihte sihðe þolien. Ah swa
he schaweð him ow.· as þah he seide. lowr ich her hwet wulle
ȝe. seggeð me hwet were ow leof. hwerto neodeð ow? Meaneð
ower neode. ȝef þe feondes ferd. ꝥ beoð his temptatíuns asailið
ow swiðe.· ondswerieð hím ⁊ seggeð. Metati sumus castra iuxta
15 lapidem adiutoríí. Porro philistíím venerunt in afech. ȝe (M. 264)
lauerd wunder is. we beoð iloget her bi þe þet art stan of help.·
tur of treowe sucurs. castel of strengðe. ⁊ te deofles ferd is
woddre up on us þen up on eaní oþre. Þis ich neome of re

Transparency (see the recto) affects the bottom of this page, especially the beginnings of 26, 27, 28; *the decorations of the* A *on the recto are visible in right margin.*

f. 72a. 1 fatiget, *sic for* -etis (*as* M): *Vulgate* -emini; *in right margin a mark* ×. 1 *to* 5: *downward scribble in the right margin; a faint mark* + *opposite* 5; *underlining of* 1 sein)te pawel hwen ȝe; 4 nab)be ȝe nawt wiðston; 5 aþet te schedunge of ower blod. 5 *after* blod. M 262, 18 *to* blod 20, *omitted.* 14 Metati: *first* t *partly overwritten and stem raised.* 14 *mark* × *in right margin.* 14 *to* 16 *underlining of* Metati *to* adiutorii, *and* we beoð *to* help.

gum. for þer hit teleð al þus ꝥ israel godes folc com ⁊ logede him
bi þe stan of help. ⁊ te philistews comen in to afech. Philist 20
ews beoð unwihtes. Afech on ebreisch.' spealeð neowe wod- schí
pe. Swa hit is witerliche. hwen mon logeð him bi ure lauerd.'
þenne on earst biginneð þe deouel to weden. ah þer
hit teleð ꝥ israel wende sone þe rug. ⁊ weren fowr þusent iþe
fluht sariliche isleíne. Ne wende ȝe nawt te rug mine leo 25
ue sustren. ah wiðstondeð þe feondes ferd amidde þe for
heaued as is iseid þruppe wið stronge bileaue. ⁊ wið þe go
de Iosaphath sendeð beode sondesmon sone efter sucurs to þe
prince of heouene. IN parabolis. In nobis quidem non est tanta forti f. 72b
tudo ut possimus huíc multitudíni resistere que irruit super
nos. Set cum ignoremus quid agere debeamus.' hoc solum habemus
residuí. ut oculos nostros dirigamus ad te. sequitur. Hec dicit dominus uobis.
Nolite timere ⁊ ne paueatis hanc multitudínem. Non ením 5
est uestra pugna set dei. tantum modo confidenter state ⁊ uidebitis auxilium
dominí super uos. Credite in domino deo uestro.' ⁊ securi eritis. þis is ꝥ
englisch. IN us nis nawt deorewurðe lauerd swa muchel
ȝtrengðe. ꝥ we mahen wiðstonden þe deofles ferd þe is se
strong up on us. Ah hwen we swa beoð bisteaðet. swa stron 10
ge bistonden. ꝥ we mid alle na read ne cunnen bi us seol
uen.' þis an we mahe don. heouen ehnen up to þe mild
fule lauerd. þu send us sucurs. þu todreaf ure fan.' for to þe
we lokið. þus wið þe gode iosaphath hwen godd kímeð bi
uoren ow ⁊ freineð hwet ȝe wulleð. ⁊ in euch time hwen 15

22 logeð: g *altered from some other letter partly erased* (*probably* k).
23 lihen *crossed out, after* deouel to.

f. 72b. 1 parabolis: pabl' (*wrongly for* paralipomenon, *or* -is). IN pabl'. In *underlined with thick stroke. In left margin mark* ×, *and below it* Josaphat (*same hand as seen on* f. 70). *Scribbled line in left margin from* 2 *to* 13. 8 IN us *to* muche(l *underlined.* 14 god)e iosaphat(h *underlined.*

ȝe neode habbeð. schawið hit swa sweteliche to his swote
earen. ȝef he sone ne hereð ow:· ȝeieð luddre ⁊ meadleslu (M. 266)
ker. ⁊ þreatið ꝥ ȝe wulleð ȝelden up þe castel bute he
sende ow sonre help:· ⁊ hihi þe swiðere. Ah wite ȝe hu he ond
20 swerede iosaphath þe gode:· þus o þisse wise. Nolite timere
⁊cetera.
þus he onswereð ow hwen ȝe help cleopieð. Ne beo ȝe nawt
offearede. ne drede ȝe ham nawiht þah ha beon stronge
⁊ monie:· þe feht is min:· nawt ower. Sulement stondeð
sikerliche ⁊ ȝe schulen mí sucurs. hab
25 beð ane to me trusti bileaue:· ⁊ ȝe beoð al sikere. lokið
nu hwuch help is hardi bileaue. for al ꝥ help þe godd
bihat. þe strengðe to stonde wel:· al is in hire ane. Hardi
bileaue makeð stonden upriht. ⁊ te unwiht nís nawt laðre.
f. 73a For þi þis is his word ín ysaíe. Incuruare ut transeamus.
Buh þe
he seið duneward ꝥ ich mahe ouer þe. þeo buheð hire. þe to
hise fondunges buheð hire heorte. for hwil ha stont upriht:·
ne mei he nowðer up on hire rukín ne riden. Lo þe treitre
5 hu he seið. Incuruare ut transeamus. Buh þe let me leapen
up
nule ich þe nawt longe riden. ah ich chulle wenden ouer.
he liheð seið sein beornard. ne lef þu nawt þen traitre. Non
uult transire:· set residere. Nule he nawt wenden ouer:· ah
wule
ful feaste sitten. Sum wes ꝥ lefde hím. þohte he schulde sone
10 adun as he bihat eauer. Do he seið þis enchearre. ⁊ schrif
þe þrof to marhen. Buh þin heorte let me up. schec me wið
schrift adun ȝef ich alles walde ride þe longe. Sum as ich
seide lefde hím ⁊ beah him ⁊ he leop up. ⁊ rad hire baðe
dei ⁊ niht twenti ȝer fulle. ꝥ is. ha dude a sunne i þe il
15 niht þurh his procunge. ⁊ þohte ꝥ ha walde hire schríuen
ine marhen. ⁊ dude hit eft ⁊ eft ⁊ fealh swa i uuel wune. ꝥ ha
lei ⁊ rotede þrín swa longe as ich seide. ⁊ ȝef a miracle nere:·

24 *after* ȝe schulen: stonden sikerliche (*replacing* seon) *is crossed out in two strokes:* ston *and* den *to* liche.

f. 73a. 1 *mark* × *in right margin;* Buh þe *underlined with thick stroke.* 2 he *to* þeo *underlined.* 7 traitre: ra *abbreviated.* 14 il, *sic* (*? for* ilke *as* M). 26 swilli, *sic.*

þe pufte adun þen deouel þe set on hire se feaste.' ha hefde i
(M. 268) turplet wið him baðe hors ⁊ lade dun in to helle grunde. for
þi mine leoue sustren haldeð ow efne upriht i treowe bileaue. 20
Hardiliche ileueð ꝥ al þe deofles strengðe mealteð þurh
þe grace
of ꝥ hali sacrement hest ouer oþre. ꝥ ȝe seoð as ofte as þe preo
st measseð. þe meidene bearn iesu godd godes sune þe licomli
che lihteð oðerhwiles to ower ín. ⁊ inwið ow eadmodliche ní
með his herbearhe. Deuleset ha beoð to wake ⁊ to unwreaste 25
iheortet.' þe wið swilli gest hardiliche ne fehteð. ȝe schulen
bileaue habben. ꝥ al hali chirche deð. red. oþer singeð. ⁊ alle
hire sacremenz. strengeð ow gasteliche. ah nan ase forð ase
þis. for hit bríngeð to noht al þes deofles wiheles. Nawt f. 73b
ane his strengðes ⁊ his stronge turnes. ah deð his wiltfule
crokes. his wrenchfule wicchecreftes. ⁊ alle his ȝulunges.
ase lease swefnes. false schawunges. dredfule offearunges.
fikele ⁊ sweokele reades. ah þah hit were o godes half. ant 5
god forte donne. for ꝥ is his unwrench. as ich ear seide. ꝥ
hali men meast dredeð. ꝥ he haueð moni hali mon grim
liche biȝulet. hwen he ne mei nawt bringen to nan open
vuel.' he sput to a þing ꝥ þuncheð god. þu schuldest he
seið beo mildre. ⁊ leoten iwurðe þi chast. nawt trubli þín 10
heorte ⁊ sturien in to wreaððe. þis he seið for þi þet tu ne
schuldest nawt chastien for hire gult ne tuhte wel þí
meiden. ⁊ bringe þe in to ȝemeles i stude of eadmodnes
se. Eft riht þer toȝeines. ne let tu híre na gult toȝeues.'
he seið. ȝef þu wult ꝥ ha drede þe.' hald hire nearowe. 15
Rihtwisnesse he seið mot beo nede sturne. ant þus he liteð
cruelte.' wið heow of rihtwisnesse. Me mei beon al to riht
wis. Noli esse iustus nímís. In ecclesiaste. Betere is wis
liste þen
luðer strengðe. Hwen þu hauest longe íwaket ⁊ schuldest
gan to slepen.' nu is uertu he seið wakien hwen hit greueð 20
(M. 270) þe. Sei ȝet a Nocturne. for hwi deð he swa? for ꝥ tu
schuldest

f. 73b. 1 *to* 3: *small patch* (*corresponding to hole in* f. 74) *in which several letters in* 1, 2, 3 *are partly effaced.* 5 ah, *sic for* as. 7 he: *mistaken insertion, or* wið *omitted after* haueð.

slepen eft hwen time were to wakien. Eft riht þer toȝeines.
ȝef ꝥ maht wakien wel:' he leið on þe an heuínesse. oþer
deð i þi þoht. wisdom is þinge best. Ich chulle ga nu to slep
25 en. ⁊ arise nunan ⁊ don cwicluker þene nu:' ꝥ ich don nuðe
schulde. ⁊ swa ofte inohreaðe ne dest tu hit i nowðer time. of
þis ilke materie ich spec muchel þruppe. I þulliche temptatiuns
nis nan se wis ne se war bute godd him warni ꝥ nis bigilet
f. 74a ofte. Ah þis hehe sacrement in hardi bileaue ouer alle oð
re þing unwrið hise wrenches. ⁊ brekeð hise strengðes.
Iwis leoue sustren hwen ȝe neh ow feleð him for hwon ꝥ ȝe
habben hardi bileaue:' nulle ȝe bute lahhen him lude to
5 bismere ꝥ he is se muchel ald cang þe kimeð his pine to e
chen:' ⁊ breiden ow crune. Sone se he sið ow hardi ⁊ bald i go
des grace:' his mihte mealteð ⁊ he flið sone. Ah ȝef he mei un
derȝeoten ꝥ ower bileaue falsi. swa ꝥ ow þunche ꝥ ȝe mah
ten beon allunge ilead forð ouer ȝef ȝe weren swiðe i þe ilke
10 stude itemptet:' þerwið ȝe unstrengeð ⁊ his mihte waxeð.

We redeð i Regum ꝥ ysboset lei ⁊ slepte. ⁊ sette a wummon
ȝeteward þe windwede hweate. ⁊ comer recabes sunen
remon. ⁊ banaa. ⁊ funden þe wummon istunt of hire wínd
wunge ⁊ ifolen o slepe. ⁊ wenden in ⁊ slohen ysboset þe un
15 seli. ꝥ lokede him se uuele. þe bitacnunge herof is muche
neod
to understonden. ysboset on ebrew:' is mon bimeaset on en
glisch. ant nis he witerliche ameaset. ⁊ ut of his witte. þe
amidden his unwines leið him to slepen? þe ȝeteward is
wittes skile ꝥ ah to windwin hweate. schaden þe eilen ⁊ te
20 ⁊ te chef. from þe cleane cornes. ꝥ is. þurh bisi warschipe:'

23 ꝥ *error for* þu *or* ꝥ tu.

f. 74a. 2 *between* hise *and* strengðes *a hole; round it a patch in which several letters are partly effaced; three small holes in right margin opposite* 3/4, 6, 8. 11 *large red initial* W (ƿ), *resembling* V *but distinct, being narrower, leaning to right, with long tail now cut off at* 17, *together with ornament, by folded inner edge of* f. 73; *a few blue lines to right, within, and in margin from top to end of tail. In right margin mark* ×. 11 *to* 16 *marginal scribble; from* 11 redeð *to* 14 slohen *underlined with hasty strokes leaving gaps.* 12 comer, *sic for* comen. 19, 20 ⁊ te | ⁊ te, *sic.*

(M. 272) sundri god from uuel. don þe hweate igerner. ⁊ puffen ea
uer awei þe deofles chef ꝥ nis noht :' bute to helle smorðre.
Ah þe bimeasede ysboset lo hu measeliche he dude. sette a
wummon to ȝeteward. ꝥ is feble warde. weila as feoledoð
þus. wummon is þe reisun. ꝥ is wittes skile. hwen hit un 25
strengeð þe schulde beo monlich. stealewurðe ⁊ kene ín
treowe bileaue. þis ȝeteward lið to slepen :' sone se me bi
gínneð consenti to sunne. leoten lust gan inward :' ⁊ te delít
waxen. Hwen Recabes sunen. ꝥ beoð helle bearnes ifindeð f. 74b
swa
unwake r. ⁊ swa nesfhe ȝeteward :' ha gað in ⁊ sleað ys
boset. ꝥ is þe bimeasede gast þe in a slepi ȝemeles forȝemeð
him seoluen. ꝥ nis nawt to forȝeoten. ꝥ as hali writ seið. Ha
þurhstichden him dun in to þe schére. Her seið seín gregoire. 5
In iguine ferire est uitam mentis carnis delectatione perforare.
þe
feond þurhsticheð þe schére :' hwen delit of leccherie þurleð
þe heorte. ⁊ þis nis bute i slep of ȝemeles ⁊ of slawðe as seín
gregoire witneð. Antiquus hostis mox ut mentem otiosam
ínuenerit :' ad eam sub quibusdam occasionibus locuturus 10
uenit. ⁊
quedam ei de gestis preteritis ad memoriam reducit. ⁊ infra.
Putruerunt ⁊ deteriorate sunt cicatrices mee. Cicatrix quidem
est
figura uulneris :' set sanati. Cicatrix ergo ad putredinem
redit :'
quando peccati uulnus quod per penitentiam sanatum est. in
delectationem
suí animum concutit. þis is ꝥ englisch. Hwen þe alde unwíne 15
sið slepi ure skile :' he draheð him anan toward hire ⁊ feleð
wið hire i speche. þenchest tu he seið huþe spec oþer þeo of
flesches galnesse. ⁊ spekeð þus þe alde sweoke toward hire
heorte wordes ꝥ ha ȝare herde fulliche iseide. oðer sihðe ꝥ
ha seh. oðer hire ahne fulðen ꝥ ha sumhwile wrahte. Al 20

f. 74b. 2 *separating* unwake r *a hole; round it several letters are partly effaced; three small holes in left margin* 3/4, 6, 8. nesfhe, *sic, but* f *is probably alteration of tall* s *to* c, *without erasure of top.* 6 iguine, *sic for* inguine. 24 sunnnen, *sic, with small point inside first* n.

þis he put forð biuore þe heorte ehnen. forte bifulen híre
wið þoht of alde sunnen.· hwen he ne mei wið neowe. ⁊ swa
he bríngeð ofte aȝeín in to þe adotede sawle þurh licunge
þe ilke suṇnnen. þe þurh reowðful sar weren ibet ȝare. swa
25 ꝥ heo mei wepen ⁊ meanen sari man wið þe salmwruhte. Pu (M. 274)
truerunt ⁊ cetera. weilawei míne wunden þe weren feire ihealet.
gede
rið neowe wursum ⁊ foð on eft to rotien. Ihealet wunde þen
ne biginneð to rotien.· hwen sunne þe wes ibet.· kimeð eft
wið
f. 75a licunge.· in to munegunge. ⁊ sleað þe unwarre sawle. Gregorius.
ysboset inopinate morti nequaquam succumberet.· nisi ad
ingressum
mentis. mulierem. id est. mollem custodiam deputasset. Al
þis unlímp
iwarð þurh þe ȝetewardes slep ꝥ nes war ⁊ waker. ne nes
nawt
5 monlich.· ah wes wummonlich. eð to ouerkeasten. Beo hit
wummon
beo hit mon. þenne is al þe strengðe efter þe bileaue. ⁊ efter
þet
me haueð trust to godes help ꝥ is neh.· bute bileaue trukie. as
ich ear buuen seide. heo unstrengeð þe unwiht ⁊ deð him
fleon
anan riht. for þi beoð eauer aȝeín hím hardi ase líun i treowe
10 bileaue. nomeliche i þe fondunge ꝥ ysboset deide on. ꝥ is gal
nesse. lo hu ȝe mahe cnawen ꝥ he is earh ⁊ unwreast hwen
he smit þiderward. Nis he earh champiun þe skirmeð tow
ard te uét. þe secheð se lahe on his kempe ifére. flesches
lust is fo
tes wunde. as wes feor iseid þruppe. Ant þis is þe reisun.
As ure
15 fet beoreð us. alswa ure lustes beoreð us ofte to þing ꝥ us
luste
efter. Nu þenne þah þi va hurte þe o þe vet. ꝥ is to seggen. fon

f. 75a. *In top right corner, opposite hole in* f. 74, *several letters ar partly effaced.*

deð wið flesches lustes:' for se lah wunde ne dred tu nawt
to sare.
bute hit to swiðe swelle þurh skiles ȝettunge wið to muchel
delit up toward te heorte. ah drinc þenne atterlaðe ⁊ drif þet
swealm aȝeinward frommard te heorte. ꝥ is to seggen. 20
þench o
þe attri pine ꝥ godd dronc o þe rode. ⁊ te swealm schal setten.
PRude. ⁊ Onde. ⁊ Wreaððe. Heorte sar for worltlich þing.
Dreori
of longunge. ⁊ ȝisceunge of ahte. þeose beoð heorte wunden. ⁊
al ꝥ of ham floweð. ⁊ ȝeoueð deaðes dunt anan buten ha beon
isaluet. Hwen þe feond smit þiderward:' þenne is iwis to 25
dreden.
ant nawt for fot wunden.

(M. 276) PRude salue is eadmodnesse. Ondes:' feolahlich luue.
Wreaððes:' þolemodnesse. Accidies:' Redunge. misliche
werkes. gastelich froure. ȝisceunges:' ouerhohe of eorðliche f. 75b
þinges.
festschipes:' freo heorte. ꝥ is to seggen. Nu of þe earste on alre
earst. ȝef þu wult beon eadmod:' þench eauer hwet te wonteð
of halinesse. ⁊ of gasteliche þeawes. þench hwet tu hauest
of þe seolf. þu art of twa dalen. of licome ⁊ of sawle. In eiðer 5
beoð twa þinges þe mahen muchel meokin þe ȝef þu ham
wel bihaldest. I þe licome is fulðe ⁊ unstrengðe. Ne kimeð
of ꝥ
vetles swuch þíng as þer is ín ? Of þi flesches fetles kimeð
þer smeal of aromaz oðer of swote basme ? Deale drue sprit
len beoreð wín berien. Breres:' rose blostmen. þi flesch hwet 10
frut bereð hit ín alle his openunges. Amid te menske of
þi neb. ꝥ is þe fehereste deal. bitweonen muðes smech. ⁊ nea
ses smeal. ne berest tu as twa priue þurles ? Nart tu icumen
of

21 dronc, *sic.* 27 *large blue initial* P, *the bow cutting* R *of* PRude, *the stem standing two line-spaces down into bottom margin; ornamented with red line-patterns to right, within, and in margin from* 22 *to near bottom of the page; in left margin directing* p.

f. 75b. *In left margin between* 3 *and* 5 *a faint* C-*like scrawl. Between* 7/8 *and* 11 *a hand (in yellow-brown ink) pointing to* wel, *first word of* 7. 14 fette, *sic, probably for* fetles.

ful slím? nart tu fulðe fette. ne bist tu wurme fode? Philo-
sophus.
15 Sperma es fluidum. Vas stercorum. Esca uermium. Nu a
flehe
mei eili þe. makie þe to blenchen. eaðe Maht tu pruden.
Bihald
hali men þe weren sum hwile. hu ha feasten. hu ha wakeden.
i hwuch passiun. i hwuch swinc ha wéren. ⁊ swa þu maht i
cnawen þin ahne wake unstrengðe. Ah wast tu hwet awild
20 geð monnes feble ehnen ꝥ is hehe iclumben.' ꝥ he bihalt
duneward. Alswa hwa se bihalt to þeo þe beoð of lah lif.' þet (M. 278)
makeð him þunchen ꝥ he is of heh lif. Ah bihald aa upp
art toward heouenliche men þe clumben se hehe.' ⁊ þenne
schalt tu seon hu lahe þu stondest. Augustinus. Sicut
incentiuum
25 est elationis respectus inferioris.' sic cautela est humilitatis.'
consideratio superioris. feasten a seoue niht to weater ⁊ to
brea
de. þreo niht to gederes wakien. hu walde hit unstrengen
þi fleschliche strenge. Þus þeos twa þinges bihald i þi licome
f. 76a fulðe ⁊ unstrengðe. Iþi sawle oþer twa. sunne ⁊ ignorance. ꝥ
is unwisdom ⁊ unweotenesse. for ofte ꝥ tu wenest godd.' is u
uel ⁊ sawle morðre. Bihald wið wet ehe þine scheome sunnen.
Dred ȝet þi wake cunde ꝥ is eð warpe. ⁊ sei wið þe hali mon
5 þe bigon to wepen. ⁊ seide þa me talde him ꝥ an of his feren
wes
wið a wummon i flesches fulðe ifallen. Ille hodie. ego cras.
ꝥ is.
he to dei. ⁊ ich to marhen. as þah he seide. Of as unstrong
cun
de ich am as he wes. ⁊ al swuch mei me ilímpen bute ȝef godd
me halde. þus lo þe hali mon nefde he of þe oþres fal na wun
10 derlich ouerhohe. ⁊ biweop his unhap ⁊ dredde ꝥ him a swuch
mahte bitiden. O þis wise eadmodieð ⁊ meokið ow seoluen.
Bernardus. Superbia est appetitus proprie excellencie.
Humilitas.' con

f. 76a. 2 godd, *sic for* god. *In right margin,* 3 *to* 7, *a hand pointing to* sunnen, *end of* 3; *a hole at edge of ruling, between* 17 *and* 18.

temptus eiusdem. ꝥ alswa as prude is wilnunge of wurð-
schipe.ʼ
riht alswa þer toȝeines. eadmodnesse is forkeastunge of
wurðschipe. ⁊ luue of lutel hereword ⁊ of lahnesse. þis þeaw 15
is alre þeawene moder. ⁊ streoneð ham alle. þe is umben
wið
uten hire to gederin gode þeawes.ʼ he bereð dust i þe wind as
sein gregoire seið. Qui sine humilitate uirtutes congregat.ʼ
quasi
qui in uento puluerem portat. þeos ane bið iborhen. þeos ane
wiðbuheð þe deofles grunen of helle. as ure lauerd schawde to 20
seint Antonie þe seh al þe world ful of þe deofles tildunge.
A lauerd qð he hwa mei wið þeose witen him ꝥ he ne beo
wið sum ilaht. Ane þe þolemode qð he ure lauerd. Swa sutil
þing is eadmodnesse. ⁊ swa gentilliche smeal ⁊ se smuhel.ʼ
ꝥ na grune ne mei hire edhalden. ant lo muche wunder. 25
(M. 280) þah ha hire makie swa smeal ⁊ se meoke.ʼ ha is þinge stren
gest. swa ꝥ of hire is euch gastelich strengðe. Seint Cassi
oðre hit witneð. Omnis fortitudo ex humilitate. Ah Salo
mon seið þe reisun hwi. Vbi humilitas.ʼ ibi humilitas.ʼ ibi f. 76b
sapi
entia. þer as eadmodnesse is.ʼ þer he seið is iesu crist. ꝥ is his fea
der wisdom ⁊ his feader strengðe. Nis na wunder þenne þah
strengðe beo þer as he is þurh his inwuniende grace. þurh þe
strengðe of eadmodnesse he weorp þe þurs of helle. þe ȝape 5
wreastlere nimeð ȝeme hwet turn his fere ne kunne nawt. ꝥ
he wið wreastleð. for wið ꝥ turn he mei him unmundlunge
warpen. Alswa dude ure lauerd. ⁊ seh hu feole þe grimme
wreastle
re of helle breid up on his hupe ⁊ weorp wið þe hanche turn
ín to galnesse þe rixleð i þe lenden. hef on heh monie ⁊ wen 10
de abuten wið ham ⁊ swong ham þurh prude dun in to hel
le grunde. þohte ure lauerd þe biheold al þis. Ich schal do þe a
turn ꝥ tu ne cuðest neauer. ne ne maht neauer cunnen. þe
turn of eadmodnesse. ꝥ is þe fallinde turn. ⁊ feol from heo
uene to eorðe. ⁊ strahte him swa bi þe eorðe. ꝥ te feond wende 15

f. 76a. 28 oðre: *MS.* ð (*not normal* ð).
f. 76b. 1 ibi humilitas, *sic* (*false repetition*).

ꝥ he were al eorðlich. ⁊ wes bilurd wið ꝥ turn. ⁊ is ȝet euche
dei of eadmode men ⁊ wummen þe hine wel cunnen. On oðer
half as Iob seið. He ne mei for prude ȝet bute bihalden hehe.
Omne sublime uident oculi eius. Hali men þe haldeð ham lut
20 le ⁊ of lah lif.' beoð ut of his sihðe. Þe wildebar ne mei nawt
buhen him to smiten. Hwa se falleð adun ⁊ þurh meoke ead
modnesse strecheð him bi þer eorðe.' he is carles of his tuskes
þis nis nawt toȝeines ꝥ þet ich habbe iseid ear. ꝥ me schal
stonden eauer toȝeínes þe deouel. for ꝥ stondinge is treowe trust
25 of hardi bileaue up o godes strengðe. þis fallunge is eadmod
cnawunge of þin ahne wacnesse. ⁊ of þin unstrengðe. Ne nan
ne mei stonde swa bute he þus falle. ꝥ is leote lutel tale ⁊ unwurð
⁊ eðelich eauer of him seoluen. Bihalde his blac ⁊ nawt his hwit (M. 282)
f. 77a for hwit awilgeð þe ehe. Eadmodnesse ne mei beon neauer ful preiset.
for ꝥ wes þe lesceun ꝥ ure lauerd inwardlukest learde his icorene.'
wið werc ba ⁊ wið worde. Discite a me quia mitis sum ⁊ hu. c. In hire
he healdeð nawt ane dropemel.' ah flowinde ȝeotteð weallen of
5 his graces. as seið þe salmiste. Qui emittis fontes in con- uallibus. Iþe
dealen þu makest he seið weallen to springen. heorte to- bollen ⁊
ihouen ase hul.' ne edhalt na wete of grace. A bleddre ibollen of
wind ne deueð nawt in to þeose halwende weattres. Ah a nelde
prichunge warpeð al þe wind ut. an eðelich stiche oðer eche
10 makeð to understonden hu lutel prude is wurð.' hu egede is

f. 76b. 16 *faint red underlining,* wið *to* ȝet, *offset from* f. 77. *In left margin near edge of ruling a hole, between* 17 *and* 18. 27 *MS.* butęhe.
f. 77a. 3 hu. c.*: read* humilis corde. 4 ȝeotteð, *sic.*

ONdes salue ich seide wes feolahlich luue ⁊ god un ¶.orhel.
nunge ⁊ god wil.' þer mihte of dede wonteð. Swa muchel
strengðe haueð luue ⁊ god wil.' ꝥ hit makeð oþres god ure god
ase wel.' as his ꝥ hit wurcheð. Sulement luue is god. beo wilcwé
me ⁊ glead þrof. þus þu turnest hit to þe.' ⁊ makest hit þin 15
ahne. Seín Gregoire hit witneð. Aliena bona si diligis.' tua fa
cis. ȝef þu hauest onde of oþres god.' þu attrest te wið healewi.'
⁊ wundest te wið salue. þi salue hit is ȝef þu hit luuest aȝeín
sawle hurtes. ⁊ ti strengðe aȝeín þe feond.' is al þe god ꝥ oðer
deð ȝef þu hit wel unnest. witerliche ich leue ne schulen 20
flesches fondunges namare þen gasteliche meistrín þe nea
uere. ȝef þu art swote iheortet. eadmod ⁊ milde. ⁊ luuest se in
wardliche alle men ⁊ wummen. ⁊ nomeliche ancres þíne leoue
sustren ꝥ tu art sari of hare uuel. ⁊ of hare god glead as of
þin ahne. Vnnen ꝥ al þe luueð þe.' luuede ham ase þe ⁊ dude ham 25
froure as þe. ȝef þu hauest cnif oðer clað. oðer mete oþer drunch.
(M. 284) scrowe. oðer cwaer. hali monne froure. oðer ei oþer þing ꝥ ham
walde freamien. Vnnen ꝥ tu hefdest wonte þe seolf þrof.' wið
þon ꝥ heo hit hefden. ȝef eaní is þe naueð nawt þe heorte þus f. 77b
afeitet.' wið sorhfule sikes ba bi dei ⁊ bi niht grede on ure la
uerd. ne neauer grið ne ȝeoue him aðet he þurh his grace
habbe hire swuch aturnet.

Salue of wreaððe ich seide. is þolemodnesse. ꝥ haueð 5
þreo steiren. heh. ⁊ herre. ⁊ alre hest ⁊ nest te hehe heo
uene. Heh is þe steire.' ȝef þu þolest for þi gult. herre ȝef þu

11 *large red initial* O *between* 10 *and* 13, *right bow cutting* N; *a few blue lines in left margin from* 9 *to* 15; *inside in blue a face, with lines representing tonsure and beard.* *A red paragraph between* un *and* .orhel. (*to follow* 10 egede is) *with top curl out into right margin.* 16 Sei)n Gregoire hit w(itneð *underlined with red chalk.*

f. 77b. 5 *large blue initial* S *between* 4 *and* 7, *with tail to* 9; *red line-patterns within, in margin, and along tail from* 1 *to* 12.

nauest gult. alre hest ȝef þu þolest for þi goddede. Nai seið
sum ameaset þíng. ȝef ich hefde gult þer to.· nalde ich nea
10 uer meanen. Art tu ꝥ swa seist ut of þe seoluen? Is þe leouere
to beon iudase feol⟨ah⟩e. þen iesu cristes fere? Ba weren ahonget. ah
Iudas for his gult.· iesu wið ute gult for his muchele godlec
wes ahon o rode. Hweðeres fere wult tu beon? wið hweðer wult
tu þolien? Of þis is þruppe iwriten muchel. hu he is þi file. þe
15 misseið oðer misdeð þe. líme is þe frensch of file. Nis hit or
acurset. þe iwurðeð swartre ⁊ ruhre se hit is ifilet mare? ant
rusteð þe swiðere ꝥ me hit scureð hearde? Gold. seoluer. Stel.
Irn. al is or. Gold ⁊ seoluer cleansið ham of hare dros i þe
fur. ȝef þu gederest dros þrín.· ꝥ is aȝeín cunde. Þe chaliz þe
20 wes þerín imealt ⁊ strongliche iweallet. ⁊ seoððen þurh se mo
ní dunt. ⁊ frotunge to godes nep. se swiðe feire afeitet. walde
he ȝef he cuðe speoken.· awearien his cleansing fur. ⁊ his wruh
te honden. Argentum reprobum uocate eos. Al þis world is
godes smið to smeoðien his icorene. wult tu þet godd nabbe
25 na fur in his smiððe. ne bealies ne homeres? fur is scheome ⁊
pine. þíne bealies beoð þe þe misseggeð. þíne homeres.· þe
þe hearmið. Þench of þis essample. Hwen dei of riht is iset. (M. 286)
ne deð he scheome þe deme. þe aþishalf þe isette dei brekeð
f. 78a þe triws ⁊ wrekeð hím. o þe oðer on hím seoluen. Augustinus. Quid
gloriatur impius si de ipso flagellum fatiat pater meus? Ant hwa nat
ꝥ domesdei nis þe dei iset to don riht alle men? Hald þe triws
þe hwiles. hwet woh se me deð þe. ne do þu nawt him scheo
5 me. forhohie wrake of his dom. ⁊ neomen to þín ahne? Twa

11 feol⟨ah⟩e: ah *interlined with caret.* 18 *small red initial* G *touched with blue lines.* 23 *small blue initial* A *touched with red lines.*

f. 78a. 1 on: *false addition.* 4 *after* deð þe *twelve words referring to Judge* (him) *omitted.* 5 ahne? : *the ? is erroneous.* Twa *underlined; in right margin mark* ×, *and marginal scribble down to* 8.

þinges beoð ꝥ godd haueð edhalden to him seoluen. ꝥ beoð.
wurðschipe ⁊ wrake. as hali writ witneð. Gloriam meam alteri
non dabo. Item. Michi vindictam. Ego retribuam. Hwa se eauer on
him seolf takeð owðer of þeos twa.’ he robbeð godd ⁊ reaueð.
Deale art tu se wrað wið mon oþer wið wummon. ꝥ tu wult 10
forte wreoke þe reauín godd mid strengðe ?

Accidies salue is. gastelich gleadschipe. ⁊ froure of glead
ful hope. þurh redunge. þurh hali þoht. oðer of mon
nes muðe. Ofte leoue sustren ȝe schulen uri leasse.’ forte reden
mare. Redunge is god bone. Redunge teacheð hu ⁊ hwet me 15
bidde.’ ⁊ beode biȝet hit efter. Amidde þe redunge hwen þe
heorte likeð. kimeð up a deuotiun ꝥ is wurð monie benen.
for þi seið sein Ierome. Ieronimus. Semper in manu tua sacra
sit lectio. tenenti tibi librum sompnus subripiat. ⁊ cadentem fací
em pagina sancta suscipiat. Hali redunge beo eauer i þine hon 20
den. Slep ga up o þe as þu lokest þron. ant te hali pagne
ikepe þi fallinde neb. swa þu schalt reden ȝeornliche ⁊ longe.
Euch þing þah me mei ouerdon.’ best is eauer mete. Aȝeínes
ȝisceunge ich walde ꝥ oþre schuneden as ȝe doð gederunge.
To muche freolec cundleð hire ofte. freo iheortet ȝe schule 25
beon. Ancre of oþer freolec. haueð ibeon oðerhwiles to freo of
Galnesse kimeð of ȝiuernesse. ⁊ of flesches ¶ .hire seoluen.
(M. 288) eise. for as as seín Gregoire seið. Mete ⁊ drunch ouer riht.’
temeð þreo teames. lihte wordes. lihte werkes. ⁊ leccheries f. 78b
lustes. Vre lauerd beo iþonket þe haueð of ȝiuernesse iheal
et ow mid alle. ah galnesse ne bið neauer allunge clea
ne acwenct of flesches fondunge. Ah ꝥ understondeð wel.

8 vindictam, *sic.* 12 *large red initial* A *between* 11 *and* 13, *with tail to* 18; *blue line-patterns to right within, in margin from* 10, *and down tail to* 21. 23 *small red initial* A *touched with faint blue lines.* 27 *small blue initial* G *touched with red lines; before* .hire seoluen. *a blue paragraph with tails into right margin, the upper elaborated with red rings and lines.* 28 as as, *sic.*

5 ꝥ þreo degrez beoð þrín as seint Beornard witneð. Þe forme is cogitatiun. Þe oþer is affectiun. Þe þridde is cun sence. Cogitatiuns beoð fleonninde þohtes. þe ne leasteð nawt. ant teo as seín Beornard seið ne hurteð nawt te sawle.' ah þah ha bispottið hire wið hare blake speckes.
10 swa.' ꝥ nis ha nawt wurðe ꝥ iesu hire leofmon ꝥ is al feier bicluppe hire ne cusse hire ear ha beo iwesschen. Swuch fulðe as hit kimeð lihtliche. lihtliche geað awei wið veni es. wið Confiteor. wið alle goddeden. Affectiun is. hwen þe þoht geað inward. ⁊ delit kimeð up. ⁊ te lust waxeð. þen
15 ne as wes spot ear up o þe hwite hude.' þer waxeð wunde ⁊ deopeð in toward te sawle efter ꝥ te lust geað ⁊ te delit þrín forðre ⁊ forðre. þenne is neod toȝeiȝen. Sana me domine. A lauerd heal me for ich am iwundet. Ruben primogenitus meus ne crescas. Ruben þu reade þoht. þu blodi delit ne wa
20 xe þu neauer. Cunsense ꝥ is skiles ȝettunge. hwen þe delit i þe lust is igan se ouerforð. ꝥ ter nere nan wiðsegg unge ȝef þer were eise to fulle þe dede. þis is hwen þe heor te draheð to hire unlust as þing þe were amaínet. ⁊ feð on as to winkin. to leote þe feond iwurðen. ⁊ leið hire seolf du
25 neward. Buheð him as he bit. ⁊ ȝeieð crauant crauant ase softe swohninde. þenne is he kene þe wes ear curre. þenne leapeð he to.' þe stod ear feorrento. ⁊ bit deaðes bite o godes deore spuse. iwiss deaðes bite.' for his teð beoð attrie as of a
f. 79a wed dogge. Dauið i þe sawter cleopeð hine dogge. Erue a fra mea deus animam meam ⁊ de manu canis unicam meam.

FOR þi mí leoue suster sone se þu eauer underȝetest (M. 290) ꝥ tes dogge of helle cume snakerinde wið his blodi
5 flehen of stinkinde þohtes.' ne li þu nawt stille ne ne site nowðer. to lokin hwet he wule don. ne hu feor he wule gan.' ne sei þu nawt slepinde. ame dogge ga her ut. hwet wult tu nu her inne? þis tolleð him inward. Ah ním anan þe rode steaf mid nempnunge i þi muð. mid te mearke i þín

f. 78b. 13 Affectiun: *the* A *a miniature form of the large initials.* 28 iwiss, *sic* (*cf.* f. 68b. 18).

f. 79a. 3 *large red initial* F *between* 2 *and* 5, *with curved arms and long tapered tail to* 12; *blue line-patterns to right, within, and in margin from above* 1 *down tail, with trails to* 20; *directing* f *in left margin.*

hond. mid þoht i þin heorte. ⁊ hat him ut heterliche þe fule 10
cur dogge. ⁊ liðere to hím luðerliche mid te hali rode steaf stron
ge bac duntes. ꝥ is. Rung up sture þe. hald up ehnen on heh
⁊ honden toward heouene. Gred efter sucurs. Deus in adiutori
um meum intende. Domine ad adiu. Veni creator spiritus. Exurgat deus
⁊ dissipentur inimici eius. Deus in nomine tuo saluum me 15 fac.
Domine quid multiplicati sunt. AD te domine leuaui animam meam.
AD te leuaui oculos meos. leuaui oculos meos in montes.
ʒef þe ne kimeð sone help:· gred luddre wið hat heorte. Vs
quequo domine obliuisceris me in fínem. us. auer. fa. t. a me. ⁊ swa al
þe salm ouer. Pater noster. Credo. aue Maria. wið halsinde 20 bonen
o þín ahne ledene. Smit smeortliche adun þe cneon to þer
eorðe. ⁊ breid up þe rode steaf. ⁊ sweng him o fowr half aʒeín
helle dogge. ꝥ nis nawt elles bute blesce þe al abuten wið
þe eadi rode taken. spite him amid te beard to hoker ⁊ to
scarne þe flikereð swa wið þe ⁊ fikeð dogge fahenunge. 25
Hwen he for se liht wurð. for þe licunge of alust ane hwile
stucche chapeð þi sawle godes deore bune ꝥ he bohte mid
his blod. ⁊ mid his deorewurðe deað o þe deore rode. aa bihald
hire wurð ꝥ he paide for hire. ⁊ dem þrefter hire pris ⁊ beo f. 79b
on hire þe deorre. ne sule þu neauer se eðeliche his fa ⁊ þín
eiðer his deorewurðe spuse ꝥ costnede him se deore. makie
deofles hore of hire:· is reowðe ouer reowðe. To unwreast
mid alle ha is þe mei wið to heouen up hire þreo fing 5
res:· ouercumen hire fa ⁊ ne luste for slawðe. hef for þi wið
(M. 292) treowe ⁊ hardi bileaue up þine þreo fingres. ⁊ wið þe

11 ⁊ liðere to hím *on an erasure.* 14 adiu.: *read* adiuuandum; spiritus: sp̄c. 19 us. auer. fa. t. a me: *read* usquequo auerteris faciem tuam a me. 21 ledene: l *altered from some other letter, resembles* b.

hali rode steaf ꝥ him is laðest cuggel lei o þe dogge deo
uel. nempne ofte iesu. cleope his passiunes help. halse bi his
10 pine. bi his deorewurðe blod. bi his deað o rode. flih to his
wunden. Muchel he luuede us þe lette makien swucche
þurles in him forte huden us ín. Creop in ham wið þi
þoht. ne beoð ha al opene ? ⁊ wið his deorewurðe blod biblod
de þin heorte. Ingredere in petram abscondere fossa humo.
15 Ga in to þe stan seið þe prophete. ⁊ hud te i þe deoluen eorðe.
ꝥ is i þe wunden of ure lauerdes flesch þe wes as idoluen
wið þe dulle neiles as he i þe sawter longe uore seide. Fo
derunt manus meas ⁊ pedes meos. ꝥ is. ha duluen me ba
ðe þe vet ⁊ te honden. ne seide he nawt þurleden. for efter
20 þis leattre as ure meistres seggeð. swa weren þe neiles
dulle.ˏ ꝥ ha duluen his flesch ⁊ tobreken þe ban mare
þen þurleden.ˏ to pínín him sarre. He him seolf cleopeð
þe toward teose wunden. Columba mea in foraminibus
petre.
in cauernis macerie. Mi culure he seið cum hud te i míne
25 limen þurles. i þe hole of mi side. Muche luue he cudde to
his leoue culure ꝥ he swuch hudles makede. loke nu ꝥ tu
þe he cleopeð culure. habbe culure cunde. ꝥ is wið ute galle.
⁊ cum to him baldeliche. ⁊ make scheld of his passiun.ˏ ⁊
f. 80a sei wið Ieremie. Dabis scutum cordis laborem tuum. ꝥ is. þu
schalt
ȝeoue me lauerd heorte scheld aȝeín þe feond. þi swincfule pí
ne ꝥ hit swincful wes. he schawde hit witerliche inoh. þa
he sweatte ase blodes swat dropen þe runnen to þer eorðe.
5 Me schal halden scheld i feht up abuuen heaued. oðer a
ȝeín þe breoste. nawt ne drahen hit bihinden. Al riht swa
ȝef þu wult ꝥ te rode scheld ⁊ godes stronge passiun fal
si þe deofles wepnen.ˏ ne dragse þu hit nawt efter þe.ˏ ah
hef hit on heh buue þin heorte heaued i þine breoste ehnen.

f. 79b. 13, 14 biblod|de, *sic, for* biblodge. 14 Isa. ii. 10 in fossa humo. 15 deoluen, *sic. In left margin a mark* × ; *the line is underlined as far as* deoluen. 24/25 *in left margin* × *with scribble beneath.* 24 Mi culure he seið cum hud te i m *underlined;* 25 limen þurles. i þe . . . mi side. Mu *underlined.*

f. 80a. 1 *in right margin a mark* × ; 1 *to* 3 *from* þu schalt *to* swincful wes. he *underlined.*

(M. 294) hald hit up toȝein þe feond. schaw hit him witerliche. þe 10
sihðe þrof ane bringeð hím o fluhte. for ba him scheomeð
þerwið ⁊ griseð ut of witte efter þe ilke time ꝥ ure lauerd
þer wið brohte swa to grunde his coínte couerschipe. ⁊ his
prude strengðe. ȝef þu þurh þi ȝemeles werest te earst
wacliche. ⁊ ȝeuest to þe feond inȝong to forð iþe frumðe.՛ 15
swa ꝥ tu ne mahe nawt reculin him aȝeinward for þí
muchele unstrengðe. ah art ibroht se ouerforð.՛ ꝥ tu ne
maht þis scheld halden o þin heorte ne wrenchen hire
þer under frommard te deofles earowen.՛ nim þe aleast
forð sein Beneites salue. þah ne þearf hit nawt beon se 20
ouerstrong as his wes. þe of þe walewunge. rug. ⁊ side. ⁊ wom
be. ron al o gure blode. ah lanhure ȝef þe seolf hwen þe
strongest stont.՛ a smeort discepline. ⁊ drif as he dude þet
swete licunge ín to smeortunge. ȝef þu þus ne dest nawt.՛
slepinde werest te.՛ he wule gan to feor on þe ear þu least 25
wene. ⁊ bringe þe of ful þoht.՛ in to delit of ful lust. ant
swa he bringeð þe al ouer to skiles ȝettunge. ꝥ is dead
lich sunne wið uten þe dede. ant swa is ec þe delit of ꝥ stín
kinde lust wið ute grant of þe werc.՛ se longe hit mei leas f. 80b
ten. Nunquam enim iudicanda est delectatio esse morosa.՛ dum
ratio reluctatur ⁊ negat assensum. þenne hit least to lon
ge. hwen þe skile ne fehteð na lengre þer toȝeines. for þi
leoue suster as ure lauerd leareð. totred te neddre heaued ꝥ 5
is þe biginnung of his fondunge. Beatus qui tenebit et
allidet paruulos suos ad petram. Eadi is seið Dauið. þe wið
halt hire on earst. ⁊ tobrekeð þe stan. þe earste sturun
ges beoð.՛ hwen þe flesch ariseð hwil ꝥ ha beoð ȝunge.
Vre lauerd is icleopet stan for his treownesse. Et in canticis. 10
Capite nobis uulpes paruulas que destruunt uíneas.
Nim ⁊ keche us leofmon anan þe ȝunge foxes he seið
ure lauerd þe strueð þe win ȝardes. ꝥ beoð þe earste pro
(M. 296) cunges þe strueð ure sawlen. þe mot muche tilunge to.՛
to beoren win berien. þe deouel is beore cunnes. ⁊ haueð 15

25 ah *probably omitted before* slepinde.

f. 80b. 8, 9 *erroneously reproduced;* to *omitted after* tobrekeð; beoð *falsely inserted after* sturunges. 12 *in left margin mark* ×. 12, 13 Nim *to* se(ið *and* þe strueð þe win ȝard *underlined.*

asse cunde. for he is bihinden strong:⸝ ⁊ i þe heaued feble.
swa is beore ⁊ asse. ꝥ is i þe frumðe. Ne ȝef þu hím neauer
inȝong:⸝ ah tep hím o þe sculle. for he is earh as beore
þron. ⁊ hihe him swa þeoneward. ⁊ askur him se scheo
20 meliche sone se þu underȝetest him:⸝ ꝥ him grise wið þe
stude ꝥ tu wunest inne. for he is þinge prudest:⸝ ant
him is scheome laðest.

Alswa leoue suster. sone se þu eauer felest ꝥ tín heorte
wið luue falle to eani þing eawt ouer mete:⸝ ananrihtes
25 beo war of þe neddre atter:⸝ ⁊ totred his heaued. þe cwene
seide ful soð þe wið a strea ontende alle hire wanes. þet
muchel kimeð of lutel. Ant ním nu ȝeme hu hit fea
reð. þe sperke þe wint up:⸝ ne bringeð nawt ananriht þe
f. 81a hus al o leie:⸝ ah lið ⁊ kecheð mare fur. ⁊ fostreð forð. ⁊
waxeð from leasse to mare. aðet al þe hus bleasie forð:⸝
ear me least wéne. ant te deouel blaweð to from ꝥ hit
earst cundleð. ⁊ mutleð his beali bleas eauer as hit wax
5 eð. Vnderstond tis bi þe seolf. a sihðe ꝥ tu sist. oðer anlepi
word ꝥ tu misherest. ȝef hit eawt stureð þe:⸝ cwench hit
wið teares weater. ⁊ mid iesu cristes blod hwil hit nis bute
a sperke. ear þen hit waxe ⁊ ontende þe swa:⸝ ꝥ tu hit ne mahe
cwenchen. for swa hit timeð ofte. ant hit is riht godes dom.
10 ꝥ hwa ne deð hwen ha mei:⸝ ne schal ha hwen ha walde.
Ecclesiasticus.
A scíntilla una augetur ignis. Moní cunnes fondunge (M. 298)
is i þis feorðe dale. Misliche frouren ⁊ monifalde saluen.
Vre lauerd ȝeoue ow grace. ꝥ ha ow moten helpen. Of alle þe
oþre þenne is schrift þe biheueste. Of hit schal beon þe
15 fifte dale as ich bihet þruppe. ant neomeð ȝeme hu euch
an dale falleð in to oþer as ich þear seide.

Twa þinges neomed
ȝeme of schrift i þe bi
ginnunge. Þe earre:⸝ of
20 hwuch mihte hit beo. Þe oþer:⸝

23 *blue initial* A *between* 22 *and* 24 *with added tail; red line-patterns from* 21, *trailing into bottom margin.* 24 ananrihtes: s *written above as flourish from* e. 28 *MS.* sperke.
f. 81a. 4 mutleð, *sic.* 8 *MS.* sperke. 11 *small red*

hwuch hit schule beon. Þis beoð nu as twa limen ⁊ eiðer
is todealet. Þe earre o sixe. Þe oþer o sixtene stucchen.
Nu is þis of þe earre.

Schrift haueð monie mihtes. ah nulle ich of alle:
seggen bute sixe. þreo aȝeín þe deouel: ⁊ þreo on 25
us seoluen. Schrift schent þen deouel. hackeð of his hea
ued. ⁊ todreaueð his ferd. Schrift wescheð us of alle u
re fulðen. ȝelt us alle ure luren. Makeð us godes children.
Eider haueð hise þreo. Pruuie we nu alle. þe earste þreo f. 81b
beoð alle ischawde i Iudithe deden. Iudith ꝥ is schrift. as
wes ȝare iseid: sloh oloferne. ꝥ is þe feond of helle. Turn
þruppe þer we speken of fuhelene cunde. þe beoð ieuenet to
ancre. Ha hackede of his heaued ⁊ seoððen com ⁊ schawde 5
hit to þe burh preostes. þenne is þe feond ischend: hwen
me schaweð alle hise cweadschipes. his heaued is ihacket
of. ⁊ he isleín i þe mon: sone se he eauer is riht sari for
his sunnen. ⁊ haueð schrift on ⟨h⟩eorte. Ah he nis nawt þe
ȝet ischend: hwil his heaued is ihulet. as dude on earst 10
iudith: ear hit beo ischawet. ꝥ is ear þe muð i schrift do
(M. 300) ut þe heaued sunne. nawt te sunne ane: ah al þe bigín
nunge þrof. ⁊ te foreridles þe brohten in þe sunne. ꝥ is
þe deofles heaued ꝥ me schal totreoden anan as ich ear
seide. þenne flih his ferd anan as dude olofernes his wihe 15
les ⁊ his wrenches ꝥ he us wið asaileð. doð ham alle o fluh
te ⁊ te burh is arud ꝥ ha hefden biset. ꝥ is to seggen. þe
sunfule is delifret. Iudas Macabeu hwa stod aȝeín him?
Alswa i Iudicum. ꝥ folc þa hit easkede efter Iosues deað:
hwa schulde beon hare dug ⁊ leaden ham i ferde. Quis 20

initial M *touched with blue lines.* 17 neomed, *sic. Very large blue initial* T (*marking beginning of Part V*) *between* 16 *and* 21; *line-patterns to right, within, and in margin from* 13 *to* 22; *the top partly overlies* an dale; *in left margin directing* t. 19 *small red initial* Þ *touched with blue lines.* 20 *small blue initial* Þ *crossed with red lines.* 24 *large red initial* S *between* 23 *and* 26 *with long tail; blue line-patterns to right, within, and in margin from* 23 *trailing down towards bottom edge; in left margin directing* s.

f. 81b. 1 Eider, *sic.* 9 ⟨h⟩eorte*:* h *interlined.* nawt*:* n *altered from some other letter with ascender* (*probably* þe *was begun by anticipation*). 15 flih his, *sic for* flið his*; punctuation mark omitted after* olofernes.

erit dux noster? vre lauerd ham ondswerede. Iudas schal gan
biuoren ow. ⁊ ich chulle ower faes lond biteachen in his
honden. lokið nu ful ȝeorne hwet tis beo to seggen. Io
sue spealeð heale. ⁊ Iudas schrift as Iudith. þenne is iosue
25 dead: hwen sawle heale is forloren þurh eani deadlich sun
ne. þe sunfule seolf is þe unwihtes lond þe is ure dead
liche fa. ah þis lond ure lauerd bihat to biteachen i Iuda
se honden: for hwon ꝥ he ga biuoren. Schrift lo is gun
f. 82a fanuner. ⁊ bereð þe banere biuoren al godes ferd. ꝥ beoð
gode þeawes. Schrift reaueð þe feond his lond. ꝥ is þe sun
fule mon. ⁊ al todriueð chanaan þe feondes ferd of
helle. Iudas hit dude licomliche. ant schrift ꝥ hit bitac
5 neð: deð gasteliche ꝥ ilke. þis beoð nuðe þreo þring þet
hit deð us seoluen. ꝥ beoð þeose her efter. Schrift wescheð
us of alle ure fulðen. for swa hit is iwriten. Omnia in con
fessione lauantur. Glosa super. Confitebimur tibi deus confitebimur. Ant ꝥ
wes bitacnet þa iudith wesch hire. ⁊ despulede hire of wi
10 dewene schrud. ꝥ wes merke of sorhe. ant sorhe nis bute
of sunne. lauit corpus suum ⁊ exuit se uestimentis sue uidue (M. 302)
tatis. Schrift eft al ꝥ god ꝥ we hefden forloren þurh hea
ued sunne: bringeð al aȝein ⁊ ȝelt al togederes. Ioel. Red
dam uobis annos quos comedit locusta. brucus. Rubigo. ⁊
15 erugo. þis wes bitacnet þurh ꝥ dauið schrudde hire mid
halidahne weden. ⁊ feahede hire utewið: as schrift deð us
inwið. wið alle þe feire urnemenz þe blisse bitacnið. ant
ure lauerd seið þurh zacharie. Erunt sicut fuerant antequam
proieceram eos. ꝥ is. Schrift schal makie þe mon alswuch
20 as he wes biuore ꝥ he sunegede. ase cleane ⁊ ase feier. ant
ase riche of alle god þe limpeð to sawle. þe þridde þing

f. 82a. 3 lond *crossed out between* sun| fule *and* mon. 5 þring, *sic for* þing. 11 uidue|tatis, *sic* (*but* e *altered from* i). 15 erugo, *sic* (*Vulg.* eruca; *but other versions including* L *have also* erugo). dauið, *sic, for* iudith; *on* dau *a faint circular scribble.* 19 *in right margin a mark* ×. 19, 20 *from* schrift schal *to* sunegede. ase *underlined. In faint pale ink* (*possibly same as the scribble on* dauið 15) a *mark* × *in left margin* 6, *and in right margin two faint letters, probably* f f.

is ꝥ schrift deð us seoluen. þe frut of þes oþre twa ⁊ end
eð ham baðe. ꝥ is makeð us godes children. þis is bitacnet
þerbi ꝥ iudas i genesy. biwon of iacob beniamín. Benía
min seið ase muchel ase sune of riht half. Iudas þet is 25
schrift alswa as is iudith. for ba ha spealieð an on ebreis
che ledene. þes gasteliche iudas. biȝet of iacob his feader
ꝥ is ure lauerd to beon his rihthondes sune. ⁊ bruken buten
ende þe eritage of heouene. Nu we habbeð iseid of hw f. 82b
uch mihte schrift is. hwucch efficaces hit haueð.' ⁊ inemp
net sixe. loki we nu ȝeornliche hwuch schrift schule
beon þe beo of swuch strengðe. ⁊ forte schawin hit bet.'
deale we nu þis lím o sixtene stucchen. 5

Schrift schal beo Wreiful. Bitter mid sorhe. Ihal. Na
ket. Ofte imaket. Hihful. Eadmod. Scheomeful. Ho
peful. Wis. Soð. ⁊ Willes. Ahne. ⁊ Studeuest. Biþoht bi
uore longe. Her beoð nu as þah hit weren sixtene stuch
en þe beoð ifeiet to schrift. ant we of euchan sum word 10

Schrift schal beo wreiful. ¶. sunderliche seggen.
(M. 304) Mon schal wreien him i schrift. nawt werien hím
ne seggen. Ich hit dude þurh oþre. Ich wes ined þer to.
þe feond hit makede me don. Þus eue ⁊ Adam wereden
ham. Adam þurh eue. ⁊ eue þurh þe neddre. þe feond 15
ne mei neden namon to na sunne þah he eggi þer to.'
ah ful wel he let of hwen ei seið ꝥ he makede him to
sunegín. as þah he hefde strengðe þe naueð nan mid al
le bute of us seoluen. Ah me ah to seggen. Mín ahne un
wrestlec hit dude. ⁊ willes ⁊ waldes ich beah to þe deouel. 20
ȝef þu witest ei þing þi sunne bute þe seoluen.' þu ne
schriuest te nawt, ȝef þu seist ꝥ tín unstrengðe ne
mahte nawt elles.' þu wrenchest þi sunne up o godd
þe makede þe swuch. ꝥ tu bi þin tale wiðstonde ne mah
test. wreie we þenne us seoluen. for lo hwet seinte pawel 25

f. 82b. 6 *large blue initial* S *between* 5 *and* 7, *with tail to* 11; *red line-patterns within, and in margin down to* 12. 7 Dredful *omitted after* Scheomeful (*cf.* f. 90a. 14). 10 wule *omitted after* word. 11 *large red initial* S *between* 10 *and* 13, *with tail to* 16; *blue line-patterns within and down tail, trailing to* 22. *Before* .sunderliche *a blue paragraph touched with red.*

seið. Si nos ipsos díiudaremus·:· non utique iudicaremur.
ꝥ is. ȝef we wreieð wel her. ⁊ demeð her us seoluen·:· we
schule beo cwite of wreíunge ed te muchele dome. þear
f. 83a as seínt Anselme seið þeos dredfule wordes. Hinc erunt
accusancia peccata. Illinc terens iusticia. Supra·:· iratus
iudex.
Subtra patens horridum chaos inferní. Intus·:· urens consciencia.
foris·:· ardens mundus. Peccator sic deprehensus in quam
partem
5 se premet? O þe an half o domes schulen ure swarte sun
nen strongliche bicleopien us of ure sawle morðre. O þe
oþer half stont rihtwisnesse ꝥ na reowðe nis wið. dredful
⁊ grislich. ⁊ grureful to bihalden. buuen us þe eorre de
me. for ase softe as he is her·:· ase heard he bið þer. ase
10 milde as he is nu·:· ase sturne þenne. lomb her liun þer.
as þe prophete witneð. leo rugiet quis non timebit? þe li
un schal greden he seið. hwa ne mei beon offearet? her
we cleopieð him lomb as ofte as we singeð. Agnus dei quí
tollis peccata mundi. Nu as ich seide. schule we seon buuen
15 us þe ilke eorre deme ꝥ is ec witnesse ⁊ wat alle ure gul
tes. Bineoðen us ȝeoniende þe wide þrote of helle. Inwið
us seoluen·:· ure ahne conscience. ꝥ is ure ínwit forculiende (M. 306)
hire seoluen. wið þe fur of sunne. wið uten us al þe world
leitinde o swart lei up in to þe skiwes. Þe sari sunfule
20 þus biset hu schal him stonde þenne? to hwuch of þes
fowre mei he him biwenden? Nis þer buten héren þet
hearde word. ꝥ wa word. ꝥ grisliche word. grureful ouer
alle. Ite maledicti ín ignem eternum qui paratus est diabo
lo ⁊ angelis eius. Gað ȝe aweariede ut of mín ehsihðe·:· into
25 ꝥ eche fur ꝥ wes igreiðet to þe feond ⁊ to his engles. ȝe
forbuhe monne dom ꝥ ich demde mon to. ꝥ wes to lib
ben i swinc. ⁊ i sar on eorðe. ⁊ ȝe schulen nu for þi hab

26 díiudaremus: *second* d (*resembling* cl) *is abnormal;* da *crossed out and expuncted, above it* dica *small and thin in pale ink.*

f. 83a. 2 terens, *sic for* terrens. 3 subtra, *sic* (*MS.* subt*ra*), *for* subtus. 5 domes, *sic:* dei *omitted.* 23 qui: qð *with* ð *erased and* i *added above* q.

ben deofles dom. bearne wið him echeliche i þe fur of helle. Wið þis schulen þe forlorene warpen a swuch ʒur.' þ heouene ⁊ eorðe mahen ba grimliche agrisen. for þi seint austin leofliche us leareð. Ascendat homo tribunal mentis sue. si illud cogitat quod oportet eum exi beri ante tribunal christi. Assit accusatrix cogitatio. testis.' Consciencia. Carnifex.' timor. þ is. þenche mon o domes dei ⁊ deme her him seoluen þus o þisse wise. Skile sitte as domes mon up o þe dom seotel. Cume þrefter forð his þohtes munegunge. wreie him ⁊ bicleopie him of mis liche sunnen. Beal ami þis þu dudest þear. ⁊ tis þear. ⁊ tis þear. ⁊ o þisse wise. His inwit beo icnawes þrof ant beore witnesse. Soð hit is. soð hit is. þis ⁊ muchele mare. Cume forð þrefter fearlac þurh þe deme heast þe heter liche háte. Tac bínd hím heteueste for he is deaðes wurðe. Bind him swa euch lím þ he haueð wið isuneget.' þ he ne mahe wið ham sunegi namare. Fearlac haueð ibun den him.' hwen he ne dear for fearlac sturie toward sun ne. ʒet nis nawt þe deme þ is skile ipaiet. þah he beo i bunden ⁊ halde him wið sunne.' bute ʒef he abugge þe sunne þ he wrahte. ⁊ cleopeð forð píne ⁊ sorhe. ⁊ hat þet sorhe þersche inwið þe heorte wið sar bireowsunge. swa.' (M. 308) þ hire suhie. ⁊ píni þe flesch utewið mid feasten ⁊ wið oþre fleschliche sares. Hwa se o þisse wise biuoren þe mu chele dom demeð her him seoluen.' eadi he is ⁊ seli. For as þe prophete seið. Non iudicabit deus bis in id ipsum. Nule nawt ure lauerd þ a mon for a þing beo twien idemet. hit nis nawt i godes curt as i þe schíre. þer as þe þ nickeð wel mei beon iborhen.' ⁊ te ful þe is icnawen.' Biuore godd is oþerweis. Si tu accusas.' deus excusat. ⁊ vice uersa. ʒef þu wrei est te her.' godd wule werie þe þear. ⁊ skerín mid alle ed te nearewe dome. for hwon þ tu deme þe as ich itaht habbe.

f. 83b. 5 accusatrix: accusat*r*ix *altered from* accusatio; x *clumsily from* i, o *erased.* 25 þe prophete seið *and* Nule *underlined.* 26 *in left margin mark* ×, *and marginal scribble* 26, 27; nawt ure *to* idemet *underlined.* 28 ⁊ te ful þe is icnawen.' Biuore godd: *punctuation correct* (*not so all versions*); ful *has sense* '*convicted*' (*as OE.* fūl). L *has* Ibi qui negat poterit liberari et dampnari qui fatetur.

Schrift schal beo bitter. aȝeín ꝥ te sunne þuhte sum
5 Schearre swéte. Iudith þe spealeð schrift as ich ofte hab
be iseid wes Merarihtes dohter. Ant iudas ꝥ is ec schrift. wí
uede o thamar. Merariht ⁊ thamar ba ha spealieð an.'
on ebreische ledene. Neomeð nu ȝeorne ȝeme of þe bi
tacnunge. Ich hit segge scheortliche. Bitter sar ⁊ schrift.'
10 þet an mot cumen of þe oþer. as Iudith dude of mera
riht. Ant ba beon somet ifeiet.' as iudas ⁊ thamar. For
nowðer wið uten oðer.' nis noht wurð oðer lutel. Pha
res ⁊ zaram ne temið ha neaure. Iudas streonede of
thamar.' phares ⁊ zaram. Phares.' diuisio. zaram.' oriens
15 interpretatur. þe gasteliche bitacnið tweamunge from sunne.
⁊ i þe heorte þrefter arisinde grace. Fowr þinges ȝef mon
þencheð ꝥ heaued sunne dude him.' mahen makien
hím to sorhin.' ⁊ bittrín his heorte. Lo þis þe forme. ȝef
a mon hefde ilosed in a tíme of þe dei his feader ant his
20 moder. his sustren ⁊ his breðren. ⁊ al his cun ⁊ alle his
freond ꝥ he eauer hefde weren asteoruen ferliche. nalde
he ouer alle men sorhful beon ⁊ sari as he eaðe mahte?
Godd wat he mei beon muche deale sorhfulre ꝥ haueð
wið deadlich sunne gasteliche islein godd inwið his
25 sawle. nawt ane forloren þe swete feader of heouene. ⁊
seinte Marie his deorewurðe moder. oþer hali chirche.
hwen he of hire naueð ne leasse ne mare. Ant te eng
les of heouene. ⁊ alle hali halhen þe weren him ear
f. 84b for freond. for breðren ⁊ for sustren.' as to him ha beoð (M. 310)
deade. as onont him is. he haueð isleín ham alle. ant
haueð þear as ha líuíeð aa.' leaððe of ham alle as Ie
remie witneð. Omnes amici eius spreuerunt eam. facti sunt
5 ei ínimici. ꝥ is. al ꝥ him luuede ȝeieð spi him on.' ant
heatieð him alle. ȝet mare. his children sone se he su

f. 84a. 4 *large blue initial* S, *with red line-patterns within, and in margin from* 2 *down tail, with trailer to* 14. 6, 7 Merarihtes, Merariht, *sic, for* Merari (*forms with* th, ht *aso occur in other versions*). 7 spealieð an, *sic; the 'interpretation'* bitternesse *omitted or replaced by* an. 13 *to* 16 : Iudas *to* grace *not in* M. 14 oriens : ns *as* f. 18b. 8. 18 sorhin : h *clumsily formed on an erasure.* 21 asteoruen, *sic; cf.* f. 84b. 16.

f. 84b. 4 *in right margin mark* ×; Ie)remie *underlined.* 5 al ꝥ *to* spi him on *underlined.*

negede deadliche.ˊ deiden alle clane. ꝥ beoð his gode wer
kes. þe beoð forloren alle. ȝet up on al þis ilke he is
him seolf biwrixlet ⁊ bicumen of godes child.ˊ þe deof
les bearn of helle. eatelich to seonne as godd seolf i þe 10
godspel seið. Vos ex patre diabolo estis. Þenche euch of
his estat ꝥ he is oðer wes ín.ˊ ⁊ he mei seon hweruore
he ah to siken sare. for þi seið Ieremie. luctum unigeniti
fac tibi planctum amarum. Make bitter man as wif deð
for hire child þe nefde bute him ane. ⁊ sið hit biuoren 15
hire fearliche asteoruen. Nu þe oþer ꝥ ich bihet. A
mon þe were idemet for a luðer morðre to beo forbearnd
al cwic. oðer scheomeliche ahonget. hu walde his heorte
stonden? Me þu unseli sunful þa þu þurh deadlich sun
ne murðredest godes spuse. ꝥ is þi sawle. þa þu were i 20
demet forte beon ahonget o bearninde wearitre i þe
eche lei of helle. Þer þu makedest foreward mid te deo
uel of þi deað. ⁊ seidest in ysaie wið þe forlorene. Pepi
gimus cum morte fedus. ⁊ cum inferno iniuimus pactum. ꝥ
is. we habbeð treowðe ipliht deað. foreward ifeast mid 25
helle. for þis is þe feondes chaffere. He ȝeoue þe sunne.ˊ
⁊ tu him þi sawle. ⁊ ti bodi mid al to weane ⁊ to wontrea
ðe world abuten ende. Nu þe þridde scheortliche. þench.
A mon þe hefde al þe world o walde. ⁊ hefde for his cwead f. 85a
schipe forloren al on a stunde. hu he walde murnin ⁊ sa
ri iwurðen.ˊ þenne ahest tu to beon hundret siðe sarure
þe þurh an heaued sunne forlure þe riche of heoue
ne. forlure ure lauerd ꝥ is hundret siðen. ȝe þusent þu 5
sent siðen betere þen is al þe world.ˊ eorðe ba ⁊ heouene.
Que enim conuentio christi ad Belial. Nu ȝet þe feorðe. ȝef
þe
(M. 312) king hefde bitaht his deore sune to his an cniht to lok
ín. ⁊ unþeode leadde forð þis child in his warde. swa ꝥ tet
child seolf weorrede up on his feader wið ꝥ unþeode.ˊ 10
nalde þe cniht beo sari ⁊ scheomien ful sare? we beoð alle

16 asteoruen *probably intended for inf.* (F morir) *but cf.* ff. 84a. 21,88b.8.
17 forbearnd: H-*shaped* n *and* d *combined, projecting into margin.*
21 wearitre *sic.* 23 *in left margin mark* ×; in ysaie *underlined.*
25 is. we *to* ifeast *underlined.* 26 helle *underlined.*

godes sunen þe kinges of heouene þe haueð bitaht ure
euch an engel i warde. Sari is he on his wise hwen unþeo
de leat us forð. hwen we ure gode feader wreaðeð wið sun
15 ne. Beo we sari ꝥ we eauer schulen wreaðen swuch feader
⁊ sweamen swuch wardeín. þe wit ⁊ wereð us eauer wið þe
unseli gastes. for elles uuele us stode. Ah we schuhteð him
awei hwen we doð deadlich sunne. ant heo leapeð þenne
to.ˀ sone se he us firseð. Halde we him neh us wið smeal of
20 gode werkes. ⁊ us in his warde. wac crist ure euchan
to segil wardeín bereð to lutel menske. ⁊ kunnen him
to lutel þonc of his seruise. Þeos ⁊ monie reisuns beoð
hwi mon mei beo bitterliche sari for his sunnen. ⁊ wep
en ful sare. ⁊ wel is him þe swa mei.ˀ for wop is sawle hea
25 le. Vre lauerd deð toward us as me deð to uuel deattur.
nimeð leasse þen we ahen him. ⁊ is þah wel ipaiet. we
ahen him blod for blod. ant ure blod þah aȝeín his
blod ꝥ he schedde for us.ˀ were ful unefne change. Ah wast
f. 85b tu hu me ȝeddeð. Me nimeð ed uuel dettur aten for hweate.
ant ure lauerd nimeð ed us ure teares aȝeín his blod.ˀ ⁊ is
wilcweme. He weop o þe rode. o lazre. O ierusalem. for oðer
mon
ne sunnen. ȝef wepeð for ure ahne.ˀ nis na muche wunder.
5 wepe we qð þe hali mon i Vitas patrum. þa me hefde longe
on him iȝeiet efter sarmun. leote we qð he teares leste
ure ahne teares forseoðen us in helle.

Schrift schal beon ihal. ꝥ is. iseid al to a mon ut of
child hade. þe poure widewe hwen ha wule hire (M. 314)
10 hus cleansin.ˀ ha gedereð al þe greaste on an heap on
alre earst.ˀ ⁊ schuueð hit ut þenne. Þrefter kimeð eft
aȝeín ⁊ heapeð eft to gederes ꝥ wes ear ileauet ⁊ schu
ueð hit ut efter. Þrefter o þe smeale dust. ȝef hit dus
teð swiðe.ˀ ha flaskeð weater ⁊ swopeð ut efter al þet oðer.

20 wac crist, *sic.* 21 segil *sic, for* se gentil*; in left margin mark* ×.

f. 85b. 4 *between* ȝef *and* wepeð *interlined with caret* we (pe) *in pale ink, small, sloping up from left to right.* 8 *large red initial* S *between* 7 *and* 10, *with tail to* 13; *blue line-patterns within, and in margin from* 7 *down tail to* 16, *with trailer to* 20. 13 schu|ueð: ð *altered from* n.

Alswa schal þe schriueð him efter þe greate schuuen 15
ut te smealre. ȝef dust of lihte þohtes windeð to swiðe
up:· flaski teares on ham. ne schulen ha nawt þenne
ablende þe heorte ehnen. hwa se heleð eawiht. he naueð
iseid nawiht for hwon he beo þe skerre. as is ilich þe
mon þe haueð on him monie deadliche wunden. ant 20
schaweð þe leche alle ⁊ let healen buten an:· ꝥ he deieð
up on as he schulde on alle. he is ase men in a schíp
þe haueð monie þurles þer þe weater þreasteð in. ⁊
heo dutteð alle buten an þurh hwam ha druncnið
alle clane. Me teleð of þe hali mon þe lei on his deað 25
uuel ⁊ wes lað to seggen a sunne of his childhad ant
his abbat bed hím allegate seggen. Ant he ondswerede
ꝥ hit nere na n⟨e⟩od for þi ꝥ he wes lute child þa he hit
hit wrahte. O least þah unneaðe þurh þe abbates rop f. 86a
unge ꝥ he hit seide ⁊ deide þrefter sone. Efter his deað:·
com a niht ⁊ schawde him to his abbat i snaw hwite
schrudes as þe ꝥ wes iborhen. ⁊ seide ꝥ sikerliche ȝef he
nefde ꝥ ilke þing ꝥ he dude ichild had. i schrift utter 5
liche iseid:· he were idemet bimong þe forlorene. Alswa
of an oþer ꝥ wes for neh fordemet for þi ꝥ he hefde en
chearre i ned a mon to drinken ⁊ deide þrof unschri
uen. Alswa of þe leafdi for þi ꝥ ha hefde ileanet to a wa
ke a wummon an of hire weden. Ah hwa se haueð ȝeor 10
(M. 316) ne isoht alle þe hurnen of his heorte. ne ne con rungi
mare ut:· ȝef þer eawiht edluteð. hit is ich hopie iþe
schrift ischuuen ut mid tet oþer. hwen þer ne lið na
ȝemeles ⁊ he walde feín mare ȝef he cuðe seggen.

Schrift schal beo naket. ꝥ is naketliche imaket. nawt 15
bisamplet feire. ne hendeliche ismaket:· ah schulen
þe wordes beon ischawet efter þe werkes. ꝥ is tacne of hea
tunge. ꝥ me tukeð towundre þing ꝥ me heateð swiðe. ȝef
þu heatest ti sunne:· hwi spekest tu menskeliche þrof. hwi

15 *in right margin blue mark, offset from* S *in* f. 86. 19 as *sic for* ah. 28 n⟨e⟩od: e *interlined with caret.*

f. 86a. 1 hit *last word of prec. folio repeated.* 15 *large blue initial* S *between* 14 *and* 17 *with red line-patterns to right, within, and in margin from* 14 *to* 22. 17 ischawet, *? for* ischapet (F taillez, *but* L exponi)*; cf.* ff. 53b. 8, 114a. 20 (F taillez).

20 hudest tu his fulðe? Spec hit scheome schendfulliche ant
tuk hit al towundre. alswa as þu wel wult schende þen
schucke. Sire ha seið þe wummon ich habbe ihaued leof
mon. oðer ich habbe ibeon ha seið fol of me seoluen. þis
nis nawt naket schrift. biclute þu hit nawt. do awei þe
25 totagges. Vnwrih þe ⁊ sei. Sire godes are ich am a ful stod
meare. a stinkinde hore. ȝef þi fa a ful nome ⁊ cleope þi
sunne fule. Make hit i schrift steort naket. ꝥ is. ne hel
þu nawiht of al ꝥ lið þer abuten. þah to fule me mei
f. 86b seggen. Me ne þearf nawt nempnín ꝥ fule dede bi his
ahne fule nome. ne þe schendfule límes bi hare ahne
nome. inoh is to seggen swa:· ꝥ te hali schrift feader
witerliche understonde hweat tu wulle meanen. Abu
5 te sunne liggeð six þing ꝥ hit hulieð. O Latin circumstan
ces. On englisch totagges mahe beon icleopede. Persone.
Stude. Time. Manere. Tale. Cause. Persone:· þe dude þe sun
ne. oðer wið hwam me hit dude:· unwreo ⁊ segge. Sire
ich am a wummon ⁊ schulde bi rihte beo mare scheome
10 ful to habben ispeken as ich spec. oðer idon as ich dude.
for þi mí sunne is mare þen of a wepmon. for hit bi
com me wurse. Ich am an ancre. A nunne. A wif iweddet. (M. 318)
a meiden. a wummon ꝥ me lefde se wel. a wummon þe
habbe ear ibeon ibearnd wið swuch þing:· ⁊ ahte þe be
15 tere forte beon iwarnet. Sire hit wes wið swuch mon. ⁊
nempni þenne:· munek. Preost. oðer clearc. ⁊ of ꝥ ordre.
a weddet mon. a ladles þing. a wummon as ich am. Þis
is nu of persone. Alswa of þe Stude. Sire þus ich pleide oðer
spec ichirche. Eede o Ríng i chirchȝard. biheold hit oþer
20 wreastlunge. ⁊ oðre fol gomenes. spec þus oðer pleide biuo
ren worltliche men. biuoren recluse in ancre hus. ed oþer
þurl þen ich schulde. neh hali þing. Ich custe him þer.
hondlede him i swuch stude:· oðer me seoluen. I chirche ich
þohte þus. biheold him ed te weouede. Of þe time alswa.
25 Sire ich wes of swuch ealde. ꝥ ich ahte wel to habben wis
luker iwite me. Sire ich hit dude in lenten. i feasten da

21 tuk *sic: final* k *indicating* tuke *with phonetic elision.*

f. 86b. 7 *MS.* PerSone. 19 Eede *sic, for* Eode; *the last* e *is altered from* o.

hes. in hali dahes. hwen oþre weren ed chirche. Sire ich
wes sone ouercumen. ⁊ is þe sunne mare þen ȝef ich hefde
ibeon akeast wið strengðe. ⁊ feole swenges. Sire ich wes þe f. 87a
bigínnunge hwi swuch þing hefde forðȝong. þurh ꝥ
ich com i swuch stude ⁊ i swuch time. Ich biþohte me ful
wel ear þen ich hit eauer dude. hu uuele hit were idon.᾽
⁊ dude hit noðeleatere. Þe Manere alswa seggen. ꝥ is þe 5
feorðe totagge. Sire þis sunne ich dude þus ⁊ o þisse
wise. þus ich leornede hit earst. þus ich com earst þrin. þus
ich dude hit forðward o þus feole wisen. þus fulliche. þus
scheomeliche. þus ich sohte delit hu ich meast mahte pai
(M. 320) en mí lustes brune. ⁊ seggen al þe wise. Tale is þe feorðe 10
totagge. Cause is hwi þu hit dudest. oðer hulpe oþre þer
to. oðer þurh hwet hit bigon. Sire ich hit dude for delit.
for uuel luue. for biȝete. for fearlac. for flatrunge. Sire
ich hit dude for uuel þah þer ne come nan of. Síre mí
lihte ondswere. oðer míne lihte lates tulden him earst up 15
o me. Sire of þis word com oþer. of þis dede wreaððe ⁊ vue
le wordes. Sire þe acheisun is þis hwi ꝥ uuel leasteð ȝet.
þus wac wes mín heorte. Euch efter ꝥ he is segge his totagg
es. Mon as limpeð to him.᾽ wummon ꝥ hire rineð. for her
nabbe ich nan iseid bute forte munegín mon oðer wummon 20
of þeo þe to ham falleð þurh þeo þe beoð her iseide as on
urn. þus of þeose six wriheles despoile þi sunne ⁊ make
hit naket i þi schrift as Ieremie leareð. Effunde sicut aquam
cor tuum. Sched ut ase weater þín heorte. ȝef eoile schet.᾽
of a feat.᾽ ȝet ter wule leauen in sumhwet of þe licur. 25
ȝef milc schet.᾽ þe heow leaueð. ȝef wín sched.᾽ þe smeal
leaueð. ah weater geað al somet ut alswa sched þin heor
te. ꝥ is. al ꝥ uuel þet is i þín heorte. ȝef þu ne dest nawt.᾽
lo hu grurefulliche godd seolf þreateð þe. þurh Naum f. 87b
þe prophete. Ostendam gentibus nuditatem tuam ⁊ regnis
ignominiam tuam ⁊ proitiam super te abhominationes tuas.

f. 87a. 10 feorðe, *sic for* fifte; *passage dealing with* Tale (M. 320, 1–8) *omitted, between* 11 totagge *and* [Cause is þe seste totagge.] Cause is.

f. 87b. 1 Naum *underlined.* 1/2 *in left margin mark* × *and marginal scribble from* 2 *to* 5.

Þu naldest nawt unwreo þe to þe preost i schrifte.' ⁊ ich (M. 322)
5 schal schawin al naket to al folc þi cweadschipe. ⁊ to al
le kinedomes þíne scheome sunnen. to þe kinedom of
eorðe. to þe kinedom of helle. to þe kinedom of heoue
ne. ⁊ trussin al þi schendfulnesse o þín ahne necke. as
me deð o þe þeof þe me leat to demen. ⁊ swa wið al þe
10 schendlac þu schalt trusse ⁊ al torplin in to helle. O
seið sein Beornard. Quid confusionis quid ignominie
erit quando dissipatis folíís ⁊ dispersis uniuersa nudabitur
turpitudo. Saníes apparebit. O seið seín beornard. Hwuch
schendlac ⁊ hwuch sorhe bið þer ed te dome. hwen alle þe
15 leaues schule beon to warplet. ⁊ al ꝥ fulðe schaweð him.
⁊ wríngeð ut ꝥ wursum biuoren al þe wide worlt. eorð
ware ⁊ heouenes. nawt ane of werkes.' ah of idelnesses. of
wordes ⁊ of þohtes þe ne beoð ibet her.' as seint anselme
witneð. Omne tempus impensum requiretur a uobis qualiter sit
20 expensum. Euc tide ⁊ time schal beo þer irikenet hu hit
wes her ispenet. Quando dissipatis folíís ⁊ cetera. Hwen
alle þe
leaues he seið seín Beornard schulen beo towarplet. he
biheold hu adam ⁊ eue þa ha hefden i þe frumðe isune
get.' gedereden leaues ⁊ makeden wriheles of ham to hare
25 schentfule límen. þus doð monie efter ham. Declinantes
cor suum in uerba malicie ad excusandas excusationes in pec
Schrift schal beon ofte i maket. for þi is ¶ .catis.
i þe sawter. Confitebimur tibi deus confitebimur. Ant
f. 88a ure lauerd seolf seið to his deciples. Eamus iterum in iudeam.
Ga we eft seide he in to Iudee. Iudee spealeð schrift. ⁊ swa
we ifindeð ꝥ he wende ofte ut of galilee in to Iudee. Gali
lee spealeð hweol. forte learen us ꝥ we of þe worldes tur
5 pelnesse ⁊ of sunne hweol.' ofte gan to schrifte. for þis is
þe sacrement efter þe weofdes sacrement. ⁊ efter fulluht.'
ꝥ te feond is laðest. as he haueð to hali men hím seolf sare

4, 5 Þu nal(dest *and* schal s(chawin *underlined.* 13 turpitudo: *second* t *altered from* d. 27 *large red initial* S *between* 26 *and a line-space below* 28*: blue line-patterns to right, within, and in margin from* 26 *down tail to present bottom edge. A blue paragraph touched with red before* .catis.

his unþonckes ibeon hit icnawen. wule a web beon ed en
(M. 324) chearre wið a weater wel ibleachet ? A sol clað wel iweschen ?
þu weschest þine honden in anlepi dei twien oðer þrien. 10
ant nult nawt þe sawle iesu cristes spuse. þe eauer se ha is
hwittre:' se fulðe is senre up on hire. bute ha beo iwesschen.
nult nawt to godes cluppunge ofte umbe seoueniht wes
schen hire eanes. Confiteor. hali weater. Beoden. hali þohtes.
Blesceunges. Cneolunges. Euch god word. euch god werc:' 15
wesscheð smeale sunnen þe me ne mei alle seggen. Ah
eauer is schrift þe heaued.

Schrift schal beon on hihðe imaket. ȝef sunne tím
eð bi niht:' anan oðer ine marhen. ȝef hit timeð
bi dei:' ear þen me slepe. Hwa durste slepen hwil his dea 20
dliche fa heolde an itohe sweord up on his heaued ? Þe
neappið up on helle breord:' ha torplið ofte al in ear ha
least wenen. Hwa se is ifallen amid te bearninde fur.
nis he mare þen amead ȝef he lið biþencheð him hwen
ne he wule arisen ? A wummon þe haueð ilosed hire nel 25
de. oðer a sutere his eal:' secheð hit ananriht ⁊ towent
euch strea aþet hit beo ifunden. ⁊ godd þurh sunne forlo
(M. 326) ren schal liggen unsoht seoue dahes fulle. Nihe þínges
beoð ꝥ ahten hihín to schrift. þe píne ꝥ okereð. for sunne f. 88b
is þe deofles feh ꝥ he ȝeueð to okere ⁊ to gauel of píne.
⁊ eauer se mon lið lengre in his sunne:' se þe gauel waxeð
of pine i purgatoire. oðer her oðer in helle. Ex usuris ⁊
iniquitate ⁊ cetera. Þe oðer þing is þe muchele ⁊ te reowð- 5
fule lu
re ꝥ he leoseð. ꝥ na þing ꝥ he deð nis gode licwurðe. Alieni
comederunt robur eius. þe þridde is deað ꝥ he nat hweðer
he schule ꝥ ilke dei ferliche asteoruen. fili ne tardes ⁊ cetera.
Þe feorðe is secnesse ꝥ he ne mei þenche wel. bute ane of

f. 88a. 15 *to* 18 *a tear in right margin.* 18 *large blue initial* S *with red line-patterns within, and in margin from* 16 *to* 24. 24 biþencheð, *sic: probably for* biþenched (F gist sei purpensant); *cf.* biswenchet, f. 112b. 7. 28 Circumdederunt me canes multi *to* swuch beatunge (M. 324–6) *is placed later*, f. 88b. 24 *to* f. 89a. 12. 28 *on* þinges *red offset from* S *on* f. 87b.

f. 88b. 1 *after* hihín: þe *interlined with caret (erroneously) in pale ink, small, sloping up from left to right.*

10 his uuel:· ne speoken as he schulde. bute granin for his eche.
⁊ grunte mare for his stiche:· þen for his sunne. Sanus confiteberis
⁊ viuens. Þe fifte þing is muche scheome ꝥ hit is efter val:·
to liggen se longe. ⁊ hure under þe schucke. Þe seste is þe
wunde ꝥ eauer wurseð on hond ⁊ strengre is to healen. Principi
15 is obsta. Medicina paratur cum mala perlongas. Þe seoueðe þing
is uuel wune. ꝥ lazre bitacneð. þe stonc se longe he hefde ileín
i þer eorðe. o hwam ure lauerd weop as þe godspel teleð. ⁊ risede
⁊ mengde hím seoluen. ⁊ ȝeide lude up on him ear he hím
arearde. forte schawin hu strong hit is to arisen of uuel wune
20 þe roteð ín his sunne. Seinte Marie. lazre stonc of fowr dahes. (M. 328)
hu stínkeð þe sunfule of fowr ȝer oðer of fíue. Quam difficile
surgit quem moles male consuetudinis premit. O seið seínt
austín hu earmliche he ariseð þe under wune of sunne ha
ueð ileín longe. Círcumdederunt me canes multi. Monie
25 hundes seið dauið habbeð biset me. Hwen gredi hundes ston
deð biuore þe bord:· nis hit neod ȝerde? As ofte as eani lecheð
toward te ⁊ reaueð þe of þi mete. nult tu as ofte smíten?
elles ha walden kecchen of þe al ꝥ tu hefdest. Ant tu alswa
f. 89a þenne. ním þe ȝerde of þi tunge. ⁊ as ofte as þe dogge of hel
le kecheð ei god from þe:· smít him ananriht mid te ȝerde
of þi tunge i schrift. ⁊ smit him se luðerliche ꝥ him laði ⁊ drede
to snecchen eft toward te. ꝥ dunt of alle duntes is him dunte
5 laðest. þe hund þe fret leðer oðer awurið ahte. me hit beat
ananriht ꝥ he understonde for hwi he is ibeaten. þenne ne
dear he nawt eft do ꝥ ilke. Beat alswa mid ti tunge schrift:·
þe hund of helle ananriht. ⁊ he wule beon ofdred to do þe eft

15 sero *omitted before* Medicina; perlongas, *sic*, *for* per longas [conualuere moras]. *In the left margin two hands, the first pointing to* ⁊ grunte 11; *the second to* þe roteð 20.

f. 89a. 5 awurið, *sic*. 7 i *omitted after* tunge.

swuch þucke. Hwa is se fol ꝥ he seið bi þe hund ꝥ fret leðer.
Abid aþet to marhen. ne beat tu hím nawt ȝetten. Ah anan 10
riht beat. beat beat ananriht. nis þing i þe world ꝥ smeor
teð him sarre. þen deð swuch beatunge. Se me deoppre
wadeð i þe feondes leíuen.' se me kimeð up leatere. Þe eahtu
ðe þing is ꝥ seint gregoire seið. Peccatum quod per penitentiam non di
luitur.' mox suo pondere ad aliud trahit. ꝥ is. sunne þet nis 15
sone ibet.' draheð anan an oðer. ant ꝥ eft þe þridde. ⁊ swa
euchan cundleð mare ⁊ wurse cundel.' þen þe seolue moder.
Þe Niheðe reisun is. se he ear biginneð her.' to don his pe
nitence.' se he haueð to beten leasse i pine of purgatoire. Þis
beoð nu nihe reisuns. ⁊ monie ma þer beoð hwi schrift ah 20
to beon imaket aa on hihðe.

Schrift ah to beon eadmod as þe puplicanes wes. nawt
as þe phariseus wes þe talde his goddeden. ⁊ schawde
þet hale forð.' þa he schulde habben unwihen hise wunden.
for þi he wende unhealet as ure lauerd seolf teleð ut of þe tem 25
ple. Eadmodnesse is ilich þeose coínte hearloz. hare gute
feastre. hare flowinde cweise ꝥ ha putteð eauer forð. ⁊
ȝef hit is eatelich.' ha schawið hit ȝet eateluker i riche
monnes ehnen. ꝥ ha habben reowðe of ham ⁊ ȝeouen ham f. 89b
god þe reaðere. hudeð hare hale clað. ⁊ doð on alre uuem
est fiterokes al totorene. O þis ilke wise eadmodnesse ead
(M. 330) modliche bigileð ure lauerd. ⁊ biȝet of his god wið seli tru
andise. hudeð eauer hire god.' schaweð forð hire pouerte. 5
put forð hire cancre. wepinde ⁊ graninde biuore godes
ehnen. halseð meadlesliche on his derue passíun. on
his deorewurðe blod. on his fif wunden. on his moder teares.
o þe ilke tittes ꝥ he seac. þe milc ꝥ híme fedde. on alle his
halhene luue. o þe deore druerie ꝥ he haueð to his deore 10
spuse. ꝥ is to cleane sawle.' oðer to hali chirche. on his deað

12 *a hole between* Se me *and* deoppre. 22 *large red initial* S *between* 21 *and* 24, *with long tail; blue line-patterns to right, within, and in margin from* 19 *to below tail; directing* S *in left margin.* 24 unwihen, *sic for* unwrihen. 27 *before* flowinde: gı *crossed out* (*probably beginning of erroneous repetition of* gute).

f. 89b. 4 ead|modliche *for* eadiliche. 9 híme: m *has first stroke expuncted, to restore the older form* hine.

o rode. for hire to biȝeotene. wið þus anewil ropunge hal
seð efter sum help to þe wrecche meoseise. to lechni wið þe
seke. to healen hire cancre. Ant ure lauerd ihalset swa.· ne mei
15 for reowðe wearnen hire ne sweamen hire wið warne. no
meliche swa as he is se unimete large. ꝥ him nis na þíng
leouere. þen þet he mahe ifinden acheisun forte ȝeoue
ne. Ah hwa se ȝelpeð of his god as doð i schrift þeos prude.·
hwet neod is ham to helpe ? Moni haueð a swuch manere
20 to seggen hire sunnen. ꝥ hit is wurð a dearne ȝelp ant
hunteð efter hereword of mare halinesse.

Schrift ah to beon scheomeful. bi ꝥ te folc of israel wende
ut þurh þe reade sea ꝥ wes read ⁊ bitter.· is bitacnet ꝥ
we moten þurh rudi scheome. ꝥ is isoð schrift. ⁊ þurh bitter
25 penitence passín to heouene. God riht is wat crist ꝥ us scheo
míe biuore mon.· þe forȝeten scheome þa we duden þe sunne
biuore godes sihðe. Nam omnia nuda sunt ⁊ aperta oculis
eius.
ad quem nobis sermo. for al ꝥ is al is naket seið seinte pawel.
⁊ o
f. 90a pen to his ehnen. wið hwam we schulen rikenín alle ure de
den. Scheome is þe measte deal as seint austin seið of ure pe
nitence. Verecundia pars est magna penetentíe. ant sein
Bernard
seið. ꝥ na deorewurðe ȝimstan ne deliteð swa muchel mon
5 to bihalden.· as deð godes ehe þe rude of monnes neb.· þe
riht seið hise sunnen. Vnderstond wel þis word. Schrift is
a sacrement. ⁊ euch sacrament haueð an ilicnesse utewið.·
of ꝥ hit wurcheð inwið. as hit is i fulluht. Þe wesschunge (M. 332)
wið uten.· bitacneð þe wesschunge of sawle wið innen. Al
10 swa i schrift. þe cwike rude of þe neb.· deð to understonden
ꝥ te sawle þe wes bla. ⁊ nefde bute dead heow.· haueð icaht
cwic heow ⁊ is irudet feire. Interior tamen penitentia non
dicitur sacramen
tum. set exterior uel puplica uel Solempnis.

12 *a hole between* rode. *and* for hire. 22 *large blue initial* S; *red line-patterns within, and in margin* 19 *down into bottom margin.* 27 Nam om(nia *underlined.* 28 *in left margin mark* ×; ad quem, *and* al is *to end, underlined.*

f. 90a. 1 *underlined to* ure. *In left margin a hole between* 4 *and* 7.

Schrift schal beo dredful. ꝥ tu segge wið Ierome. Quoci
ens confessus sum.· uideor michi non esse confessus. As 15
ofte as
ich am ischríuen.· eauer me þuncheð me unschriuen. for
eauer is sum forȝeten of þe totagges. for þi seið seint au
stin. Ve laudabili hominum uíte si remota misericordia discu
tias eam. ꝥ is. þe beste mon of al þe world. ȝef ure lauerd
demde him al efter rihtwisnesse. ⁊ nawt efter mearci.· Wa 20
schulde him iwurðen. Set misericordia superexaltat iudicium.
Ah his mearci toward us.· weieð eauer mare þen þe rihte
Schrift schal beon hopeful. Hwa se seið ¶.nearewe.
as he con. ⁊ deð al ꝥ he mei.· godd ne bit namare. Ah
hope ⁊ dred schulen aa beon imengt togederes. Þis forte bi 25
tacnín.· wes i þe alde lahe ihaten ꝥ te twa grindelstanes.
ne schulde namon twínnín. Þe neoðere þe lið stille ⁊ bereð
heuí charge.· bitacneð fearlac þe teieð mon from sunne.
⁊ is iheueget her wið heard forte beo quite of heardre. Þe f.90b
vuere stan bitacneð hope þe eorneð ⁊ stureð hire igode
werkes eauer wið trust of muche mede. Þeos twa namon
ne parti from. for as seín gregoire seið. Spes sine timore
luxuriat in presumptionem. Tímor sine spe.· degenerat in 5
desperationem. Dred wið uten hope.· makeð mon untrus
ten. ant hope wið ute dred.· makeð ouertrusten. þeos twa
unþeawes. Vntrust ⁊ ouertrust.· beoð þe deofles tristen. þer
ꝥ wrecche beast seldene edstearteð. Triste is þer me sit mid
(M. 334) te greahunz forte kepe þe heare. oðer tildeð þe nettes a 10
ȝeín him. Toward an of þeos twa is al ꝥ he sleateð. for
þer beoð his greahunz. þer beoð his nettes. Vntrust ⁊ o
uertrust beoð of alle sunnen nest te ȝete of helle. wið
dred wið uten hope. ꝥ is wið untrust.· wes Caymes schrift
⁊ Iudasen. for hwi ha forferden. wið hope wið ute dred.· þet 15
is wið ouertrust.· is þe unselies sahe þe seið i þe sawter.
Secundum

14 *large red initial* S *between* 13 *and* 16 *with tail to* 19; *blue line-patterns to right, within, and in margin from* 12 *to* 22. 23 *large blue initial* S *between* 22 *and* 24; *red line-patterns to right, within, and in margin from* 22 *to present bottom edge* (*tip cut off*). *Before* .nearewe. *a red paragraph ornamented with blue.*

f. 90b. 4 *after* from *a caret; above it* oþer *in pale ink, small, sloping up from left to right. In right margin a hole between* 5 *and* 6.

multitudinem ire sue non queret. Nis nawt godd qð ha
se grím as ȝe him fore makieð. Na he seið dauið. ȝeoi he
⁊ seið þenne. Propter quid irritauit impius deum? dixit enim
20 in corde suo non requiret. On alre earst he cleopeð þe
ouertrusti unbileuet. Þe unbileuet wið hwon gremeð he
godd almihti? wið þon ꝥ he seið. Nule he nawt se nea
rowliche demen as ȝe seggeð. ȝeoi siker ah he wule. þus þeos
twa unþeawes beoð to grimme robberes ieuenet. for þe an ꝥ
25 is ouertrust. reaueð godd his rihte dom ⁊ his rihtwisnesse.
Þe oðer ꝥ is untrust.' reaueð him his milce. ant swa ha
beoð umben to fordon godd seolf. for godd ne muhte nawt
beon wið uten rihtwisnesse. ne wið uten milce. Nu þenne
f. 91a hwucche unþeawes beoð euening to þeose þe wulleð godd
acwellen on hare fule wise? ȝef þu art totrusti ⁊ haldest
godd to nessche forte wreoke sunne.' sunne likeð him bi
þin tale. ah bihald hu he wrec in his heh engel. þe þohte
5 of a prude. hu he wrec in adam þe bite of an eappel. hu
he bisencte sodome ⁊ gommorre. were. ⁊ wif. ⁊ wenchel. þe
nomecuðe burhes. al a muche schire dun in to helle grun
de. þer as is nu þe deade sea ꝥ nawiht cwikes nis inne. hu he
i Noes flod al þe world adrencte. bute eahte iþe arche. hu he
10 ín his ahne folc israel his deorling. grimliche awrec hím ase (M. 336)
ofte as ha gulten. Dathan. ⁊ Abyron. Chore. ⁊ his feren. Þe
oþre alswa þe he sloh bi feole þusendes ofte for hare gruch
unge ane. On oþer half loke. ȝef þu hauest untrust of
his unimete milce.' hu lihtliche ⁊ hu sone. seinte peter efter
15 ꝥ he hefde forsaken hím. ⁊ ꝥ for a cwene worð.' wes wið him
isahtnet. O þe þeof o rode þe hefde aa ilíued uuele in a stert
hwile hefde ed him milce wið a feier speche. for þi bitweone
þeos twa. Vntrust. ⁊ ouertrust. hope ⁊ dred beon aa. ifeiet
to ge

Schrift ȝet schal beo wis. ⁊ to wis mon ímaket. . deres.
20 Of uncuðe sunnen. nawt to ȝunge preostes. ȝun

f. 91a. 16 O þe þeof: *between* O *and* þ *tall* f *inserted with thin stem sloping back, and flourished top, in pale ink; but* O *is error for* Hu. 15 worð, *sic.* 19 *large red initial* S *between* 18 *and* 21 *with tail to* 23; *blue line-patterns within, and a few to right and in margin from* 16 *to* 24; *directing* S *in left margin. Paragraph omitted before* . deres. *Between and of* 19 *and* 22 *a narrow hole* (*stitches now lost*) *avoided*

ge ich segge of wit.' ne to sotte alde. Bigín earst ed pru de.
⁊ sech alle þe bohes þrof. as ha beoð þruppe iwríte
ne hwuch falle to þe. Þrefter alswa of onde. ⁊ ga we swa du
neward rawe bi rawe. aþet to þe leaste. ant drah to gedere
al þe team under þe moder. 25

Schrift ah to beo soð. ne lih þu nawt o þe seolf. for as seínt
Saustín seið. Quí causa humilitatis de se mentitur.' fit quod
prius ipse non fuit .id est. peccator. Þe seið leas on him seolf þurh
to muchel eadmodnesse.' he is ímaket sunful þah he ear nere. f. 91b
Sein Gregoire seið þah. Bonarum mentium est culpam agnoscere
ubi culpa non est. Cunde of god heorte is to beon offea
ret of sunne þer as nan nis ofte. oðer weie swiðre his
sunne sumchearre þen he þurfte. weien hit to lutel.' is 5
ase uuel oðer wurse. þe middel wei of meosure is eauer
guldene. Drede we us eaure. for ofte we weneð forte don a
lutel uuel.' ⁊ doð a great sunne. ofte wel to donne.' ⁊ doð al
(M. 338) to cweade. Segge we eauer þenne wið seinte anselme. Etiam
bonum nostrum est aliquo modo corruptum. ut possit non placere.' 10
aut certe displicere deo. Paulus. Scio quod non est in me.' hoc est
in carne mea bonum. Na god in us nis of us.' ure god is
godes. ah sunne is of us ⁊ ure ahne. Godes god hwen ich
hit do. qð he seínt anselme. swa o summe wise min uuel
hit forgneaieð.' oþer ich hit do ungleadliche. oþer to ear 15
oðer to leate.' oðer leote wel þrof. þah namon hit nute. oþ
er walde ꝥ ei hit wiste. oðer ȝemelesliche do hit. oðer to un
wisliche. to muchel oðer to lutel. þus eauer sum uuel mon
gleð hím wið mi god ꝥ godes grace ȝeueð me.' ꝥ hit mei

by scribe, dividing pru de 21, *and separating* þruppe iwríte 22. 22 *before* beoð: weren *crossed out.* 26 *large blue initial* S; *red line-patterns within, and a few lines in margin running from* 24 *to edge of large hole in bottom left-hand corner; directing* S *in left margin.* 28 leas *on an erasure* (*probably of* fals). *From a hole in bottom edge a tear* (*stitches now lost*) *runs up to ruling of* 27, *separating* 28 on *from* him.

20 lutel likin godd.ˀ ant mislikin ofte. Seinte Marie
hwen þe hali mon seide þus bi him seolf.ˀ hu ma
he we hit witerliche seggen bi us wrecches ?

Schrift ah to beon willes. ꝥ is willeliche unfreinet.
Snawt idrahen of þe as þin unþonkes.ˀ Hwil þu const
25 seggen eawt.ˀ sei al uneasket. Me ne schal easki nan.ˀ bute
for neode ane. for of þe easkunge mei uuel fallen bute hit
beo þe wisre. On oðer half moni mon abit forte schriuen
him aðet te nede tippe. Ah ofte him liheð þe wrench. ꝥ he
f. 92a ne mei hwen he wule.ˀ þe nalde þa he mahte. Na mare cang
schipe nis. þen setten godd tearme. as þah grace were his.ˀ
as he bere hire in his purs. to neomen up o grace þrín iþe
tearme as he him seolf sette. Nai beal ami nai. þe tearme
5 is igodes hond.ˀ nawt i þi bandun. Hwen godd beot hit te.ˀ
reach to ba þe honden. for wiðdrahe he his hond.ˀ þu maht
þrefter lokin. ȝef uuel oðer oþerhwet ned te to schrifte.ˀ lo
hwet seið seint austín. Coacta seruicia deo non placent.
Seruises inedde ne cwemeð nawt ure lauerd. þah noðeleatere (M. 340)
10 betere is o þene no. Nunquam sera penitentía si tamen uera.
Nis neauer
to leate penitence ꝥ is soðliche imaket. he seið eft him seol
uen. Ah betere is as dauið seið. Refloruit caro mea ⁊ ex
uolun
tate mea confitebor ei. ꝥ is. mí flesch is ifluret. bicumen al
neowe. for ich chulle schriue me ⁊ herie godd willes. wel seið
15 he ifluret to bitacnín wil schrift. for þe eorðe al unnet. ⁊ te
treon alswa openið ham ⁊ bringeð forð misliche flures. In
Canticis. flores apparuerunt in terra nostra. Eadmodnesse.
absti
nence. Culures unlaðnesse. ⁊ oþre swucche uertuz beoð fei
re i godes ehnen. ⁊ swote i godes nease smeallinde flures.
20 Of ham make his herbearhe inwið þe seoluen. for his de
lices he seið beoð þer forte wunien. Et delicie mee esse. cum
filíís hominum in libro prouerbiorum.

f. 91b. 20 *to* 22*: narrow hole* (*see recto*) *occupies beginning of* 20 *and* 21 *and separates* he we *from* hit 22. 23 *large red initial* S *between* 22 *and* 25, *with tail below* 28; *blue line-patterns within, and in margin from* 21 *with trailers to present bottom edge* (*tip cut off*). 28 *tear* (*see recto*) *divides* nede *and* tippe; *top of the* t *in two strokes, as if altered from* c.

Schrift ah to beon ahne. Namon ne schal i schrift wrei
Sen bute him seoluen.' ase forð as he mei. þis ich segge
for þi þet swuch auenture bitimeð to sum mon oðer to 25
sum wummon.' ꝥ ha ne mei nawt fulleliche wreien
hire seoluen.' bute ha wreie oþre. ah bi nome noðeleatere
ne nempni ha nawt þe ilke. þah þe schrift feader wite wel
toward hwam hit turne. Ah a munk. oðer a preost. nawt f. 92b
wilȝam ne water.' þah þer ne beo nan oþer.

Schrift schal beo studeuest to halde þe penitence.' ⁊ lea
Sue þe sunne. ꝥ tu segge to þe preost. Ich habbe stude
festliche i þonc ⁊ in heorte þis sunne to forleten. ⁊ do þe pe 5
nitence. Þe preost ne schal nawt easki þe ȝef þu wult þeon
ne uorð forhate þi sunne.' Inoh is ꝥ tu segge. ꝥ tu hit ha
uest on heorte treoweliche to donne.' þurh godes grace. ⁊
ȝef þu fallest eft þrín.' ꝥ tu wult anan riht arisen þurh
(M. 342) godes help.' ⁊ cumen aȝein to schrift. Vade ⁊ amplius no 10
li peccare. Ga qð ure lauerd to a sunful wummon. ⁊ ha
ue wil ꝥ tu nult sungi namare. Þus ne easkede he nan oðer

Schrift ah to beon biþoht biuore. ¶ .sikernesse.
Slonge. Of fif þinges wið þi wit gedere þine sunnen
of alle þine ealdes. of childhad of ȝuheðe had gedere al 15
to gederes. þrefter gedere þe studen ꝥ tu ín wunedest. ant
þench ȝeorne hwet tu dudest in euch stude sunderliche
⁊ in euch ealde. þrefter sech al ut ⁊ trude þine sunnen bi
þine fif wittes. þrefter bi alle þine límen. i hwuch þu ha
uest isuneget meast oðer oftest. Aleast sunderliche bi 20
NV ȝe habbeð alle ihaued ¶ .dahes ⁊ bi tiden.

f. 92a. 23 *large blue initial* S; *red line-patterns within, and in margin from* 31 *down tail to deep in bottom margin.* 26 hire *crossed out with bold stroke after* wreien.

f. 92b. *This page has four large initial letters,* S, S, N, Þ, *alternating red/blue; their marginal ornament, alternating blue/red, forms a continuous border from* 2 *to the bottom edge* (*the end of the trailers of* Þ *are now cut off*). S, S, Þ *have tails, and ornament in line-patterns within and on both sides;* N, *the smallest, only a few blue lines.* 2 wilȝam *has* w, *not* ƿ; *the bottom of* wilȝ *is covered by the top of* S. 3 *initial* S *between* 2 *and* 5. 13 *initial* S *between* 12 *and* 15; *before* .sikernesse. *a red paragraph touched with blue.* 21 *initial* N *between* 20 *and* 22; *before* .dahes ⁊ bi tiden. *a blue paragraph touched with red.*

as ich understonde þe sixtene stucchen þe ich bihét to
dealen. ⁊ alle ich habbe tobroken ham ow míne leoue
sustren. as me deð to children. þe mahten wið unbroke
25 bread deien on hunger. ah me is ꝥ wite ȝe moni crome
edfallen. secheð ham ⁊ gederið for ha beoð sawle fode.

Þulli schrift ꝥ haueð þus þes sixtene stucchen.· haueð þe
þilke muchele mihten þet ich earst seide. Þreo aȝeín þe
f. 93a deouel. Þreo on us seoluen. Ant þreo aȝeines þe world. deo
rewurðe ouer gold or.· ⁊ ȝímmes of ynde. Míne leoue
sustren þis fifte dale þe is of schrift.· límpeð to alle men ili
che. for þi ne wundri ȝe ow nawt. ꝥ ich toward ow nomeli
5 che nabbe nawt ispeken iþis dale. Habbeð þah to ower biho
ue þis lutle leaste ende. of alle cuðe sunnen. as of prude. of
great oðer of heh heorte. of onde. of wreaððe. of slawðe. of
ȝemeles. of Idel word. of untohene þohtes. of sum idel herun
ge. of sum fals gleadunge. oðer of heui murnunge. of ypo
10 cresie. of mete. of drunch to muchel oðer to lutel. of gruch (M. 344)
unge. of grim chére. of silences ibrokene. of sitten longe ed
þurl. of vres mis iseide. wið ute ȝeme of heorte.· oðer ín untí
me. of sum fals word. of sware. of plohe of ischake lahtre.
of schede cromen oðer ale. of leote þinges muhelín. Rustín
15 oðer rotien. claðes unseowet. bireinet. unwesschen. breoke
nep oðer disch. oðer biseo ȝemelesliche ei þíng ꝥ me wið
feareð. oðer ahte toȝemen. of keorfunge. of hurtunge.
þurh unbisehenesse. Of alle þe þinges þe beoð i þis riwle.
þe beoð mis numene. of alle þulliche þing schriue hire
20 euche wike eanes ed te leaste. for nan se lutel nis of þeos.·
ꝥ te deouel naueð enbreuet on his rolle. Ah schrift hit
schrapeð of. ⁊ makeð him to leosen muchel of his hwile.
Ah al ꝥ schrift ne schrapeð of.· al he wule o domes dei rede
ful witerliche forte bicleopie þe wið. a word ne schal þer
25 wontín. Nu þenne ich reade ȝeoueð him to writen þet
leaste ꝥ ȝe eauer mahen. for na meoster nis him leouere.
ant hwet se he writ.· beoð umben to schrapien hit of clean
liche. wið na þing ne mahe ȝe matin hím betere. To euch

27 *initial* Þ *between* 26 *and below* 28.

f. 93a. 2 *small, poorly executed, initial* M *in red, with a few blue lines.*

preost mei ancre schriuen hire of swucche utterliche sunnen f. 93b
þe to alle bifalleð. Ah ful trusti ha schal beon o þe preostes
godlec. ꝥ ha allunge schaweð to. hu hire stonde abute fles
ches temptatiuns. ȝef ha is swa ifondet. bute ideaðes dute. Þus
þah me þuncheð ꝥ ha mei seggen. Sire flesches fondunge
ꝥ ich habbe oðer habbe ihaued.' geað to uorð up o me þurh
mi þeafunge. Ich am ofdred leste ich ga dríuínde oðerhwiles
to swiðe forðward mine fol þohtes. ⁊ fule umbe stunde. as
þah ich huntede efter licunge. Ich mihte þurh godes streng
(M. 346) ðe schaken ham ofte of me.' ȝef ich were cwicliche ⁊ stealew
urðliche umben. Ich am offearet sare ꝥ te delit iþe þoht
leaste to longe ofte. swa ꝥ hit cume neh skiles ȝettunge. Ne
dear ich ꝥ ha deopluker ne witerluker schriue hire to
ȝung preost her abuten. Ant ȝet of þis inohreaðe hím
walde þunche wunder. Ah to hire ahne schrift feader. oðer
to sum lif hali mon ȝef ha mei him habben.' culle al þe
pot ut. þer speowe ut al ꝥ wunder. þer wið fule wordes ꝥ
fulðe efter ꝥ hit is tuki al towundre. swa ꝥ ha drede ꝥ ha
hurte his earen ꝥ hercneð hire sunnen. ȝef ei ancre nat
nawt of þulliche þinges.' þonki ȝeorne iesu crist.' ⁊ halde
hire i drede. Þe deouel nis nawt dead.' ꝥ wite ha þah he slepe.

Lihte gultes beteð þus anan bi ow seoluen. ⁊ þah seggeð
ham i schrift hwen ȝe þencheð ham on as ȝe speokeð mid
preoste. for þe leaste of alle sone se ȝe underȝeoteð hit.' falleð
biuoren ower weoued o cros to þer eorðe. ⁊ seggeð mea culpa.
Ich gulte mearci lauerd. Þe preost ne þearf for na gult bute
hit beo þe greattre.' leggen oþer schrift on ow.' þen ꝥ lif ꝥ ȝe
leadeð efter þeos riwle. Ah efter þe absolutiun.' he schal þus seg
gen. Al ꝥ god ꝥ tu eauer dest. ⁊ ⟨al⟩ ꝥ vuel ꝥ tu eauer þolest f. 94a
for þe luue of iesu crist inwið þine ancre wahes.' al ich en

f. 93b. 22 *large red initial* L; *stem in margin between* 19 *and* 22; *blue ornament in angle and in margin from* 14 *to* 27.

f. 94a. 1 al *written above* ⁊.

goíní þe. al ich legge up o þe i remissiun of þeose. ⁊ i forȝe
uenesse of alle þine sunnen. Ant þenne sum lutlesihweat
5 he mei leggen up on ow. as a salm oðer twa. Pater nostres.
auez
tene oðer tweolue. Disceplines. echi to:· ȝef him swa
þuncheð.
efter þe totagges þe beoð iwriten þruppe:· he schal þe sun
ne demen mare oðer leasse. A sunne ful forȝeuelich. mei
wurðe ful deadlich þurh sum uuel totagge þe lið þer bi
10 siden. Efter schrift falleð to speoken of penitence. ꝥ is dead (M. 348)
bote. ant swa we habbeð inȝong ut of þis fifte dale:· in
to þe Seste.

A l is penitence.
ant strong penitence
15 þet ȝe eauer dreheð mine leoue sustren.
Al þet ȝe eauer doð of god. Al ꝥ ȝe þoli
eð is ow martirdom i se derf ordre. for ȝe beoð niht ⁊
dei up o godes rode. bliðe mahe ȝe beon þrof. for as seín
te pawel seið. Si compatimur:· conregnabimus. As ȝe scot
20 tið wið him of his pine on eorðe:· ȝe schule scotti wið
him of his blisse in heouene. for þi seið seinte pawel. Michi
absit gloriari nisi in cruce dominí mei iesu christi. Ant hali
chirche
síngeð. Nos opportet gloriari in cruce dominí nostri iesu
christi. Al ure
blisse mot beon i iesu cristes rode. Þis word nomeliche
límpeð
25 to recluses. hwas blisse ah to beon allunge i godes rode. Ich
chulle biginnen herre. ⁊ lihten swa herto. neomeð nu go
de ȝeme. for al meast is seín Beornardes sentence.

Þ reo manere men of godes icorene líuíeð on eorðe. Þe

13 *very large blue initial* A (*marking the beginning of Part VI*) *between* 12 *and* 17 *with tail to* 20; *ornamented with red lines and patterns, especially within, and down tail.* 15 *written large* (*especially* mine). 19/20 *in right margin mark* × *and scribble.* 23 síngeð: *long* S *lying on back to avoid small hole. In right margin mark* ×; Al ure *underlined;* christi: $\frac{i}{x}$. 24 blisse *to* Þis word *underlined.* 28 *large red initial* Þ *partly below line; blue lines within, and in margin from* 23 *and down tail* (*trailers cut off at bottom edge*).

ane mahe beon to gode pilegrimes ieuenet. Þe oþre:· to dea f. 94b
de. Þe þridde to ihongede wið hare gode wil o iesuse rode.
Þe forme beoð gode. þe oþre beoð betere. Þe þridde best of
To þe forme gredeð seinte peter inwardliche. ℂ .alle.
Obsecro uos tanquam aduenas ⁊ peregrinos ut abstin- 5
eatis uos
a carnalibus desideriís que militant aduersus animam. Ich hal
si ow he seið as elþeodie ⁊ pilegrimes. ꝥ ȝe wiðhalden ow
from fleschliche lustes þe weorrið aȝeín þe sawle. þe gode
pilegrim halt eauer his rihte wei forðward. þah he seo oðer
here idele gomenes ⁊ wundres bi þe weie:· he ne edstont 10
(M. 350) nawt as foles doð:· ah halt forð his rute ⁊ hiheð toward
his giste. he ne bereð na gersum bute his speonse gnedeli
che. ne claðes bute ane þeo ꝥ him to neodeð. þis beoð hali
men þe þah ha beon i þe world:· ha beoð þrin as pilegrimes.
⁊ gað wið god liflade toward te riche of heouene. ⁊ seggeð 15
wið þe apostle. Non habemus hic manentem ciuitatem:· set
futuram inquirimus. ꝥ is. nabbe we na wununge her:· ah we
sech.
eð oþer. beoð bi þe leaste ꝥ ha mahen. ne ne haldeð na ta
le of na worltlich froure:· þah ha beon i worltlich wei as ich
seide of pilegrim. ah habbeð hare heorte eauer toward heo 20
uene. ⁊ ahen wel to habben. for oðer pilegrimes gað muche
swinc to sechen ane sontes banes as seín Iames oðer seín
giles. Ah þeo pilegrimes þe gað toward heouene:· ha gað
to beon isontet. ⁊ to finden godd seolf ⁊ alle his hali halh
en. líuíende i blisse. ⁊ schulen líuíen wið hím i wunne bu 25
ten ende. Ha ifindeð iwis seín Iulienes ín. þe wei fearinde
men ȝeornliche bisecheð. NV beoð þeose gode. ah ȝet beoð

f. 94b. 4 *tall square initial* T *in blue, the stem in margin from* 3 *to curled end at* 10; *ornamented with red lines from* 1 *down tail to* 18, *a single trailer running to a curl in bottom margin. Before* .alle. *a red paragraph touched with blue.* 6 *marginal scribble crossing* T *and down to* 12; Ich hal *underlined.* 7 *in left margin mark* ×; si ow he seið as el *underlined.* 8 from fleschliche lust *underlined.* 17 *in left margin mark* ×; nabbe *to* ah w(e *underlined.* 17, 18 sech.|eð, *sic.* 18 eð oþer *underlined.* 21 i *omitted between* gað muche. 23 *small hole at end after* gað. 27 *red initial* N *touched with blue lines.*

þe oþre betere. for allegate pilegrimes as ich ear seide al gan
f. 95a ha eauer forðward. ne bicumen burhmen iþe worldes burh.·
ham þuncheð sum chearre god of ꝥ ha seoð bi weie. ant ed
stuteð sumdeal.· þah ha ne don mid alle. ⁊ moní þing ham
falleð to.· hwer þurh ha beoð ilette. swa ꝥ mare hearm is. sum
5 kímeð leate hám.· sum neauer mare. Hwa is þenne skerre.· ⁊
mare ut of þe world þen pilegrimes ? ꝥ is to seggen. þen þeo
men þe habbeð wortlich þing. ⁊ ne luuieð hit nawt.· ah ȝeo
ueð hit as hit kimeð ham. ⁊ gað untrusset lihte as pilegri
mes doð toward heouene. Hwa beoð betere þene þeos ? Godd
10 wat þeo beoð betere. þe þe apostle spekeð to. ⁊ seið in his epist
le. Mortuí estis. ⁊ Vita uestra abscondita est. cum christo in deo. Cum
autem apparuerit uita uestra.· tunc ⁊ uos apparebitis cum ipso
in gloria. ȝe beoð deade ⁊ ower lif is ihud mid criste. Hwen he (M. 352)
ꝥ is ower lif eadeaweð ⁊ spríngeð as þe dahunge efter nihtes
15 þeosternesse.· ant ȝe schulen wið him springen schenre þen
þe sunne in to eche blisse. þe nu beoð þus deade.· hare liflade
is herre. for pilegrim eileð monihwet. þe deade nis noht of.·
þah he ligge unburiet. ⁊ rotie buuen eorðe. preise him laste
him. do him scheome. sei him scheome.· al him is iliche leof.
20 þis is a seli deað. ꝥ makeð cwic mon þus oðer cwic wummon.·
ut of þe worlde. Ah sikerliche hwa se is þus dead in hire seoluen.·
godd liueð in hire heorte. for þis is ꝥ te apostle seið. Víuo ego
iam non ego. Viuít autem in me christus. Ich líuíe nawt ich.
ah crist liueð in me þurh his inwuniende grace. ⁊ is as þah
25 he seide. worltlich speche. worltlich sihðe. ⁊ euch worltlich þing
ifindeð me deade. ah ꝥ te límpeð to crist. ꝥ ich seo ⁊ hére.
⁊ wurche i cwicnesse. þus riht is euch religius dead to þe

f. 95a. 10 *in right margin* ×; *marginal scribble from* 10 *to* 15.
14 eadeaweð, *sic.* 23 Ich líuíe nawt ich. *underlined; in right margin mark* ×. *Marginal scribble from* 23 *to* 26.

worlde.' ⁊ cwic þah to criste. Þis is an heh steire.' ah ȝet is þah
an herre. Ant hwa stod eauer þrín? Godd wat þe þe seide. f. 95b Michi
absit gloriari nisi in cruce domini mei iesu christi. per quam michi mundus
crucifixus est ⁊ ego mundo. þis is ꝥ ich seide þruppe. Crist me
schilde forte habben eani blisse i þis world.' bute i iesu cristes
rode mi lauerd. þurh hwam þe world is me unwurð.' ant ich 5
am unwurð híre as weari þe is ahonget. A lauerd hehe
stod he þe spec o þisse wise. ant þis is ancre steire ꝥ ha þus
segge. Michi autem absit gloriari ⁊ cetera. I na þing ne blissi ich me bu
te i godes rode. ꝥ ich þolie nu wa ⁊ am itald unwurð as godd
wes o rode. lokið leoue sustren hu þis steire is herre þen 10
eani beo of þe oþre. Þe pilegrim i þe wordes wei þah he
ga forðward toward te hám of heouene.' he sið ⁊ hereð un
net. ⁊ spekeð umbe hwile. wreaðeð him for weohes. ⁊ moni
þing mei letten him of his Iurnee. Þe deade nis nama
re of scheome þen of menske. of heard.' þen of nesche.' for 15
he ne feleð nowðer. ⁊ for þi ne ofearneð he nowðer wa.' ne
wunne. ah þe þe is o rode ⁊ haueð blisse þrof.' he wendeð
(M. 354) scheome to menske.' ⁊ wa ín to wunne. ⁊ ofearneð for þi hu
re ouer hure. Þis beoð þeo þe neauer ne beoð gleade i
heortet.' bute hwen ha þolieð sum wa oðer sum scheome 20
wið iesu on his rode. for þis is þe selhðe on eorðe.' hwa se
mei for godes luue habben scheome ⁊ teone. Þus lo rih
te ancres ne beoð nawt ane pilegrimes.' ne ȝet nawt ane
deade.' ah beoð of þeos þridde. for al hare blisse is forte
beon ahonget sariliche ⁊ scheomeliche wið iesu on his ro 25
de. Þeos mahe bliðe wið hali chirche singen. Nos oppor
tet gloriari. ⁊ cetera. ꝥ is as ich seide ear. hwet se beo of ordre. þe hab

f. 95b. 2 christi: x with i above. 4 *in left margin mark* ×; schilde fo(rte *underlined*. 5 rode m(i *underlined*. 11 wordes, *sic*. 13 weohes, *sic for* wohes. 27 ordre, *sic for* oðre.

beð hare blisse summe i flesches licunge. summe i worldes
f. 96a dweole. summe in oþres uuel. we mote nede blissin us i iesu
cristes rode. ꝥ is i scheome ⁊ i wa ꝥ he droh o rode. Moni wal
de summes weis þolien flesches heardschipe.' ah beon itald
unwurð.' ne scheome ne mahte he þolien. ah he nis bute
5 halflunge up o godes rode.' ȝef he nis igreiðet to þolien ham
Vilitas ⁊ asperitas. Vilte ⁊ asprete. þeos twa. scheo ¶ .baðe.
me ⁊ píne. as sein Beornard seið. beoð þe twa leaddre steolen
þe beoð up iriht to heouene. ⁊ bitweone þeose steolen beoð
of alle gode þeawes þe tindes ifestnet. bi hwucche me clím
10 beð to þe blisse of heouene. for þi ꝥ dauið hefde þe twa steo
len of þis leaddre.' þah he kíng wére.' he clomb uppard ⁊
seide baldeliche to ure lauerd. Vide humilitatem meam
⁊ labo
rem meum ⁊ dimitte uniuersa delicta mea. Bihald qð he
⁊ sih mín eadmodnesse ⁊ mí swínc.' ⁊ forȝef me mine sun
15 nen alle to gederes. Notið wel þes twa word þe dauið fei
eð somet. Swinc.' ⁊ eadmodnesse. Swinc i píne ⁊ i wa. i sar.
⁊ i sorhe. Eadmodnesse aȝeín woh of scheome ꝥ mon dre (M. 356)
heð. þe is itald unwurð. Ba þeos bihald in me qð dauið godes
deorling. Ich habbe þeos twa leaddre steolen. Dimitte
uniuersa
20 delicta mea. leaf qð he bihinde me ⁊ warp awei from me al
le míne gultes. ꝥ ich ilihtet of hare heuinesse.' lihtliche
stihe up to heouene bi þeos leaddre. Þeose twa þinges. ꝥ is
wa ⁊ scheome ifeiet to gederes.' beoð helyes hweoles þe wé
ren furene hit teleð. ⁊ beren him up to parais.' þer he líueð
25 ȝetten. Fur is hat ⁊ read. Iþe heate is understonden euch
wa ꝥ eileð flesch. Scheome bi þe reade. Ah wel mei duhen
ha beoð her.' hweolinde ase hweoles. ouerturneð sone ne leas
teð nane hwile. þis ilke is ec bitacnet bi cherubines sweord.
f. 96b biuore paraise ȝeten þe wes of lei ⁊ hweolinde. ⁊ turninde
abuten. Ne kimeð nan in to parais.' bute þurh þis leitin
de sweord þe wes hat ⁊ read. ⁊ in helyes furene hweoles.
ꝥ is. þurh sar ⁊ þurh scheome þe ouerturneð tidliche.' ant

f. 96a. 6 *red initial* V *between* 5 *and* 7, *ornamented with a few blue lines* (*in margin from* 3 *to* 9); *directing* v *in left margin. Before* .baðe. *a blue paragraph touched with red.* 15 *in right margin a hand, pointing to* dauið fei. 18 dauið: dð.

agað sone. Ant nes godes rode wið his deorewurðe blod 5
irudet ⁊ ireadet. forte schawin on him seolf. ꝥ pine. ⁊ sorhe.
⁊ sar. schulden wið scheome beon iheowet. Nis hit iwriten
bi him. Factus est obediens patri usque ad mortem. mortem autem
crucis. ꝥ is. he wes buhsum his feader. nawt ane to deað.' ah
to deað o rode. þurh ꝥ he seide earst deað.' is pine under 10
stonden. þurh ꝥ he þrefter seið deað o þe rode.' is schendlac
bitacnet. for swuch wes godes deað o þe deore rode. pínful. ⁊
schentful ouer alle oþre. Hwa se eauer deieð ine godd.
⁊ o godes rode.' þeos twa ha mot þolien. scheome for hím
⁊ pine. Scheome ich cleopie eauer her. beon itald unwurð. 15
⁊ beggin as an hearlot ȝef neod is hire liueneð. ⁊ beon oþ
res beodes mon. as ȝe beoð leoue sustren. ⁊ þolieð ofte dan
ger of swuch oðerhwile þe mahte beon ower þreal. þis
is ꝥ eadi scheome þet ich of talie. Pine ne trukeð ow
(M. 358) nawt. I þeos ilke twa þing ꝥ al penitence is ín.' blissið ow ⁊ 20
gleadieð. for aȝein þeos twa ow beoð twafald blissen iȝar
ket. aȝeín scheome.' menske. aȝein pine.' delit ⁊ reste buten
ende. ysa. In terra ínquit sua duplicia possidebunt. Ha schulen
seið ysaie. ín hare ahne lond wealden twauald blisse. aȝein
twauald wa ꝥ ha her dreheð. In hare ahne lond seið ysa 25
ie. for alswa as þe vuele nabbeð na lot in heouene.' ne þe
þe gode nabbeð na lot in eorðe. Super epistolam ia. Mali nichil
habent in celo. Boni uero nichil in terra. In hare ahne lond
ha schulen wealden blisse. twafald cunne mede. aȝeín twa f. 97a
uald sorhe. as þah he seide. Ne þunche ham na feorlich.'
þah ha her þolien as in uncuð lond. ⁊ in uncuð eard.'
bituh hen unþeode.' scheome ba ⁊ sorhe.' for swa deð moni
gentil mon þe is uncuð in uncuððe. Me mot ute swín 5
ken.' ed hame me schal resten. ant nis he a cang cniht
þe secheð reste i þe feht ⁊ eise i þe place? Milicia est vita

f. 96b. 8 *above* him, *in thin hand sloping back*, seolf. 9 *in left margin mark* ×; 9, 10 he wes buhsum *to* rode. þurh *underlined*. 23 ysa, *sic for* ysaie. 23, 24 *in left margin mark* ×; Ha schulen *to* twauald blisse *underlined*. 25, 26 þe|þe *for* þe. 27 ia.: *read* iacobi.

hominis super terram. Al þis lif is a feht as Iob witneð. ah ef
ter þis feht her. ȝef we wel fehteð.' menske ⁊ reste abit us
10 ed hame in ure ahne lond.' ꝥ is heoueriche. lokið nu hu
witerliche ure lauerd seolf hit witneð. Cum sederit filius hominis
in sede maiestatis sue.' sedebitis ⁊ uos iudicantes ⁊cetera. Ber
nardus. In sedibus quies.' inperturbata. In iudicio honoris emi
nencia commendatur. Hwen ich sitte forte demen seið ure lauerd.'
15 ȝe schulen sitten wið me ⁊ deme wið me al þe world þet
schal beon idemet. Kinges. ⁊ keisers. Cnihtes. ⁊ clearkes. Iþe
sete is reste ⁊ eise bitacnet.' aȝeín þe swínc ꝥ her is. I þe mens
ke of þe dom ꝥ ha schulen demen.' is hehschipe menskeful
ouer alle understonden. aȝeín scheome ⁊ lahschipe ꝥ ha her
20 for godes luue mildeliche þoleden. NiS þer nu þenne
bute þolien gleadliche. for bi godd seolf is iwriten. Quod per
penam ignominiose passionis.' peruenit ad gloriam resurrec
tionis. ꝥ is. þurh schentful píne.' he com to gloire of blis (M. 360)
ful ariste. Nis na selcuð þenne ȝef we wrecche sunfule þo
25 lien her píne. ȝef we wulleð o domes dei blisfule arisen.'
ant ꝥ we mahen þurh his grace.' ȝef we us seolf wulleð.
Quoniam si complantati fuerimus similitudini mortis eius.' simul
⁊ resurrectionis erimus. Seinte paweles sahe þe seið se wel eauer.
f. 97b ȝef we beoð íímpet to þe ilicnesse of godes deað.' we schulen
of his ariste. ꝥ is to seggen. ȝef we libbeð i scheome ⁊ i pine
for his luue.' i hwucche twa he deide.' we schulen beon iliche
his blisful ariste. ure bodi briht as his is world buten ende
5 as seinte pawel witneð. Saluatorem expectamus qui reforma

f. 97a. 4 bituh hen, *sic*. 17 mens: ns *as* f. 18 b. 8. 20 *small red initial* N *touched with blue; it is partly drawn over a small capital* N, *the first stroke and bar of which appear to the left; the bow obscures* i *of* Nis. 22, 23 resurreć|tionis, *see* p. xiii.

f. 97b. 1, 2 ȝef we *to* ariste *underlined; in left margin mark* ×.

bit corpus humilitatis nostre configuratum corpori claritatis sue.
let oþre acemín hare bodi þe eorneð biuoren hond. Abide
we ure healent þe schal acemín ure efter his ahne. Si compa
timur.' conregnabimus. ȝef we þolieð wið hím.' we schule blis
sin wið hím. Nis þis god foreward? Wat crist nis he nawt 10
god feolahe ne treowe.' þe nule scottin i þe lure.' as eft i þe
biȝete. Glosa. Illis solis prodest sanguis christi. qui uolup-tates de
serunt ⁊ corpus affligunt. Godd schedde his blod for alle. ah
heom ane hit is wurð.' þe fleoð flesches licunge ⁊ pínið
ham seoluen. ant is ꝥ eani wunder? Nis godd ure heaued 15
⁊ we his limen alle? Ah nis euch lim sar wið sorhe of þe
heaued? His lím þenne nis he nawt. þe naueð eche un
der se sar akinde heaued. Hwen þe heaued sweat wel.' ꝥ
lím þe ne swet nawt. Nis hit uuel tacne? He þe is ure
heaued sweatte blodes swat for ure secnesse. to turnen 20
us of ꝥ lond uuel ꝥ alle londes leien on.' ⁊ liggeð ȝette
monie. þe lím þe ne sweat nawt i swincful pine for his
luue.' deuleset hit leaueð in his secnesse. ⁊ nis þer bute
forkeoruen hit.' þah hit þunche sar godd. for betere is
finger offe.' þen he ake eauer. Cwemeð he nu wel godd 25
(M. 362) þe þus bilimeð him of hím seolf þurh ꝥ he nule sweaten?
Oporetbat christum pati ⁊ sic íntrare in gloriam suam. Seinte
Marie mearci. hit moste swa beon hit seið. crist þolie pí
ne ⁊ passiun. ant swa habben inȝong ín to his riche. lo dea f. 98a
le hwet he seið. swa habben inȝong in to his riche. swa.' ⁊
nan oðerweis. ant we wrecches sunfule wulleð wið eise sti
hen to heouene ꝥ is se hehe buuen us ⁊ se swiðe muchel
wurð. ant me ne mei nawt wið uten swinc.' a lutel cote 5

7 *to* 9 Abide *to* acemin, *and* ȝef we *to* blis *underlined; in left margin two marks* ×. *In left margin a hand pointing between* 10 *and* 11. 12 christi: $\frac{\text{i}}{\text{x}}$. 27 *in left margin mark* ×; oporteb(at *underlined.* 28 hit moste swa beon *underlined.*

f. 98a. 1 *from the right-hand edge extends a forearm and hand with long clubbed forefinger on the ruled margin pointing to* dea (*end of line*). *The line is underlined as far as* lo.

areoren. ne twa þwongede scheos habbe wið ute bune.
Oðer þeo beoð canges þe weneð wið lihtleapes buggen
eche blisse.' oðer þe hali halhen þe bohten hit se deore.
Nes seinte peter ⁊ seinte andrew. þeruore istraht o rode?
10 Seín lorenz o þe gridil. ⁊ laðlese meidnes þe tittes ítor
en of. tohwiðeret o hweoles. heafdes bicoruen? Ah ure sot
schipe is sutel. ant heo weren ilich þeose ȝape children þe
habbeð ȝape feaderes. þe willes ⁊ waldes toteoreð hare
claðes. forte habbe neowe. Vre alde curtel is þe flesch ꝥ we
15 of adam ure alde feader habbeð. þe neowe we schulen
underuon of godd ure riche feader i þe ariste of domes
dei. hwen ure flesch schal blikien schenre þen þe sunne.'
ȝef hit is totoren her wið wontreaðe ⁊ wið weane. Of þeo
þe hare curtles toteoreð o þisse wise.' seið ysaie. Deferetur
20 munus domino exercituum a populo díuulso ⁊ dilacerato.' a
populo terribili. A folc tolaimet ⁊ totoren. A folc he seið fear
lich. schal makien to ure lauerd present of him seoluen.
Folc tolaimet. ⁊ totoren wið strong liflade ⁊ wið heard.'
he cleopeð folc fearlac. for þe feond is of swucche offruht
25 ⁊ offearet. For þi ꝥ Iob wes þullich.' he meande him ant
seide. Pellem pro pelle ⁊ uni ⁊ cetera. ꝥ is. he wule ȝeouen
fel for

fel. þe alde for þe neowe. as þah he seide. Ne geineð me
nawt to asailín him. he is of ꝥ totore folc. he tereð his
f. 98b alde curtel. ⁊ torendeð þe alde pilche of his deadliche fel.
for þe fel is undeadlich ꝥ i þe neowe ariste schal schíne **(M. 364)**
seoueuald brihtre þen þe sunne. Eise ⁊ flesches este beoð
þes deofles mearken. Hwen he sið þeos mearken i mon.
5 oðer i wummon.' he wat þe castel is his.' ⁊ geað baldeli
che ín.' þer he sið i riht up swucche baneres as me deð i
castel. I þet totore folc he misseð his merken. ⁊ sið in ham
iriht up godes banere. ꝥ is heardschipe of lif. ⁊ heaueð
muche dred þrof as ysaie witneð. Me leoue sire seið

7 lihtleapes, *sic*, *cf.* liht chap, f. 107b. 23. 11 o hweoles *to* sot *underlined.* 13 ȝape *false repetition for* riche. 21, 22 *from first* A folc *to* him seoluen *underlined; in right margin mark* ×. 24 fearlac, *sic for* fearlic(h). 26 uni, *sic for* uniuersa.
f. 98b. 7 *MS.* merken. 9 *small red initial* M *touched with blue.*

sum ⁊ is hit nu wisdom. to don se wa him seoluen? ant 10
tu ȝeld me ondswere of tweie men hweðer is wisre. Ha
beoð ba seke. Þe an forgeað al ꝥ he luueð of metes ⁊
of drunches. ⁊ drinkeð bitter sabraz forte acourin hea
le. Þe oþer folheð al his wil ⁊ fordeð his lustes aȝein his
secnesse.· ⁊ leoseð his lif sone. Hweðer is wisre of þes twa? 15
hweðer is betere his ahne freond? Hweðer luueð hím seolf
mare? Ant hwa nis sec of sunne? Godd for ure secnesse
dronc
attri drunch o rode. ant we nulleð nawt bittres biten for
us seoluen. Nis þer nawiht þrof. Sikerliche his folhere
mot wið pine of his flesch folhin his pine. Ne wene nan 20
wið este stihen to heouene. Me sire seið sum eft wule
godd se wracfulliche wreoken up o sunne? ȝe mon. for
loke nu hu he hit heateð swiðe. Hu walde nu þe mon
beate ꝥ þing seolf hwer se he hit ifunde. þe for muchel hea
tunge beote þrof þe schadewe. ⁊ al ꝥ hefde þer to eani lic 25
nesse? Godd feader almihti hu beot he bitterliche his deo
rewurðe sune iesu ure lauerd ꝥ neauer nefde sunne. bute
ane ꝥ he ber flesch ilich ure.· ꝥ is ful of sunne. ant we
(M. 366) schulden beon ispearet þe beoreð on us his sune deað. Þe f. 99a
wepne ꝥ sloh hím ꝥ wes ure sunne. ant he þe nefde nawt
of sunne bute schadewe ane.· wes i þe ilke schadewe se
scheomeliche ituket. se sorhfulliche ipinet. ꝥ ear hit come
þer to.· for þe þreatunge ane þrof swa him agras þer a 5
ȝeín.· ꝥ he bed his feader are. Tristis est anima mea usque ad
mortem. Pater mi si possibile est.· transeat a me calix iste.
SARe
qð he me grulleð aȝeín mi muchele píne. Mi feader ȝef
hit mei beon.· speare me ed tis time. Þi wil þah ⁊ nawt mín.·
eauer beo iuorðet. His deorewurðe feader for þi ne forber 10
him nawt. ah leide on him se luðerliche. ꝥ he bigon to gre
den wið reowðfule steuene. Heloy. heloy. lamazabatani.
Mi godd mi godd. mi deorewurðe feader hauest tu al for
warpe me þin anlepi sune þe beatest me se hearde? for al
þis ne lette he nawt. ah beot se swiðe longe ⁊ se swiðe grimlí 15

14 fordeð, *sic for* forðeð. 21 *small blue initial* M *touched with red.*
f. 99a. 3 *between* schadewe *and* se *an erasure.*

che.ꝛ ꝥ he stearf o rode. Disciplina pacis nostre super eum seið
ysaie. þus ure beatunge feol on him. for he dude him seoluen
bitweonen us ⁊ his feader þe þreatte us forte smiten ase
moder ꝥ is reowðful deð hire bitweonen hire child. ant te
20 wraðe sturne feader hwen he hit wule beaten. þus dude ure
lauerd iesu crist. ikepte on him deaðes dunt forte schilden
us þer wið.ꝛ igracet beo his milce. Hwer se muchel dunt is. hit
bulteð aȝein up o þeo þe þer neh stondeð. soðliche hwa se
is neh hím þe ikepte se heui dunt.ꝛ hit wule bulten on him
25 ne nule he him neauer meanen. for ꝥ is þe preoue þet he
stont neh him. ⁊ liht is þe bultunge to þolien for his luue
þe underueng se heui dunt us forte burhen from þe deof
les botte i þe píne of helle. Ȝet seið moni mon. hweat
f. 99b is godd þe betere þah ich pini me for his luue ? leoue mon
⁊ wummon godd þuncheð god of ure god. Vre god is ȝef
we doð ꝥ tet we ahen. Ním ȝeme of þis essample. A mon
þe were feor ifearen. ⁊ me come ⁊ talde him ꝥ his deore spu
5 se se swiðe murnede efter him. ꝥ heo wið uten him delit (M 368)
nefde i na þing. ah were for þoht of his luue leane ⁊ elheow
et. nalde him betere likin. þen ꝥ me seide him ꝥ ha gleowde
⁊ gomnede ⁊ wedde wið oþre men. ⁊ líuede i delices ? Alswa
ure lauerd ꝥ is þe sawle spus ꝥ sið al ꝥ ha deð þah he hehe
10 sitte.ꝛ he ⟨is⟩ ful wel ipaiet ꝥ ha murneð efter him ⁊ wule hih
in toward hire mucheles þe swiðere. wið ȝeoue of his grace
oðer fecchen hire allunge to him to gloire ⁊ to blisse
þurh wuniende. Ne grapi hire nan to softeliche hire
seoluen to bichearren. Ne schal ha for hire lif witen
15 hire al cleane. ne halden riht hire chastete wið uten twa
þinges. as seint ailred þe abbat wrat to his suster. Þet

17 þus ure beatunge feol on him. for *underlined; in right margin mark* ×. 28 *small blue initial* Ȝ (*yogh*); *directing* ȝ *in right margin* (*blurred*).

f. 99b. *In left margin four hands:* (*1*) *large, pointing to beginning of* 1; (*2, 3, 4*) *small, with forearms in sleeves, projecting from left edge, and pointing approximately to lines* 7 et. nalde, 10 sitte, 11 in toward. 10 is *interlined with tail of* s *prolonged to act as caret;* hamurneð *separated by caret.* 13 *small red initial* N *touched with blue.*

an is pinsunge i flesch wið feasten. wið wecchen. wið dis
ceplines. wið heard werunge. heard leohe. wið uuel. wið
muchele swinkes. Þe oþer is heorte þeawes. Deuotiun.
Reowfulnesse. Riht luue. Eadmodnesse. ⁊ uertuz oþre swuc 20
che. Me sire þu ondswerest me. suleð godd his grace ? Nis
grace
wil ȝeoue ? Míne leoue sustren þah cleannesse of chastete
ne beo nawt bune ed godd. ah beo ȝeoue of grace.· Vn-
graciuse
stondeð þer toȝeines. ⁊ makieð ham unwurðe to halden se
heh þing. þe nulleð swinc þeruore bliðeliche þolien. Bitweon 25
en delices. ⁊ eise. ⁊ flesches este. hwa wes eauer chaste ? hwa
bredde
eauer inwið hire fur ꝥ ha ne bearnde. Pot þe walleð swiðe nu
le he beon ouerleden. oðer cald weater iwarpe þrín. ⁊ brondes
wiðdrahene ? þe wombe pot þe walleð of metes. ⁊ of drunches. f. 100a
is se neh nehbur to ꝥ ful⟨í⟩tohe lím. ꝥ ha dealeð þerwið þe
brune of hire heate. ah moníe mare hearm is beoð se flesch
wise. ⁊ swa ouerswiðe ofdred leste hare heaued ake. leste hare
licome febli to swiðe. ⁊ witeð swa hare heale.· ꝥ te gast 5
unstren
geð ⁊ secleð i sunne. ant þeo þe schulden ane lechnín hare
(M. 370) sawle wið heorte bireowsunge ⁊ flesches pinsunge.· forwurð
eð fisitiens ⁊ licomes leche. Dude swa seínte Agace þe ondswe
rede. ⁊ seide to ure lauerdes sonde. þe brohte sonde o
godes half
to healen hire títtes ? Medicinam carnalem corpori meo nun 10
quam adhibui. ꝥ is. fleschlich medecine ne dude ich me
neaure.
Nabbe ȝe iherd tellen of þe þreo hali men. Bute þe an wes
iwunet for his calde mahe to nutten hate speces. ⁊ wes ornre
of mete ⁊ of drunch þen þe tweien oþre þah ha weren seke.
ne nomen neauer ȝeme hweat wes hal hwet unhal to eo 15
ten ne to drinken. ah nomen eauer forðriht hwet se godd
ham sende. ne makeden neauer strengðe of gingiure ne of

f. 100a. 2 ful⟨í⟩tohe: l *altered from* i; *a small* í *interlined with caret.*
9 *second* sonde *crossed out, and* salue (*small back-sloping letters*) *interlined to replace it with long caret stroke.* 14 þe *omitted after* oþre.

zedual. ne of clowes de gilofre. A dei as ha þreo weren ifolen
o slepe. ⁊ lei bitweone þes twa þe þridde ꝥ ich seide. Com þe
20 cwen of heouene ⁊ twa meidnes wið hire. Þe an as þah hit
wére ber a letuaire. þe oþer of gold a sticcke. vre leafdi wið þe
sticke nom ⁊ dude i þe anes muð of þe letuaire. ⁊ te meidnes
eoden forðre to þe midleste. Nai qð ure leafdi he is his ah
ne leche. ga ouer to þe þridde. Stod an hali mon of feor
25 biheold al þis ilke. Hwen sec mon haueð ed hond þing ꝥ
wule don him god.' he hit mei wel notien. ah beon
þrefter se ancreful. nomeliche religius.' nis nawt godd
icweme. Godd ⁊ his desciples speken of sawle lechecreft.
f. 100b ypocras. ⁊ Galien.' of licomes heale. þe an þe wes best ilea
ret of iesu cristes lechecreft. seið flesches wisdom is deað to
þe sawle. Prudencia carnis.' mors. Procul odoramus bellum.
as Iob seið. Swa we dredeð flesches uuel ofte ear þen hit
5 cume.' ꝥ sawle uuel kimeð up. ⁊ we þolieð sawle uuel for
te edstearten flesches uuel. as þah hit were betere to þolien
galnesses brune. þen heaued eche oðer grucchunge of a
mistohe wombe. ant hweðer is betere i secnesse to beo godes
freo child.' þen i flesches heale.' to beo þreal under sunne?
10 ant þis ne segge ich nawt swa.' ꝥ wisdom ⁊ meosure ne (M. 372)
beon ouer al iloket.' þe moder is ⁊ nurrice of alle gode
þeawes. Ah we cleopieð ofte wisdom ꝥ nis nan. for soð wis
dom is. don eauer sawle heale.' biuore flesches heale. ⁊ hwen
he ne mei nawt ba somet halden.' cheose ear licomes
15 hurt.' þen þurh to strong fondunge.' sawle þrowunge
Nichodemus brohte to smírien ure lauerd an hundret wei
es hit seið of mirre ⁊ of aloes. ꝥ beoð bittre speces. ⁊ bitac
nið bittre swinkes ⁊ flesches pínsunges. Hundret is ful
tale. ⁊ noteð perfectiun. ꝥ is ful dede. forte schawin ꝥ me
20 schal ful do flesches pine. ase forð as eauer euene mei
þolien. Iþe weie is bitacnet meosure ⁊ wisdom. ꝥ euch
mon wið wisdom weie hwet he mahe don. ne beo nawt
se ouer swiðe igast.' ꝥ he forȝeme þe bodi. ne eft se tendre

26 wel notien: *MS.* wel him notien; him *crossed out;* wel *somewhat roughly written* (*on erasure or imperfection of surface*).

f. 100b. 23 igast *for* i gast.

of his flesch:· ꝥ hit iwurðe untohen ⁊ makie þe gast þeowe.
Nu is al þis meast iseid of bitternesse utewið. Of bitter 25
nesse inwið segge we nu sumhweat. for of þes twa bitter
nesses:· awakeneð swetnesse. her ȝet i þis world:· nawt
ane in heouene. AS ich seid riht nu ꝥ nichodemus
brohte smirles to ure lauerd:· alswa þe þreo Maries bohten f. 101a
deorewurðe aromaz his bodi forte smirien. Neomeð nu go
de ȝeme míne leoue sustren. Þeos þreo maries bitacnið
þreo bitternesses. for þis nome marie as meraht ⁊ merariht
ꝥ ich spec þruppe of:· spealeð bitternesse. Þe earste bitter- 5
nesse is.
i sunne bireowsunge ⁊ i deadbote. hwen þe sunfule is iturnd
earst to ure lauerd. Ant þeos is understonden bi þe earste
Marie. marie magdaleíne. ⁊ bi god rihte. for ha wið mu
che bireowsunge ⁊ bitternesse of heorte leafde hire sunnen.
⁊ turnde to ure lauerd. Ah for þi ꝥ sum mahte þurh to 10
muche bitternesse fallen in to unhope:· Magdaleine þe spea
leð tures hehnesse:· is to Marie ifeiet. þurh hwet is bitacnet
(M. 374) hope of heh mearci ⁊ of heouene blisse. Þe oðer bitternesse is.
i wreastlunge ⁊ i wragelunge aȝeines fondunges. Ant þeos
is bitacnet bi þe oðer Marie. marie iacobi. for Iacob spealeð 15
wreastlere. þis wreastlunge is ful bitter to monie þe beoð ful
forð i þe wei toward heouene. for þe ȝet i fondunges. ꝥ beoð
þe deofles swenges. waggið oðerhwiles. ⁊ moten wreastlín a
ȝeín wið strong wraglunge. for as seínt austin seið. Pharao
contemptus surgit in scandalum. hwil eauer israeles folc wes 20
in
egypte under hParaones hond:· ne leadde he neauer ferd
þron:· ah þa hit fleah from hím:· þa wið al his strengðe
wende he þrefter. for þi is eauer bitter feht:· neod aȝeín
pharaon. ꝥ is aȝein þe deouel. for ase seið ezechiel. Sanguí
nem fugies. ⁊ sanguis persequetur te. Flih sunne. ⁊ sunne 25
wule
folhín eauer efter. Inoh is iseid þruppe hwi þe gode nís
neauer sker of alle fondunges. Sone se he haueð þe an

28 *small blue initial* A *with tail into lower margin, ornamented with red lines.*

f. 101a. 17 þe ȝet *for* þeo ȝet '*they still*'. 21 hParaones, *sic*: P *is an alteration* (*on an erasure*); *scribe probably began* hond.

ouercumen.' ikeþe anan an oþer. Þe þridde bitternesse is i
lon
f. 101b gunge toward heouene. ⁊ i þe ennu of þis world. hwen
ei is se hehe ꝥ he haueð heorte reste onont unþeawes
weorre. ⁊ is as in heouene ȝeten. ⁊ þuncheð bitter alle
worltliche þinges. Ant tis þridde bitternesse is underston
5 den bi marie Salomee þe þridde marie. for Salome spea
leð pes. ⁊ þeo ȝet þe habbeð pes. ⁊ reste of cleane inwit
habbeð in hare heorte bitternesse of þis lif ꝥ edhalt
ham from blisse ꝥ ham longeð to. from godd ꝥ ha lu
uieð. þus lo in euch stat rixleð bitternesse. earst i þe
10 bigínnunge hwen me sahtneð wið godd i þe forðȝong
of god lif.' ⁊ i þe leaste ende. Hwa is þenne o godes half
þe wilneð i þis world eise oðer este? AH neomeð nu
ȝeme míne leoue sustren hu efter bitternesse kimeð
swetnesse. bitternesse buð hit. for as ꝥ godspel teleð. þeose
15 þreo maries bohten swote smeallinde aromaz to smi (M. 376)
rien ure lauerd. Þurh aromaz þe beoð swote.' is under
stonden swotnesse of deuot heorte. þeos maries hit bug
geð. ꝥ is. þurh bitternesse me kimeð to swotnesse. bi
þis nome marie ním eauer bitternesse. Þurh Maries
20 bone wes ed te neoces weater iwent to wine. ꝥ is to un
derstonden. þurh bone of bitternesse ꝥ me dreheð for
godd.' þe heorte þe wes weattri. smechles ne ne felde na
sauur of godd namare þen i weater.' schal beon iwent
to wíne. þet is ifinden smech in him swete ouer alle wí
25 nes. for þi seið þe wise. Vsque in tempus sustinebit paci
ens. ⁊ postea redditio iocunditatis. þe þolemode þolie
bitter ane hwile. he schal sone þrefter habben ȝeld of
blisse. ant anna i tobie seið bi ure lauerd. Qui post tempesta
f. 102a tem tranquillum facit. ⁊ post lacrimationem ⁊ fletum.' exul
tationem infundit. þet is. iblescet ibeo þu lauerd þe mak
est stille efter storm. ⁊ efter wopi weattres ȝeldest bliðe murh

f. 101b. 12 *small red initial* A *touched with blue.* 18 me: *produced by alteration, without erasure, of* hit. 25 seið þe wise *underlined.* 27, 28 *side-scribble in ruled margin, right, and beyond it a mark* ×.

f. 102a. 2 ibeo, *sic* (*after* iblescet) *for* beo.

ðes. Salomon. Esuriens etiam amarum.' pro dulci sumet.
ȝef
þu art ofhungret efter þet swete.' þu most earst witerliche 5
biten o þe bittre. In canticis. Ibo michi ad montem myrre.
⁊ad
colles turis. Ich chulle ha seið godes deore spuse gan to rech
leses hul.' bi þe dun of myrre. lo hwuch is þe wei to rech
leses swotnesse.' bi myrre of bitternesse. ant eft iꝥ ilke luue
boc. Que est ista que ascendit per desertum sicut uirgula 10
fumi ex aromatibus myrre ⁊ thuris. Aromaz me makeð
of myrre ⁊ of rechles. ah myrre he set biuoren. ⁊ rechles
kimeð efter. Ex aromatibus myrre ⁊ thuris. Nu meaneð
hire sum. ꝥ ha ne mei habben na swotnesse of godd.' ne
swetnesse wið ínnen. Ne wundri ha hire nawiht ȝef ha 15
nis marie. for ha hit mot buggen wið bitternesse wið uten.
nawt wið euch bitternesse.' for sum geað frommard godd.
as euch worltlich sar ꝥ nis for sawle heale. for þi iþe god
spel of þe þreo maries is iwriten þisses weis. Vt uenien
tes ungerent iesum. non autem recedentes. þeos maries hit 20
(M. 378) seið. þeose bitternesses.' weren cuminde to smirien ure lauerd.
þeo beoð cuminde to smirien ure lauerd.' þe me þoleð for
his luue. þe strecheð him toward us as þing ꝥ ismired
is. ⁊ makeð him nesche ⁊ softe to hondlín. Ant nes he
him seolf reclus i maries wombe? þeos twa þing limpeð 25
to ancre. nearowðe. ⁊ bitternesse. for wombe is nearow
wunun
ge. þer ure lauerd wes reclus. ant tis word marie as ich of
te habbe iseid.' spealeð bitternesse. ȝef ȝe þenne i nearow
stude
þolieð bitternesse.' ȝe beoð his feolahes reclus as he wes i f. 102b
Marie wombe. Beo ȝe ibunden inwið fowr large wahes?
⁊ he in a nearow cader. i neilet o rode. i stanene þruh bi

5 efter*:* f *altered from* t. 6 myrre*:* *second* r *altered from* e.
28 stude*:* de *written below* tu. *The first eight lines have received special attention from the reader interested in translation; in right margin:* toby*; side-scribble at ends of* 2, 3*; marks* × *approx. opposite* 1, 5, 7*; underlinings in text* 2 iblescet *to* mak, 5 þu *to* wit(erliche, 6 biten *to* cantic(is, 7 Ich chulle *to* rech, 8 leses *to* myrre. *Hole or triangular incision in bottom edge.*

cluset hete feste. Marie wombe ⁊ þis þruh:· weren his
5 ancre huses. I nowðer nes he worltlich mon:· ah as ut of
þe world forte schawin ancren ꝥ ha ne schulen wið þe
world na þing habben imeane. ȝe þu ondswerest me.
ah he wende ut of ba. ȝe went tu alswa of baþíne ancre
huses. as he dude wið ute bruche. ⁊ leaf ham ba ihale.
10 ꝥ schal beon hwen þe gast went ut on ende wið uten
bruche ⁊ wem of his twa huses. ꝥ an is þe licome. þet.
oþer is þe uttre hus. ꝥ is as þe uttre wah abute þe castel.

Al ꝥ ich habbe iseid of flesches pínsunge:· nis nawt
for ow míne leoue sustren. þe oðerhwile þolieð ma
15 re þen ich walde. Ah is for sum ꝥ schal rede þis inohreaðe:·
þe grapeð hire to softe. Noðeles ȝunge ímpen me bigurd
wið þornes leste beastes freoten ham hwil ha beoð meare
we. ȝe beoð ȝunge impen iset i godes orchard. þornes beoð
þe heardschipes ꝥ ich habbe ispeken of. ⁊ ow is neoð ꝥ ȝe
20 beon biset wið ham abuten. ꝥ te beast of helle hwen he **(M. 380)**
snakereð toward ow forte biten on ow:· hurte him o þe
scharpschipe ⁊ schunche aȝeínwardes wið alle þeose heard
schipes beoð gleade ⁊ wel ipaiet ȝef lutel word is of ow:·
ȝef ȝe beoð unwurðe. for þorn is scharp ⁊ unwurð. wið
25 þeose twa beoð bigurde. ȝe ne ahen nawt to unnen þet
uuel word beo of ow. Scandle is heaued sunne. ꝥ is. þing
swa iseid oðer idon:· ꝥ me mei rihtliche turnen hit to u
uele. ⁊ sunegín þrefter þer þurh:· wið mis þoht. wið uuel
f. 103a word. on hire. on oþre. ⁊ sungín ec wið dede. ah ȝe ahen
unnen.
ꝥ na word ne beo of ow:· ne mare þen of deade. ⁊ beon bliðe
iheortet. ȝef ȝe þolieð danger of sluri þe cokes cneaue:·
þe wescheð ⁊ wipeð disches i cuchene:· þenne beo ȝe dunes i
5 hehet toward heouene. for lo hu spekeð þe leafdi iꝥ swete
luue boc. venit dilectus meus saliens in montibus. transiliens
col
les. Mí leof kimeð leapinde ha seið o þe dunes. ꝥ is. totret

f. 102b. 13 *large red initial* A *between* 12 *and* 15, *with tail to* 18; *blue line-patterns within, and in margin from* 8 *to* 25. 19 neoð, *sic.* 26 *ff. the definition of* Scandle *is not in* M.

f. 103a. 7 Mi leof kimeð *to* þe dunes *underlined; mark* × *in right*

ham tofuleð ham. þoleð ꝥ me totreode ham. tuki ham
al to wundre. schaweð ín ham his ahne troden. ꝥ me trud
de him in ham. ifinden hu he wes totreden as his trode 10
schaweð. þis beoð þe hehe dunes as munt of muntgiw.
Dunes of armeníe. þe hulles þe beoð lahre. þeo as þe leaf
di seið hire seolf:· he ouerleapeð. ne trust nawt se wel on
ham for hare feblesce. ne ne mahte nawt þolien swuch to
treodunge. ant he leapeð ouer ham. forbereð ham. ⁊ for 15
buheð aþet ha waxen herre:· from hulles to dunes. His scha
dewe lanhure ouergeað ⁊ wrið ham hwil he leapeð ouer
ham. ꝥ is. sum ilicnesse he leið on ham of his lif on eorðe
as þah hit were his schadewe. ah þe ⟨dunes⟩ underuoð þe tro
den of him seoluen. ⁊ schaweð in hare lif hwuch his liflade 20
wes. hu ⁊ hwer he eode. i hwuch vilte. i hwuch wa:· he leadde
his lif on eorðe. þulliche dunes þe gode pawel spek of:· ⁊
eadmodliche seide. Deicimur set non perímus. Mortifica-
tionem
iesu in corpore nostro circumferentes. ut ⁊ uíta iesu in
corporibus
(M. 382)
nostris manifestetur. Alle wa qð he ⁊ alle scheome we þolieð. 25
ah
ꝥ is ure selhðe. ꝥ we beoren on ure bodi iesu cristes deadlic
nesse. ꝥ hit suteli in us:· hwuch wes his lif on eorðe. Godd hit
wat þe þus doð:· ha pruuieð us hare luue toward ure lauerd.
luuest tu me ? cuð hit. for luue wule schawin him wið uttre f. 103b
werkes. Gregorius. Probatio dilectionis:· exhibitio est operis.
Ne beo nea
uer þing se heard:· soð luue lihteð hit ⁊ softeð ⁊ sweteð. Amor
omnia fatilia reddit. Hweat þolieð men ⁊ wummen for
fals luue ⁊ for ful luue:· ⁊ mare walden þolien ? Ant hweat
is mare wunder ꝥ siker luue ⁊ treowe ⁊ ouer alle oþre 5
swéte. ne mei meistrin us se forð:· as deð þe luue of sunne ?

margin; after dunes *two lines omitted*: M. 380, 12 *to* 14 hulles (*error for* dunes). 10 ifinden *for* ifinde. 11 munt *for* mun(t)z. 13 seolf:· he *for* leof. 14 feblesce. ne ne *for* feblesce ne. 19 dunes *interlined above* troden *crossed out.* 25 Alle *to* 27 deadlic| nesse *underlined.*

f. 103b. 2 Probatio: *the* b *written thickly, an alteration* (*probably of* a).

nawt for þi ich wat swuch þ bereð ba togederes heuí bru
níe. ⁊ hére. ibunden hearde wið írn. middel. þeh. ⁊ earm
10 es. míd brade þicke bondes. swa þ tet swat þrof:' is passíun
to þolien. Feasteð. wakeð. Swinkeð. ⁊ crist hit wat meaneð
hím þ hit ne greueð hím nawt. ⁊ bit me ofte teachen hím
sumhwet wið hwet he mahte his licome deruen. Al þ is
bitter for ure lauerdes luue:' al him þuncheð swete. Deu le
15 set ȝet he wepeð to me wíuene sarest. ⁊ seið godd forȝet him
for þi þ he ne sent him na muchel secnesse. Godd hit wat
þ makeð luue. for as he seið me ofte. for na þing þ godd
mahte don uuele bi hím. þah he wið þe forlorene wurpe
him in to helle:' ne mahte he neauer him þuncheð luuien
20 him þe leasse. ȝef ei mon eani swuch þing ortrowi bi him.
he is mare mat þen þeof ínume wið þeofðe. Ich wat ec
swuch wummon þ þoleð lutel leasse. ah nis þer bute þonc
ki godd i strengðe þ he ȝeueð ham. ⁊ icnawen eadmodli
che ure wacnesse. luuie we hare god:' ⁊ swa hit is ure ahne.
25 for as sein Gregoire seið. of swa muchel strengðe is luue:' þ
hit makeð oþres god:' wið ute swinc ure ahne. as is iseid
þruppe. Nu me þuncheð we beoð icumen in to þe seoue
ðe dale þ is al of luue:' þe makeð schir heorte.

f. 104a S eínte pawel witneð (M. 384)
þ alle uttre heardschipes.
alle flesches pinsunges. ant
licomliche swínkes. al is ase nawt aȝeínes lu
5 ue þe schireð ⁊ brihteð þe heorte. Exercitio corporis ad modi
cum ualet. pietas autem ualet ad omnia. þ is. licomlich bisi
schipe:' is to lutel wurð. ah swote ⁊ schir heorte is god
to alle
þinges. Si linguis hominum loquar ⁊ angelorum ⁊ cetera. Si
tradidero

15 wíuene, *sic* (*so also* T). 23 i, *probably for* þe.

f. 104a. 1 *Very large blue initial* S (*marking the beginning of Part VII*), *rising from* 5 *to two line-spaces in upper margin, with tail to* 9; *elaborately ornamented with red line-patterns within, above, and in margin from present top edge down tail to* 18; *the top of the decoration is now shaved off.* 1 *to* 3, *and* 5 *to* 8: *side-scribbles at the line-ends, and right margin corresponding marks* × (*opposite* 1 *and* 8). 5 Exercitio, *sic; cf.* f. 1b. 6.

corpus meum ita ut ardeam ⁊ cetera. Si distribuero omnes faculta
tes meas in cibos pauperum. caritatem autem non habeam·ˏ ní 10
chil michi prodest. þah ich cuðe he seið monne ledene ⁊ englene.
þah ich dude o mi bodi alle píne ⁊ passíun ꝥ bodi mahte
þolien. þah ich ȝeue poure al ꝥ ich hefde·ˏ ȝef ich nefde luue
þerwið·ˏ to godd ⁊ to alle men in hím ⁊ for hím·ˏ al were i
spillet. for as þe hali abbat moyses seide. Al ꝥ wa ⁊ al þet 15
heard ꝥ we þolieð o flesch. ⁊ al ꝥ god ꝥ we eauer doð. alle swuc
che þinges. ne beoð nawt bute as lomen to tilie wið þe heorte.
ȝef þe axe ne kurue. ne spitelsteaf ne dulue. ne þe su⟨l⟩h ne ere
de. hwa kepte ham to halden ? Alswa as na mon neluueð lo
men for ham seolf·ˏ ah deð for þe þinges ꝥ me wurcheð wið 20
ham·ˏ alswa na flesches derf nis to luuien bute for þi·ˏ þet
godd te reaðere þiderward loki mid his grace. ⁊ makeð þe
heorte schir ⁊ of briht sihðe. ꝥ nan ne mei habben wið mong
lunge of unþeawes. ne wið eorðlich luue of worltliche þinges.
(M. 386) for þis mong woreð swa þe ehnen of þe heorte·ˏ ꝥ ha ne mei 25
cnawen godd. ne gleadien of his sihðe. Schir heorte as seínt
Bernard seið·ˏ makieð twa þinges. ꝥ tu al ꝥ tu dest. do hit
oðer for luue ane of godd·ˏ oðer for oþres god ⁊ for his bihé·ue·
Haue in al ꝥ tu dest·ˏ an of þes twa ententes·ˏ oðer ba togederes. f. 104b
for þe leatere falleð in to þe earre. haue eauer schire heorte þus.
⁊ do al ꝥ tu wult. haue wori heorte·ˏ al þe sit uuele. Omnia
munda mundis. coínquinatis uero nichil est mundum. Apostolus.
Item. Augustinus. Habe caritatem·ˏ ⁊ fac quicquid uis. uolun- 5
tate uidelicet

18 su⟨l⟩h: l *interlined with caret.* 28 bihéue: .ue. *written below* hé. *A large mark × is scratched in the bottom margin below* 28 oðer *to* for his.

rationis. for þi mine leoue sustren ouer alle þing beoð bisie to habben schír heorte. Hwet is schir heorte? Ich hit habbe iseid
ear. ꝥ is ꝥ ȝe na þing ne wilnín ne ne luuien.' bute godd ane. ⁊ te ilke þinges for godd.' þe helpeð ow toward him. for
10 godd ich segge luuien ham.' ⁊ nawt for ham seoluen. as ís mete oðer clað. mon oðer wummon. þe ȝe beoð of igodet. for ase seið seint austin. ⁊ spekeð þus to ure lauerd. Mínus te amat qui preter te aliquid amat. quod non propter te amat. ꝥ is.
lauerd leasse ha luuieð þe.' þe luuieð eawt bute þe. bute ha
15 luuien hit for þe. Schirnesse of heorte is godes luue ane. I þis is al þe strengðe of alle religiuns. þe ende of alle ord res. Plenitudo legis est dilectio. luue fulleð þe lahe seið seín te pawel. Quicquid precipitur.' in sola caritate solidatur. Alle go
des heastes as sein gregoire seið beoð i luue i rotet. luue
20 ane schal beon ileid i seinte Mihales weie. Þeo þe meast lu uieð.' schulen beo meast iblisset. nawt þeo þe leadeð hear dest lif.' for luue hit ouerweieð. luue is heouene stiward. for hire muchele freolec. for heo ne edhalt na þing.' ah ȝeueð al ꝥ ha haueð ⁊ ec hire seoluen. elles ne kepte
25 godd nawt of þet hiren wére.

Godd haueð ofgan ure luue on alle cunne wise. he haueð muchel idon us.' ⁊ mare bihaten. Muchel ȝeoue ofdraheð luue. Me al þe world he ȝef us in adam (M. 388)
f. 105a ure alde feader. ⁊ al ꝥ is i þe world he weorp under ure fét. beastes ⁊ fuheles ear we weren forgulte. Omnia subiecisti sub pedibus eius. o. ⁊ bo. u. insuper ⁊ pe. c. volucres ce. ⁊ p. ma. qui peram.
se. maris. ant ȝet al ꝥ is. as is þruppe iseid.' serueð þe gode
5 to sawle bihéue. ȝet te uuele seruið. eorðe. sea. ⁊ sunne. He

f. 104b. 17 *mark* × *in left margin;* 17, 18 luue fulleð þe lahe . . . te pawel *underlined.* 20 Mihales, *sic; cf.* f. 111b. 26 *large red initial* G *between* 25 *and* 28*; blue line-patterns within, and in margin from* 22 *to low in bottom margin.*

f. 105a. 3, 4 *read* oues ⁊ boues uniuersas insuper ⁊ pecora campi volucres celi ⁊ pisces maris qui perambulant semitas maris.

dude ȝet mare. ȝef us. nawt ane of his.' ah dude al him
seoluen. Se heh ȝeoue nes neauer iȝeuen.' to se lahe wrecch
ces. Apostolus. christus dilexit ecclesiam ⁊ dedit semet ipsum
pro ea.
Crist seíð seinte pawel. luuede swa his leofmon.' ꝥ he ȝef for
hire þe pris of him seoluen. Neomeð nu gode ȝeme mine 10
leoue sustren for hwi me ah⟨h⟩im to luuien. Earst as a mon
þe woheð. as a king ꝥ luuede a gentil poure leafdi of feor
rene londe. he sende his sonden biuoren. ꝥ weren þe patriarches
⁊ te prophetes. of þe alde testament wið leattres isealet. On
en
de he com him seoluen. ⁊ brohte þe godspel as leattres 15
iopenet.
⁊ wrat wið his ahne blod saluz to his leofmon. luue gretun
ge. forte wohín hire wið. ⁊ hire luue wealden. Herto falleð a
A leafdi wes mid hire ¶ .tale.' a wrihe forbisne.
fan.' biset al abuten. hire lond al destruet. ⁊ heo al
poure inwið an eorðene castel. A mihti kinges luue wes þah 20
biturnd up on hire swa unimete swiðe.' ꝥ he for wohlech sen
de hire his sonden. an efter oðer. ofte somet monie. sende
hire beawbelez baðe feole ⁊ feire. sucurs of liueneð. help
of his hehe hird to halden hire castel. Heo underfeng al as on
unrecheles. ⁊ swa wes heard iheortet.' ꝥ hire luue ne mahte he 25
neauer beo þe neorre. hwet wult tu mare he com him seolf
on ende. schawde hire his feire neb. as þe þe wes of alle men.'
(M. 390) feherest to bihalden. spec se swiðe swoteliche. ⁊ wordes se
murie.'
þet ha mahten deade arearen to líue. wrahte feole wundres f. 105b
⁊ dude muchele meistries biuoren hire ehsihðe. schawde
hire his mihte. talde hire of his kínedom. bead to makien

7–8 wrecch|ces, *sic.* 9, 10 Crist *to* him seoluen *underlined.*
11 ah⟨h⟩im: ⟨h⟩ *interlined with caret.* 13 patriarches: rches
crowded together (h *blotted*) *at end of line.* 14 *MS.* prophes.
18 *large blue initial* A *between* 17 *and* 20, *with tail to* 22; *red line-patterns to right, within, and in margin from* 16 *down tail to* 27; *directing* a *in left margin. Before* .tale.' a wrihe forbisne. *a blue paragraph touched with red.*

hire cwen of al ꝥ he ahte. al þis ne heold nawt. nes þis
5 hoker wunder? for heo nes neauer wurðe forte beon his
þuften. ah swa þurh his deboneírte luue hefde ouercumen
him.' ꝥ he seide on ende. Dame þu art iweorret. ⁊ þine van
beoð se stronge.' ꝥ tu ne maht nanesweis wið ute mi sucurs
edfleon hare honden. ꝥ ha ne don þe to scheome deað efter
10 al þi weane. Ich chulle for þe luue of þe.' neome ꝥ feht up
o me. ⁊ arudde þe of ham þe þi deað secheð. Ich wat þah
to soðe ꝥ ich schal bituhen ham neomen deaðes wunde.
⁊ ich hit wulle heorteliche forte ofgan þin heorte. Nu
þenne biseche ich þe for þe luue ꝥ ich cuðe þe. ꝥ tu luuíe
15 me lanhure efter þe ilke dede dead.' hwen þu naldest lí
ues. þes king dude al þus. arudde hire of alle hire van.
⁊ wes him seolf to wundre ituket ⁊ isleín on ende. þurh
miracle aras þah from deaðe to líue. Nere þeos ilke
leafdi of uueles cunnes cunde. ȝef ha ouer alle þing
20 ne luuede him her efter?

Þes king is iesu godes sune. ꝥ al o þisse wise wohede
ure sawle þe deoflen hefden biset. Ant he as noble wo
here efter monie messagers ⁊ feole goddeden.' com to pru
uien his luue. ⁊ schawde þurh cnihtschipe ꝥ he wes luue
25 wurðe. as weren sumhwile cnihtes iwunet to donne. du
de him i turneiment. ⁊ hefde for his leoues luue his
scheld i feht as kene cniht on euche half iþurlet. his
scheld þe wreah his godd head.' wes his leoue licome þet
f. 106a wes ispread o rode. brad as scheld buuen.' in his istrahte ear
mes. nearow bineoðen as þe an fot efter moníes wéne set
up o þe oðer. ꝥ þis scheld naueð siden.' is for bitacnunge. (M. 392)
ꝥ his deciples þe schulden stonden bi hím. ⁊ habben ibeon
5 his siden.' fluhen alle from him ⁊ leafden him as fremede.'
as þe godspel seið. Relicto eo omnes fugerunt. Þis scheld is i
ȝeuen us aȝeín alle temptatiuns. as Ieremie witneð. Dabis
scutum cordis laborem tuum. nawt ane þis scheld ne schilt
us from alle uueles.' ah deð ȝet mare. cruneð us in heouene.
10 Scuto bone uoluntatis. Lauerd he seið dauið wið þe scheld

f. 105b. 21 *large red initial* Þ *between* 20 *and* 23 *with stem in margin from* 18 *to tail at* 26; *blue line-patterns within, and in margin from* 15 *to low in bottom margin.*

of þi gode wil þu hauest us icrunet. scheld he seið of god
wil. for willes he þolede al ꝥ he þolede. ysaias. Oblatus est
quia
Me lauerd þu seist hwerto. ne mahte he wið ¶ .uoluit.
leasse gref habben arud us? ȝeoi iwiss ful lihtliche. ah he
nalde. for hwi? forte bineomen us euch bitellunge aȝein 15
hím of ure luue ꝥ he se deore bohte. Me buð lihtliche
þing ꝥ me luueð lutel. He bohte us wið his heorte blod.
deorre pris nes neauer. forte ofdrahen of us ure luue to
ward hím. ꝥ costnede him se sare. I scheld beoð þreo þinges.
þe treo. ⁊ te leðer. ⁊ te litunge. alswa wes i þis scheld. þe treo 20
of þe rode. ꝥ leðer of godes licome. þe litunge of þe reade
blod ꝥ heowede hire se feire. Eft þe þridde reisun. Efter
kene
cnihtes deað. me hongeð hehe ichirche his scheld on his
mungunge. alswa is þis scheld. ꝥ is þe crucifix. ichirche i
set i swuch stude. þer me hit sonest seo. forte þenchen þer 25
bi o iesu cristes cnihtschipe ꝥ he dude o rode. his leofmon
bihalde þron hu he bohte hire luue. lette þurlín his scheld
openín his side. to schawín hire his heorte. to schawin híre
openliche hu inwardliche he luuede hire. ⁊ to ofdrahen hire f. 106b
Fowr heaued luuen me ifind i þis world. bi ¶ .heorte.
tweone gode iféren. bitweone mon ⁊ wummon. bi
(M. 394) wif ⁊ hire child. bitweone licome ⁊ sawle. þe luue ꝥ iesu crist
haueð to his deore leofmon. ouergeað þeos fowre. passeð 5
ham
alle. Ne teleð me him god fere þe leið his wed i giwerie to
acwi
tin ut his fére? Godd almihti leide him seolf for us i giwerie.
⁊ dude his deorewurðe bodi to acwitin ut his leofmon of giwe

f. 106a. 13 *small blue initial* M *with a few hasty red lines within, and in margin from* 10 *to* 16; *before* .uoluit. *a red paragraph with flourish into right margin, scribbled with blue.* 14 iwiss, *sic* (*cf.* f. 68b). 26 cristes: c *resembles* r.

f. 106b. 2 *large square red initial* F *between* 1 *and* 4, *with stem in margin down to* 6/7, *the lower arm cuts top of* wif ⁊ h(ire; *blue line-patterns within, and in margin from above* 1 *to* 9; *before* .heorte. *a blue paragraph touched with red.* 3 *between* bitweone *and* mon: gode *crossed out; after* bi: tweone *omitted.*

ne honden. neauer fére ne dude swuch fordede for his fere.
10 Muche luue is ofte bitweone mon ⁊ wummon. ah þah ha wé
re iweddet him.' ha mahte iwurðen se unwreast. ⁊ swa longe ha
mahte forhorín hire wið oþre men.' ꝥ þah ha walde aȝein
cumen.' he ne kepte hire nawt. for þi crist luueð mare. for
þah þe sawle his spuse forhori hire wið þe feond under hea
15 ued sunne. feole ȝeres ⁊ dahes.' his mearci is hire eauer ȝarow
hwen ha wule cumen hám.' ⁊ leten þen deouel. Al þis he seið
him seolf þurh Ieremie. Si dímiserit uir uxorem suam. ⁊ cetera.
Tu autem fornicata es cum multis amatoribus.' tamen reuer- tere ad me
dicit dominus. ȝet he ȝeiȝeð al dei. þu ꝥ hauest se unwreaste idon
20 biturn þe ⁊ cum aȝeín.' welcume schalt tu beo me. Immo ⁊ oc
currit prodigo uenienti. ȝet he eorneð hit seið aȝeín híre ȝeín
cume ⁊ warpeð earmes anan abuten hire swire. Hweat is
mare milce ? ȝet her gleadfulre wunder. Ne beo neauer his
leof forhoret mid se monie deadliche sunnen.' sone se ha ki
25 með to hím aȝeín.' he makeð hire neowe meiden. for as seint
austín seið. Swa muchel is bitweonen. bituhhen godes neo
leachunge. ⁊ monnes to wummon.' ꝥ monnes neoleachunge
makeð of meiden wif.' ⁊ godd makeð of wif meiden. Restituit
f. 107a inquit Iob ín íntegrum. Gode werkes ⁊ treowe bileaue. þeose twa
þinges beoð meiðhad isawle. Nu of þe þridde luue.
Child ꝥ hefde swuch uuel. ꝥ him bihofde beað of blod ear hit
were ihealet.' muchel þe moder luuede hit. þe walde þis beað
5 him makien. þis dude ure lauerd us þe weren se seke of sunne. (M. 396)
⁊ swa isulet þerwið.' ꝥ na þing ne mahte healen us ne clean
sín us bute his blod ane. for swa he hit walde. his luue ma

9 fordede, *for or derived from* forðdede (OE. forðdæd). 10 *small blue initial* M *with a few red lines within, and in margin from* 9 *to* 16/17. 22 abuten: b *and first stroke of* u *thickly written on an erasure.*

f. 107a. 2 *small red initial* N *touched with blue; in* Nu *the* u *has exceptional form like* ıȷ (*cf.* ff. 5a, 108b); *top bar of* F *on preceding page has offset at the end of the line.*

keð us beað þrof. iblescet beo he eaure. þreo beaðes he greiðe
de to his deore leofmon forte weschen hi⟨re⟩ in ham se hwit ⁊
se feier :· þ ha were wurðe to his cleane cluppunges. þe earste 10
beað is fulluht. þe oðer beoð teares inre oðer uttre. efter þe
forme beað ȝef ha hire suleð. Þe þridde is iesu cristes blod þ
halheð ba þe oþre as seín iuhan seið iþe apocalipse. Qui di
lexit nos ⁊ lauit nos in sanguine suo :· þ he luueð us mare
þen eani moder hire child :· he hit seið him seoluen þurh 15
ysaie. Nunquid potest mater oblíuisci filíí uteri sui. Et si
illa obliuiscatur :· ego non obliuiscar tui. Mei moder he seið
for
ȝeoten hire child ? ant þah heo do :· ich ne mei þe forȝeoten
neauer. ant seið þe resun efter. In manibus meis descripsi te.
Ich habbe he seið depeínt te i míne honden. swa he dude 20
mid read blod up o þe rode. Me cnut his gurdel to habben
þoht of a þing. ah ure lauerd for he nalde neauer forȝeo
ten us :· dude mearke of þurlunge. in ure munegunge i
ba twa his honden. NV þe feorðe luue. þe sawle luueð þe
licome swiðe mid alle. ant þet is etscene iþe twinnunge. for 25
leoue freond beoð sari hwen ha schulen twínnin. ah ure
lauerd willeliche totweamde his sawle from his bodi forte
veien ure baðe togederes world buten ende i þe blisse of heo
uene. þus lo iesu cristes luue toward his deore spuse. þ is hali f. 107b
chirche. oðer cleane sawle. passeð alle ⁊ ouerkimeð þe fowr
measte luuen þ me ifínd on eorðe. wið al þis luue ȝetten
he woheð hire o þis wise. Þí luue he seið oðer hit is
forte ȝeouen allunge :· oðer hit is to sullen. oðer hit is to 5
(M. 398) reauín ⁊ to neomen wið strengðe. ȝef hit is forte ȝeouen :·
hwer maht tu biteon hit betere þen up o me ? Nam ich þin
ge feherest. nam ich kinge richest. nam ich hest icunnet.
nam ich weolie wisest. nam ich monne hendest. nam ich

9 hi⟨re⟩: re *interlined above* m *crossed out.* 17 *to* 20: 17 Mei moder he seið, 18 ȝeoten *to* forȝeoten, 19 neauer. ant seið, 20 Ich habbe *to* honden, *underlined; in right margin marks* × *opposite* 17, 19. 19 resun, *sic.* 24 *small square blue initial* N *with a few red lines about and within.*

f. 107b. 4 *small red initial* Þ *touched with blue.* 9 weolie, *sic; original word probably* weore '*of men*' (*as* T). L peritorum *suggests intermediate stage* weote, weotie.

10 þinge freoest ? for swa me seið bi large mon þe ne con nawt
edhalden.' ꝥ he haueð þe honden as mine beoð iþurlet.
Nam ich alre þinge swotest ⁊ swetest ? Þus alle þe reisuns
hwi me ah to ȝeoue luue.' þu maht ifinden in me. nome
liche ȝef þu luuest chaste cleannesse. for nan ne mei lu
15 uíe me.' bute ha hire halde. Ah ha is þreouald. i widewe
had. i spus had. i meidenhad. þe heste.' ȝef þi luue nis nawt
toȝeouene.' ah wult ꝥ me bugge hire.' buggen hire ? oðer
wið oðer luue oðer wið sumhweat elles.' Me suleð wel lu
ue.' ⁊ swa me ah to sulle luue. ⁊ for na þing elles. ȝef þin is
20 swa to sullen.' ich habbe iboht hire wið luue ouer alle oþre.
for of þe fowr measte luuen. ich habbe icud toward te.'
þe measte of ham alle. ȝef þu seist þu nult nawt leote
þron se liht chap. ah wult ȝette mare.' nempne hweat
hit schule beon. sete feor o þi luue. þu ne schalt seggen se
25 muchel.' ꝥ ich nule ȝeoue mare. wult tu castles. kinedom
es. wult tu wealden al þe world ? Ich chulle do þe betere. ma
kie þe wið al þis.' cwen of heoueriche. þu schalt te seolf
beo seoueuald brihtre þen þe sunne. nan uuel ne schal
f. 108a nahhi þe. na wunne ne schal wonti þe. al þi wil schal beon i
wraht in heouene ⁊ ec in eorðe. ȝe ⁊ ȝet ín helle. ne schalnea
uer heorte þenchen hwuch selhðe.' ꝥ ich nule ȝeouen for þi
luue. unmeteliche. vneuenliche. unendeliche mare. Al Crea
5 suse weole.' þe wes kinge richest. Absalones schene wlite.
þeas
ofte as me euesede hím. salde his euesunge. þe her ꝥ he kearf
of.' for twa hundret sicles of seoluer iweiet. Asaeles swiftschi
pe þe straf wið heortes of urn. Samsones strengðe. þe sloh a
þusent of his fan al ed a tíme. ⁊ ane bute fére. Cesares freo
10 lec. Alixandres hereword. Moysese heale. Nalde amon for
an
of þeos ȝeouen al ꝥ he ahte ? ant alle somet aȝeín mi bodi.' (M. 400)
ne beoð nawt wurð a nelde. ȝef þu art se swiðe anewil. ⁊ swa

18, 19 me suleð wel luue: *after this* for luue *is omitted.*

f. 108a. *On this page the lines are crowded and words written unusually close together.* 5 weole *written* wule; *first stroke of* u *altered to* e, *above second stroke a small* o *in paler ink. Correction probably by main hand.* wule *shows attraction of* suse; *cf. reverse in* M. kresules weole.

ut of þi wit. ꝥ tu þurh nawt to leosen forsakest swuch biȝe
te.᛫ wið alles cunnes selhðe.᛫ lo ich halde her heatel sweord up
o þín heaued todealen lif ⁊ sawle. ⁊ bisenchen ham ba in to þe 15
fur of helle. to beon deofles hore schentfulliche ⁊ sorhfulliche
world abuten ende. Ondswere nu ⁊ were þe ȝef þu const a
ȝeín me.᛫ oðer ȝette me þi luue þe ich ȝirne se swiðe. nawt
for min.᛫ ah for þín ahne muchele biheue.
Lo þus ure lauerd woheð. Nis ha to heard iheortet ꝥ a 20
þulli
wohere ne mei to his luue turnen? ȝef ha wel þencheð
þeose
þreo þinges. hwet he is ⁊ hwet heo is.᛫ ⁊ hu muchel is þe luue
of se heh as he is.᛫ toward se lah as heo is. for þi seið þe salm
wruhte. Non est qui se abscondat a calore eius. Nis nan
ꝥ mahe
edlutien.᛫ ꝥ ha ne mot him luuien. þe soðe sunne iþe under 25
tid wes for þi istihen on heh.᛫ o þe hehe rode. forte spreaden
ouer
al hate luue gleames. þus neodful he wes ⁊ is aþet tes dei to on
tenden his luue. ⁊ his leoues heorte. ⁊ seið iþe godspel.
Ignem
uení mittere in terram. & quid uolo nisi ut ardeat? Ich com f. 108b
to brin
gen he seið fur in to eorðe. ꝥ is. bearninde luue in to eorðlich
heorte. ant hwet ȝirne ich elles bute ꝥ hit bleasie? wlech lu
ue is him lað. as he seið þurh sein iuhan i þe apocalipse.
Vtinam frigidus esses aut calidus. set quia tepidus es.᛫ 5
incipiam
te euomere de ore meo. Ich walde he seið to his leofmon.
ꝥ tu
were i mí luue. oðer allunge cald.᛫ oðer hat mid alle. ah for
þi ꝥ tu art ase wlech bitweone twa. nowðer hat. ne cald.᛫ þu
makest me to wleatien. ⁊ ich wulle speowe þe ut.᛫ bute þu

15 todealen, *sic, for* to dealen *or* to todealen. 20 *large blue initial* L *with stem in margin between* 17 *and* 21; *red line-patterns in angle, and in margin from* 14 *to* 24.

f. 108b. *In left margin a large hand pointing up, with forefinger at level of* 4; *behind, a mark* × *at level of* 6; Ich walde he seið to his leof *underlined.*

10 wurðe hattre. Nu ȝe habbeð iherd mine leoue sustren (M. 402)
hu ⁊ for hwi godd is swiðe to luuíen. forte ontenden ow wel:
gederið wude þerto: wið þe poure wummon of Sarepte
þe burh þe spealeð ontendunge. En inquit colligo duo
ligna. Regum .iii. lauerd qð ha to helye þe hali prophete. lo
15 ich gederi twa treon. þeos twa treon bitacnið. ꝥ a treo þet
stod upriht. ⁊ ꝥ oþer þe eode þwertouer: o þe deore rode. of
þeos twa treon ȝe schulen ontende fur of luue inwið ower
heorte. biseoð ofte towart ham. þencheð ȝef ȝe ne ahen eaðe
to luuien þe king of blisse. þe tospreat swa his earmes tow
20 ard ow. ⁊ buheð as to beoden cos duneward his heaued. Si
kerliche ich segge hit. ȝef þe soðe helye. ꝥ is godd almihti
ifint ow þeose twa treon bisiliche gederín: he wule gestnín
wið ow. ⁊ monifalden in ow: his deorewurðe grace. as helie
dude hire liueneð. ⁊ gestnede wið hire. ꝥ he ifond þe twa
25 treon gederín i Sarepte. GRickisch fur is imaket of
reades monnes blod. ⁊ ꝥ ne mei na þing. bute Migge. ant
Sond. ⁊ eisil: as me seið acwenchen. Þis grickisch fur is
þe luue of iesu ure lauerd. ⁊ ȝe hit schule makien of reade
f. 109a monnes blod. ꝥ is iesu crist ireadet wið his ahne blod o þe deore
rode. ant wes ínread cundeliche alswa as me weneð. þis blod for
ow isched up o þe earre twa treon: schal makien ow sareptiens.
ꝥ is ontende mid tis grickisch fur. ꝥ as Salomon seið: nane
5 weattres. ꝥ beoð worldliche tribulatíuns. nane temptatiuns. now
ðer ínre ne uttre: ne mahen þis luue acwenchen. Nu nis þen
ne on ende bute witen ow warliche wið al ꝥ hit acwencheð. (M. 404)
ꝥ beoð Migge. ⁊ sond. ⁊ eisil. as ich ear seide. Migge is stench
of sunne. O sond ne groweð na god ⁊ bitacneð idel. Idel akel
10 deð ⁊ acwencheð þis fur. Sturieð ow cwicliche aa i gode
werkes. ⁊ ꝥ schal heaten ow ⁊ ontenden þis fur aȝeín þe

10 *small red initial* N *touched with blue;* Nu: *the* u *has same shape as in* Nu f. 107a. 25 *small blue initial* G *filled and surrounded with red lines.* 27 Sond: s *has form* ꝏ, *but some other letter was first begun.* f. 109a. 3. sareptiens: ns *as* f. 18b. 8.

brune of sunne. for alswa as þe an neil driueð ut þen o
þer:· alswa þe brune of godes luue. driueð brune of ful lu
ue ut of þe heorte. Þe þridde þing is eisil. ꝥ is sur heorte
of nið oðer of onde. Vnderstondeð þis word. þa þe niðfu 15
le giws offreden ure lauerd þis sure present up o þe rode:·
þa seide he ꝥ reowðfule word. Consumatum est. neauer
qð he ear nu nes ich ful pinet. nawt þurh ꝥ eisil:· ah
þurh hare ondfule nið:· ꝥ tet eisil bitacnede ꝥ heo hím
duden drinken. ant is ilich as þah a mon ꝥ hefde longe 20
iswunken. ⁊ failede efter long swinc:· on ende of his hu
re. Alswa ure lauerd mare þen twa ⁊ þritti ȝer tilede ef
ter hare luue. ⁊ for al his sare swinc ne wilnede na þing:·
bute luue to hure. Ah i þe ende of his lif. ꝥ wes as i þe
euentid. hwen me ȝelt wercmen hare deies hure. loke 25
hu ha ȝulden him for piment of huní luue:· eisil of
sur nið. ⁊ galle of bitter onde. O qð ure lauerd þa:· Con
sumatum est. Al mí swínc on eorðe. Al mi pine o rode.
ne sweameð ne ne derueð me nawiht aȝeín þis. ꝥ ich þus f. 109b
biteo
al ꝥ ich idon habbe. þis eisil ꝥ ȝe beodeð me. þis sure hure
þurh
filleð mi píne. þis eisil of sur heorte ⁊ of bitter þonc ouer alle
oðre þing acwencheð grickisch fur ꝥ is þe luue of ure lauerd
ant hwa se hit bereð i breoste toward wummon oðer mon:· ha 5
is giwes make. ha offreð godd þis eisil. ⁊ þurhfulleð onont
hire iesues pine o rode. Me warpeð grickisch fur upon his fa
men. ⁊ swa me ouerkimeð ham. ȝe schule don alswa hwen
godd
areareð ow of ei va eani weorre. Hu ȝe hit schule warpen:· Sa
lomon teacheð. Si esurierit inimicus tuus:· ciba illum. Si sí 10
tierit:· potum da illi. Sic enim carbones ardentes congeres
super

17 *and* 28 consumatum, *sic*. 20 duden drinken: duden *can still be read, but is now covered by a transparent gum-drop (also covering bottom of* þu *in* þurh *above); on this patch faint writing is visible, apparently offset from* heaued (*in* 20 *of preceding page*) *which is now faint.*

f. 109b. 7 iesues, *sic*. 10 Sa)lomon *underlined; in left margin a mark* ×, *and side-scribble down to* 19.

caput eius. ꝥ is. ȝef þi fa hungreð.˙/ fed him. to his þurst ȝef (M. 406)
him drunch. ꝥ is to understonden. ȝef he efter þin hearm
haueð hunger oðer þurst.˙/ ȝef him fode of þine beoden ꝥ
15 godd do him are. ȝef hím drunch of teares. wep for his sun
nen. þus þu schalt seið Salomon rukelin on his heaued bear
ninde gleden. ꝥ is to seggen. þus þu schalt ontenden his heorte
forte luuie þe. for heorte is in hali writ bi heaued underston
den. O þulli wise wule godd seggen ed te dome. Hwi luuedest
20 tu þe mon oðer þe wummon? Sire ha luueden me. ȝe he wu
le seggen. þu ȝulde ꝥ tu ahtest. her nabbe ich þe nawt mu
ches to ȝelden. ȝef þu maht ondswerien. alle wa ha duden
me. ne na luue ne ahte ich ham. ah sire ich luuede ham for
þi luue.˙/ ꝥ luue he ah þe. for hit wes iȝeuen him.˙/ ⁊ he hit
25 wule þe ȝelden. Migge as ich seide ꝥ acwencheð grickisch
fur.˙/ is stinkinde flesches luue. þe acwencheð gastelich luue.˙/
ꝥ grickisch fur bitacneð. Hweat flesch wes on eorðe se swete
⁊ se hali as wes iesu cristes flesch? ant þah he seide him seolf
f. 110a to his deore deciples. Nisi ego abiero.˙/ paraclitus non veniet ad
uos. ꝥ is. bute ich parti from ow. þe hali gast ꝥ is mín ⁊ mines
feaderes luue.˙/ ne mei nawt cumen to ow. ah hwen ich beo from
ow.˙/ ich chulle senden him ow. Hwen iesu cristes ahne deci- ples
5 hwil ꝥ ha fleschliche luueden hím neh ham.˙/ foreoden þe swet
nesse of þe hali gast. ne ne mahte nawt habben baðe to- gederes.˙/
demeð ow seoluen. nis he wod oðer heo þe luueð to swiðe hire
ahne flesch. oðer eani mon fleschliche. swa ꝥ ha ȝirne to swi
ðe his sihðe oðer his speche.˙/ ne þunche hire neauer wunder

17 his heorte: h *of* his *altered from* l. 25 *small red initial* M *touched with blue.*

f. 110a. 4 iesu, *sic.* 6, 10, 11 *some spots of gum seem to have been present, which in rubbing off have partly effaced* uu *of* luueð 7, an o þ *of* euchan of þes 10, *and* or þ *of* for þet 11.

ȝef hire wonti þe hali gastes froure. Cheose nu euchan of þes twa:· 10
eorðlich elne ⁊ heouenlich. to hweðer ha wule halden. for þet
oðer ha mot léten. for i þe tweire monglunge ne mei ha hab
ben neauer mare schirnesse of heorte. ꝥ is as we seiden ear. þet
god ⁊ te strengðe of alle religiuns ⁊ in euch ordre. luue makeð
hire schír. griðful ⁊ cleane. luue haueð a meistrie biuoren 15
(M. 408) alle oþre. for al ꝥ ha ríneð:· al ha turneð to hire:· ⁊ makeð al
hire ahne. Quemcumque locum calcauerit pes uester:· pes videlicet
amoris:· uester erit. Deore walde moní mon buggen a swuch þing
ꝥ al ꝥ he rine to:· al were his ahne:· ant ne seide hit þruppe
feor. Ane þurh ꝥ tu luuest ꝥ god ꝥ is in an oðer. wið þe ri 20
nunge of þi luue. þu makest wið uten oþer swínc his god:·
þin ahne god. as sein Gregoire witneð. lokið nu hu muchel
god þe ontfule leoseð. streche þi luue to iesu crist:· þu hauest
him iwunnen. Rín him wið ase muche luue. as þu hauest
sum mon sum chearre. he is þín to don wið al ꝥ tu wilnest. 25
ah hwa luueð þíng ꝥ leaueð hit for leasse þen hit is wurð?
Nis godd betere uneuenlich þen al ꝥ is i þe world? Chearite is
cherte of leof þíng ⁊ of deore. Vndeore he makeð godd ⁊ to un
wurð mid alle:· ꝥ for ei worltlich þing of his luue leaskeð f. 110b
for na þing ne con luuien riht:· bute he ane. Swa ouer swiðe
he luueð luue:· ꝥ he makeð hire his euening. ȝet ich dear
segge mare. he makeð hire his meistre. ⁊ deð al ꝥ ha hat
as þah he moste nede. Mei ich pruuíen þis? ȝe witerliche 5
ich bi his ahne wordes. for þus he spekeð to moyses þe mon
ne meast him luuede. In Numerí. Dimisi iuxta uerbum tuum.
non dicit preces. Ich hefde qð he imunt to wreoke mine
wreaððe i þis folc. Ah þu seist i ne schal nawt:· þi word beo
iforðet. Me seið ꝥ luue bindeð. witerliche luue bint swa 10
ure lauerd. ꝥ he ne mei na þing don:· bute þurh luues lea

10 þes twa: *written small running into the margin; probably by main hand, though not required:* euchan *is subject of* Cheose. 19 þerwið *omitted after* rine.

ue. Nu preoue her of for hit þuncheð wunder. Ysaias.
Domine non est qui consurgat ⁊ teneat te. Lauerd þu wult smiten
seið ysaie. weilawei þu maht wel.· nis nan ꝥ te halde. As
15 þah he seide. ȝef ei luuede þe riht.· he mahte halden þe. ⁊
wearnen þe to smiten. In Genesy. ad loth. festina ⁊ cetera. Non
potero ibi quicquam facere.· donec egressus fueris illinc. ꝥ is. (M. 410) þa u
re lauerd walde bisenchen Sodome þer lot his freond wes
ínne.· hihe þe qð he utward. for hwil þu art bimong
20 ham.· ne mei ich nawt don ham. Nes þes wið luue ibunden?
hwet wult tu mare. luue is his chamberleng. his Conseiler.
his spuse. ꝥ he ne mei nawt heole wið.· Ah teleð al þet he
þencheð. In Genesy. Num celare potero abraham que gestu
rus sum? Mei ich qð ure lauerd heolen abraham þing ꝥ
25 ich þenche to donne? Nai o nane wise. Nu con þes luui
en þe þus spekeð ⁊ þus deð. to alle þe him inwardliche leueð
⁊ luuieð. þe blisse ꝥ he ȝarkeð ham.· as ha is uneuenlich
to alle worldes blissen.· alswa as ha is untalelich to world
f. 111a liche tungen. ysaias. Oculus non uidit deus absque te que prepa
rasti diligentibus te. Apostolus. Oculus non uidit. nec auris audi
uit. ⁊ cetera. ȝe habbeð of þeos blissen iwriten elleshwer míne
leoue sustren. þis luue is þe riwle þe riwleð þe heorte. Confi
5 tebor tibi in directione. id est. in regulatione cordis. Exprobratio
malorum. Generatio que non direxit cor suum. Þis is þe leafdi
riwle. alle þe oþre seruið hire. ⁊ ane for hire sake.· me hat
ham to luuien. lutel strengðe ich do of ham.· for hwon þet
þeos beo deorewurðliche ihalden. habbeð ham þah scheort
10 liche i þe eahtuðe dale.

f. 110b. 14 weilawei *to* halde *underlined; in left margin mark* ×.
28 alswa as: as *is probably an erroneous addition.*
f. 111a. 7 hat, *sic for* ah.

Bíuoren on earst ich
seide. ꝥ ȝe ne schulden nawiht
as i vu bihaten forte halden nan
of þe uttre riwlen. ꝥ ilke ich segge ȝetten.
ne nane ne write ich ham buten ow ane. Ich segge þis for 15
þi ꝥ oþre ancren ne seggen nawt þet ich þurh mi meistrie
(M. 412) makie ham neowe riwle. Ne bidde ich nawt ꝥ ha halden
ham. ah ȝe ȝet moten changín hwen se ȝe eauer wulleð.'
þeose for betere. aȝeín þinges þe beoð biuoren.' of ham is
lutel strengðe. Of sihðe. ⁊ of speche. ⁊ of þe oþre wittes is 20
inoh iseid. nu is þis leaste dale as ich bihet on earst.' todea
let ⁊ isundret.' o lutle seoue stucchen.

Me let leasse of þe þing ꝥ me haueð ofte. for þi ne
schule ȝe beon bute as ure breðren beoð ihuslet
·i·
inwið tweolf moneð fiftene siðen. Midwinter dei. Tweofte 25
·ii· ·iii·
dei. Condelmeasse dei. A sunne dei mid wei bitweonen
ꝥ ⁊ easter. oðer ure leafdi dei ȝef he is neh þe sunne dei.
·iiii· ·v· ·vi·
for þe hehnesse. Easter dei. Þe þridde sunne dei þrefter.
·vii· ·viii· ·ix·
Hali þursdei. Witsunne dei. Midsumerdei. Seinte Marie f. 111b
x· xi· xii·
dei magdaleine. Þe Assumptiun. Þe Natiuite. Seinte
xiii· xiiii· xv·
Mihales dei. Alle halhene dei. Seint andrews dei. aȝein
alle þeose beoð cleanliche i schriuene. ⁊ neomeð disceplin
es. neauer þah of namon bute of ow seoluen. ⁊ forgað an 5
dei ower pitance. ȝef ewt ilimpeð misliche ꝥ ȝe ne beon

11 *very large blue initial* B (*marking the beginning of Part VIII*) *between* 10 *and* 15, *stem in the margin, the top bow covers bottom of* he i þ *of* liche i þe eahtuðe *above; elaborate ornament with line-patterns to right, within, and in margin flourishing up to* 4 *and trailing to* 21; *directing* b *in left margin.* 20 *small blue initial* O *touched with red and two small flourishes; directing* o *in left margin.* 23 *red initial* M *between* 22 *and* 25; *blue line-patterns within, and in margin from* 21 *to low in bottom margin; directing* M *in left margin.* 25 Tweofte, *sic* (*probably a genuine form*).

f. 111b. 1 Witsunne, *sic* (T witsunendai)*: cf.* þe Hooly Gost ȝaf to apostlis wit at Wit Sunday for to knowe al maner langagis (*Wiclif*, De Officio Pastorali, *ch. xv*). 3 Mihales, *sic; cf.* f. 104b.

nawt ihuslet i þeose isette tearmes.' beoð hit þe neste sun
ne dei. oðer ȝef þe oþer terme is neh.' abideð aþet tenne.
Ȝe schulen eoten from easter.' aþet te hali rode dei þe lea
10 tere þe is in heruest euche dei twien bute þe fridahes. ne i
þe aduent ne schule ȝe nawt eoten hwit bute neode hit
makie. þe oþer half ȝer feasten al.' bute sunne dahes
ane. hwen ȝe beoð in heale ⁊ i ful strengðe. ah riwle ne
tweast nawt seke ne blodletene. Ȝe ne schulen nawt
15 eoten flesch ne seím.' bute for muche secnesse. oðer hwa
se is ouer feble. Potage eoteð bliðeliche. ⁊ wunieð ow to lu
tel drunch. noðeles leoue sustren ower mete ant ower
drunch haueð iþuht me ofte leasse þen ich walde. Ne
feaste ȝe na dei to bread ne to weattre. bute ȝe habben
20 Sum ancre makeð hire bord wið hire gest ¶ .leaue.
utewið. ꝥ is to muche freondschipe. for of alle ordres þen (M. 414
ne is hit uncundelukest. ⁊ meast aȝein ancre ordre þe
is al dead to þe world. me haueð iherd ofte ꝥ deade speken
wið cwike. ah ꝥ ha eten wið cwike.' ne fond ich ȝet n eauer.
25 Ne makie ȝe nane gestnunges. ne ne tulle ȝe to þe ȝe
te. nane uncuðe hearloz. þah þer nere nan oðer uuel
bute hare meadlese nurð.' hit walde letten oðerhwile
heouenliche þohtes. Ne límpeð nawt to ancre of oþer
f. 112a monnes ealmesse.' to makien hire large. Nalde me lahhen
a beggere lude to bismere. þe leaðede men to feaste? Ma
rie ⁊ Marthe ba weren sustren. ah hare lif sundrede. ȝean
cren beoð inumen ow to Marie dale. þe ure lauerd seolf
5 herede. Maria optimam partem elegit. Marthe marthe
qð he þu art muche baret. Marie haueð icore bet. ⁊ ne
schal hire na þing reauín hire dale. Husewifschipe is
marthe dale. Marie dale is stilnesse ⁊ reste of alle worl
des noise. ꝥ na þing ne lette hire to heren godes steuene.
10 Ant lokið hwet godd seið. ꝥ na þing ne schal ow reauín

8 *MS.* terme. 9 *small blue initial* Ȝ *touched with red.* 10 [umbridahes ȝongdahes ⁊ uigilies. I þeos dahes] *omitted before* ne; *cf.* f. 17b. 3 *to* 6. 14 *small red initial* Ȝ *touched with blue.* 20 *small blue initial* S *touched with red; before* .leaue. *a blue paragraph touched with red.* 24 n eauer: *in space first half of* a *erased but still visible.* 25 *a small red initial* N *touched with red.*

f. 112a. 6 i *omitted before* muche.

þis dale. Marie haueð hire meoster. leoteð hire iwurðen.
ȝe sitten wið Marie stan stille ed godes fét ⁊ hercnið hím
ane. Marthe meoster is to feden poure ⁊ schruden as hus
leafdi. Marie ne ah nawt to entremeatin þr⟨o⟩f. ȝef ei bla
með hire:· godd seolf ihwer wereð híre. as hali writ wit 15
neð. Contra Symonem:· duo debitores ⁊ cetera. Contra
Martham:·
Maria optimam par. ⁊ cetera. Contra apostolos:· murmur-
antes. Vt quid
perditio hec ? Bonum inquit opus ⁊ cetera. On oðer half nan
ancre
ne ah to neomen bute meaðfulliche ꝥ hire to neodeð.
hwer of þenne mei ha makien hire large ? ha schal lib 20
ben bi ealmesse ase meaðfulliche as ha eauer mei. ⁊ nawt ge
(M. 416) derín forte ȝeouen. ha nis nawt husewif:· ah is a chirch
ancre. ȝef ha mei spearien eaní poure schraden:· sende
ham al dearnliche ut of hire wanes. Vnder semblant
of god:· is ofte ihulet sunne. Ant hu schulen þeose 25
chirch ancres þe tilieð oðer habbeð rentes isette. don to
poure nehburs dearnliche hare ealmesse ? Ne wilni ha
nawt to habbe word of a large ancre. ne forte ȝeouen
muchel:· ne beo nan þe gnedure. forte habben mare. for f. 112b
hwon ꝥ gredinesse beo rote of ꝥ gederunge. of hire bit
ternesse. al beoð þe bohes bittre þe of hire spruteð. Bid
den hit forte ȝeouen hit:· his nawt ancre rihte. Of ancre
curteisie. of ancre largesce:· is icumen ofte sunne ant 5
scheome on ende. Wummen. ⁊ children. ⁊ nomeliche
ancre meidnes þe cumeð iswenchet for ow. þah ȝe
spearien hit on ow:· oðer borhin oðer bidden hit:· ma
kieð ham to eotene wið chearitable chere. ⁊ leaðieð to
herbarhin. Na mon ne eote biuoren ow bute bi ow 10

11 Marie *sic for* Marthe. 14 þr⟨o⟩f: o *interlined above* i *expuncted.* 17 par.: *read* partem. 26 chirch, *sic for* riche. 27 nehburs, *sic.*

f. 112b. *In outer left margin, written sideways from* 20 *to* 2, *in a 16th-century hand:* J J J Joh[ann]es Mannyng Elizabeth dei gratia Anglie ffranc[i]e et hib[ern]ie. 1 gnedure, *for* grediure. 6 *small blue initial* W (ƿ) *with red lines forming a tail through* 7 *to* 8. 10 *small red initial* N *touched with blue.* 10 bute *to* 14 leaue[2] *not in* M.

er meistres leaue. general oðer spetial. as of freres
preachurs. ⁊ meonurs. spetial:ʹ of alle oþre. Ne leaðie
ȝe nane oþre to eoten ne to drinken:ʹ bute alswa þurh
his leaue. liht is me seið leaue. Nawiht ne ȝirne ich
15 ꝥ me for swucche boden telle ow hende ancren. Ihwear
þah ant eauer ȝemeð ow ꝥ nan from ow þurh ower
untuhtle ne parti wið scandle.

ED gode men neomeð al ꝥ ow to nedeð. Ah ꝥ lokið
ow wel. ꝥ ȝe ne kecchen þe no⟨m⟩e of gederinde
20 ancren. Of mon ꝥ ȝe misleueð þurh his fol semblant
oðer bi his wake wordes:ʹ nowðer ne neome ȝe ne leasse
ne mare. neode schal dríuen ow forte bidden ei þing.
þah eadmodliche schawið to gode men ⁊ wummen:ʹ ow
er meoseise. Ȝe mine leoue sustren bute ȝef neod
25 ow dríue ⁊ ower meistre hit reade. ne schulen habbe
na beast bute cat ane. Ancre þe haueð ahte. þuncheð
bet husewif ase Marthe wes. ne lihtliche ne mei ha
nawt beo Marie marthe suster wið griðfullnesse
f. 113a of heorte. for þenne mot ha þenchen of þe kues fod
dre. of heordemonne hure. Olhnin þe heiward. wearien (M. 418)
hwen he punt hire. ⁊ ȝelden þah þe hearmes. ladlich
þing is hit wat crist hwen me makeð i tune man of
5 ancre ahte. Nu þenne ȝef eani mot nedlunge habben
hit:ʹ loki ꝥ hit namon ne eili ne ne hearmí. ne ꝥ hire
þoht ne beo nawiht þron ifestnet. ancre ne ah to hab
ben na þing ꝥ utward drahe hire heorte. Na chaffere
ne driue ȝe. Ancre ꝥ is chepilt. ꝥ is. buð forte sullen efter
10 biȝete:ʹ ha chepeð hire sawle þe chapmon of helle. þing
þah ꝥ ha wurcheð ha mei þurh hire meistres read:ʹ for hi
re neode sullen. Hali men sumhwile liueden bi hare hon
Nawt deore dehtren ne wite ȝe in ower hus:ʹ of ¶ den.
oðer monne þinges. ne ahte ne claðes. ne boistes. ne char

18 *blue initial* E *between* 17 *and* 20; *red line-patterns within, and a few lines in margin.* 19 no⟨m⟩e: m *interlined above* n̤ *crossed out.* 22 *before* neode *an omission* (*?* muche). 24 *small red initial* Ȝ *touched with blue.*

f. 113a. *From* f. 113a, 8 Na *to* f. 115a, 20 Ancre *each item begins with a small coloured initial, alternating red/blue and touched with lines of the opposite colour: on this page* 8 Na; 13 Nawt, *and*

tres. Scoren ne cyrograffes. ne þe chirch uestemenz. ne þe 15
calices. bute neode oðer strengðe hit makie.' oðer muchel
eie.
Of swuch witunge is muchel vuel ilumpen ofte siðen. IN
wið ower wanes ne leote ȝe namon slepen. Ȝef muchel
neod mid alle makeð breoken ower hus. hwil hit eauer 20
is ibroken.' habbeð þrinne wið ow a wummon of cleane
lif deies ⁊ nihtes. FOR þi ꝥ wepmen ne seoð ow neȝe
ham.' wel mei don of ower clað beo hit hwit beo hit blac bu
te hit beo unorne. warm ⁊ wel iwraht. felles wel itawet. ⁊
habbeð ase monie as ow to neodeð to bedde ⁊ to rugge. 25
Nest flesch ne schal nan werien linnene clað bute hit
beo of hearde ⁊ of greate heorden. Stamín habbe hwa se wu
le.' hwa se wule beo buten. Ȝe schulen in an hetter ant
igurd liggen. swa leoðeliche þah ꝥ ȝe mahen honden put f. 113b
ten þer under. Nest lich nan ne gurde hire wið na cunne
gurdles.' bute þurh schriftes leaue. ne beore nan irn ne hére.
ne ilespiles felles. ne ne beate hire þer wið.' ne wið scurge i
(M. 420) leadet. wið holín ne wið breres. ne biblodgi hire seolf.' wið 5
ute schriftes leaue. nohwer ne binetli hire. ne ne beate bi
uoren. ne na keoruunge ne keorue. ne ne neome ed eanes
to luðere disceplines. temptatiuns forte acwenchen. ne for na
bote aȝein cundeliche secnesses. nan uncundelich lechecreft
ne leue ȝe ne ne fondín. wið uten ower meistres read.' les 10
te ow stonde wurse. Ower schon i winter beon meoke.
greate ⁊ warme. I sumer ȝe habbeð leaue bearuot gan ⁊
sitten ⁊ lihte scheos werien. Hosen wið ute vampez.'
ligge ín hwa se likeð. Ischeoed ne slepe ȝe nawt. ne noh
wer bute i bedde. Sum wummon inohreaðe wereð þe brech 15
of hére ful wel icnottet. þe streapeles dun to þe vet ilacet
ful feaste. ah eauer is best þe swete ⁊ te swote heorte. Me is

paragraph before den. (*included in alternation*); 17 IN; 18 Ȝef: 21 FOR; 25 Nest; 27 Ȝe. 23 felles: fe *thick; an erasure above* e, *extending to* w *of* hwit *in line above. The bottom right-hand corner is torn off; old stitching-hole at edge. Of the directing letters only* N, N *in left margin* 13, 25 *are now to be seen.*

f. 113b. *The small coloured initials on this page are:* 10 Ower; 12 Hosen; 18 Ȝef (*the top cuts bottom of* leo *in* 17 *above; a letter-space is left before* ef).

leouere ꝥ ȝe þolien wel an heard word.' þen an heard hére.
Ȝ ef ȝe muhen beo wímpelles ⁊ ȝe wel wullen.' beoð bi
warme cappen. ⁊ þer uppon.' hwite oðer blake veiles. Ancren
20 summe sungið in hare wímplunge.' na leasse þen leafdis.
Ah þah seið sum ꝥ hit límpeð to euch wummon cunde
liche forte werien wímpel. Nai. wímpel ne heaued clað
nowðer ne nempneð hali writ.' ah wriheles ane. Ad corín
thios. Mulier uelet caput suum. wummon seið þe apostle.
25 schal wreon hire heaued. wrihen he seið nawt wimplin.
wrihen ha schal hire scheome. as eue sunfule dohter.
i mungunge of þe sunne ꝥ schende us on earst alle. ant
nawt drahe þe wriheles to tiffunge ⁊ to prude. Eft wule
f. 114a þe apostle ꝥ wummon wreo i chirche hire neb ȝetten.
leste uuel þoht arise þurh hire onsihðe. Et hoc est propter
angelos. Hwi þenne þu chirch ancre iwímplet openest
þi neb to wepmonnes ehe.' toȝeines þe sist men.' spekeð
5 þe apostle. ȝef þu þe ne hudest. ah ȝef ꝥ ei þing wriheð
þi neb from monnes ehe. beo hit wah beo hit clað. i wel i
tund windowe. wel mei duhen ancre of oðer wimplunge.
Toȝeines þe þe þus ne dest.' spekeð þe apostle nawt toȝeín
es oþre. ꝥ hare ahne wah wriheð wið euch monnes sihðe.
10 þer awakenið ofte wake þohtes of. ⁊ werkes oðerhwiles.
Hwa se wule beon isehen.' þah ha atiffi hire nis nawt mu
che wunder. ah to godes ehnen ha is lufsumre.' þe is for
þe luue of him.' untiffet wið uten. Ríng ne broche
ne habbe ȝe. ne gurdel ímembret. ne glouen ne nan swuch
15 þíng ꝥ ow ne deh to habben. A meoke surpliz ȝe mahen
in hat sumer werien. Eauer me is leouere se ȝe doð gre
attre werkes. Ne makie ȝe nane purses forte freondín
ow wið. bute to þeo ꝥ ower meistre ȝeueð ow his leaue.
ne huue ne blodbinde of seole. ne laz buten leaue. Ah
20 schapieð ⁊ seowið. ⁊ mendið chirche claðes. ⁊ poure monne
hettren. na swuch þing ne schule ȝe ȝeouen wið uten

19 Ancren *to end of* f. 114a. 10, *not in* M. 24 *in left margin mark* ×; thios *underlined.* 25 schal wreon hire hea(ued *underlined.* 26 eue sunfule, *sic* (*reversed*).

f. 114a. 4 þe sist, *sic, for* þe þe sist. 11 isehen: he *awkwardly produced on erasure.* 13, 16, 17 *small coloured initials* R, E, N (*blue, red, blue*) *touched with lines of opposite colour.*

schriftes leaue. namare þen neomen.· þ ȝe ne seggen him
fore.· as of oðre þinges. kun oðer cuððe. hu ofte ȝe under
uengen. hu longe ȝe edheolden. tendre of cun ne límpeð
nawt ancre beonne. A mon wes of religiun. ⁊ com to hím 25
efter help his fleschliche broðer. ⁊ he tahte him to his
þridde breðer. þe wes dead biburiet. þe ondswerede wun
drinde. Nai qð he nis he dead? Ant ich qð þe hali mon
am dead gasteliche. Na fleschlich freond ne easki me flesch f. 114b
lich froure. Amites ⁊ parures. worldliche leafdis mahen inoh
wurchen. Ant ȝef ȝe ham makieð.· ne makie ȝe þrof na
mustreisun. Veíne gloire attreð alle gode þeawes. ⁊ alle go
de werkes. Criblín ne schal nan of ow for luue ne for hure. 5
Taueles ne forbeode ich nawt. ȝef sum ríueð surpliz oðer
measse kemese.· oþre riuunges ne ríue ha nawt nomeliche
oueregede.· bute for muche neode. Helpeð ow wið ower ah
(M. 422) ne swínc se forð se ȝe eauer mahen to schruden ow seoluen
⁊ feden ȝef neod is. ⁊ þeo þe ow seruið. AS sein Ierome 10
leareð. ne beo ȝe neauer longe ne lihtliche of sum þing al
lunges idel. for anan rihtes þe feond beot hire his werc.· þe
i godes werc ne swinkeð. ⁊ tuteleð anan toward híre. for
hwil he sið hire bisi.· he þencheð þus. for nawt ich schulde
nu cume neh hire.· ne mei ha nawt iȝemen to lustní mí 15
lare. Of idelnesse awakeneð muchel flesches fondunge. Iní
quítas Sodome.· saturitas panis ⁊ ocium. þ is. Sodomes
cwedschipe com of idelnesse ⁊ of ful wombe. Irn þ lið stille
gedereð sone rust. weater þe ne stureð nawt.· readliche stín
Ancre ne schal nawt forwurðe scolmeistre. ne ¶ .keð. 20

22 namare *to verso* 8 neode, *not in* M. 26 to his*; owing to a defect in surface* i *written a letter-space from* h *to which it is joined by enlarged head bent back; two spaces are left at line end.* 28 he nis: bednis *emended by alteration of* b, *and erasure of* d. *Long slit in lower margin, curving in, from ruled margin right, up towards centre of bottom line; holes at edges for lost stiches.*

f. 114b. *Surface defect causing ink-spread affects the writing towards ends of* 1 *to* 4, *esp.* ask *of* easki, fd *of* leafdis. 8 *small red initial* H *touched with blue.* 9 schruden: schrrden *with second* r *altered to* u *by adding a minim.* 10 *small blue initial* A *touched with red; directing* a *in right margin.* 20 *red initial* A *with tail in margin to* 23*; a few blue lines, one flourished below* 28*; before* .keð. *a red paragraph touched with blue.*

turnen ancre hus to childrene scole. hire meiden mei lea
ren sum oðer meiden. ꝥ were pliht of to leornín among
wepmen. oðer bimong gromes. ah ancre ne ah to ȝemen
bute godd ane. þah bi hire meistres read ha mei sum
25 rihten ⁊ helpen to learen. Ȝe ne schulen senden leat
tres. ne underuon leattres. ne writen bute leaue. Ȝe
schulen beon idoddet. oðer ȝef ȝe wulleð ischauen fowr
siðen i þe ȝer. to lihtin ower heaued. beo bi þe hér ieueset.'
f. 115a hwa se swa is leouere. ant as ofte ileten blod ⁊ ȝef neod is
oftre. Þe mei beon þer buten.' ich hit mei wel þolien.
Hwen ȝe
beoð al greiðe ilete blod.' ȝe ne schule don na þing þe
þreo dahes ꝥ ow greueð. ah talkið to ower meidnes. ⁊
5 wið þeawfule talen schurteð ow to gederes. ȝe mahen
swa don ofte hwen ow þuncheð heuíe.' oðer beoð for sum
worltlich þíng sare oðer seke. þah euch worltlich froure
is unwurðe to ancre. Swa wisliche witeð ow in ower
blodletunge.' ⁊ haldeð ow i swuch reste.' ꝥ ȝe longe þrefter
10 mahen i godes seruise þe monluker swinken. ant alswa
hwen ȝe feleð eani secnesse. Muchel sotschipe hit is leos (M. 424)
en for an dei.' téne oðer tweolue. Wesscheð ow hwer se
neod is as ofte as ȝe wulleð. ⁊ ower oþre þinges. Nes nea
uer fulðe godd leof. þah pouerte ⁊ unorneschipe beon hím
15 licwurðe. VNderstondeð eauer of alle þeose þinges. ꝥ
nan nis heast ne forbod ꝥ beoð of þe uttre riwle. þet is
lute strengðe of. for hwon ꝥ te ínre beo wel iwist as ich sei
de i þe frumðe. þeos mei beon ichanget hwer se eaní neod
oðer eaní skile hit easkeð. efter ꝥ ha best mei þe leafdi
riw

25 *small blue initial* Ȝ *touched with red.* 26 *the same with reversed colour; directing* ȝ *in right margin. Slit (see recto) in bottom margin. from left ruled margin to centre.*

f. 115a. *Tear, with stitching-holes, from top edge towards* 1 leoue(re. 3 al greiðe *crossed out with weak stroke in pale ink* (cf. f. 4b. 28). 4 *in* second e *of* meidnes *a worm-hole that continues to* f. 117*; another in right margin beyond end of* 5. 8, 12, 15, 21 *small coloured initials* S, W (þ), V, A, *alternating red/blue, touched with opposite colour: the* þ *is clearly distinguished from* V *by sloping to right, with narrower angle and lower apex. Three small holes in bottom right-hand corner.* 13 ⁊ ower *to* 21 towundre *not in* M.

le seruín as hire eadmode þuften. ah sikerliche wið uten
hire þe leafdi feareð towundre. Ancre þe naueð nawt
neh honde hire fode.' beoð bisie twa wummen. An eauer
þe leaue ed háme.' an oþer þe wende ut. hwenne driueð
neod. ⁊ þeo beo ful unorne wið uten euch tiffunge. oðer
a lutel þuftene.' oðer of feier ealde. Bi þe wei as ha geað.' 25
ga singinde hire beoden. ne ne halde na tale wið mon ne
wið wummon. ne sitte ne ne stonde. bute ꝥ leaste þet ha
eauer mei ear þen ha ham cume. Nohwider elles ne ga
heo bute þider as me send híre. wið ute leaue. ne ne eote f. 115b
ha ne ne drínke ute. þe oþer beo eauer ínne. ne wið uteþe
ȝeten.' ne ga wið ute leaue. Ba beon obedient to hare da
me in alle þíng.' bute i sunne ane. na þíng nabben þet
heo hit nute. ne underuo na þing. ne ne ȝeoue nowðer.' 5
wið uten hire leaue. Na mon ne leote ȝe ín. ne þe ȝungre
ne speoke wið namon bute leaue. ne ga ha nawt ut of
tune.' wið uten siker fere. ȝef hit swa mei beon.' ne ne
ligge ute. ȝef heo ne con o boke.' segge bi pater nostres. ant bí
auez hire ures. ⁊ wurche ꝥ me hat hire wið ute gruchun 10
ge. habbe eauer hire earen opene toward hire dame.
Nowðer of þe wummen ne beore from hare dame. ne
ne bringe to híre nane idele talen.' ne neowe tidinges.
ne bitweonen ham seolf.' ne singen ne ne speoken na
ne worldliche spechen. ne lahhen swa ne pleien.' þet ei 15
mon ꝥ hit sehe.' mahte hit to uuel turnen. Ouer alle
þinges. leasunges ⁊ luðere wordes heatien. hare her beo i
coruen. hare heaued clað sitte laḥhe. eiðer ligge ane.
hare cop beo hehe isticchet. ⁊ bute broche. namon ne
seo ham unleppet ne open heaued. lah locunge habben. 20
heo ne schulen cussen na mon. ne cuðmon ne cunnes
mon. ne for na cuððe cluppen. ne weschen hare heaued.
ne lokin feaste o na mon.' ne toggín wið ne pleien. Hare
(M. 426) weden beon of swuch schape. ⁊ al hare aturn swuch.' þet
hit beo edscene hwerto ha beoð iturnde. Hare lates lokín 25
warliche. ꝥ nan ne mahe edwiten ham.' ín hus ne ut of
hus. On alle wise forbeoren to wreaðen hare dame. ⁊ as

f. 115b. 4 *worm-hole in* n *of* in. 6 leote ȝe, *sic, for* leoten
ha.

ofte as heo hit doð:˒ ear ha drínken oþer eoten:˒ makien
f. 116a hare veníe. o cneon dun biuoren hire. ⁊ seggen. mea
culpa. ⁊ underuon þe penitence ꝥ ha leið up on hire
lutinde hire lahe. Þe ancre þrefter neauer mare ꝥ ilke
gult ne upbreide for na wreaððe. bute ȝef ha eft sone
5 falle i ꝥ ilke. ah do hit allunge ut of hire heorte. ȝef ei
strif ariseð bitweone þe wummen:˒ þe ancre makie eiðer
to makien oþer venie o cneon to þer eorðe. ⁊ eiðer rihte
up oþer:˒ ⁊ cussen on ende. ant te ancre legge on eiðer:˒
sum penitence. mare up o þe ilke þe greatluker gulte.
10 þis is a þing witen ha wel ꝥ is gode leouest:˒ Sahtnesse ⁊
some. ⁊ te feond laðest. for þi he is eauer umben to area
ren sum leaððe. Nu sið þe sweoke wel. ꝥ hwen fur is wel
o brune:˒ ⁊ me wule ꝥ hit aga:˒ me sundreð þe brondes. ⁊
he deð hond ꝥ ilke. luue is iesu cristes fur. ꝥ he wule ꝥ blea
15 sie aa i þín heorte. ant te deouel blaweð forte puffen hit
ut. Hwen his blawunge ne geíneð nawt:˒ he bringeð up
sum uuel word. oðer sum oþer nohtunge. hwer þurh
ha to hurten eiðer frommard oþer. ⁊ te hali gastes fur:˒
cwencheð hwen þebrondes þurh wreaððe beoð isundret.
20 for þi halden ham i luue feaste to gederes. Ant ne beo ham
nawt of hwen þe feond blawe. nomeliche ȝef moníe beon
iueiet somet:˒ ⁊ wel wið luue ontende. Þah þe ancre on hi
re meidnes for openliche gultes legge penitence:˒ to þe
preost noðeleater schriuen ham hwen neod is. ah eauer
25 þah wið leaue. Ȝef ha ne cunnen nawt þe mete graces:˒
seggen in hare stude:˒ pater noster biuoren:˒ ⁊ Aue Maria.
⁊ efter

mete alswa. ant a Credo mare. ⁊ segge þus on ende. Feader.
Sune. hali gast al mihti godd. ȝeoue ure dame his grace. (M. 428)
f. 116b se lengre se mare. ⁊ leue hire ⁊ us ba neomen god ende. for
ȝelde alle þe us god doð. ⁊ milcí hare sawle þe us god idon
habbeð. hare sawle. ⁊ alle cristene sawles. Bitweone

f. 116a. 14 hond, *sic, probably for* on hond (*cf.* f. 88b. 14). 25 *small red initial* Ȝ *touched with blue, directing* ȝ *in left margin.*

f. 116b. 1 *to* 6*: a dirty patch runs through the left part of these lines, particularly affecting* 3 hare, 4 gruchesi, 5 bute, *probably due to alteration producing* gruchesi. 3 *small blue initial* B *touched with red; directing* b *in right margin.*

mel ne gru[cħ]esi ȝe nawt. nowðer frut ne oðerhwet.' ne
drinken bute leaue ⁊ te leaue beo liht in al ꝥ nis sunne 5
Ed te mete na word. oðer lut.' ⁊ teo stille. Alswa efter þe an
cre complie. aþet prime. ne don na þing ne seggen.' hwer
þurh hire silence mahe beon isturbet. Nan ancre ser
uant ne ahte bi riht to easkin iset hure. bute mete ⁊ hure
ꝥ ha mei flutte bi.' ant godes milce. Ne mis leue nan godd.' 10
hwet se tide of þe ancre. ꝥ he hire trukie. þe meidnes wið u
ten ȝef ha seruið þe ancre alswa as ha ahen.' hare hure
schal beon þe hehe blisse of heouene. Hwa se haueð ehe of
hope toward se heh hure.' gleadliche wule ha seruin ⁊ liht
liche alle wa ⁊ alle teone þolien. wið eise ⁊ wið este ne buð 15
Ȝe ancreș ahen þis leaste stucche . me nawt blisse.
reden to ower wummen euche wike eanes. aþet ha
hit cunnen. Ant muche neod is ꝥ ȝe neomen to ham mu
che ȝeme. for ȝe mahen muchel beon þurh ham igodet. ⁊
iwurset. On oðer half ⟨ȝef⟩ þet ha sungið þurh ower ȝe 20
meles.' ȝe schule beo bicleopet þrof biuore þe hehe deme. ⁊
for þi as ow is muche neod. ⁊ ham ȝet mare.' ȝeornliche
leareð ham to halden hare riwle. ba for ow ⁊ for ham seolf.'
liðeliche ⁊ luueliche. for swuch ah wummone lare to beonne.
luuelich ⁊ liðe. ⁊ selthwenne sturne. Ba is riht ꝥ ha ow dred 25
en ⁊ luuien. ant þah ꝥ ter beo eauer mare of luue.' þen of
drede. þenne schal hit wel fearen. Me schal healden eoli ⁊
wín
ba i wunden efter godes lare. ah mare of softe eoli.' þen of
bitinde wín. ꝥ is. Mare of liðe wordes.' þen of suhinde. for þer f. 117a
(M. 430) of kímeð þinge best.' ꝥ is luue eie. Lihtliche ⁊ sweteliche for
ȝeoueð ham hare gultes. hwen ha ham icnaweð ⁊ bihateð

4 gru[cħ]esi: cħ *cramped on an erasure, written with black ink and scratchy pen (which also touched up top of second stroke of* u); *MS. may have had* grulefi *for* grufeli ; ȝe *is, as context shows, an error for* ha *or* heo. 8 *small red initial* N *touched with blue; directing* n *in right margin.* 9 *second* hure*: erroneous repetition replacing* hetter *or* clað. 16 *large blue initial* Ȝ *between* 15 *and* 18*; ornamented with red lines, and elaborated tail in margin, from* 13 *to* 27*; no paragraph before* .me nawt blisse. *which is written slightly higher than first part of the line.* 20 ȝef *interlined above* þurh *crossed out.*

bote. Ase forð as ȝe mahen of mete ⁊ of claðes. ⁊ of oþre
5 þinges þet neode of flesch easkeð.ʼ beoð large toward ham.ʼ
þah ȝe nearowe beon ⁊ hearde to ow seoluen. Swa deð þe wel
blaweð.ʼ went te nearewe of þe horn to his ahne muð.ʼ ant
utward ꝥ wide. Ant ȝe don alswa as ȝe wulleð ꝥ ower beod
en bemín wel ⁊ dremen.ʼ i drihtines earen. nawt ane to ower
10 ahnes.ʼ ah to alle folkes heale. as ure lauerd leue þurh þe grace
of him seolf ꝥ hit swa mote amen. Hwen ower sustres
meidnes cumeð to ow to froure.ʼ cumeð to ham to þe þurl.ʼ
earunder ⁊ ouerunder. eanes oðer twien. ⁊ gað aȝein sone.ʼ
to ower note gastelich. ne biuore Complie ne sitte ȝe nawt
15 for ham ouer riht tíme. swa ꝥ hare cume beo na lure of ow
er religiun.ʼ ah gastelich biȝete. ȝef þer is eani word iseid
ꝥ mahte hurten heorte.ʼ ne beo hit nawt iboren ut.ʼ ne ibroht
to oþer ancre.ʼ ꝥ is eð hurte. To him hit schal beon iseid.ʼ þe
lokeð ham alle. Twa niht is ínoh ꝥ ei beo edhalden. ant ꝥ
20 beo ful seldene. ne for heom ne breoke silence ed te mete.ʼ ne
for blodletunge. bute ȝef sum muche god oðer neod hit
makie. Þe ancre ne hire meiden ne plohien worldliche go
menes ed te þurle. ne ne ticki to gederes. for ase seið seint
Beornard. Vnwurðe þíng is to euch gastelich mon. ⁊ nome
25 liche to ancre.ʼ euch swuch fleschlich froure. ⁊ hit bínímeð
gastelich ꝥ is wiðute met utnume murhðe. ⁊ ꝥ is uuel chan

Of þis boc redeð hwen ȝe ¶ .ge as is iseid þruppe.
beoð eise euche dei.ʼ leasse oðer mare. Ich hopie ꝥ hit
f. 117b schal beon ow ȝef ȝe hit redeð ofte.ʼ swiðe biheue.ʼ þurh go
des muchele grace. elles ich hefde uuele bitohe mi muchele
hwile. Me were leouere godd hit wite do me toward rome.ʼ
þen forte biginnen hit eft forte donne. ȝef ȝe findeð ꝥ
5 ȝe doð alswa as ȝe redeð.ʼ þonckið godd ȝeorne. ȝef ȝe
ne doð nawt.ʼ biddeð godes are. ⁊ beoð umben þeronuuen
ꝥ ȝe hit bet halden efter ower mihte.

f. 117a. 4 *small red initial* A *touched with blue.* 11 *small blue initial* H *touched with red;* Hwen *to* 27 þruppe *not in* M. 22 *after* plohien: nane *interlined with caret.* 27 *red initial* O *with a few blue lines within, and in margin from* 23 *to low in bottom margin; before* .ge as is iseid þruppe. *a blue paragraph without red. Worm-holes in* n *of* na 15, n *of* eani 16; *leaf pierced below* ib *of* ibroht 17 (*see verso*).

f. 117b. 1, 2 go|des: d *altered from g without erasure of tail.*

Feader. Sune. Hali gast. An almihti godd wite ow in his warde. he gleadie ow ⁊ frouri ow mine leoue sustren. ant for al ꝥ ȝe for him drełeð ⁊ dreaieð. ne ȝeoue ow neauer 10 leasse.' þen al to gedere hím seoluen. Beo he aa iheiet from world in to worlde aa on ecnesse. AMeN. ASe ofte as ȝe habbeð ired eawiht her on.' greteð þe leafdi wið an aue.' for him ꝥ swonc her abuten. Inoh meaðful ich am þe bidde se lutel. ℭ Explicit. Iþench o þi writere i þine 15 beoden sumchearre.' ne beo hit ne se lutel. hit turneð þe to gode.' ꝥ tu bidest for oþre.

8 *blue initial* F *with tapered tail in margin from* 7 *to* 12; *a few red lines within, and in margin from* 5 *to* 14. 12 *small red initial* A *touched with blue.* 15 *before* Explicit. *a red paragraph touched with blue;* Iþench *has small blue* I *without ornament. Worm-holes in text at* 5 doð, 15 lutel, 16 chearre. *The last (blank) leaf was pierced in three places; the two upper points affect the text: abrasion under* 9; *abrasion and small hole under* od *of* 17 gode.

In the footnotes a few references are given to other versions printed by the E.E.T.S. G *refers to the Gonville and Caius MS.;* T *to MS. Titus;* L *to the Latin version; and* F *to the French version of MS. Vitellius. But to avoid confusion* M *has been used throughout in references to MS. Nero, as in the side-notes.*

PRINTED IN GREAT BRITAIN
AT THE UNIVERSITY PRESS, OXFORD
BY VIVIAN RIDLER
PRINTER TO THE UNIVERSITY

Early English Text Society

OFFICERS AND COUNCIL

THE Subscription to the Society, which constitutes full membership, is £2. 2*s*. a year for the annual publications, from 1921 onwards, due in advance on the 1st of JANUARY, and should be paid by Cheque, Postal Order, or Money Order crossed 'National Provincial Bank Limited', to the Hon. Secretary, R. W. Burchfield, 40 Walton Crescent, Oxford. Individual members of the Society are allowed, after consultation with the Secretary, to select other volumes of the Society's publications instead of those for the current year. The Society's Texts can also be purchased separately from the Publisher, Oxford University Press, through a bookseller, at the prices put after them in the List, or through the Secretary, by members only, for their own use, at a discount of 2*d*. in the shilling.

The Early English Text Society was founded in 1864 by Frederick James Furnivall, with the help of Richard Morris, Walter Skeat, and others, to bring the mass of unprinted Early English literature within the reach of students and provide sound texts from which the New English Dictionary could quote. In 1867 an Extra Series was started of texts already printed but not in satisfactory or readily obtainable editions. At a cost of nearly £35,000, 159 volumes were issued in the Original Series and 126 in the Extra Series before 1921. In that year the title *Extra Series* was dropped, and all the publications of 1921 and subsequent years have since been listed and numbered as part of the Original Series. Since 1921 some ninety volumes have been issued. In this prospectus the Original Series and Extra Series for the years 1867–1920 are amalgamated, so as to show all the publications of the Society in a single list. In 1955 the prices of all volumes issued for the years up to 1936 and still available, were increased by one-fifth.

LIST OF PUBLICATIONS

Original Series, 1864–1962. Extra Series, 1867–1920

(*One guinea per annum for each series separately up to* 1920, *two guineas from* 1921)

O.S. 1. **Early English Alliterative Poems,** ed. R. Morris. 20*s*. 1864
2. **Arthur,** ed. F. J. Furnivall. (*Out of print.*) „
3. **Lauder on the Dewtie of Kyngis, &c.,** 1556, ed. F. Hall. (*Out of print.*) „
4. **Sir Gawayne and the Green Knight,** ed. R. Morris. (*Out of print, see* O.S. 210.) „
5. **Hume's Orthographie and Congruitie of the Britan Tongue,** ed. H. B. Wheatley. 5*s*. 1865
6. **Lancelot of the Laik,** ed. W. W. Skeat. (*Out of print.*) „
7. **Genesis & Exodus,** ed. R. Morris. (*Out of print.*) „
8. **Morte Arthure,** ed. E. Brock. (*Reprinted* 1961.) 25*s*. „
9. **Thynne on Speght's ed. of Chaucer,** A.D. 1599, ed. G. Kingsley and F. J. Furnivall. (*Out of print.*) „
10. **Merlin,** Part I, ed. H. B. Wheatley. (*Out of print.*) „
11. **Lyndesay's Monarche, &c.,** ed. J. Small. Part I. (*Out of print.*) „
12. **The Wright's Chaste Wife,** ed. F. J. Furnivall. (*Out of print.*) „
13. **Seinte Marherete,** ed. O. Cockayne. (*Out of print, see* O.S. 193.) 1866
14. **Kyng Horn, Floris and Blancheflour, &c.,** ed. J. R. Lumby, re-ed. G. H. McKnight. (*Out of print.*) „
15. **Political, Religious, and Love Poems,** ed. F. J. Furnivall. (*Out of print.*) „
16. **The Book of Quinte Essence,** ed. F. J. Furnivall. (*Out of print.*) „
17. **Parallel Extracts from 45 MSS. of Piers the Plowman,** ed. W. W. Skeat. (*Out of print.*) „
18. **Hali Meidenhad,** ed. O. Cockayne, re-ed. F. J. Furnivall. (*Out of print.*) „
19. **Lyndesay's Monarche, &c.,** ed. J. Small. Part II. (*Out of print.*) „
20. **Richard Rolle de Hampole, English Prose Treatises of,** ed. G. G. Perry. (*Reprinted* 1920.) 7*s*. „
21. **Merlin,** ed. H. B. Wheatley. Part II. (*Out of print.*) „
22. **Partenay** or **Lusignen,** ed. W. W. Skeat. 7*s*. 6*d*. „
23. **Dan Michel's Ayenbite of Inwyt,** ed. R. Morris. (*Out of print.*) „
24. **Hymns to the Virgin and Christ; The Parliament of Devils, &c.,** ed. F. J. Furnivall. (*Out of print.*) 1867
25. **The Stacions of Rome, the Pilgrims' Sea-voyage, with Clene Maydenhod,** ed. F. J. Furnivall. (*Out of print.*) „
26. **Religious Pieces in Prose and Verse,** from R. Thornton's MS., ed. G. G. Perry. 6*s*. (*See under* 1913.) „
27. **Levins' Manipulus Vocabulorum, a rhyming Dictionary,** ed. H. B. Wheatley. 14*s*. „
28. **William's Vision of Piers the Plowman,** ed. W. W. Skeat. A–Text. (*Reprinted* 1956.) 20*s*. „
29. **Old English Homilies** (1220–30), ed. R. Morris. Series I, Part I. (*Out of print.*) „
30. **Pierce the Ploughmans Crede,** ed. W. W. Skeat. (*Out of print.*) „

E.S. 1. **William of Palerne** or **William and the Werwolf,** re-ed. W. W. Skeat. (*Out of print.*) „
2. **Early English Pronunciation,** by A. J. Ellis. Part I. (*Out of print.*) „

O.S. 31. **Myrc's Duties of a Parish Priest,** in Verse, ed. E. Peacock. (*Out of print.*) 1868
32. **Early English Meals and Manners: the Boke of Norture of John Russell, the Bokes of Keruynge, Curtasye, and Demeanor, the Babees Book, Urbanitatis, &c.,** ed. F. J. Furnivall. (*Out of print.*) „
33. **The Book of the Knight of La Tour-Landry,** ed. T. Wright. (*Out of print.*) „
34. **Old English Homilies** (before 1300), ed. R. Morris. Series I, Part II. (*Out of print.*) „
35. **Lyndesay's Works,** Part III: The Historie and Testament of Squyer Meldrum, ed. F. Hall. 2s. 6*d*. „

E.S. 3. **Caxton's Book of Curtesye,** in Three Versions, ed. F. J. Furnivall. (*Out of print.*) „
4. **Havelok the Dane,** re-ed. W. W. Skeat. (*Out of print.*) „

E.S. 5. **Chaucer's Boethius,** ed. R. Morris. 14*s*. 1868

6. **Chevelere Assigne,** re-ed. Lord Aldenham. 3*s*. 6*d*. „

O.S. 36. **Merlin,** ed. H. B. Wheatley. Part III. On Arthurian Localities, by J. S. Stuart Glennie. 14*s*. 1869

37. **Sir David Lyndesay's Works,** Part IV, Ane Satyre of the thrie Estaits, ed. F. Hall. (*Out of print.*) „

38. **William's Vision of Piers the Plowman,** ed. W. W Skeat. Part II. Text B. (*Reprinted* 1951.) 18*s*. 6*d*. „

39. **The Gest Hystoriale of the Destruction of Troy,** ed. D. Donaldson and G. A. Panton. Part I. (*Out of print.*) „

E.S. 7. **Early English Pronunciation,** by A. J. Ellis. Part II. 12*s*. „

8. **Queene Elizabethes Achademy, &c.,** ed. F. J. Furnivall. Essays on early Italian and German Books of Courtesy, by W. M. Rossetti and E. Oswald. (*Out of print.*) „

9. **Awdeley's Fraternitye of Vacabondes, Harman's Caveat, &c.,** ed. E. Viles and F. J. Furnivall. 9*s*. „

O.S. 40. **English Gilds,** their Statutes and Customs, A.D. 1389, ed. Toulmin Smith and Lucy T. Smith, with an Essay on Gilds and Trades-Unions, by L. Brentano. (*Out of print.*) 1870

41. **William Lauder's Minor Poems,** ed. F. J. Furnivall. (*Out of print.*) „

42. **Bernardus De Cura Rei Famuliaris,** Early Scottish Prophecies, &c., ed. J. R. Lumby. (*Out of print.*) „

43. **Ratis Raving,** and other Moral and Religious Pieces, ed. J. R. Lumby. (*Out of print.*) „

E.S. 10. **Andrew Boorde's Introduction of Knowledge, 1547, Dyetary of Helth, 1542, Barnes in Defence of the Berde, 1542–3,** ed. F. J. Furnivall. (*Out of print.*) „

11. **Barbour's Bruce,** ed. W. W. Skeat. Part I. 14*s*. „

O.S. 44. **The Alliterative Romance of Joseph of Arimathie, or The Holy Grail: from the Vernon MS.;** with W. de Worde's and Pynson's Lives of Joseph: ed. W. W. Skeat. (*Out of print.*) 1871

45. **King Alfred's West-Saxon Version of Gregory's Pastoral Care,** ed., with an English translation, by Henry Sweet. Part I. (*Reprinted* 1958.) 30*s*. „

46. **Legends of the Holy Rood, Symbols of the Passion and Cross Poems,** ed. R. Morris. (*Out of print.*) „

47. **Sir David Lyndesay's Works,** ed. J. A. H. Murray. Part V. (*Out oj print.*) „

48. **The Times' Whistle,** and other Poems, by R. C., 1616; ed. J. M. Cowper. 7*s*. 6*d*.

E.S. 12. **England in Henry VIII's Time:** a Dialogue between Cardinal Pole and Lupset, by Thom. Starkey Chaplain to Henry VIII, ed. J. M. Cowper. Part II. (*Out of print*, Part I is E.S. 32, 1878.) „

13. **A Supplicacyon of the Beggers,** by Simon Fish, A.D. 1528–9, ed. F. J. Furnivall, with **A Supplication to our Moste Soueraigne Lorde, A Supplication of the Poore Commons, and The Decaye of England by the Great Multitude of Sheep,** ed. J. M. Cowper. (*Out of print.*) „

14. **Early English Pronunciation,** by A. J. Ellis. Part III. (*Out of print.*) „

O.S. 49. **An Old English Miscellany,** containing a Bestiary, Kentish Sermons, Proverbs of Alfred, and Religious Poems of the 13th cent., ed. R. Morris. (*Out of print.*) 1872

50. **King Alfred's West-Saxon Version of Gregory's Pastoral Care,** ed. H. Sweet. Part II. (*Reprinted* 1958.) 30*s*. „

51. **Þe Liflade of St. Juliana,** 2 versions, with translations; ed. O. Cockayne and E. Brock. (*Reprinted* 1957.) 25*s*. „

52. **Palladius on Husbondrie,** englisht, ed. Barton Lodge. Part I. 12*s*. „

E.S. 15. **Robert Crowley's Thirty-One Epigrams, Voyce of the Last Trumpet, Way to Wealth, &c.,** ed. J. M. Cowper. (*Out of print.*) „

16. **Chaucer's Treatise on the Astrolabe,** ed. W. W. Skeat. (*Out of print.*)

17. **The Complaynt of Scotlande,** with 4 Tracts, ed. J. A. H. Murray. Part I. (*Out of print.*) „

O.S. 53. **Old-English Homilies,** Series II, and three Hymns to the Virgin and God, 13th-century, with the music to two of them, in old and modern notation, ed. R. Morris. (*Out of print.*) 1873

54. **The Vision of Piers Plowman,** ed. W. W. Skeat. Part III. Text C. (*Reprinted* 1959.) 35*s*. „

55. **Generydes,** a Romance, ed. W. Aldis Wright. Part I. 3*s*. 6*d*. „

E.S. 18. **The Complaynt of Scotlande,** ed. J. A. H. Murray. Part II. (*Out of print.*) „

19. **The Myroure of oure Ladye,** ed. J. H. Blunt. (*Out of print.*) „

O.S. 56. **The Gest Hystoriale of the Destruction of Troy,** in alliterative verse, ed. D. Donaldson and G. A. Panton. Part II. 12*s*. 6*d*. 1874

57. **Cursor Mundi,** in four Texts, ed. R. Morris. Part I, with 2 photolithographic facsimiles. (*Reprinted* 1961.) 25*s*. „

58. **The Blickling Homilies,** ed. R. Morris. Part I. (*Out of print.*) „

E.S. 20. **Lovelich's History of the Holy Grail,** ed. F. J. Furnivall. Part I. (*Out of print.*) „

21. **Barbour's Bruce,** ed. W. W. Skeat. Part II. (*Out of print.*) „

22. **Henry Brinklow's Complaynt of Roderyck Mors** and **The Lamentacyon of a Christen Agaynst the Cytye of London,** made by Roderigo Mors, ed. J. M. Cowper. (*Out of print.*) „

23. **Early English Pronunciation,** by A. J. Ellis. Part IV. (*Out of print.*) „

O.S. 59. **Cursor Mundi,** in four Texts, ed. R. Morris. Part II. 18*s*. 1875

60. **Meditacyuns on the Soper of our Lorde,** by Robert of Brunne, ed. J. M. Cowper. 3*s*. „

61. **The Romance and Prophecies of Thomas of Erceldoune,** ed. J. A. H. Murray. 12*s*. 6*d*. „

E.S. 24. **Lovelich's History of the Holv Grail,** ed. F. J. Furnivall. Part II. (*Out of print.*) „

25. **Guy of Warwick,** 15th century Version, ed. J. Zupitza. Part I. (*Out of print.*) „

O.S. 62. **Cursor Mundi,** in four Texts, ed. R. Morris. Part III. 18*s*. 1876

63. **The Blickling Homilies,** ed. R. Morris. Part II. (*Out of print.*) „

64. **Francis Thynne's Embleames and Epigrams,** ed. F. J. Furnivall. 8*s*. 6*d*. „

65. **Be Domes Dæge** (Bede's *De Die Judicii*), &c., ed. J. R. Lumby. (*Out of print.*) „

E.S. 26. **Guy of Warwick,** 15th-century Version, ed. J. Zupitza. Part II. (*Out of print.*) „

E.S. 27. **The English Works of John Fisher,** ed. J. E. B. Mayor. Part I. (*Out of print.*) 1876

O.S. 66. **Cursor Mundi,** in four Texts, ed. R. Morris. Part IV, with 2 autotypes. 12*s*. 1877

67. **Notes on Piers Plowman,** by W. W. Skeat. Part I. 25*s*. ,,

E.S. 28. **Lovelich's Holy Grail,** ed. F. J. Furnivall. Part III. (*Out of print.*) ,,

29. **Barbour's Bruce,** ed. W. W. Skeat. Part III. 25*s*. ,,

O.S. 68. **Cursor Mundi,** in 4 Texts, ed. R. Morris. Part V. 30*s*. 1878

69. **Adam Davie's 5 Dreams about Edward II, &c.,** ed. F. J. Furnivall. 6*s*. ,,

70. **Generydes,** a Romance, ed. W. Aldis Wright. Part II. 5*s*. ,,

E.S. 30. **Lovelich's Holy Grail,** ed. F. J. Furnivall. Part IV. (*Out of print.*) ,,

31. **The Alliterative Romance of Alexander and Dindimus,** ed. W. W. Skeat. 7*s*. 6*d*. ,,

32. **Starkey's England in Henry VIII's Time.** Part I. **Starkey's Life and Letters,** ed. S. J. Herrtage. 9*s*. 6*d*. ,,

O.S. 71. **The Lay Folks Mass-Book,** four texts, ed. T. F. Simmons. (*Out of print.*) 1879

72. **Palladius on Husbondrie,** englisht, ed. S. J. Herrtage. Part II. 6*s*. ,,

E.S. 33. **Gesta Romanorum,** ed. S. J. Herrtage. (*Out of print.*) ,,

34. **The Charlemagne Romances: 1. Sir Ferumbras,** from Ashm. MS. 33, ed. S. J. Herrtage. (*Out of print.*) ,,

O.S. 73. **The Blickling Homilies,** ed. R. Morris. Part III. 12*s*. 1880

74. **English Works of Wyclif,** hitherto unprinted, ed. F. D. Matthew. (*Out of print.*) ,,

E.S. 35. **Charlemagne Romances: 2. The Sege off Melayne, Sir Otuell, &c.,** ed. S. J. Herrtage. (*Out of print.*) ,,

36. **Charlemagne Romances: 3. Lyf of Charles the Grete,** ed. S. J. Herrtage. Part I. 19*s*. ,,

O.S. 75. **Catholicon Anglicum,** an English-Latin Wordbook, from Lord Monson's MS., A.D. 1483, ed., with Introduction and Notes, by S. J. Herrtage and Preface by H. B. Wheatley. 24*s*. 1881

76. **Ælfric's Metrical Lives of Saints,** in MS. Cott. Jul. E VII, ed. W. W. Skeat. Part I. 20*s*. ,,

E.S. 37. **Charlemagne Romances: 4. Lyf of Charles the Grete,** ed. S. J. Herrtage. Part II (*Out of print.*) ,,

38. **Charlemagne Romances: 5. The Sowdone of Babylone,** ed. E. Hausknecht. (*Out of print.*) ,,

O.S. 77. **Beowulf,** the unique MS. autotyped and transliterated, ed. J. Zupitza. (*Re-issued as* No. 245. *See under* 1958.) 1882

78. **The Fifty Earliest English Wills,** in the Court of Probate, 1387–1439, ed. F .J. Furnivall. (*Out of print.*) ,,

E.S. 39. **Charlemagne Romances: 6. Rauf Coilyear, Roland, Otuel, &c.,** ed. S. J. Herrtage. 18*s*. ,,

40. **Charlemagne Romances: 7. Huon of Burdeux,** by Lord Berners, ed. S. L. Lee. Part I. (*Out of print.*) ,,

O.S. 79. **King Alfred's Orosius,** from Lord Tollemache's 9th-century MS., ed. H. Sweet. Part I. (*Reprinted* 1959.) 30*s*. 1883

79 *b*. *Extra Volume.* **Facsimile of the Epinal Glossary,** ed. H. Sweet. (*Out of print.*) ,,

E.S. 41. **Charlemagne Romances: 8. Huon of Burdeux,** by Lord Berners, ed. S. L. Lee. **Part II.** (*Out of print.*) ,,

42. **Guy of Warwick:** 2 texts (Auchinleck MS. and Caius MS.), **ed. J. Zupitza.** Part I. (*Out of print.*) ,,

O.S. 80. **The Life of St. Katherine,** B.M. Royal MS. 17 A. xxvii, &c., and its Latin **Original,** ed. E. Einenkel. (*Out of print.*) 1884

81. **Piers Plowman:** Glossary, &c., ed. W. W. Skeat. Part IV, completing the work (*Out of print.*) ,,

E.S. 43. **Charlemagne Romances: 9. Huon of Burdeux,** by Lord Berners, ed. S. L. Lee. Part III. (*Out of print.*) ,,

44. **Charlemagne Romances: 10. The Foure Sonnes of Aymon,** ed. Octavia Richardson. Part I. (*Out of print.*) ,,

O.S. 82. **Ælfric's Metrical Lives of Saints,** MS. Cott. Jul. E VII, ed. W. W. Skeat. Part II. 20*s*. 1885

83. **The Oldest English Texts, Charters, &c.,** ed. H. Sweet. (*Reprinted* 1957.) 42*s*. ,,

E.S. 45. **Charlemagne Romances: 11. The Foure Sonnes of Aymon,** ed. O. Richardson. **Part II.** (*Out of print.*) ,,

46. **Sir Beves of Hamtoun,** ed. E. Kölbing. Part I. (*Out of print.*) ,,

O.S. 84. **Additional Analogs to 'The Wright's Chaste Wife',** O.S. 12, by W. A. Clouston. 1*s*. 1886

85. **The Three Kings of Cologne,** ed. C. Horstmann. 20*s*. 6*d*. ,,

86. **Prose Lives of Women Saints,** ed. C. Horstmann. 14*s*. ,,

E.S. 47. **The Wars of Alexander,** ed. W. W. Skeat. (*Out of print.*) ,,

48. **Sir Beves of Hamtoun,** ed. E. Kölbing. Part II. (*Out of print.*) ,,

O.S. 87. **The Early South-English Legendary,** Laud MS. 108, ed. C. Horstmann. (*Out of print.*) 1887

88. **Hy. Bradshaw's Life of St. Werburghe** (Pynson, 1521), ed. C. Hortsmann. 12*s*. ,,

E.S. 49. **Guy of Warwick,** 2 texts (Auchinleck and Caius MSS.), ed. J. Zupitza. Part II. (*Out of print.*) ,,

50. **Charlemagne Romances: 12. Huon of Burdeux,** by Lord Berners, ed. S. L. Lee. **Part IV.** (*Out of print.*) ,,

51. **Torrent of Portyngale,** ed. E. Adam. (*Out of print.*) ,,

O.S. 89. **Vices and Virtues,** ed. F. Holthausen. Part I. (*Out of print.*) 1888

90. **Anglo-Saxon and Latin Rule of St. Benet,** interlinear Glosses, ed. H Logeman. 20*s*. ,,

91. **Two Fifteenth-Century Cookery-Books,** ed. T. Austin. (*Out of print.*) ,,

E.S. 52. **Bullein's Dialogue against the Feuer Pestilence, 1578,** ed. M. and A. H. Bullen. 12*s*. ,,

53. **Vicary's Anatomie of the Body of Man, 1548,** ed. 1577, ed. F. J. and Percy **Furnivall.** Part I. 18*s*. ,,

54. **The Curial made by maystere Alain Charretier, translated by William Caxton,** 1484, ed. F. J. Furnivall and P. Meyer. 6*s*. ,,

O.S. 92. **Eadwine's Canterbury Psalter,** from the Trin. Cambr. MS., ed. F. Harsley, Part II. 14*s*. 1889

93. **Defensor's Liber Scintillarum,** ed. E. Rhodes. 20*s*. ,,

E.S. 55. **Barbour's Bruce,** ed. W. W. Skeat. Part IV. 6*s*. ,,

56. **Early English Pronunciation,** by A. J. Ellis. Part V, the present English Dialects. (*Out of print.*) 1889

O.S. 94. **Ælfric's Metrical Lives of Saints,** MS. Cott. Jul. E VII, ed. W. W. Skeat. Part III. 30*s*. 1890

95. **The Old-English Version of Bede's Ecclesiastical History,** re-ed. T. Miller. Part I, 1. (*Reprinted* 1959.) 30*s*. ,,

E.S. 57. **Caxton's Eneydos,** ed. W. T. Culley and F. J. Furnivall. (*Reprinting.*) 30*s*. ,,

E.S. 58. **Caxton's Blanchardyn and Eglantine,** c. 1489, ed. L. Kellner. (*Reprinting.*) 42*s*. 1890
O.S. 96. **The Old-English Version of Bede's Ecclesiastical History,** re-ed. T. Miller. Part I, 2. (*Reprinted* 1959.) 30*s*. 1891
97. **The Earliest English Prose Psalter,** ed. K. D. Buelbring. Part I. 18*s*. ,,
E.S. 59. **Guy of Warwick,** 2 texts (Auchinleck and Caius MSS.), ed. J. Zupitza. Part III. (*Out of print.*) ,,
60. **Lydgate's Temple of Glas,** re-ed. J. Schick. 18*s*. ,,
O.S. 98. **Minor Poems of the Vernon MS.,** ed. C. Horstmann. Part I. 24*s*. 1892
99. **Cursor Mundi.** Preface, Notes, and Glossary, Part VI, ed. R. Morris. 12*s*. ,,
E.S. 61. **Hoccleve's Minor Poems, I,** from the Phillipps and Durham MSS., ed. F. J. Furnivall. 18*s*. ,,
62. **The Chester Plays,** re-ed. H. Deimling. Part I. (*Reprinted* 1959.) 25*s*. ,,
O.S. 100. **Capgrave's Life of St. Katharine,** ed. C. Horstmann, with Forewords by F. J. Furnivall. 24*s*. 1893
101. **Cursor Mundi.** Essay on the MSS., their Dialects, &c., by H. Hupe. Part VII. 12*s*. ,,
E.S. 63. **Thomas à Kempis's De Imitatione Christi,** ed. J. K. Ingram. (*Out of print.*) ,,
64. **Caxton's Godeffroy of Boloyne, or The Siege and Conqueste of Jerusalem,** 1481, ed. Mary N. Colvin. 18*s*. ,,
O.S. 102. **Lanfranc's Science of Cirurgie,** ed. R. von Fleischhacker. Part I. 24*s*. 1894
103. **The Legend of the Cross,** &c., ed. A. S. Napier. 15*s*. ,,
E.S. 65. **Sir Beves of Hamtoun,** ed. E. Kölbing. Part III. (*Out of print.*) ,,
66. **Lydgate's and Burgh's Secrees of Philisoffres** ('Governance of Kings and Princes'), ed. R. Steele. (*Out of print.*) ,,
O.S. 104. **The Exeter Book** (Anglo-Saxon Poems), re-ed. I. Gollancz. Part I. (*Reprinted* 1958.) 30*s*. 1895
105. **The Prymer or Lay Folks' Prayer Book,** Camb. Univ. MS., ed. H. Littlehales. Part I. (*Out of print.*) ,,
E.S. 67. **The Three Kings' Sons,** a Romance, ed. F. J. Furnivall. Part I, the Text. (*Out of print.*) ,,
68. **Melusine,** the prose Romance, ed. A. K. Donald. Part I, the Text. (*Out of print.*) ,,
O.S. 106. **R. Misyn's Fire of Love and Mending of Life** (Hampole), ed. R. Harvey. 18*s*. 1896
107. **The English Conquest of Ireland,** A.D. 1166–1185, 2 Texts, ed. F. J. Furnivall. Part I. 18*s*. ,,
E.S. 69. **Lydgate's Assembly of the Gods,** ed. O. L. Triggs. (*Reprinted* 1957.) 25*s*. ,,
70. **The Digby Plays,** ed. F. J. Furnivall. (*Out of print.*) ,,
O.S. 108. **Child-Marriages and -Divorces, Trothplights, &c.** Chester Depositions, 1561–6, ed. F. J. Furnivall. 18*s*. 1897
109. **The Prymer or Lay Folks' Prayer Book,** ed. H. Littlehales. Part II. (*Out of print.*) ,,
E.S. 71. **The Towneley Plays,** ed. G. England and A. W. Pollard. (*Re-issued* 1952.) 30*s*. ,,
72. **Hoccleve's Regement of Princes, and 14 Poems,** ed. F. J. Furnivall. (*Out of print.*) ,,
73. **Hoccleve's Minor Poems, II,** from the Ashburnham MS., ed. I. Gollancz. (*Out of print.*) ,,
O.S. 110. **The Old-English Version of Bede's Ecclesiastical History,** ed. T. Miller. Part II, 1. 18*s*. 1898
111. **The Old-English Version of Bede's Ecclesiastical History,** ed. T. Miller. Part II, 2. (*Reprinting.*) ,,
E.S. 74. **Secreta Secretorum,** 3 prose Englishings, one by Jas. Yonge, 1428, ed. R. Steele. Part I. 24*s*. ,,
75. **Speculum Guidonis de Warwyk,** ed. G. L. Morrill. 12*s*. ,,
O.S. 112. **Merlin.** Part IV. Outlines of the Legend of Merlin, by W. E. Mead. 18*s*. 1899
113. **Queen Elizabeth's Englishings of Boethius, Plutarch, &c.,** ed. C. Pemberton. (*Out of print.*) ,,
E.S. 76. **George Ashby's Poems, &c.,** ed. Mary Bateson. (*Out of print.*) ,,
77. **Lydgate's DeGuilleville's Pilgrimage of the Life of Man,** ed. F. J. Furnivall. Part I. (*Out of print.*)
78. **The Life and Death of Mary Magdalene,** by T. Robinson, *c.* 1620, ed. H. O. Sommer. 6*s*. ,,
O.S. 114. **Ælfric's Metrical Lives of Saints,** ed. W. W. Skeat. Part IV and last. (*Reprinting.*) 1900
115. **Jacob's Well,** ed. A. Brandeis. Part I. 12*s*. ,,
116. **An Old-English Martyrology,** re-ed. G. Herzfeld. 20*s*. ,,
E.S. 79. **Caxton's Dialogues, English and French,** ed. H. Bradley. 12*s*. ,,
80. **Lydgate's Two Nightingale Poems,** ed. O. Glauning. 6*s*. ,,
81. **The English Works of John Gower,** ed. G. C. Macaulay. Part I. (*Reprinted* 1957.) 40*s*. ,,
O.S. 117. **Minor Poems of the Vernon MS.,** ed. F. J. Furnivall. Part II. 18*s*. 1901
118. **The Lay Folks' Catechism,** ed. T. F. Simmons and H. E. Nolloth. 6*s*. ,,
119. **Robert of Brunne's Handlyng Synne,** and its French original, re-ed. F. J. Furnivall. Part I. (*Out of print.*) ,,
E.S. 82. **The English Works of John Gower,** ed. G. C. Macaulay. Part II. (*Reprinted* 1957.) 40*s*. ,,
83. **Lydgate's DeGuilleville's Pilgrimage of the Life of Man,** ed. F. J. Furnivall. Part II. (*Out of print.*) ,,
84. **Lydgate's Reason and Sensuality,** ed. E. Sieper. Part I. (*Out of print.*) ,,
O.S. 120. **The Rule of St. Benet** in Northern Prose and Verse, and Caxton's Summary, ed. E. A. Kock. 18*s*. 1902
121. **The Laud MS. Troy-Book,** ed. J. E. Wülfing. Part I. 18*s*. ,,
E.S. 85. **Alexander Scott's Poems,** 1568, ed. A. K. Donald. (*Out of print.*) ,,
86. **William of Shoreham's Poems,** re-ed. M. Konrath. Part I. (*Out of print.*) ,,
87. **Two Coventry Corpus Christi Plays,** re-ed. H. Craig. 15*s*. (*See under* 1952.) ,,
O.S. 122. **The Laud MS. Troy-Book,** ed. by J. E. Wülfing. Part II. 24*s*. 1903
123. **Robert of Brunne's Handlyng Synne,** and its French original, re-ed. F. J. Furnivall. Part II. (*Out of print.*) ,,
E.S. 88. **Le Morte Arthur,** re-ed. J. D. Bruce. (*Reprinted* 1959.) 30*s*. ,,
89. **Lydgate's Reason and Sensuality,** ed. E. Sieper. Part II. (*Out of print.*) ,,
90. **English Fragments from Latin Medieval Service-Books,** ed. H. Littlehales. (*Out of print.*) ,,
O.S. 124. **Twenty-six Political and other Poems** from Digby MS. 102, &c., ed. J. Kail. Part I. 12*s*. 1904
O.S. 125. **Medieval Records of a London City Church,** ed. H. Littlehales. Part I. 12*s*. 1904
126. **An Alphabet of Tales,** in Northern English, from the Latin, ed. M. M. Banks. Part I. 12*s*. ,,
E.S. 91. **The Macro Plays,** ed. F. J. Furnivall and A. W. Pollard. (*Out of print.*) ,,
92. **Lydgate's DeGuileville's Pilgrimage of the Life of Man,** ed. Katherine B. Locock. Part III. (*Out of print.*) ,,
93. **Lovelich's Romance of Merlin,** from the unique MS., ed. E. A. Kock. Part I. 12*s*.

O.S. 127. **An Alphabet of Tales,** in Northern English, from the Latin, ed. M. M. Banks. Part II. 12*s*. 1905

128. **Medieval Records of a London City Church,** ed. H. Littlehales. Part II. 12*s*. „

129. **The English Register of Godstow Nunnery,** ed. A. Clark. Part I. 12*s*. „

E.S. 94. **Respublica,** a Play on a Social England, ed. L. A. Magnus. (*Out of print. See under* 1946.) „

95. **Lovelich's History of the Holy Grail.** Part V. **The Legend of the Holy Grail,** ed. Dorothy Kempe. (*Out of print.*) „

96. **Mirk's Festial,** ed. T. Erbe. Part I. 14*s*. „

O.S. 130. **The English Register of Godstow Nunnery,** ed. A. Clark. Part II. 18*s*. 1906

131. **The Brut,** or **The Chronicle of England,** ed. F. Brie. Part I. (*Reprinted* 1960.) 25*s*. „

132. **John Metham's Works,** ed. H. Craig. 18*s*. „

E.S. 97. **Lydgate's Troy Book,** ed. H. Bergen. Part I, Books I and II. (*Out of print.*) „

98. **Skelton's Magnyfycence,** ed. R. L. Ramsay. (*Reprinted* 1958.) 30*s*. „

99. **The Romance of Emaré,** re-ed. Edith Rickert. (*Reprinted* 1958.) 15*s*. „

O.S. 133. **The English Register of Oseney Abbey, by Oxford,** ed. A. Clark. Part I. 18*s*. 1907

134. **The Coventry Leet Book,** ed. M. Dormer Harris. Part I. 18*s*. „

E.S. 100. **The Harrowing of Hell,** and **The Gospel of Nicodemus,** re-ed. W. H. Hulme. (*Reprinted* 1961.) 30*s*. „

101. **Songs, Carols, &c.,** from Richard Hill's Balliol MS., ed. R. Dyboski. 18*s*. „

O.S. 135. **The Coventry Leet Book,** ed. M. Dormer Harris. Part II. 18*s*. 1908

135 *b*. *Extra Issue.* Prof. Manly's **Piers Plowman and its Sequence,** urging the fivefold authorship of the *Vision.* (*Out of print.*) „

136. **The Brut,** or **The Chronicle of England,** ed. F. Brie. Part II. 18*s*. „

E.S. 102. **Promptorium Parvulorum,** the 1st English-Latin Dictionary, ed. A. L. Mayhew. 25*s*. 6*d*. „

103. **Lydgate's Troy Book,** ed. H. Bergen. Part II, Book III. (*Out of print.*) „

O.S. 137. **Twelfth-Century Homilies** in MS. Bodley 343, ed. A. O. Belfour. Part I, the Text. (*Reprinting.*) 25*s*. 1909

138. **The Coventry Leet Book,** ed. M. Dormer Harris. Part III. 18*s*. „

E.S. 104. **The Non-Cycle Mystery Plays,** re-ed. O. Waterhouse. (*Out of print.*) „

105. **The Tale of Beryn, with the Pardoner and Tapster,** ed. F. J. Furnivall and W. G. Stone. (*Out of print.*) „

O.S. 139. **John Arderne's Treatises on Fistula in Ano, &c.,** ed. D'Arcy Power. 18*s*. 1910

139 *b*, *c*, *d*, *e*, *f*, *Extra Issue.* **The Piers Plowman Controversy:** *b*. **Dr. Jusserand's 1st Reply to Prof. Manly;** *c*. **Prof. Manly's Answer to Dr. Jusserand;** *d*. **Dr. Jusserand's 2nd Reply to Prof. Manly;** *e*. **Mr. R. W. Chambers's Article;** *f*. **Dr. Henry Bradley's Rejoinder to Mr. R. W. Chambers.** (*Out of print.*) „

140. **Capgrave's Lives of St. Augustine and St. Gilbert of Sempringham,** ed. J. Munro. (*Out of print.*) „

E.S. 106. **Lydgate's Troy Book,** ed. H. Bergen. Part III. (*Out of print.*) „

107. **Lydgate's Minor Poems,** ed. H. N. MacCracken. Part I. **Religious Poems.** (*Reprinted* 1961.) 40*s*. „

O.S. 141. **Earth upon Earth,** all the known texts, ed., with an Introduction, by Hilda Murray. (*Out of print.*) 1911

142. **The English Register of Godstow Nunnery,** ed. A. Clark. Part III. 12*s*. „

143. **The Prose Life of Alexander,** Thornton MS., ed. J. S. Westlake. 12*s*. „

E.S. 108. **Lydgate's Siege of Thebes,** re-ed. A. Erdmann. Part I, the Text. (*Reprinted* 1960.) 24*s*. „

109. **Partonope,** re-ed. A. T. Bödtker. The Texts. (*Out of print.*) „

O.S. 144. **The English Register of Oseney Abbey, by Oxford,** ed. A. Clark. Part II. 12*s*. 1912

145. **The Northern Passion,** ed. F. A. Foster. Part I, the four parallel texts. 18*s*. „

E.S. 110. **Caxton's Mirrour of the World,** with all the woodcuts, ed. O. H. Prior. (*Out of print.*) „

111. **Caxton's History of Jason,** the Text, Part I, ed. J. Munro. 18*s*. „

O.S. 146. **The Coventry Leet Book,** ed. M. Dormer Harris. Introduction, Indexes, &c. Part IV. 12*s*. 1913

147. **The Northern Passion,** ed. F. A. Foster, Introduction, French Text, Variants and Fragments, Glossary. Part II. 18*s*. „

[An enlarged reprint of O.S. 26, **Religious Pieces in Prose and Verse,** from the Thornton MS., ed. G. G. Perry. 6*s*.] „

E.S. 112. **Lovelich's Romance of Merlin,** ed. E. A. Kock. Part II. (*Reprinted* 1961.) 30*s*. „

113. **Poems by Sir John Salusbury, Robert Chester, and others,** from Christ Church MS. 184, &c., ed. Carleton Brown. 18*s*. „

O.S. 148. **A Fifteenth-Century Courtesy Book and Two Franciscan Rules,** ed. R. W. Chambers and W. W. Seton. (*Out of print.*) 1914

149 **Lincoln Diocese Documents, 1450–1544,** ed. Andrew Clark. 18*s*. „

150. **The Old-English Rule of Bp. Chrodegang,** and the **Capitula of Bp. Theodulf,** ed. A. S. Napier. 15*s*. „

E.S. 114. **The Gild of St. Mary, Lichfield,** ed. F. J. Furnivall. 18*s*. „

115. **The Chester Plays,** re-ed. J. Matthews. Part II. (*Reprinted* 1959.) 25*s*. „

O.S. 151. **The Lanterne of Light,** ed. Lilian M. Swinburn. (*Out of print.*) 1915

152. **Early English Homilies,** from Cott. Vesp. D. XIV, ed. Rubie Warner. Part I, Text. (*Out of print.*) „

E.S. 116. **The Pauline Epistles,** ed. M. J. Powell. (*Out of print.*) „

117. **Bp. Fisher's English Works,** ed. R. Bayne. Part II. 18*s*. „

O.S. 153. **Mandeville's Travels,** ed. P. Hamelius. Part I, Text. (*Reprinted* 1960.) 25*s*. 1916

154. **Mandeville's Travels,** ed. P. Hamelius. Part II, Notes and Introduction. (*Reprinted* 1961.) 25*s*. „

E.S. 118. **The Earliest Arithmetics in English,** ed. R. Steele. 18*s*. „

119. **The Owl and Nightingale,** 2 Texts parallel, ed. G. F. H. Sykes and J. H. G. Grattan. (*Reprinted* 1959.) 20*s*. „

O.S. 155. **The Wheatley MS.,** ed. Mabel Day. 36*s*. 1917

E.S. 120. **Ludus Coventriae,** ed. K. S. Block. (*Reprinted* 1961.) 30*s.* 1917
O.S. 156. **Reginald Pecock's Donet,** from Bodl. MS. 916, ed. Elsie V. Hitchcock. 42*s.* 1918
E.S. 121. **Lydgate's Fall of Princes,** ed. H. Bergen. Part I. (*Out of print.*) ,,
122. **Lydgate's Fall of Princes,** ed. H. Bergen. Part II. (*Out of print.*) ,,
O.S. 157. **Harmony of the Life of Christ,** from MS. Pepys 2498, ed. Margery Goates. (*Out of print.*) 1919
158. **Meditations on the Life and Passion of Christ,** from MS. Add., 11307, ed. Charlotte D'Evelyn. (*Out of print.*) ,,
E.S. 123. **Lydgate's Fall of Princes,** ed. H. Bergen. Part III. (*Out of print.*) ,,
124. **Lydgate's Fall of Princes,** ed. H. Bergen. Part IV. (*Out of print.*) ,,
O.S. 159. **Vices and Virtues,** ed. F. Holthausen. Part II. 14*s.* 1920
[A re-edition of O.S. 18, **Hali Meidenhad,** ed. O. Cockayne, with a variant MS., Bodl. 34, hitherto unprinted, ed. F. J. Furnivall. (*Out of print.*)] ,,
E.S. 125. **Lydgate's Siege of Thebes,** ed. A. Erdmann and E. Ekwall. Part II. 24*s.* ,,
126. **Lydgate's Troy Book,** ed. H. Bergen. Part IV. 18*s.* ,,

---

O.S. 160. **The Old English Heptateuch,** MS. Cott. Claud. B. IV, ed. S. J. Crawford. (*Out of print.*) 1921
161. **Three O.E. Prose Texts,** MS. Cott. Vit. A. XV, ed. S. Rypins. (*Out of print.*) ,,
162. **Facsimile of MS. Cotton Nero A. x (Pearl, Cleanness, Patience and Sir Gawain),** Introduction by I. Gollancz. (*Reprinted* 1955.) 100*s.* 1922
163. **Book of the Foundation of St. Bartholomew's Church in London,** ed. N. Moore. 12*s.* 1923
164. **Pecock's Folewer to the Donet,** ed. Elsie V. Hitchcock. (*Out of print.*) ,,
165. **Middleton's Chinon of England, with Leland's Assertio Arturii and Robinson's translation,** ed. W. E. Mead. (*Out of print.*) ,,
166. **Stanzaic Life of Christ,** ed. Frances A. Foster. (*Out of print.*) 1924
167. **Trevisa's Dialogus inter Militem et Clericum, Sermon by FitzRalph, and Bygynnyng of the World,** ed. A. J. Perry. (*Out of print.*) ,,
168. **Caxton's Ordre of Chyualry,** ed. A. T. P. Byles. (*Out of print.*) 1925
169. **The Southern Passion,** ed. Beatrice Brown. (*Out of print.*) ,,
170. **Walton's Boethius,** ed. M. Science. (*Out of print.*) ,,
171. **Pecock's Reule of Cristen Religioun,** ed. W. C. Greet. (*Out of print.*) 1926
172. **The Seege or Batayle of Troye,** ed. M. E. Barnicle. (*Out of print.*) ,,
173. **Hawes' Pastime of Pleasure,** ed. W. E. Mead. 18*s.* 1927
174. **The Life of St. Anne,** ed. R. E. Parker. (*Out of print.*) ,,
175. **Barclay's Eclogues,** ed. Beatrice White. (*Reprinted* 1961.) 35*s.* ,,
176. **Caxton's Prologues and Epilogues,** ed. W. J. B. Crotch. (*Reprinted* 1956.) 30*s.* ,,
177. **Byrhtferth's Manual,** ed. S. J. Crawford. (*Out of print.*) 1928
178. **The Revelations of St. Birgitta,** ed. W. P. Cumming. 12*s.* ,,
179. **The Castell of Pleasure,** ed. R. Cornelius. 15*s.* ,,
180. **The Apologye of Syr Thomas More,** ed. A. I. Taft. (*Out of print.*) 1929
181. **The Dance of Death,** ed. F. Warren. (*Out of print.*) ,,
182. **Speculum Christiani,** ed. G. Holmstedt. 30*s.* ,,
183. **The Northern Passion (Supplement),** ed. W. Heuser and Frances Foster. 9*s.* 1930
184. **The Poems of John Audelay,** ed. Ella K. Whiting. 33*s.* 6*d.* ,,
185. **Lovelich's Merlin,** ed. E. A. Kock. Part III. 30*s.* ,,
186. **Harpsfield's Life of More,** ed. Elsie V. Hitchcock and R. W. Chambers. (*Reprinting.*) 45*s.* 1931
187. **Whittinton and Stanbridge's Vulgaria,** ed. B. White. 14*s.* ,,
188. **The Siege of Jerusalem,** ed. E. Kölbing and Mabel Day. 18*s.* ,,
189. **Caxton's Fayttes of Armes and of Chyualrye,** ed. A. T. Byles. 25*s.* 6*d.* 1932
190. **English Mediæval Lapidaries,** ed. Joan Evans and Mary Serjeantson. (*Reprinted* 1960.) 20*s.* ,,
191. **The Seven Sages,** ed. K. Brunner. (*Reprinting.*) ,,
191A. **On the Continuity of English Prose,** by R. W. Chambers. (*Reprinted* 1957.) 14*s.* ,,
192. **Lydgate's Minor Poems,** ed. H. N. MacCracken. Part II, **Secular Poems.** (*Reprinted* 1961.) 40*s.* 1933
193. **Seinte Marherete,** re-ed. Frances Mack. (*Reprinted* 1958.) 30*s.* ,,
194. **The Exeter Book,** Part II, ed. W. S. Mackie. (*Reprinted* 1958.) 25*s.* ,,
195. **The Quatrefoil of Love,** ed. I. Gollancz and M. Weale. 6*s.* 1934
196. **A Short English Metrical Chronicle,** ed. E. Zettl. 24*s.* ,,
197. **Roper's Life of More,** ed. Elsie V. Hitchcock. (*Reprinted* 1958.) 20*s.* ,,
198. **Firumbras and Otuel and Roland,** ed. Mary O'Sullivan. (*Out of print.*) ,,
199. **Mum and the Sothsegger,** ed. Mabel Day and R. Steele. 14*s.* ,,
200. **Speculum Sacerdotale,** ed. E. H. Weatherly. 20*s.* 1935
201. **Knyghthode and Bataile,** ed. R. Dyboski and Z. M. Arend. 20*s.* ,,
202. **Palsgrave's Acolastus,** ed. P. L. Carver. 24*s.* ,,
203. **Amis and Amiloun,** ed. MacEdward Leach. (*Reprinted* 1960.) 30*s.* ,,
204. **Valentine and Orson,** ed. Arthur Dickson. 24*s.* 1936
205. **Tales from the Decameron,** ed. H. G. Wright. 20*s.* ,,
206. **Bokenham's Lives of Holy Women (Lives of the Saints),** ed. Mary S. Serjeantson. 21*s.* 6*d.* ,,
207. **Liber de Diversis Medicinis,** ed. Margaret S. Ogden. 12*s.* ,,

The Original and Extra Series of the 'Early English Text Society'

208. **The Parker Chronicle and Laws** (facsimile), ed. R. Flower and A. H. Smith. 84*s*. — 1937
209. **Middle English Sermons from MS. Roy. 18 B. xxiii,** ed. W. O. Ross. (*Reprinted* 1960.) 42*s*. — 1938
210. **Sir Gawain and the Green Knight,** ed. I. Gollancz. With Introductory essays by Mabel Day and M. S. Serjeantson. (*Reprinted* 1957.) 10*s*. — ”
211. **Dictes and Sayings of the Philosophers,** ed. C. F. Bühler. (*Reprinted* 1961.) 45*s*. — 1939
212. **The Book of Margery Kempe,** Part I, ed. S. B. Meech and Hope Emily Allen. (*Reprinted* 1961.) 42*s*. — ”
213. **Ælfric's De Temporibus Anni,** ed. H. Henel. 30*s*. — 1940
214. **Morley's Translation of Boccaccio's De Claris Mulieribus,** ed. H. G. Wright. 31*s*. 6*d*. — ”
215. **English Poems of Charles of Orleans,** Part I, ed. R. Steele. 31*s*. 6*d*. — 1941
216. **The Latin Text of the Ancrene Riwle,** ed. Charlotte D'Evelyn. (*Reprinted* 1957.) 31*s*. 6*d*. — ”
217. **Book of Vices and Virtues,** ed. W. Nelson Francis. 52*s*. 6*d*. — 1942
218. **The Cloud of Unknowing and the Book of Privy Counselling,** ed. Phyllis Hodgson. (*Reprinted* 1958.) 40*s*. — 1943
219. **The French Text of the Ancrene Riwle,** B.M. Cotton MS. Vitellius. F. VII, ed. J. A. Herbert. 28*s*. — ”
220. **English Poems of Charles of Orleans,** Part II, ed. R. Steele and Mabel Day. 10*s*. 6*d*. — 1944
221. **Sir Degrevant,** ed. L. F. Casson. 52*s*. 6*d*. — ”
222. **Ro. Ba.'s Life of Syr Thomas More,** ed. Elsie V. Hitchcock and Mgr. P. E. Hallett. (*Reprinted* 1957.) 35*s*. — 1945
223. **Tretyse of Loue,** ed. J. H. Fisher. 28*s*. — ”
224. **Athelston,** ed. A. McI. Trounce. (*Reprinted* 1957.) 15*s*. — 1946
225. **The English Text of the Ancrene Riwle,** B.M. Cotton MS. Nero A. XIV, ed. Mabel Day. (*Reprinted* 1957.) 25*s*. — ”
226. **Respublica,** re-ed. W. W. Greg. 18*s*. 6*d*. — ”
227. **Kyng Alisaunder,** ed. G. V. Smithers. Vol. I, Text. (*Reprinted* 1961.) 35*s*. — 1947
228. **The Metrical Life of St. Robert of Knaresborough,** ed. J. Bazire. 25*s*. — ”
229. **The English Text of the Ancrene Riwle,** Gonville and Caius College MS. 234/120, ed. R. M. Wilson. With Introduction by N. R. Ker. (*Reprinted* 1957.) 25*s*. — 1948
230. **The Life of St. George by Alexander Barclay,** ed. W. Nelson. (*Reprinted* 1960.) 28*s*. — ”
231. **Deonise Hid Diuinite,** and other treatises related to *The Cloud of Unknowing*, ed. Phyllis Hodgson. (*Reprinted* 1958.) 30*s*. — 1949
232. **The English Text of the Ancrene Riwle,** B.M. Royal MS. 8 C. 1, ed. A. C. Baugh. (*Reprinted* 1958.) 20*s*. — ”
233. **The Bibliotheca Historica of Diodorus Siculus translated by John Skelton,** ed. F. M. Salter and H. L. R. Edwards. Vol. I, Text. 42*s*. — 1950
234. **Caxton: Paris and Vienne,** ed. MacEdward Leach. 30*s*. — 1951
235. **The South English Legendary,** Corpus Christi College Cambridge MS. 145 and B.M. M.S. Harley 2277, &c., ed. Charlotte D'Evelyn and Anna J. Mill. Text, Vol. I. 35*s*. — ”
236. **The South English Legendary.** Text, Vol. II. 35*s*. — 1952

[E.S. 87. **Two Coventry Corpus Christi Plays,** re-ed. H. Craig. Second Edition. 15*s*.] — ”

237. **Kyng Alisaunder,** ed. G. V. Smithers. Vol. II, Introduction, Commentary, and Glossary. 37*s*. 6*d*. — 1953
238. **The Phonetic Writings of Robert Robinson,** ed. E. J. Dobson. 28*s*. — ”
239. **The Bibliotheca Historica of Diodorus Siculus translated by John Skelton,** ed. F. M. Salter and H. L. R. Edwards. Vol. II. Introduction, Notes, and Glossary. 15*s*. — 1954
240. **The French Text of the Ancrene Riwle,** Trinity College, Cambridge, MS. R. 14. 7, ed. W. H. Trethewey. 45*s*. — ”
241. **Þe Wohunge of ure Lauerd,** and other pieces, ed. W. Meredith Thompson. 32*s*. — 1955
242. **The Salisbury Psalter,** ed. Celia Sisam and Kenneth Sisam. 84*s*. — 1955–56
243. **George Cavendish: The Life and Death of Cardinal Wolsey,** ed. Richard S. Sylvester. (*Reprinted* 1961.) 35*s*. — 1957
244. **The South English Legendary.** Vol. III, Introduction and Glossary, ed. Charlotte D'Evelyn. 25*s*. — ”
245. **Beowulf** (facsimile). With Transliteration by J. Zupitza, new collotype plates, and Introduction by N. Davis. 70*s*. — 1958
246. **The Parlement of the Thre Ages,** ed. M. Y. Offord. 28*s*. — 1959
247. **Facsimile of MS. Bodley 34** (Katherine Group). With Introduction by N. R. Ker. 42*s*. — ”
248. **Þe Liflade ant te Passiun of Seinte Iuliene,** ed. S. R. T. O. d'Ardenne. 30*s*. — 1960
249. **Ancrene Wisse,** Corpus Christi College, Cambridge, MS. 402, ed. J. R. R. Tolkien. With an Introduction by N. R. Ker. (*At press.*) 30*s*. — ”

The following is a select list of forthcoming volumes. Other texts are under consideration:

Facsimile of the Cotton and Jesus Manuscripts of the Owl and the Nightingale. With Introduction by N. R. Ker. (*At press.*) (*Part of issue for* 1962.)
Ælfric: Catholic Homilies, First Series, ed. P. Clemoes.
The Paston Letters, ed. N. Davis.
The English Text of the Ancrene Riwle, edited from all the extant manuscripts:
- Bodleian MS. Vernon, ed. G. V. Smithers.
- B.M. Cotton MS. Titus D. XVIII, ed. Frances M. Mack. (*At press.*) (*Part of issue for* 1962.)
- B.M. Cotton MS. Cleopatra C. VI, ed. A. H. Smith.

(*It is also hoped to issue a revised edition of Magdalene College, Cambridge, MS. Pepys* 2498.)

Laȝamon's Brut, ed. G. L. Brook and R. F. Leslie. (*Vol. I at press.*) (*Issue for* 1961.)
The Bodley Version of Mandeville's Travels, ed. M. C. Seymour. (*At press.*)
Ywain and Gawain, ed. Albert B. Friedman and Norman T. Harrington.
The York Plays, re-ed. Arthur Brown.
The Macro Plays, re-ed. Mark Eccles.
The Cely Letters, ed. A. H. Hanham.

January 1962

Publisher
LONDON: THE OXFORD UNIVERSITY PRESS, AMEN HOUSE, E.C. 4